Northern Ireland

Northern Ireland
The Politics of War and Peace

Paul Dixon

palgrave

First published 2001 by
PALGRAVE
Houndmills, Basingstoke, Hampshire RG21 6XS
and
175 Fifth Avenue, New York, N. Y. 10010
Companies and representatives throughout the world

PALGRAVE is the new global academic imprint of St. Martin's Press
LLC Scholarly and Reference Division and Palgrave Publishers Ltd
(formerly Macmillan Press Ltd).

ISBN 0–333–72968–4 hardback
ISBN 0–333–72969–2 paperback

This book is printed on paper suitable for recycling
and made from fully managed and sustained forest sources.

A catalogue record for this book is available
from the British Library.

Library of Congress Cataloging-in-Publication Data
Dixon, Paul, 1964–
    Northern Ireland : the politics of war and peace / Paul Dixon.
        p. cm.
    Includes bibliographical references and index.
    ISBN 0–333–72968–4 (cloth) — ISBN 0–333–72969–2 (paper)
    1. Northern Ireland—Politics and government.   2. Political
violence—Northern Ireland.   3. Peace movements—Northern
Ireland. I. Title.
DA990.U46 D598 2000
941.6—dc21   00-048297

10 9 8 7 6 5 4 3 2 1
10 09 08 07 06 05 04 03 02 01

Printed in China

For mum and dad

Contents

List of Maps, Figures and Tables

Acknowledgements

The support of friends, colleagues and family over the years has been of enormous importance, particularly through recent, difficult times. This book is dedicated to my parents. Charles Dixon encouraged me to be creative, free-thinking and constantly questioning. If he were alive, he would be immensely proud of his son but stubbornly argumentative over the content of this book. Joyce Dixon provides a great example of determination, hard work and integrity. Their support and love are appreciated. Kate Dixon has been a rock; it would be difficult to imagine a better sister. Mark Dixon and the bears have provided a helpful and lively distraction from the tribulations of research. Old friends in England have been superb (especially Ma, Da and Minxy Maguire) and new friends in Northern Ireland (the 'Sisters of Tyrone' deserve special mention – Bébhinn, Cait, Martina and Anne-Marie) have helped me settle into Belfast life. Thank you to Helen Whalley for her support over many years. Didsbury Northern Hockey Club provided an essential relief from the stresses of work, sometimes by providing a stress of their own!

I have been privileged to have had the help of many people who are not only fine academics but very decent human beings. The work of Professors Paul Bew and Henry Patterson has been inspirational. As an undergraduate at the University of Manchester Peter Mair and Lewis Minkin gave me the confidence and encouragement to take my work further. Bob Purdie provided accommodation to a stranger and intellectual stimulation. Robin Wilson was not only generous with his hospitality but his magnificent editorship of *Fortnight* magazine had a great impact on the development of many of the ideas presented in this book. The School of Peace Studies at the University of Bradford provided a fascinating, comparative environment in which to conduct PhD research. My fellow researchers there were generous with ideas and arguments: special respect to 'big Al' Bloomgarden. A fellowship at the Institute of Irish Studies provided an invaluable breathing space for me to develop my interests further. I remember fondly my time at the University of Luton where colleagues, although teaching at the sharp end, still found time to be friendly and encouraging. The University of Leeds made me a timely offer of work and provided generous space for me to pursue my teaching and research interests. Teaching Northern Irish students at the University of Ulster has been stimulating and enjoyable. My colleague Professor Colin Thain has provided much needed moral support. The editorial board of *Chartist* magazine has displayed great tolerance in allowing me space to rehearse some of my arguments on Northern Ireland over the years.

My students at the Universities of Luton, Leeds (POLI 2810) and Ulster (PUP504J1, MED702B1) have been the guinea pigs for drafts of this book. They have borne this burden stoically, and their perceptive criticisms have provided much food for thought and revision. They were a pleasure to teach.

I have pressed into service several people to read earlier drafts of chapters of this book. Thanks go to: Colin Hay, Martin Lodge, Des McCabe, Eamonn O'Kane, Henry Patterson, Bob Purdie and John Schwarzmantel. Dr Rupert Taylor of the University of the Witwatersrand, South Africa, deserves special mention for his generosity in providing some excellent comments on an earlier draft of this book. I am grateful to Mairead Crilly for her work on the maps, diagram and table. My publisher, Steven Kennedy was perceptive in his suggestions for improvement and was always sympathetic to my excuses over length and deadlines. None of the above should be held responsible for the politics, arguments or any shortcomings of this book.

PAUL DIXON

List of Abbreviations

AIA	Anglo-Irish Agreement
APL	Anti-Partition League
APNI	Alliance Party of Northern Ireland
CC	Cabinet Conclusions
CDU	Campaign for Democracy in Ulster
CSJ	Campaign for Social Justice
DCAC	Derry Citizens Action Committee
DHAC	Derry Housing Action Committee
DSD	Downing Street Declaration
DUP	Democratic Unionist Party
EEC	European Economic Community
GFA	Good Friday Agreement
GOC	General Officer Commanding
HCL	Homeless Citizens League
IGC	Intergovernmental Conference of the AIA
INLA	Irish National Liberation Army
IRA	Irish Republican Army (the Provisional IRA)
LVF	Loyalist Volunteer Force
NATO	North Atlantic Treaty Organisation
NIC	Northern Ireland Committee of the Parliamentary Conservative Party
NICRA	Northern Ireland Civil Rights Association
NILP	Northern Ireland Labour Party
NIO	Northern Ireland Office
OIRA	Official IRA
PIRA	Provisional IRA
PREM	Prime Minister's Office
PRO	Public Record Office
PTA	Prevention of Terrorism Act
PUP	Progressive Unionist Party
RIR	Royal Irish Regiment (a regiment of the British Army comprised of the UDR and Royal Irish Rangers)
RIRA	Real IRA
RUC	Royal Ulster Constabulary
SDLP	Social Democratic and Labour Party

SF	Sinn Féin
UDA	Ulster Defence Association
UDP	Ulster Democratic Party
UDR	Ulster Defence Regiment
UFF	Ulster Freedom Fighters
UUC	Ulster Unionist Council
UUP	Ulster Unionist Party
UUUC	United Ulster Unionist Council
UVF	Ulster Volunteer Force
UWC	Ulster Workers' Council
VUP	Vanguard Unionist Party
VUPP	Vanguard Unionist Progressive Party

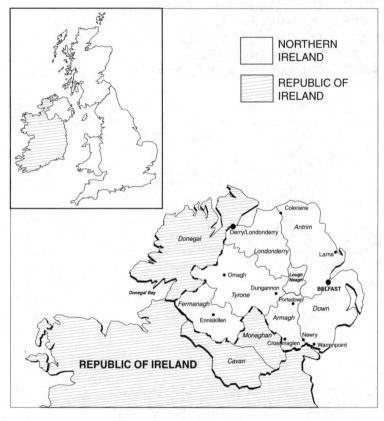

Map 1.1 Northern Ireland

1

Introduction

This chapter aims to give a brief background and introduction to the conflict in Northern Ireland, by presenting a brief history, introducing nationalist and unionist perspectives on the conflict, and considering also the extent of violence and segregation. The popular historical accounts given by nationalists and unionists of the history of the conflict in Northern Ireland tend to be very different. These accounts are not merely of historical interest but are deployed by politicians to win advantage in the propaganda war over the future of Northern Ireland. Past grievances are used to justify current claims to justice. Although these highly 'propagandistic' accounts of history are often undermined by historical research, these 'myths' continue to persist. Do these very different accounts of the history Northern Ireland, including the recent period of conflict since the 1960s, contribute to the continuation of the conflict?

The following chapter presents 'The Approach and Argument' of the book and will pick up on the concepts of 'power', 'ideology' (and the propaganda war) and 'reality' which are the key, inter-related themes. Power, it is argued, is deployed in the two, inter-connected wars being fought over Northern Ireland, the 'real war' and the propaganda war. The 'real war' is aimed at winning advantage through physical means, violence, demonstrations and repression. But these are also deployed in the propaganda war to shift the political agenda. The ideological, public rhetoric of the propaganda war by the various parties to the conflict can be contrasted with the 'realities' of the conflict which are often only privately acknowledged.

A Few Generalisations

In trying to understand the conflict in Northern Ireland a few rough generalisations can be helpful. The conflict in Northern Ireland can be most easily and quickly understood as being between two main groups. First, there are unionists, who comprise about 60 per cent of the population of Northern Ireland, and tend to see themselves as British and want Northern Ireland to continue to remain part of the UK. These unionists are mostly Protestant, but there are some Catholic unionists. Second, there are nationalists, who make up an increasing proportion of the Northern Ireland population, currently about 40 per cent, and who tend to see themselves as Irish and aspire to be part of a united Ireland. These nationalists are overwhelmingly Catholic. There is a much smaller third group, perhaps a few per cent of people in Northern Ireland, who reject the domination of nationalism and unionism and see themselves as occupying the 'moderate' centre ground between the two dominant unionist and nationalist communities. While the labels 'Catholic' and 'Protestant' are used to describe the principal contending communities, the conflict is not to any great extent about religion or religious dogma. The terms 'Protestant' and 'Catholic' are usually used to indicate someone who is either unionist or nationalist. Northern Ireland can be seen as a place where the British and Irish nations overlap and their co-nationals, British unionists and Irish nationalists, aspire to be part of two different states. This is not such an unusual state of affairs, particularly in Eastern Europe, where borders have shifted back and forward down the centuries; minorities have frequently been caught on the 'wrong side' of a border, under the sovereignty of a state which is not run by their co-nationals.

A Brief History of the Conflict

In the historical debate between nationalists and unionists there is some dispute over which group has first claim to Northern Ireland. Nationalists can point to their Celtic 'forefathers' while some unionists have claimed that their ancestors, the Cruthin, were in the territory now called Northern Ireland even before the Celts. This is not a unique debate: where there is conflict over territory there is often historical debate over 'who was here first' since this can be used in political argument to justify one or other group's legitimate claim to a territory.

Nationalists usually date Ireland's woes to the Anglo–Norman invasion of 1169 and England's domination of Ireland ever since. When Henry VIII broke with Rome in the sixteenth century England became Protestant while Ireland remained Catholic and rebellious. In 1603 the conquest of Ireland was completed. In 1609 the plantation of Ulster began, the Catholic Irish were dispossessed and (mainly Scottish) Protestant settlers were established in present day Northern Ireland. Some Catholics can still point out the lands which were taken over by the settlers. During the seventeenth century Protestant landownership in Ireland rose from 5 per cent to over 80 per cent at the expense of the Catholics. In 1641 the Irish rose up against the Protestants and massacred some of them. Cromwell triumphed bloodily over the Irish in 1649–52. In 1690 King William of Orange defeated James II, the Catholic King of England and Scotland, at the Battle of the Boyne, ensuring Protestant dominance. At the end of the seventeenth century and the beginning of the eighteenth, 'penal laws' were passed which further established Protestant domination in Ireland. Anglican Protestants enjoyed privileges over both Catholics and non-conformist Protestants. In 1798 the Protestant Wolfe Tone led the United Irishmen, combining Catholics and Presbyterians, in a republican uprising, to establish Ireland's independence from England. Again this was defeated and in 1801 the Act of Union was passed integrating the Irish Parliament into the Parliament of Great Britain and Ireland.

During the 1820s and 1830s Daniel O'Connell led a successful movement for Catholic representation in Parliament and an unsuc-cessful one for the 'Repeal of the Union'. The Irish famine (1845–51) resulted in the deaths of over a million Irish, and the emigration of another million within a decade. This diaspora has continued to play a role in Irish politics ever since, particularly Irish-Americans. Nationalists continued to agitate against English domination. The Fenians turned to violence and bombings to oust the English. A constitutional movement for Irish Home Rule developed at the end of the nineteenth century which succeeded in winning consider-able land reforms for the Irish, but by the outbreak of the First World War it had failed to achieve the implementation of Home Rule for Ireland. Throughout Ireland the unionists, mainly the Protestant descendants of the plantation, led resistance to home rule, fearing Catholic domination in an all-Ireland assembly. Unionists were particularly concentrated in Ulster and between 1912 and 1914 they mobilised, declaring their willingness to fight against Home Rule. In this they were supported by the Conservat-ive Party and had the sympathy of important sections of the British Army. By 1914 England faced civil war over the 'Irish Question' between the Conservatives and their unionist allies in Ireland, and the Liberals (and Labour) who were sympathetic to the home rule demand of nationalists.

The First World War drastically changed the political landscape. Both Irish nationalists and unionists went off to fight for Britain in the War, with the Ulster Division taking heavy casualties on the Somme. At Easter 1916 a small group of republicans entered the General Post Office in Dublin and declared an Irish republic. The 'Easter Rising' was defeated by the British but when its leaders were executed there followed a wave of public sympathy for the republicans. Public opinion shifted away from the Irish Parliamentary Party and Home Rule and towards the republicans and their demand for independence. In 1918 the republican party, Sinn Féin, decisively won the last all-Ireland election. The 'War of Independence', 1919–21, was fought by the Irish Republican Army (IRA) to drive the British state out of Ireland. On the other hand the unionists continued to resist incorporation into a united independent Ireland. In 1920 the British Government partitioned Ireland. Northern Ireland, which had its Parliament at Stormont in Belfast, consisted of six of the nine counties of Ulster. Unionists comprised a majority in just four of the six counties but held a clear majority in Northern Ireland. The Irish Free State (as the South of Ireland was known after partition until the declaration of the republic in 1948), with a Parliament in Dublin, was to rule the other 26 counties of Ireland. The treaty signed between the British Government and Sinn Féin in December 1921 gave the Irish Free State Dominion status within the British Empire and set up a boundary commission to consider redrawing the border with Northern Ireland.

The partition of Ireland was widely seen as a temporary measure and provision was made for its voluntary reunification (see Chapter 3). However, the division between the majority Protestant Northern Ireland state and the overwhelmingly Catholic state in the South grew after partition. In 1937 the new Constitution of the Irish Free state recognised the special position of the Catholic Church and in Articles 2 and 3 claimed as the national territory the whole island of Ireland. The Catholic minority within Northern Ireland was discriminated against by a unionist regime concerned to establish its control in the face of an IRA threat from the South. British politics had been dominated by the 'Irish Question' for much of the late nineteenth and early twentieth centuries. British politicians now handed over responsibility for the North to the subordinate Stormont Parliament, ignored abuses of Catholics' civil rights and minimised its involvement in Irish politics (see Chapter 4). By the 1960s unionists were concerned that their position within the Union was becoming undermined. In 1964 there was rioting during the Westminster General Election campaign and in 1966 the loyalist paramilitary Ulster Volunteer Force (UVF) reformed and murdered two Catholics. The civil rights movement drew attention to abuses occurring under the Stormont Government but, when that failed to bring about change, it took politics into the streets. The result was escalating conflict and violence which finally forced the British Government to intervene more directly. First the British put pressure on the Stormont Government to reform and then troops were deployed on the streets as communal rioting spiralled beyond the control of the local police, the Royal Ulster Constabulary (RUC: see Chapter 5). Republicans took to the streets to defend Catholic areas from attack by unionists but also went on the offensive, seizing their opportunity to drive the British out of Ireland. Unionist paramilitaries mobilised to strike back against the IRA by killing Catholics. In 1972, after a further escalation in violence, the British Government suspended the Northern Ireland Parliament and introduced direct rule (Chapter 6). From 1972 to 1974 a serious attempt was made by the British Government to introduce power-sharing between unionists and nationalists alongside an all-Ireland body. Unionist opinion turned against this first 'peace process' and it ended in failure (see Chapter 5). Opinion in Northern Ireland was polarised and the prospects for resucitating an accommodation between unionists and nationalists receded.

The British Government and the IRA settled down for a 'Long War'. The British attempted to criminalise republican prisoners who resisted, resulting in the deaths of ten republicans during the Hunger Strikes of 1980–81. The IRA's political wing, Sinn Féin, contested elections after the Hunger Strikes and performed well (Chapter 7). The British and Irish Governments embarked on an initiative which Margaret Thatcher intended would reap security benefits for Britain in the battle against the IRA (Chapter 8). In 1985 the Anglo–Irish Agreement was signed by the two governments, giving the Irish an input into the governance of Northern Ireland. Unionists were alienated by this development and a polarisation of public and political opinion followed the Agreement. However, this Agreement may have accelerated a rethink within the republican movement which, while the IRA continued its 'armed struggle', adjusted its ideological stance and entered into secret contacts with the British Government from 1990 to 1993 (Chapter 9). In 1994 the IRA announced a ceasefire and negotiations began about the conditions on which Sinn Féin would be admitted into all-party negotiations with unionists. Unionists and the British Government insisted that some decommissioning of IRA weapons must take place before Sinn Féin could be allowed to sit at the negotiating table. This condition was abandoned in return for elections to a Northern Ireland Forum. The republicans rejected this and the IRA ended its ceasefire in February 1996. Following the election of a Labour Government in 1997 the IRA renewed its ceasefire and entered negotiations with unionists in September 1997. In April 1998 the 'Good Friday Agreement' was reached between unionists and nationalists on new power-sharing institutions for Northern Ireland and a programme of reform (Chapter 10). The Agreement continues to be dogged by controversy, particularly over the issue of decommissioning IRA weapons. In December 1999 power was finally devolved to the Northern Ireland Assembly, only to be suspended in February 2000. Power was again devolved to the Assembly in May 2000.

Nationalist and Unionist Views of the Conflict

In Northern Ireland Irish nationalists and British unionists have very different perspectives on the conflict and its history. History and contemporary events are used to apportion blame and justify contrasting analyses and 'solutions' to the conflict. Yet while unionists and nationalists are divided, there are also divisions within both unionism and nationalism in their analysis of the conflict and prescriptions for settling it. Within nationalism the term 'nationalist' is often used to describe someone who aspires to a united Ireland but is opposed to the use of violence to achieve it, while a 'republican' often shares much of the analysis of the 'nationalist' but is prepared to use violence; so all republicans are nationalists, but not all nationalists are republicans. Similarly, within unionism the term 'unionist' describes a supporter of the Union who is opposed to the use of violence and uses more constitutional means to defend the Union, while a 'loyalist' is used to describe a unionist who tends to employ or advocate more militant methods to defend the Union, sometimes including violence. Loyalists and republicans tend to be drawn disproportionately from the working class.

Nationalist and Republican Views

Nationalists argue that 800 years of English oppression have followed the Anglo–Norman invasion of 1169, during which a succession of nationalist heroes have striven to drive out the English invader who has brought nothing but trouble to Ireland. However, some nationalists go even further back and draw inspiration from an idyllic Celtic past.

A consistent theme of nationalist/republican history is the brutality of the invading English/British. The propensity of the English brutally to oppress the Irish is established, from Cromwell's massacres of the Irish during the 1640s, through the execution of the Easter Rising martyrs in 1916 and the atrocities perpetrated by the British 'Blacks'n' Tans' during the War of Independence, to the Bloody Sunday 'massacre' in 1972. The responsibility of the English for the Irish famine, or genocide as some call it, is used to establish the guilt of the English then and, by implication and analogy, now both for the events of the 1840s and Ireland's stunted development ever since (Ireland's population was 25 per cent of that of the UK in 1845 but just 10 per cent by 1914). A story is told which emphasises the continuity of English/British oppression in Ireland and therefore its inevitability: 'Nothing but the same old story', according to the title of one book.

Irish history becomes a morality tale in which the brave, principally male, heroes of nationalist history take up the struggle of centuries against the English/British oppressor (the O'Neills of Tyrone, Wolfe Tone, the Fenians, Daniel O'Connell, Michael Davitt, Charles Stewart Parnell, James Connolly, Patrick Pearse, Michael Collins, Bobby Sands). As the struggle against the English continues, new events and heroes are added to the pantheon. During 'the Troubles' republicans and nationalists have commemorated Bloody Sunday and the introduction of internment. Bobby Sands and the 1981 hunger strikers are placed in the tradition of the men of 1916.

The role of Irish Protestants in the nationalist tradition is often highlighted, from Tone to Parnell, to show the way for contemporary unionists. From this perspective, unionists are seen as Irish people who have been duped by the English/British into believing they are British. Once the British leave Ireland the unionists will reassess their position and realise that they are Irish after all. Alternatively, unionists are seen as illegitimate settlers with no right to remain in

Ireland. They should be encouraged to leave when the British colonial power withdraws.

For nationalists and republicans the partition of Ireland was really an undemocratic imposition by the British to maintain their domination, rather than a compromise between the competing forces of nationalism and unionism. The 1918 all-Ireland election demonstrated the desire of the Irish people for unity and independence. Partition is undemocratic and artificial, since the border was not drawn with respect to the will of the people but as a result of power and the threat of force. Had the British imposed a united Ireland the unionists would not have resisted because they had no particular place to go. It is the British prop which has sustained unionist resistance.

Republicans view developments during 'the Troubles' in a different way to nationalists. The IRA justifies its lack of popular support for its 'armed struggle' among nationalists by reference to the Easter Rising in 1916. The Rising did not have popular support at the time (many nationalists had relatives serving in the British Army in France) but subsequently won widespread sympathy. Republicans emphasise loyalist or unionist responsibility for the recent outbreak of the conflict, pointing to the emergence of the loyalist UVF in 1966 or the brutality of the Stormont regime against the civil rights protesters. The British rather than the unionists then become the primary focus of the enmity of republican ideology. The British are held responsible for the establishment of an oppressive security regime including abuses of human rights, torture, Bloody Sunday, internment without trial, 'shoot to kill', and the suspension of civil liberties. Republicans, on the other hand, were forced to respond to British oppression and defend the Catholic community. Republicans reject the nationalist view that the British are 'neutral' and have argued that the British have economic, strategic and political reasons for retaining Northern Ireland within the Union.

Both republicans and nationalists argue that Irish unity is inevitable (Chapter 3). Since partition, British neglect of Northern Ireland has allowed the perpetration of civil rights abuses by the Unionist Government at Stormont. Republicans stress the repressive nature of the Stormont era and subsequent British policy in order to justify the IRA's 'armed struggle' after 1969. Nationalists and republicans would tend to argue that during the 1960s there was a shift towards participation in the Northern Ireland state, with Catholics emphasising 'British rights for British citizens' rather than an end to the border. When this conciliatory stance was rebuffed by the unionists, Catholics took to the streets to secure their civil rights and were met with unionist brutality (Chapter 4). Communal violence and the violence of the British Army polarised the situation in Northern Ireland. Nationalists supported power-sharing in 1974 but this was 'sold out' by the British Labour Government which did not take strong action to defend it against unionist opposition or subsequently push the unionists hard enough towards reviving power-sharing. Unlike republicans, however, nationalists have tended to accept that Britain is 'neutral' in its attitude towards Northern Ireland, meaning that it has no overriding interest in retaining the Union. Nationalists argue that the Anglo–Irish Agreement of 1985 which gave the Republic a say in the affairs of Northern Ireland was further evidence of British neutrality. The key problem in Northern Ireland for nationalists is not so much the British Government as a division among the people of Northern Ireland themselves, between unionists and nationalists. Unionists are not simply, as republicans claim, the puppets of the British; they have a considerable degree of independence or autonomy. The republican leadership presents the peace process and the Good Friday Agreement as further steps towards the inevitable unity of Ireland.

The Social Democratic and Labour Party (SDLP)　The SDLP was founded in 1970 and has been the main exponent of the nationalist view of the conflict. It is overwhelmingly Catholic in membership and support. A centre-left party with working-class support it none the less tends to do better among middle-class Catholics. In its founding constitution the SDLP supported the proposition that the unity of Ireland could only come about with the consent of the majority within Northern Ireland. The SDLP has long supported joint authority of the British and Irish Governments over Northern Ireland; but it has also supported power-sharing between nationalists and unionists, along with an 'Irish dimension' to express the Irishness and national aspiration of the minority community. In the mid-1970s factions within the SDLP supported a declaration of British intent to withdraw and independence for Northern Ireland, some as a transition stage before Irish unity, others in order to reach accommodation with unionists. The principal divide within the SDLP has been between those around John Hume who have emphasised the importance of the Irish dimension (North/South bodies and an increased role for the Republic of Ireland in the North), and

Table 1.1   Election results 1973–99 (principal parties, percentage shares)

Election	Political Parties					
	Democratic Unionist	Vanguard Unionist	Ulster Unionist	Alliance	Social Democratic & Labour Party	Provisional Sinn Féin
May 1973 L	4.3	2.1	41.4	13.7	13.4	–
Jun 1973 A	10.8	10.5	29.3	9.2	22.1	–
Feb 1974 W	8.2	10.6	32.3	3.2	22.4	–
Oct 1974 W	8.5	13.1	36.5	6.4	22.0	–
May 1975 C	14.7	12.7	25.8	9.8	23.7	–
May 1977 L	12.7	1.5	29.6	14.4	20.6	–
May 1979 W	10.2	–	36.6	11.9	18.2	–
Jun 1979 E	29.8	–	21.9	6.8	24.6	–
May 1981 L	26.6	–	26.5	8.9	17.5	–
Oct 1982 A	23.0	–	29.7	9.3	18.8	10.1
Jun 1983 W	20.0	–	34.0	8.0	17.9	13.4
Jun 1984 E	33.6	–	21.5	5.0	22.1	13.3
May 1985 L	24.3	–	29.5	7.1	17.8	11.8
Jun 1987 W	11.7	–	37.8	10.0	21.1	11.4
May 1989 L	17.7	–	31.3	6.9	21.0	11.2
Jun 1989 E	29.9	–	22.2	5.2	25.5	9.1
Apr 1992 W	13.1	–	34.5	8.7	23.5	10.0
Jun 1993 L	17.3	–	29.3	7.6	22.0	12.4
Jun 1994 E	29.2	–	23.8	4.1	28.9	9.9
May 1996 F	18.8	–	24.2	6.5	21.4	15.5
May 1997 W	13.6	–	32.7	8.0	24.1	16.1
May 1997 L	15.9	–	27.8	6.6	20.7	16.9
Jun 1998 A	18.1	–	21.3	6.5	22.0	17.6
Jun 1999 E	28.4	–	17.6	2.1	28.1	17.3

Notes:
(i)   Type of election is indicated by letter:
   A = Assembly, W = Westminster Parliament, C = Convention, E = European Parliament, F = Forum, L = Local Council Elections.
(ii)   The symbol (–) indicates the party did not exist or did not contest the election.
(iii)   Figures do not add up to 100 per cent, as assorted minor parties and independents also contested elections.

others who have prioritised power-sharing and accommodation with unionists within Northern Ireland. On security, the SDLP has been critical of the security forces, the police and the army and they refuse to 'support' the police or encourage Catholics to join the RUC. However, the SDLP has also been very strong in its condemnations of all republican and loyalist violence. The SDLP's principal electoral rivals have been firstly the moderate Alliance Party, secondly in the late 1970s and early 1980s the small, 'more nationalist' Irish

Independence Party, and thirdly throughout the 1980s and 1990s Sinn Féin, the political wing of the IRA. Although the republicans did not contest elections in the 1970s, they nevertheless represented a challenge to the SDLP for the support of the nationalist community. The SDLP has been led by Gerry Fitt (1970–79) and John Hume (1979–). The party's electoral support 1973–98 has ranged between 13.4 per cent and 28.9 per cent but has averaged around 22 per cent (see Table 1.1). Its deputy leader, Seamus Mallon, is Deputy First Minister in the Northern Ireland Assembly.

Sinn Féin/IRA   Since 1969 the republican movement has split into various factions. In 1969 the IRA split into the Official IRA and the Provisional IRA (which is the full name of today's IRA). The Official IRA (OIRA) was more left-wing than the Provisionals, emphasised the unity of the Protestant and Catholic working class and took a more defensive military stance. It declared a ceasefire in 1972. In 1975 the Irish National Liberation Army (INLA) split away from the OIRA and mounted a terrorist campaign against the security forces. The Provisional IRA (PIRA) was more Catholic, right-wing and militaristic in its outlook. It took the offensive against the British Army in 1969–70 and emerged as the dominant group within the republican movement. Republican Sinn Féin broke away from the Provisionals in 1986 over the latter's decision that their success-fully elected candidates would take their seats in the Irish Dáil (assembly) in break of the traditional republican boycott. Republican Sinn Féin's military wing is the Continuity IRA. The 'Real IRA' (RIRA) split from the Provisionals in the autumn of 1997 over growing disatisfaction with Sinn Féin's involvement in the 'peace process'. The RIRA were responsible for the Omagh bombing in the summer of 1998 which killed 29 and injured 310.

The evidence points overwhelmingly towards an inextricable link between the IRA and Sinn Féin, in spite of the attempts in recent years, for propaganda reasons, for Sinn Féin to claim a distance between itself and the IRA. Sinn Féin had long been subordinate to the military wing but during the 1980s began to play a more promin-ent role in the partnership, contesting elections and taking its seats on local councils. The republican movement does not accept parti-tion and argues for British withdrawal and a democratic socialist Irish republic. The IRA opposed power-sharing during 1972–74 and escalated its campaign to topple that experiment. In 1975–76 it announced a ceasefire in the expectation that the British were about to withdraw. 'Hardline' elements within the republican movement opposed this development and, when the British did not withdraw, the IRA leadership were discredited; subsequently a new leadership from Northern Ireland emerged as dominant within the IRA. They settled down for the 'Long War' and attempted to mobilise a political campaign alongside the military struggle. Following the Hunger Strikes in 1981 this emerged as the 'bullet and ballot box' strategy: the PIRA continued its military campaign while the political wing, Sinn Féin, fought elections. The Provisionals continued to oppose any 'internal settlement' in Northern Ireland on the grounds that it represented a return to the bad old days of the 'Stormont regime'. Republican paramilitaries have been responsible for approximately 2139 (58.8 per cent) (PIRA 1771) out of the 3636 'troubles' related deaths in Northern Ireland (McKittrick *et al.* 1999). They have killed policemen, prison officers, workers working for the security forces, soldiers and both Protestant and Catholic civilians. Reviewing the statistics of violence, Fay *et al.* argue that the IRA has 'Essentially... been an offensive rather than defensive organisation, with little evidence that it was able to protect the Nationalist population from either the security forces or sectarian attack' (Fay *et al.* 1999, p. 178). Ruairí Ó Brádaigh was President of Sinn Féin (1970–83), while Gerry Adams was Vice-President of Sinn Féin (1978–83) and has been President since 1983. Sinn Féin's electoral support 1982–99 has varied between 10.1 per cent and 17.6 per cent and averages about 13 per cent, although it has increased during the 'peace process'.

Unionist and Loyalist Views

In recent years loyalist historians have argued that the Cruthin were the original inhabitants of Northern Ireland and when the Scottish settlers settled in Ulster during the seventeenth century this was simply a return of the Cruthin to their original homeland. Unionist history highlights the plantation of the seventeenth century and suggests that the Protestant settlers brought with them 'progressive' ways to a backward land. The Irish rebellion of 1641 against the settlers is remembered as a warning to Protestants of the hostility of Catholics and the consequences of not being vigilant. At the Siege of Derry in 1689 the Protestant Apprentice Boys slammed the gates of Derry shut when the Protestant leader, Governor Lundy, proposed to surrender to the forces of the Catholic King James II. The siege was subsequently lifted and in 1690 the Protestant King William of

Orange defeated James at the Battle of the Boyne. Both of these events are highlights of the unionist marching season commemorated annually on 14 August and 12 July. The Siege of Derry is used to remind unionists that a defiant 'no surrender' posture can bring victory. Those who are perceived to be selling out the unionist cause are called 'Lundies'. Another key date in unionist history is the mobilisation of unionism, under the leadership of William Carson, during the Ulster Crisis 1912–14 when unionists rallied to demonstrate their opposition to home rule for Ireland and willingness to resort to arms to avoid it. During the Battle of the Somme in 1916 the Ulster Division took heavy casualties, demonstrating 'Ulster's' commitment to the Union in blood and consequently Britain's debt to Northern Ireland. The loyalty of Northern Ireland was again demonstrated during the Second World War when Britain 'stood alone' against the Nazis, in contrast to the neutrality of the South. During 'the Troubles' unionists have also moved to preserve its heritage, celebrate new heroes and commemorate new events. For example, following the Drumcree stand-off in 1995, a commemorative medal was struck.

Unionists see the partition of Ireland as democratic and resulting from the South's decision to secede from the Union. The border of Northern Ireland is formed in a similar way to most others, being the result of conflicts of power rather than just following natural geographical features. The threat to the new Northern Ireland state from the IRA is emphasised to justify discrimination against Catholics, or else that discrimination is denied or its impact minimised (see Chapter 4). The emergence of the civil rights movement in the 1960s is seen as a Communist/republican-inspired campaign to re-open the border question, rather than a movement genuinely seeking reform. The growing involvement of the British Government prevented unionists from taking the necessary repressive measures to deal with the terrorist threat. British negotiation with the IRA, its suspension of Stormont and the weakness of British politicians on the constitutional position of Northern Ireland encouraged IRA violence and resulted in a mobilisation of unionists to defend the Union (Chapter 5). The Republic of Ireland, with a territorial claim on the North in its Constitution and its failure to suppress the IRA, encourages and legitimises the IRA campaign against Northern Ireland. The British-inspired power-sharing experiment of 1972–74, particularly its hated Irish dimension, was designed to manipulate Northern Ireland out of the Union and only a popular revolt by unionists prevented this. The Labour Government of 1974–79 cracked down on terrorism and began to rule Northern Ireland like any other part of the UK. This resulted in a decrease in violence. The Conservative governments during 1979–97 turned their back on unionists, beginning an Anglo–Irish process in 1980 which culminated in the great 'sell-out' of 1985 when the Anglo–Irish Agreement was signed, giving the Republic a role in the running of Northern Ireland. For some loyalists this represented yet another ratchet in the expulsion of Northern Ireland from the Union. From this perspective the 'peace process' represents a 'surrender process', with Northern Ireland pushed further and further to the edge of the Union. Unionists are more likely to see the agreement as a historic accommodation from which the Union benefits and emerges stronger, ending Northern Ireland's slide from the Union.

The Ulster Unionist Party   This was the dominant party in the Stormont era 1921–72. It is a centre-right party that draws support from all classes but disproportionately from the middle class. After partition the Ulster Unionist Party (UUP) lacked a serious rival until the Northern Ireland Labour Party in the late 1950s and early 1960s. In the 1960s it was riven by conflict over reform and how to deal with the British Government's interventionism. During the 1970s the UUP began to fragment. The most serious division within its ranks was over the power-sharing experiment of 1974. The leader of the UUP, Brian Faulkner, signed up for power-sharing and an Irish dimension but this split his party and Faulkner resigned. Following the collapse of power-sharing, unionism shifted away from any further power-sharing settlements. Subsequently, the principal division has been between the 'devolutionists' who favour a strong devolved assembly in Northern Ireland and the 'integrationists' who (before the devolution of power to Scotland and Wales in 1999) prefered the region to be ruled like any other part of the UK, directly from Westminster. The UUP favoured the restoration of the powers of local government and an improvement in the way Northern Ireland affairs were dealt with under direct rule as a step towards integration. The party has been united against any Irish dimension beyond 'normal' North–South co-operation. The Good Friday Agreement has split the UUP into those supporting the Agreement and David Trimble's leadership and those against. During the recent conflict the party's principal rival has been the hardline Democratic Unionist Party (DUP) which has succeeded in making inroads into its support, most notably in the early 1980s when it almost became the leading unionist party. The UUP has been more conciliatory, more middle class and slightly less hardline on security than its DUP rival. The UUP's most recent leaders have been Terence O'Neill (1963–69), James Chichester-Clark (1969–71), Brian Faulkner (1971–74), Harry West (1974–79), James Molyneaux (1979–95) and David Trimble (1995–). The UUP's support 1969–99 has ranged from 54.3 per cent to 16.9 per cent, averaging 28 per cent over 1974–99, although in recent years UUP support has dipped well below this.

The Democratic Unionist Party   This loyalist party was founded by the Reverend Ian Paisley in September 1971. During the 1960s Paisley had warned against the apparent softening in the UUP's attitude towards Catholics and the Republic, and these warnings appeared to be vindicated by the turn of events (see Chapters 3 and 4). The DUP, after initially supporting the integration of Northern Ireland into the UK, favoured the return of a majority-rule Northern Ireland Assembly, albeit with some safeguards for the nationalist minority. The DUP is more opposed to power-sharing and an Irish dimension than the UUP and there has been some sympathy for independence. In the late 1970s it demolished its rival, the Vanguard Unionist Party (VUP), which had a more open relationship with the loyalist paramilitaries. In the early 1980s its hardline stance threatened to make it the biggest unionist party. Ian Paisley regularly tops the poll for the Northern Ireland-wide European elections, illustrating that his popularity extends beyond his party. The DUP tends to take a more 'repressive stance' on security issues than the UUP, leaning towards conservatism on social issues (contraception, gay and women's rights), but it is left of centre on economic issues, reflecting its more working-class support. There are two DUP voting constituencies, rural evangelicals and urban, working-class loyalists. The DUP has been led by Dr Ian Paisley since 1971. Between 1973 and 1999 the DUP has averaged 18 per cent of the vote.

The Loyalist paramilitaries   The Ulster Defence Association (UDA) was formed in 1971 to co-ordinate working-class, loyalist vigilante groups which had grown up to 'defend' loyalist areas. It has been involved in violence against Catholics and its political wing has tended towards support for an independent Ulster. The UDA was banned in August 1992 and carries out paramilitary activities under the name the Ulster Freedom Fighters (UFF). The political wing of the UDA is the Ulster Democratic Party (UDP) which participated in the all-party talks which led to the Good Friday Agreement but, with only 1.1 per cent of the vote, failed to win any Assembly seats in 1998. This loyalist party – like the political wing of the paramilitary Ulster Volunteer Force, the Progressive Unionist Party (PUP) – has taken a moderate, accommodating stance during the recent 'peace process'. The UVF was revived in 1966 and after it murdered two Catholics was banned by the Northern Ireland Prime Minister. It is a smaller, more elite grouping than the mass membership UDA but has been responsible for more deaths during the recent conflict. The PUP won 2.6 per cent of the vote in the 1998 Assembly elections, securing two seats. The support of the UVF and UDA for the 'peace process' resulted in a split in the UVF with Billy Wright breaking away to form the Loyalist Volunteer Force (LVF) in 1995. Wright was murdered in prison in December 1997. In 1998 the organisation declared a ceasefire and in December of that year was the first paramilitary organisation to decommission any weapons. The leader of the UDP is Gary McMichael and the leading figures in the PUP are Billy Hutchinson and David Ervine.

The Alliance Party (APNI)   This is the only party in Northern Ireland which draws significant cross-community support, and it is debatable whether it is a unionist party at all. The Alliance Party Assembly members refused to designate themselves as either nationalist or unionist. The party argues that there can be no constitutional change without the consent of the people of Northern Ireland. It was founded in April 1970 among people with little previous political record, and drew support from liberals in the UUP and the Northern Ireland Labour Party. The party supported the power-sharing experiment and after its collapse argued that there was no need for a Council of Ireland to achieve co-operation with the Republic. The Alliance Party draws its support principally from the Greater Belfast area but when it gave conditional support to the Anglo–Irish Agreement in 1985 it lost some Protestant support. The party has favoured power-sharing and been more supportive than the UUP of the Irish dimension. It has more middle-class support and its electoral rivals have been the nationalist SDLP, the unionist UUP, the Conservative Party in Northern Ireland and the Northern Ireland Women's Coalition. Alliance support over 1973–99 has ranged from 2.1 per cent to 14.4 per cent and averaged about 8 per cent, but has been lower in more recent years. The most recent leaders of the Alliance Party have been Oliver Napier (1972–84), John Cushnahan (1984–87), Lord John Alderdice (1987–98) and Sean Neeson (1998–).

History and the Current Conflict

Both nationalists and unionists have different views of history which justify current political positions. Contemporary debates over history have political implications, and can imply both guilt and blame. History can be used to emphasise past injustices and patterns of oppression which can be used to legitimise violence to redress these grievances. As the historian, Paul Bew, has commented, 'The difficulty is that many people on "both sides" as a result of the "troubles" have an investment in a highly partisan reading of that history that validates their suffering or indeed suffering they have inflicted on others.' Conflict over history is common across the world, but perhaps not with the intensity that accompanies an area which is in violent conflict (Ignatieff 1996).

Historians have been conscious of the way history has been used to justify violence. A so-called 'Revisionist' movement of professional historians has developed to undermine the 'myths' of popular unionist and nationalist history. In the 1930s and 1940s a school of professional Irish historians believed that their 'value free' approach to history could demythologise the dominant official and popular histories. This was seen as even more necessary after the recent 'troubles' exploded in the late 1960s and history was used by the protagonists on all sides to justify their violence. The revisionists criticised history as a morality tale and emphasised the discontinuities and complexity of history; they rejected and sought to explode the 'simplistic hero cults' of nationalism and unionism. Inevitably, these 'revisionists' revised the demonic, propagandistic portrayal of Britain in nationalist history and portrayed it in a more sympathetic light. Revisionists also took on unionist history and showed the support of the Pope for William of Orange in 1690 and the conciliatory character of Carson, in contrast with his 'no surrender' unionist stereotype. A more accurate (and empathetic) understanding of history and contemporary history, it could be argued, promotes the kind of understanding which can undermine the crude 'propagandistic', ideological history which (some argue) sustains the conflict.

A traditionalist or nationalist school of history has criticised revisionists for using history to justify the partition of Ireland by emphasising the historical divisions and sectarianism of unionists and nationalists. They were also accused of playing down famine and massacres in history in order to portray the British more favourably. 'Revisionists' have been accused of 'neo-colonialism' or 'anti-nationalism', and one historian has claimed they are part of British counter-insurgency strategy. Traditionalists argued that nationalism and its 'myths' could be a positive force in uniting and fortifying a community in struggle against the British imperialistic enemy (Boyce 1995).

'Myths' are used by the various parties to the conflict in Northern Ireland in the propaganda war to mobilise support and shift the political agenda in their direction (for more on the propaganda war, see Chapter 2). In attempting to communicate with and mobilise a mass audience, politicians use versions of history which resonate with popular ideologies rather than necessarily what is more 'historically accurate' (which, of course, is debatable). These myths may not reflect the latest historical findings but they may reflect certain 'truths' experienced by the people and which the politician seeks to put across to an audience using historical 'stories'. The imperatives of the propaganda war also override the need for historical accuracy, since 'distortion' can be more politically useful than 'truth'. The historical account is not necessarily about, for example, the history of past English atrocities, but about English oppression now. Michael Ignatieff argues that the 'atrocity myth' does not deny that atrocities happen:

> What is mythic is that the atrocities are held to reveal the essential identity of the peoples in whose name they were committed. The atrocity myth implies an idea of a people having some essential genocidal propensity toward the other side. All the members of the group are held to have such a propensity even though atrocity can only be committed by specific individuals. The idea of collective guilt depends on the idea of a national psyche or racial identity. The fiction at work here is akin to the nationalist delusion that the identities of individuals are or should be subsumed into their national identities. (Ignatieff 1996 p. 116)

Usually 'myths' must contain some portion of 'truth' in order to be accepted and, depending on their intent, we may be sympathetic to the sentiment and ignore the historical inaccuracy. These often competing 'myths' have been created by the protagonists during 'the

Troubles' to reinforce their ideological positions and mobilise supporters in the propaganda war (O'Doherty 1998, chs 3 and 4). This means that, as this book makes clear, there is considerable conflict over the interpretation of Northern Ireland's recent history. In the run-up to and during the peace process the British Government has attempted to address historical grievances in the hope that this will aid the process of reconciliation. The British Prime Minister has apologised for Britain's role in the famine of the 1840s, ministers have regretted England's role in Irish history, an inquiry has been set up into the events of 'Bloody Sunday' 1972 and a commission has been established on the victims of the conflict.

There are contrasting views on the impact of history and myth. To what extent does a 'distorted' view of Irish history motivate and exacerbate the conflict? Or is the debate over history more a symptom than a cause of 'the Troubles'? If nationalist and unionist ideologies have deeper, even primordial, cultural or ethnic roots, then revisionist history is less likely to be effective since it will not 'resonate' with the ideologies of the national communities. On the other hand, if nationalism and unionism are modern and malleable ideologies, then we can be optimistic that 'revisionism' may be able to dent nationalist and unionist histories by promoting empathy and a less simplistic view of the conflict.

Segregation and Sharing

The strongly contrasting nationalist and unionist views of the reasons for the Northern Ireland conflict and the means by which it can be resolved are probably related to the very different socialisation experiences of nationalists and unionists. The thinking behind this is that because Protestants and Catholics come into contact so little in Northern Ireland their prejudices and ideological views about 'the other' are reinforced instead of challenged. This creates an environment in which prejudice and violence against the other side is tolerated. To promote the resolution of conflict, it is argued, cross-community contact should be promoted. Others have disputed this and argued that unionist and nationalist identities are permanent and have to be managed and worked around rather than challenged or eroded. They argue that segregation reduces the opportunities for contact and therefore for conflict (see Dixon 1997a, 1997c, 1997d for a detailed review of these approaches).

BELFAST

Map 1.2   Residential segregation in Belfast and Derry/Londonderry
(a rough guide)

Education

There is research which suggests that even pre-school children develop sectarian attitudes. The overwhelming majority of both Catholics and Protestants are educated in single denomination Catholic or state (i.e. Protestant) schools. This limits opportunities for cross-community contact. Some attempt has been made during the conflict to establish integrated schools but these have been met with opposition from both Protestant and Catholic churches. While polls indicate many parents would like to have their children educated in integrated schools, this has not been matched by demand.

Residence

There has always been some degree of residential segregation in Northern Ireland, particularly in working-class areas. The rioting of the late 1960s and early 1970s precipitated what was until then the largest movement of population in Western Europe since Second World War. Catholics fled from Protestant areas to find safety with their co-religionists and, to a lesser extent, Protestants fled Catholic areas. Since the early 1970s there has been a gradual trend towards further residential segregation as a result of force (intimidation and fear of attack) and voluntary movement. Boyle and Hadden conclude, 'in urban areas the two communities are moving into what they regard as safe areas, while in rural areas they are staying put on their land' (Boyle and Hadden 1994 p. 7). By 1991, 'About half of the province's 1.5 million population live in areas more than 90 per cent Protestant or more than 90 per cent Catholic', and 'In the past two decades, the number of predominantly Catholic wards increased from 43 to 120. Areas almost exclusively Protestant rose from 56 to 115' (*The Independent on Sunday*, 21 March 1993). Map 1.2 illustrates residential segregation in Derry/Londonderry and Belfast.

Employment

Following discrimination during the Stormont period (see Chapter 4) there have been attempts to correct the religious imbalance in the workforce. Residential segregation has compounded the problems of achieving this balance, and Protestants and Catholics are deterred from taking jobs in areas dominated by members of the opposite

religion for safety reasons. Also, particularly in smaller firms, employment by social network, word of mouth or overt discrimination has
resulted in a high degree of segregation in employment (Boyle and
Hadden 1994 p. 46). Northern Ireland is one of the most deprived
regions of the UK and there has been increasing inequality (Coulter
1999, ch. 2).

Social

The levels of church attendance in Northern Ireland are disproportionately high for the UK. Social activities associated with the church
tend therefore to reproduce segregation. In addition sports are often
segregated, with Catholics playing the 'Gaelic sports' (e.g., hurling,
camogie, gaelic football) while Protestants play the more 'British
sports' (hockey, rugby, cricket). Even sports which are 'shared', such
as soccer, are not necessarily played in a cross-community context.
The Orange Order was founded in 1795 and now has approximately
100000 members. One of its objectives was to defend the Protestant
succession to the British throne, and it annually commemorates
Protestant victories in Irish history by parading. Catholics are
excluded from membership. Catholic organisations include the
Ancient Order of Hibernians and the Gaelic Athletic Association.
These organisations are often associated with social or community
activities: 'It is highly unlikely that anyone who frequents any of
these clubs or premises will ever meet anyone from the other
community there' (Boyle and Hadden 1994 p. 39). This results in
a low number, approximately 5 per cent, of mixed marriages.

Population

The population of Northern Ireland is approximately 1.7 million,
with nearly 500000 living in the urban area around Belfast (the
population of the Republic is approximately 3.5 million). The higher
Catholic birthrate in Northern Ireland did not lead to an increasing
Catholic proportion of the population between 1926 and 1961 due to
its higher emigration rate. But since 1971 the Catholic proportion
of the population has increased from about 33 per cent to 'at least'
40 per cent in 1991 (Boyle and Hadden 1994 pp. 30–1). This has raised
nationalist expectations that there will be a Catholic and therefore
nationalist majority by about 2020 which could vote itself into a
united Ireland. However, such projections of population growth are

notoriously inaccurate and, since some Catholics are unionists, a Catholic majority might not vote for Irish unity.

Violence and the Conflict: Who Did What to Whom

Interpretations of the violence in Northern Ireland are highly contentious because they can be used to establish victimhood and legitimise political violence. Unionists and nationalists have strongly contrasting views as to who is responsible for the violence and what is a legitimate response to it (Fay *et al.* 1999 pp. 156–7).

There are two contrasting academic perspectives on the impact of violence. The first emphasises the extent of the violence in Northern Ireland and sees this as an incentive for people and policy-makers to turn away from the abyss of all-out civil war and towards accommodation. Nearly 2 per cent of the population of Northern Ireland has been killed (0.22 per cent) or injured (1.78 per cent) during the recent conflict (see Figure 1.1) and comparative evidence is produced to argue that the Northern Ireland conflict is 'very intense' (O'Leary and McGarry 1996 pp. 13, 20). While over 3600 people have been killed 'around 100000 people in Northern Ireland live in households where someone has been injured in a Troubles-related incident' (Fay *et al.* 1999 p. 204). Padraig O'Malley argues against O'Leary's and McGarry use of comparative data:

> Scale alters the perception of the breadth of conflict: we do not think in terms of proportionality but in terms of absolutes. A bomb that kills one person in a population of 1.5 million is not the same thing, nor is it perceived as such, as a bomb that kills one hundred people in a country with a population of one hundred-fifty million people. (O'Malley 1994 p. 16)

He draws attention to the extent of the killing in Sri Lanka (50 000 killed out of 17 million population in 10 years) and Angola (100 000 killed during its civil war).

A second interpretation of the violence suggests that it is because the violence in Northern Ireland has been localised and contained that many have been unaffected by the conflict and are therefore reluctant to become involved in resolving it (Boyle and Hadden 1994 p. 107, O'Malley 1994). There is less risk of sudden death (due to terrorism/murder or road deaths) in Northern Ireland than in the

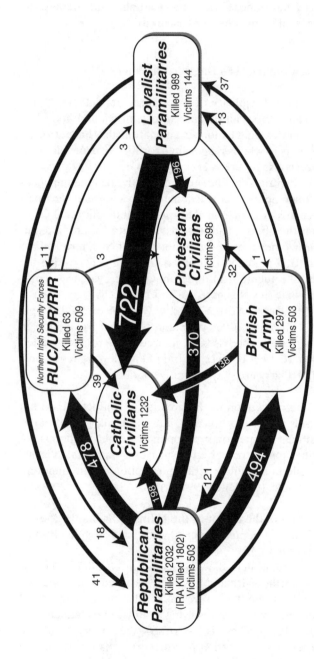

Figure 1.1 'Who killed whom during "the Troubles"' 1969–2000

Note: The primary source for this diagram is McKittrick *et al.* (2000) but where necessary this has been supplemented by figures from Sutton (1994, 1999), Fay *et al.* (1999) and McGarry and O'Leary (1996). These figures are from varying sources with different methods of classification, therefore the figures are approximate and do not add up. Nevertheless they give an idea of the perpetrators and victims of the violence.

USA: 'most people in Northern Ireland have less direct contact with death or injury from the conflict than from ordinary accidents'. They conclude, 'The vast majority of people in Northern Ireland live perfectly normal lives in the midst of the conflict' (Boyle and Hadden 1994 pp. 105–6). However, statistics on road deaths ignore the terrifying impact that the threat of paramilitary or state violence can have on the civilian population. Three areas saw most of the violent incidents: Derry, Mid-Ulster and Belfast. North and West Belfast have seen approximately 40 per cent of all deaths, and there were 600 deaths in North Belfast alone in 1969–93 (*Irish News*, 25 January 1993). Fay *et al.* argue that there is not one conflict in Northern Ireland but 'a mosaic of different types of conflict. Accordingly, the "reality" of the Troubles is different for people in different locations and in different occupations' (Fay *et al.* 1999 p. 136).

Lost Lives: The Stories of the Men, Women and Children who died as a result of the Northern Ireland Troubles is a valuable contribution to the debate because it describes the story of each victim and brings home the immense human tragedy of the conflict which risks being lost in the discussion of statistics (McKittrick *et al.* 1999).

2

The Approach and Argument: Power, Ideology and 'Reality'

The Argument Stated Briefly

This chapter explains the approach and argument of the book to analysing the conflict in Northern Ireland. It stresses the dynamic nature of the conflict and the inter-relationship between power, ideology and 'reality', which reveal the constraints and opportunities affecting the various parties (individuals, groups and governments) to the conflict. This chapter is a much more difficult read than Chapter 1, but its argument should become clearer as the book progresses.

The power of the various parties to pursue their interests is distributed unevenly, with considerable constraints operating on the British Government's ability to control the conflict.

- *Power* is used to fight both a 'real war' and an ideological or propaganda war over Northern Ireland. The 'real war' involves the use of physical force in an attempt to destroy an opponent's armed forces.
- *Ideology* is deployed in the propaganda war in which rhetoric and propaganda are used to realise the party or government's interests. In the propaganda war participants attempt to sustain the determination and morale of the domestic audience, win external support and shift the political agenda in their favour, while at the same time attempting to break their opponent's will to resist. The 'real war' and the propaganda war are inextricably inter-related.
- *'Reality'*. An attempt is made to distinguish between the ideological propaganda and rhetoric which are deployed in the 'propaganda war' and shape perceptions, and the underlying 'realities' of the conflict. However, attention is drawn to the

difficulties of this exercise, in particular the problems of objectivity and the difficulties of distinguishing between false 'propaganda' and 'reality'.

Defining Power: Structure and Agency

The problems of one-dimensional, static explanations of the Northern Ireland conflict – based solely or largely on materialism, religion, social-psychology, ethnicity or culture – have been exposed elsewhere (Whyte 1990). However, while one factor may not explain everything it could explain something. The unemployment rate may not be directly related to the statistics of violence (McGarry and O'Leary 1995 p. 289), but this does not mean that unemployment has no indirect impact on violence and the conflict. The great difficulty is attempting to weigh the importance of various factors (structural, rational and cultural) which affect the conflict and how they inter-relate (Lichbach and Zuckerman 1997 p. 273). Static and unidimensional explanations tend not to consider the dynamics of the conflict, its heights and troughs, and how the impact of its prime factor varies over time and by context (Dixon 1996b, 1996c).

This book seeks a more dynamic explanation of the conflict in Northern Ireland. It focuses on the inter-relationship of power, ideology and reality. Power is an elusive but useful concept which can be defined as the ability to shape action (and here the power of ideologies to shape action is emphasised) (Ashe *et al.* 1999). By considering the *structures* (political, economic, ideological, cultural) which empower or constrain the various *agents* (individuals, parties, organisations and governments) which seek to exert influence on the conflict we can make an assessment of the power which these agents have to pursue their interests and how this power varies over time. There is an attempt to combine the political scientist's eye for the general, structure-oriented explanation and the journalist's or contemporary historian's more agency-oriented approach, with their eye for chronology, detail and nuance (Hay 1995, Marsh *et al.* 1999).

Agency-Oriented Explanations

There is a tendency of some historians and journalists to become caught up in the minutiae of the conflict and not to see the wood for the trees, or the trees for the leaves. There is an overemphasis placed on the individual's capacity for agency (an actor's capacity to take decisions and act upon a situation), where the agents are conceived of as being 'knowledgeable and intentional subjects with complete control over the settings which frame their actions' (Hay 1995 p. 189). By contrast, the structural constraints, influences and long-term processes which shape the individual's, government's or group's (agent's) identity, experience and strategic orientation are played down (Marsh 1999 p. 217).

For example, an agency-oriented account of the Northern Ireland peace process by historians and journalists might be drawn towards the historical minutiae, the recollection of politicians and the nature of the personalities in explaining the outcome of the process. In *The Fight For Peace* the peace process is explained as the result of forceful personalities such as John Hume, Gerry Adams and Albert Reynolds who, largely through their determination and political skill produce an IRA ceasefire (Mallie and McKittrick 1997). The politicians (agents) are seen as exerting a powerful influence and so there is a focus on their intentions, strategies and perceptions. The British Government comes in for particular criticism for failing to win an IRA ceasefire. Little attention is paid to the structural constraints which operate on British policy, in particular the need to bring republicans *and unionists* simultaneously into any all-party talks process (see Chapters 9–10 and Conclusion). An agency-oriented account therefore attaches less weight to the context and constraints which operate on the politicians, such as the political, ideological, social and economic context (the 'structure') in which the politicians take their decisions and the constraints these impose upon politicians (Hay 1995 p. 195).

Structural Explanations

The tendency of some political scientists is to stand so far back that they can only see the wood and not the trees, branches or leaves. They emphasise the objective structures which constrain or are held to determine the behaviour of agents (individuals, groups, governments) and which may even lie outside the understanding of those individuals. A structuralist argument does not attribute much importance to the autonomy and influence of agents, it is not interested in the ways in which people perceive change or contribute to it. The actors appear as 'the unwitting products of their context, helpless individuals with minimal control over their destiny, floundering around in a maelstrom of turbulent currents' (Hay 1995 p. 189).

A strong structuralist account of the peace process would play down the role of politicians who are seen simply as the product of a situation determined by social, political, historical, ideological and economic forces which it is beyond their ability to control or manipulate (see Ruane and Todd 1996, 1999 for structure-oriented accounts). A 'structuralist account' might, for example, emphasise the history of antagonism which makes conflict 'inevitable'. The socio-economic disparity between Catholics and Protestants combines with social segregation to nurture widely contrasting ideologies which perpetuate division and conflict. Reflecting this polarisation, the structural constraints operating on the agents are such that the ability of political leaders to move towards the centre ground of politics or even effect change in Northern Ireland is highly constrained. Public opinion may demand a non-compromising approach from the politicians and make it very difficult to move away from an 'intransigent' stance. The activities of politicians, parties and governments do not and cannot made a difference to a conflict which is beyond their ability to influence, let alone control. Agency-oriented accounts attribute great power to agents (individuals, groups, governments) whereas structuralist accounts emphasise the limits on their power.

The Strategic-Relational Approach

The strategic-relational approach is structure-oriented but leaves scope for agency, it argues that structure and agency are completely interwoven (Hay 1995, Marsh *et al.* 1999). Structure conditions agency and the potential strategies that agents may use to realise their intentions. These structures tend to favour some strategies over others and the more powerful actors. All agents are not equally powerful and strategic opportunities are unevenly distributed; this reflects structures of power and social inequality which are constantly evolving and transforming (Marsh *et al.* 1999 pp. 39–41). Structures constrain agents, but agents also have the potential to impact on the structures in which they operate and thereby attempt to improve their scope for taking action and wielding power. The structural constraints operating on an agent will vary depending on the context in which the agent wishes to wield power. Agents' strategies are dependent on their perceptions or misperceptions of the world around them and they take decisions based on the information which is available to them. Ideology and culture are therefore relevant in explaining the perceptions and behaviour of agents. Agents can be unpredictable and make 'mistakes'; outcomes can be intended or unintended. But these actors can also 'learn' about the structures operating on them and thereby improve their ability to maximise their opportunities to exert power.

As Karl Marx put it, 'Men make their own history but they do not do so just as they please; they do not make it under circumstances chosen by themselves, but under circumstances directly encountered, given, and transmitted from the past.'

The strategic-relational account of the peace process below (Chapters 9–10 and Conclusion) is structure-oriented and emphasises and assesses the limits of the power of the various agents to the conflict (politicians, groups, governments) to impact on the structures they find themselves constrained by. Particular attention is paid to the interests of the various agents and their attempts to realise these interests and the structural constraints which face them in trying to do this. This highlights the distribution of, and limits to, the power of the various parties to the conflict. Although this strategic-relational account is 'structure-oriented', the focus of the study is on the structural limitations facing the power of agents rather than on the structures themselves (which is well done by Ruane and Todd 1996).

The relevance of the strategic-relational approach can be seen when we consider the attempts of some politicians to lead their political activists and supporters to the 'centre' ground of Northern Irish politics (see especially Chapters 3, 4, 6, 9, 10). In order to understand the power of political elites to effect change in Northern Ireland we have to understand and interpret the structural constraints operating on those politicians. Gerry Adams (Sinn Féin) and David Trimble (Ulster Unionist Party) have attempted to move the Good Friday Agreement forward. Both have been constrained by what their activists and voters will stand for. If either moves 'too far' they stand to lose support to their political rivals. The UUP is also under electoral pressure from more hardline unionist parties over the Agreement. Gerry Adams may be less concerned by the nationalist electorate, Sinn Féin having gained electoral support, than by the threat of a significant minority of republican activists splitting away and restarting the 'armed struggle'. Who should move first and how far, Adams or Trimble? By considering the structural constraints on each agent (Adams and Trimble), we attempt to understand what their room for manoeuvre is. Who has the power to move and by how far? This is a highly political and sensitive process as we are attempting to distinguish between:

(a) the moral question of who *should* move; and
(b) the pragmatic or strategic question of who *can* move.

These moral and pragmatic issues are difficult to disentangle, and there is a tendency to argue that those who should move can move. Those sympathetic to republicanism are likely to emphasise the constraints operating on Adams in order to put pressure on Trimble to move, whereas Trimble's sympathisers are likely to do the opposite. The more immediate constraints are probably related to a host of other, more long-term, structural influences (economic, political, social, historical, ideological, etc.) which have constructed a population as divided and suspicious as that in Northern Ireland and which form the wider context in which Adams and Trimble have to operate.

Power is more obviously manifested in a 'top-down' fashion by political and other elites. For example, the power of the British State is obviously manifested in its army and the resources which it has at its disposal in the propaganda war. In this view all aspects of popular daily life are formed by the dominant economic and political forces. The subordinate social groups are reduced to the status of passivity with no scope for independent action. More recent research on power suggests that, while it is distributed unevenly, it is also manifested in the culture of daily life and lived experience, from the 'bottom-up' (Ashe *et al*. 1999). While the influence of 'top-down' power is acknowledged, this is often contested from 'below'. In debates over the collapse of the former Yugoslavia, there is sometimes a concentration on the role played by the political elites for inciting the people to violence through control of the media and appeals to nationalism. But there is also the question as to why people were so responsive to such nationalist appeals rather than say, for example, appeals to class. Demagogues, to be successful, require popular prejudices to which they can appeal. It is important to consider the *inter-relationship* between elite, top-down, and mass, bottom-up, practices in order to assess opportunities for agency and change.

The strategic-relational approach raises important questions about the scope and limits of the power of politicians and other agents to effect change and pursue their interests. Some agents have more power in certain contexts than others, but who has that power and how do we determine this? What resources do actors have or can they mobilise in order to alter the structural pattern of constraint and opportunity in which they find themselves? What is the role of agents such as the British Government, Irish Government, US

Government, and civil society in Northern Ireland to bring about change? How can the structures which constrain agents be altered to maximise the power of politicians to sustain a centrist accommodation? Or are these constraints too strong to be manipulated and the gap between politicians too wide to bridge? A focus on the relationship between structure and agency allows us to understand the strategic problems facing the political elites, and also the extent and limits of their power. It should be remembered that a politically possible accommodation or settlement (such as the Good Friday Agreement) may not be a 'just' one.

The Ideological or Propaganda War

Ideology is a highly controversial concept, but arguably a useful one for analysing the conflict in Northern Ireland. Ideology is used here to describe a set of related ideas shared by a significant number of people which is connected to the nature of power within a society. Ideologies (nationalism, republicanism, unionism, loyalism, socialism, conservatism) provide firstly an intellectual map for making sense of the world as it is, secondly prescribe a vision of the ideal society of the future which can be used to inspire and mobilise support and thirdly provide a strategy for achieving the ideal society. Ideologies serve either to sustain or to undermine the legitimacy, or rightfulness, of a socio-political order. Importantly, ideologies are not just the preserve of political and intellectual elites but shape the common-sense assumptions of the 'masses' too. Ideologies are apparent in the rhetoric of politicians and political publications but extend also into the politics and culture of everyday life, such as everyday conversation, marching and demonstrations, the arts and sport. These ideologies shape people's perceptions and motivate behaviour (they can have an emotional as well as a rational appeal), and can be considered part of the structure within which politicians and other agents operate but which agents also attempt to change (Cash 1996).

Ideology is deployed to win support and pressurise opponents in the propaganda war which has been fought over Northern Ireland. The propaganda war has been fought alongside and is inextricably bound up with the 'real war': that is, the physical, military and material power-struggle. Leading British soldiers have argued from the beginning of 'the Troubles' that there was no purely military solution to the conflict, and that the army could only 'hold the ring' or promote a climate in which a political settlement could be found, perhaps by sapping the will of the enemy to resist. Leading figures in the republican movement accepted that they could not physically kill all the soldiers in the British Army, but they felt they could, through a combination of their military and propaganda activities, attempt to undermine the British will to remain in Northern Ireland, as anti-imperialist movements had done to the British in the days of Empire. In the propaganda war the British Government could not publicly declare that the conflict in Northern Ireland was a 'war' since this ran the risk of conceding legitimacy to the IRA's violence and the political nature of its struggle. However, the British behaved as though the conflict was a 'war' because of the threat it posed to the state. This was reflected in the government's attempts to extend its influence over the media since the belief was that impartiality has no place in war. As the British Prime Minister, Ted Heath, privately commented in 1972, referring to 'Bloody Sunday', 'we were in Northern Ireland fighting not only a military war but a propaganda war' (*The Guardian*, 10 November 1995). The British have attempted to undermine support for the IRA's military campaign (and the loyalists) through its rhetoric in the propaganda war, attempting to criminalise the republican movement and reduce its base of support inside and outside Northern Ireland. Yet privately the 'reality' is that, over the course of the conflict, the British have maintained contacts and even negotiated with the IRA, accepting implicitly the political nature of the republican movement. The IRA's Hunger Strike in 1981 represented in part an attempt to fight back against the British in the propaganda war, and to have the republican movement's political rather than criminal interpretation of their struggle recognised (Chapter 7). The contrast between public rhetoric and private reality has been a particular feature of British politicians' attitudes towards Northern Ireland and explains important apparent contradictions and inconsistencies in British policy (Dixon 1994b, Dixon 1995a pp. 173–8, Dixon 2000b).

Modern political propaganda has been defined as 'the deliberate attempt to influence the opinions of an audience through the transmission of ideas and values for a specific persuasive purpose, consciously designed to serve the interest of the propagandists and their political masters, either directly or indirectly' (Welch 1999 p. 26). The participants in the conflict in Northern Ireland have conflicting ideologies and interpretations of history and political events which are used to fight a propaganda war for the 'hearts and minds' of Irish, British and international opinion. Propagandistic rhetoric, while it bears some relationship to 'truth', can be contrasted with the 'realities' (which may be privately acknowledged) which underlie the conflict. Ideological positions may be adopted not because they are 'true' – the limitations of the different positions are often painfully apparent (O'Malley 1983, Whyte 1990) – but because they are effective in mobilising public opinion.

Ideology is not necessarily 'false' but, when used to mobilise political support in the propaganda war, it can simplify in a way that distorts 'reality'. Contrary to popular perceptions, propaganda does not have to be untrue and the purveyors of propaganda may or may not regard it as true. Propaganda which is based on truth and reflects 'reality' is more likely to be effective as a result. It has been argued that the IRA soon realised that deceiving the media in an obvious way lost it credibility and that being more 'truthful' could be more effective in the propaganda war (Curtis 1984 p. 268). The British Army used 'black propaganda' (*the spreading of of deliberate lies to undermine* an opponent) against both loyalist and republican paramilitaries. When the extent of this became known it undermined the effectiveness of the government's propaganda effort and the army's unit was wound up.

The propaganda war is fought on three fronts:

First, by waging a propaganda war and/or 'psychological operations' directly *against the enemy government/organisation and population* to undermine its will to resist and win over the support of waverers. This can be promoted by 'white'/ 'true' propaganda or by 'black propaganda' which involves the planting of deliberate lies and false stories to mislead and undermine the enemy; or, in the case of a 'civil war', to win over the 'hearts and minds' of those people living in the affected territory.

Second, the propaganda war is waged to win the *support and sympathy of international opinion* which may support one side or the other materially, ideologically (through propaganda) or through diplomatic pressure.

Third, the government attempts to break the opponent's will to resist in the propaganda war by showing *the determination of the domestic government, military and public opinion* to overcome the enemy. This might be achieved by demonising the opponent with stories (sometimes false) of atrocities in order to whip up popular support for war. Morale may also be sustained by censoring reports of defeats or reversals or exaggerating success against the enemy. The British Army has been sensitive to the morale of public opinion and the perceived impact this can have on soldiers. Creating the appearance (if not necessarily the reality of the determination of public opinion) strengthens the position of the government in negotiations with the enemy. It could result in victory with more 'limited' use of force, or even without any need to resort to force (for example, Kosovo: see Dixon 2000a). On the other hand, demonising your opponent can make it more difficult to negotiate with them at a later stage, and whipping up popular opinion could result in an unstoppable momentum to war or even to withdrawal. Not enough domestic interest in a conflict fails to demonstrate determination to win, whereas too much could impact on elite control of policy.

British counter-insurgency strategy placed a great premium on winning the propaganda war against the IRA through political determination. If the British government showed complete determination to defeat the IRA this would sap the will of republicans and their supporters to resist. The government was concerned that the republicans would defeat the British, not so much by physical military means, but by sapping the will of the British public and political elite to resist the IRA. The bipartisan approach of the British political parties to the conflict was designed to maintain unity and stifle domestic dissent in order to demonstrate political determination against the IRA's challenge (see Chapter 5). In 'war' some argue that censorship is necessary to defeat the enemy; the importance of the propaganda war in maintaining morale and defeating the enemy explains British censorship during Second World War, the Falklands conflict and over Northern Ireland (Dixon 2000a).

The British Government is not the only participant in the propaganda war. Since early on in 'the Troubles' the IRA leadership has demonstrated an appreciation of the importance of the propaganda war and of establishing its own legitimacy. The 'armed struggle' could be seen as a tool in the propaganda war – 'armed propaganda' according to Gerry Adams – to put pressure on the British to win a better settlement for republicans, if not outright withdrawal. Violence is a tool for increasing pressure, and the propaganda war is necessary to maintain and increase the pressure of republican and nationalist opinion against the British government. The IRA, like other parties to the conflict, was addressing and attempting to tailor its propaganda to different audiences. For example, in the US republicans tended to emphasise nationalism and Catholic Irish imagery, playing down their socialism. Socialism was played up when attempting to win sympathy amongst the British Left, particularly in the early 1980s. Republicans also understood the legitimacy that talks with the British Government lent the 'armed struggle' (Wright 1991 pp. 94–7). This helps to explain the reluctance of both the British and Irish Governments to embark on *public, official* contacts with the republican movement.

Republicans have also demonstrated an awareness of the propaganda impact of army casualties on British public opinion, producing consistent majority support for a British withdrawal (Dixon 2000a). Since the mid-1970s leading figures in the republican movement may have realised that they could not win against the British but nevertheless continued to make intransigent demands and employed the rhetoric of ultimate victory to maintain republican morale and sustain their 'struggle'. Republicans, again like other parties to the conflict, demonise their opponents to legitimise their violence (see Cash 1996 on loyalist demonisation). Joanne Wright describes the importance of 'supporting propaganda' for sustaining the IRA's violence:

> [it] emphasises the supreme importance of the cause and of the collective over the individual, thus helping to resolve any moral dilemma individuals may have about the acts they have committed or will commit. The theme of a 'war situation' is dominant, with constant references to a long war and the inevitability of victory. Also to maintain morale among active volunteers, the terrorist organisation's treatment of its imprisoned members is vital. It is essential for volunteers to believe that even if captured they will retain a place in the overall struggle, and that attempts will be made to release them. For the volunteer killed in action there is the promise of martyrdom. (Wright 1991 p. 140; see also Chapter 7 in this book)

The Irish Government has also participated in the propaganda war. It has kept up pressure on the British by advocating and demanding Irish unity and (until 1999) retaining Articles 2 and 3 of its Constitution, which laid claim to Northern Ireland. This power to influence the attitudes of Irish nationalism both North and South, and to be more or less co-operative over security, can be used as a bargaining counter in negotiations with the British. Privately, however, Irish governments have often acted in a more accommodating way than their public nationalist posturing would suggest. The Irish

Government privately opposed British withdrawal from Northern Ireland on the grounds that this would lead to civil war. Privately the Irish Government agreed to the British armed forces flying up to five miles inside the Republic, but publicly the Irish Government denied this for fear that it would be politically damaging (Miller 1993). Whether or not the use of propaganda by the political elites is as consciously cynical as suggested here is debatable, as is the extent to which people believe their own propaganda.

The War of Words

The propaganda war is contested by political elites, pressure groups, journalists and academics, but also by the people in the politics of everyday life. The language used to describe the conflict can influence an observer's understanding of it. External opinion, perhaps with little time for the details of the conflict, can more readily grasp that a conflict fits into a pre-existing category such as 'colonial', 'ethnic', 'anti-terrorist' or 'criminal'. Some argue that the use of 'inappropriate' language and characterisations has contributed to the conflict by reproducing sectarian perspectives and stereotypes. Definitions of words are strongly contested, and the most obvious conflicts occur, for example, over whether 'paramilitaries' in Northern Ireland are 'terrorists', 'freedom fighters' or 'guerrillas'. (Inverted commas are used during the text to highlight the particularly contested nature of some of these terms.) In Northern Ireland one of the ways of indicating whether someone is a nationalist or a unionist is their choice of language. Unionists who want to emphasise the separateness of Northern Ireland from the rest of the island tend to refer to Northern Ireland as 'Ulster'. Nationalists who want to stress the illegitimacy of Northern Ireland refer to it as the 'six counties' or the 'north of Ireland'. Since Sinn Féin has attempted to distance itself from the IRA, unionists more often refer to Sinn Féin as Sinn Féin/IRA or IRA/Sinn Féin to stress that the two are inextricably linked.

Conor Cruise O'Brien has gone so far as to argue that in a political and ideological struggle 'words are weapons' and the use or not of the term 'terrorism' had 'a bearing on how long the political violence is likely to continue and how many lives it will cost'. He argues that by failing to describe the IRA as 'terrorists', people are intentionally or unintentionally giving them the legitimacy which sustains their violence. The ground on which this propaganda war is fought extends from politics through to culture. There were calls in Britain for the banning of the film *Michael Collins* for fear that its romanticised portrayal of the IRA lent legitimacy to the contemporary IRA's 'armed struggle'.

Politicians have expressed a consciousness of the impact their pronouncements can have on the conflict. A clear connection is often perceived between aggressive political rhetoric, party ideology and political violence. Ideology and political rhetoric are seen to have 'real' effects, directly inciting violence or creating a permissive culture in which political violence is more likely. Nationalists, particularly in the case of Ian Paisley, tend to draw the link between the rhetoric and actions of unionist politicians and political violence. Since the 1960s some loyalists have claimed they were incited to violence by Paisley's rhetoric and actions. The IRA justified the murder of Unionist MP Robert Bradford on the grounds that he was 'responsible to a considerable degree for motivating the series of purely sectarian attacks on ordinary nationalists, and while they do not pull the trigger they provide the ideological framework for the UDA and UVF gunmen who do the murdering' (*An Phoblacht*, a republican newspaper quoted in Wright 1991 p. 157). Unionists have complained that Sinn Féin has not been banned, despite the fact that the political wing of the IRA has publicly advocated violence against the mainly Protestant RUC. It is argued that the common goals of nationalists and republicans lend legitimacy to the IRA's violence. The failure of nationalists to support the police, their support for the Hunger Strikers in 1981, for Irish unity and Articles 2 and 3 of the Irish Constitution have all been cited by some unionists as legitimising the IRA's campaign of murder against them. In 1991 Joanne Wright argued that the eradication of the IRA would only be achieved by de-legitimising or re-defining the common ideological ends which nationalists (particularly in the Republic) and republicans seek. The British, by avoiding 'security force blunders', could contribute to choking off the propaganda on which the IRA thrives (Wright 1991 p. 219).

There does appear to be evidence to support some relationship between the ideologies of public opinion and violence (Burton 1978, Sluka 1989). To some extent, the paramilitary 'fish' require a 'sea' of at least some public support or acquiescence in which to swim. When the IRA's political wing, Sinn Féin, launched itself into electoral politics in the 1980s and 1990s there developed a tension between the violent activities of the IRA which, if they went 'too far', could alienate nationalists, and the electoral struggle of Sinn Féin to win votes (see Chapter 9 below, Wright 1991 pp. 117–21, Darby 1994 pp. 62–3). Nationalists have expressed concern from time to time that the IRA was provoking loyalist retaliation (Wright 1991 p. 215). On the loyalist side, there also seems to be a relationship between the violence of loyalist paramilitaries and the perceptions of the wider unionist community. During times of extreme stress when Northern Ireland's constitutional position appears to be under threat, unionists are more tolerant of (and likely to engage in) paramilitary activity (Bruce 1999 pp. 202–3).

The problem arises in attempting *to interpret the rhetoric and intentions* of politicians. Many politicians would deny the interpretation that their words are intended to incite violence. Ian Paisley could defend his 'anti-Catholic' rhetoric on at least two grounds: first, that the rhetoric was directed at the Catholic Church and not Catholic people, and second, that the rhetoric is directed to win and consolidate the support of unionists in competition with other unionist parties, rather than inspire violence against Catholics. Paisley's rhetoric could represent a means by which his supporters 'let off steam' and vent their frustrations, as an alternative to violence. Similarly, Gerry Adams' rhetoric could be interpreted on similar grounds: that the IRA's violence is directed at the forces of the British state whose representatives often just happen to be unionists; that the rhetoric is necessary to represent republicans, express their discontents and fend off challenges to his leadership rather than incite more violence.

Ideology: Power Creates 'Reality'?

Some argue that the ideological contest over the 'truth' of any situation is not based on 'facts about reality' but on power. Ideology becomes 'true' because those with the power and authority to produce knowledge impose their definition of the 'truth' of the situation. For example, during the propaganda war the British state tried to criminalise the republican movement. Whether or not the IRA is 'really' a 'criminal' organisation is beside the point if you have the power to convince people that it is a criminal organisation. However, this power to convince people is likely to be related not just to 'political spin' but also to people's direct experience of 'reality' and what they *perceive* that 'reality' to be. Those with a republican ideology, who may know republican activists or have personal experience of the conditions which have sustained the IRA, are less likely to be susceptible to British propaganda than the British public, who are probably already disposed to accept a hostile interpretation of the IRA as criminals.

Ideology may influence action but, to be effective, it has to bear some relation to material realities. The impact of class on the conflict can be seen in the concentration of violence in working class areas and the disproportionate support of the working class for the more 'extreme' political parties. Archbishop Eames, the head of the Church of Ireland, expressed the significance of class: 'I've heard it said they're not fighting each other on the Malone Road [a middle-class suburban area of South Belfast]. It took me years to understand the implications of that remark. There are two communities here, and one is involved in violence, suffering, unemployment, and injustice. The demarcation is class.' (This is backed up by Fay *et al.* 1999. On class see O'Connor 1993, Bew, Gibbon and Patterson 1995, Ruane and Todd 1996 pp. 61–3, 73–5, Coulter 1999 ch. 2.)

The resources available to those who want to conduct the propaganda war varies. While the British Government has enormous material resources this has not ensured domination. Other agents also have resources and a varying ability to put their message across (see Conclusion). Nationalist or republican targets of British propaganda have alternative sources of information to draw upon including their own ideological predispositions and experiences. Equipped with such ideologies, their receptivity to British propaganda is not likely to be passive but will be conducive to alternative explanations of events. Summarising research on propaganda, David Welch argues that it 'is most effective when it reinforces already held ideas and beliefs'. Propaganda is not simply injected into a passive people through the mass media:

> individuals seek out opinion formers from within their own class or sex for confirmation of their own ideas and attitudes. Most writers today argue that propaganda confirms rather than converts, and is most effective when its message is in line with existing opinions and beliefs of those it is aimed at. (Welch 1999 p. 26)

Ideologies tend to reflect and perpetuate contrasting socialisation experiences and the structures which sustain them. These ideologies, although changing and adapting, also reproduce the contrasting assumptions and attitudes of the communities from which they spring, often with overtones of superiority and a lack of empathy for others. The attitude of external opinion, the British, Irish, Europeans and Americans, also reflects to some extent the cultural and ideological environment in those countries. British attitudes towards the conflict in Northern Ireland, particularly at the start of the conflict, were permeated with assumptions, prejudices and a superiority which derive from a very different cultural environment. Their receptivity to republican propaganda – when it does get through – is likely to be hostile given the cultural context and predisposition of the audience.

Ideologies are not closed and undergo constant change and remaking. The potential exists for these ideologies to be transformed in a way that reduces the demonisation of opponents, is more reflective of political 'realities' and promotes accommodation and understanding. This raises questions about to what extent these ideologies can be transformed, and is this in turn dependent on structural change? How far can political actors remake an ideology without losing popular or party support?

Winding Down the Propaganda War

The propaganda war sees participants demonising the enemy in order to mobilise support for the 'war effort', gain external support and exhibit determination to win. The triumph of propaganda over reality – it is argued – has succeeded in polarising opinion particularly within Northern Ireland. Expectations have been raised, while the gap between political rhetoric and political reality has widened and become entrenched. This has left would-be peacemakers with the difficult task of simultaneously winding down the propaganda war, in order to create an ideological environment more conducive to accommodation, while at the same time sustaining the propaganda war to maximise leverage in negotiations.

In times of 'war' it is often argued that dissent and the 'truth' are luxuries which cannot be afforded. First, dissent and the 'truth' could undermine domestic morale and the group's determination to defeat the enemy. Second, this lack of will encourages the enemy to scent victory and to continue its own physical and propaganda campaign. Adherents of an ideology may or may not believe in the 'truth' of that ideology. Indeed an ideology which is 'untrue' may prove to be a more effective tool in fighting the propaganda war because of its ability to mobilise popular prejudices. The ends justify the means, censorship and distortion are justified by the political elite in order to fight the propaganda war and sustain the struggle of the group. The 'truth' could undermine 'the struggle' and is a luxury permitted, if then, in peacetime. In 1981 the former British Prime Minister, Jim Callaghan, argued that it was now time for a full, frank and open debate on Northern Ireland:

> At present every fresh discussion is constrained by self-imposed limitations – justifiable limitations, I admit. There is the fear that anything that we may do will lead to the IRA being encouraged to renewed effort, the feeling that, of course, we must give no encouragement to it or to any terrorist organisation. There is no doubt that that has inhibited discussion in the House ... In my view, the time is ripe for a fundamental, free and open discussion here at Westminster. That is the first step. (Hansard, vol. 7, col. 1050, 2 July 1981)

Unionists and nationalists, at elite and popular levels, show sensitivity to how 'the truth' could aid the enemy in the propaganda war. This might apply, for example, to charges of discrimination; unionists may be privately aware that it occurred but publicly would not confirm this because they feel it would help the IRA in its propaganda war, feed its armed struggle and strengthen its hand in negotiations. For nationalists to acknowledge that some Protestants may have been discriminated against or else to draw attention to IRA atrocities may weaken their side in the propaganda war against unionists and the British. The winding down of the propaganda war and the re-evaluation of ideologies could take place when the climate is more peaceful and the 'real war' de-escalated, but it could also be a precondition for that de-escalation.

The peace process has been largely pursued by elites who, while they have attempted to bring their supporters to accommodation, have a highly limited ability to do this, given the accretion and polarisation of propaganda (ideology) and violence in the 'real war' built up over the years. This propaganda has adversely affected the ideological structures which constrain the politicians (and other agents) who seek an accomodation between unionism and nationalism.

The difficulty comes for the political elites in attempting to bridge that ideological gap, wind down the propaganda war and 're-educate' their communities for the 'new realities' of the post-conflict era (Dixon 2000c). The IRA's ceasefires may have opened up the space where a more 'objective' investigation of 'the Troubles' and the abuses of all sides can be investigated without giving rise to charges that this is sustaining the violence of one side or the other in the propaganda war. Investigations into 'Bloody Sunday', allegations of security force collusion and the IRA's 'disappeared' could all be seen in this context.

The Hall of Mirrors: What is 'Reality'?

In this propaganda war it is difficult to tell the difference between what is political spin necessary to keep up the political pressure on opponents and sustain domestic support, and what is argued here are the underlying political 'realities' of the conflict. Politicians may privately acknowledge 'realities' which they cannot express publicly for fear of jeopardising public or party support. John Taylor, a leading member of the UUP, has commented on the limits of leadership, 'in politics sometimes the logical thing is not necessarily what the people will allow you to do. And in Northern Ireland such are the intense feelings and deep seated fears that what an outside observer might consider logical is not the kind of thing you can deliver politically' (*Irish Times*, 27 September 1989). Public admissions of private 'realities' might provoke an adverse reaction including violence. As Garret Fitzgerald, Irish Taoiseach (Prime Minister) in the 1980s, put it:

> In any situation which is ultimately a negotiating situation, none of the parties are likely to disclose the whole of their minds in public. And that means there can be significant disparities between publicly stated attitudes and privately stated positions, you have the fact that the issues we are dealing with are ones which involve strong emotions in each of the areas – both within Northern Ireland on the Unionist and nationalist sides, in the Republic to a degree also, and in Britain perhaps sometimes to a degree greater than appreciated. And that all operates as a constraint on people stating the whole of their thought in a public forum. (Quoted in O'Malley 1983 p. 253)

The difficulty lies in trying to distinguish between public attitudes and private positions. The observer is in a 'hall of mirrors' trying to go beyond the propaganda war to distinguish between the public rhetoric of propaganda and private 'reality'. How do we know what the underlying 'realities' of the conflict are? Or are these just the author's realities or ideology? Political elites tend to have a vested interest in producing propagandised accounts of events and may be embarrassed publicly to admit a gap between rhetoric and realities, while for some this gap may not exist.

The approach taken here represents an attempt to analyse these often private 'realities' through a careful interpretation of the recent history of the conflict and by an assessment of the interests of the various parties to the conflict and how they sought to achieve them (see Conclusion). Particular attention is paid to sources which indicate the attitudes of politicians when they are not in the public eye, for example to newspaper off-the-record briefings, other leaks of information, politicians' gaffes, private papers, committee minutes and private communications between elites. One journalist wrote of interviewing politicians in Northern Ireland: 'On the record, one gets platitudes and cliches. Off the record, once can either hear unprintable sectarian bile, or well-thought out ideas on the future' (O'Farrell 1998 pp. 102–3). The lack of available government documents is a disadvantage but it seems likely that, if past experience is any indicator, some of these will be unavailable for a hundred years or so on the grounds of 'national security'. Nevertheless, even without government papers, it is possible for contemporary historians to construct an account of an event that proves reasonably accurate once papers are released (Seldon in Brivati *et al.* 1996 p. 354).

There is an attempt in this book to be 'objective' and present a 'balanced' account of the Northern Ireland conflict. However, this inevitably reflects the intellectual interests, preoccupations, conscious and unconscious assumptions and perspectives of the author (who is also 'structured') and so should be read – as all books should be – with a critical eye and a healthy dose of scepticism. Academics, as with journalists and politicians (whether wittingly or not), inevitably become caught up in the conflict they are trying to analyse and should not be blind to the political implications of their arguments. It has been argued that 'the conclusions of much of the scholarship on Northern Ireland are closely correlated with the background of those who reach the conclusions' (Fay *et al.* 1993 p. 3; see also R. Taylor 1988 on the problems of objective research on Northern

Ireland). Michael Ignatieff has argued 'truth is related to identity. What you believe to be true depends, in some measure, on who you believe yourself to be' (Ignatieff 1996 p. 114). For this reason, where possible, contesting perspectives and explanations are presented, analysed and evaluated along with the author's conclusion. Not all explanations are equally convincing; it is argued that some, based on the evidence available, are more convincing than others. There is no claim here to 'absolute truth', but it is hoped that this exercise will encourage more critical thinking about the nature of what we know and how we know it and that this will have an emancipatory effect. A consciousness of how we are socially constructed facilitates critical reflection on our ideological assumptions and actions.

This book engages with, and is a contribution to, the ongoing debates about the conflict in Northern Ireland. While the general approach has been outlined, this book also attempts to correct what the author sees as important distortions or omissions in the literature (as listed below) and this influences the character and content of the book.

1. The character of the book is affected by the author's particular interest in British policy towards Northern Ireland. The empathetic version of British policy presented here may be too positive as it attempts to counter some overly propagandistic accounts.
2. The plight of unionism has been notoriously difficult to understand or empathise with and so a particular effort has been made to understand the unionist position. This is facilitated through a better grasp of British policy, its weakness on the Union and the substance (rather than, as some claim, paranoia) that lies behind unionist concerns that they could be manipulated out of the UK.
3. The problems and limitations of British political and security policy have led to a persistent and structural bias of the security forces against the nationalist community.
4. Violence has proved to be an effective means of exerting extra-parliamentary influence on the political process. British and Irish Governments have publicly refused to deal with the 'men of violence' or legitimise the use of violence through concessions. Yet, it will be argued, the use of violence has produced significant gains (and losses) for its advocates which it seems churlish to ignore. Working-class loyalist and republican paramilitary

organisations have gained disproportionate influence through their willingness to use violence. The British state has at times also deployed considerable and illegitimate repressive violence.

5. This text is oriented towards explaining the difficulties of 'bridging the gap' between unionist and nationalist politicians and achieving an accommodation on the 'centre ground' of politics, such as the Good Friday Agreement. This explains the focus throughout the book on the problems and dilemmas of politicians and other agents attempting to construct such a settlement. Implicit is the assumption that such an accommodation is 'a good thing'.

3

The Inevitability of Irish Unity? Northern Ireland 1921–68

The partition of Ireland in 1920 was an unhappy compromise between contending interests and widely seen as a temporary measure until Ireland could be reunited. Republicans and nationalists tended to believe Ireland would be reunited as a state independent of the UK. The British and unionists, on the other hand, looked forward to a united Ireland more closely tied to Britain, either through a closer relationship within the Empire/Commonwealth or even the re-entry of Ireland into the UK. The forces of history, geography, religion, demography, anti-colonialism and economics have all been invoked to argue that the reunification of Ireland is inevitable. Belief in the inevitability of Irish unity persists among many British and Irish politicians, but now it is more often assumed that a united Ireland would be independent rather than achieved within the Union.

This chapter emphasises the importance of the economic argument for the inevitability of Irish unity for understanding British and Irish attitudes towards Northern Ireland since partition. This economic theory – known as 'Modernisation Theory' – suggests that the spread of economic integration and interdependence between states creates common interests among different social groups. These common interests then transcend, erode and ultimately end national and communal identities. Old identities and prejudices are eroded in three ways:

(a) Increased contact between peoples breaks down stereotypes, reduces prejudice and promotes understanding and tolerance;
(b) by creating common material interests between peoples these rational economic interests come to take precedence over outdated communal or religious ones;

47

(c)   the prosperity that Modernisation brings with it allows the individual to detach herself from backward or primordial identities, based on religion, nation or ethnicity. These old cleavages are left behind and a new modern politics emerges around material or class interests.

Confusingly, *Modernisation Theory* is related to the notion of *modernisation* which was used in the 1960s to mean a rejection of traditional sectarian attitudes and a growing interest in economic growth and consumerism. Modernisation Theory fails to predict the turn of events in Northern Ireland, but the widespread *belief* in the assumptions underlying Modernisation Theory continues to affect the attitudes and actions of important actors in Britain and Ireland. What was the impact of Modernisation Theory and the belief in the inevitability of Irish unity on the actions of politicians? How did growing economic integration and beliefs about economic integration affect the conflict in the key 1960s period?

Partition and Irish Unity

The Government of Ireland Act 1920 which partitioned Ireland also made provision for its reunification. It established two equal Irish parliaments and a 'Council of Ireland':

> With a view to the eventual establishment of a parliament for the whole of Ireland, and to bringing about harmonisation between the parliaments and governments of mutual intercourse and uniformity in relation to matters affecting the whole of Ireland and to providing for the administration of services which the two Parliaments mutually agree should be administered uniformly throughout the whole of Ireland, or which by virtue of this Act are to be so administered, there shall be constituted the Council of Ireland.

The Chief Secretary for Ireland claimed the government's objective with the Act was 'to frame the bill in such a manner as may lead to a union between the two parts of Ireland'. In 1921, at the opening of Stormont, King George V declared:

> The future lies in the hands of my Irish people themselves. May this historic gathering be the prelude of the day in which the Irish

people, North and South, under one Parliament or two, as those Parliaments may themselves decide, shall work together in common love for Ireland upon the sure foundation of mutual justice and respect.

Nationalists, unionists and the British did not want the partition of Ireland. The British tended to see it as a temporary expedient and Ireland was expected to be reunited within the Empire (Canning 1985 p. 312). Winston Churchill's attitude in 1922 towards the Irish Question echoed the assumptions of Modernisation Theory. He expressed impatience with an anachronistic issue which failed to become ameliorated by 'modern' developments. The Great War and 'the deluge of the world' had overturned empires, changed the map of Europe and brought 'tremendous changes' in the 'modes of thought of men'. 'But as the deluge subsides and the waters fall short, we see the dreary steeples of Fermanagh emerging once again. The integrity of their quarrel is one of the few institutions that has been unaltered in the cataclysm which has swept the world.' Churchill, on the imperialist wing of the Conservative Party, also favoured Irish unity within the Empire and he claimed that it was this dream of unity which had motivated Irish acceptance of allegiance to the Crown (Canning 1985 p. 8). Even the diehard unionist, Lord Birkenhead, shared the assumption of British Ministers in the 1920s 'that Ulster must sooner or later be absorbed into the Free State' (Campbell 1983 p. 585). The British Labour Party had been sympathetic to Irish nationalism and, while it opposed partition, the party welcomed the Treaty. Both Irish nationalists and their British supporters seemed to share the assumption 'that an independent, politically "reunited" Ireland was inevitable' (Bowman 1982 p. 30, O'Halloran 1987). If unity was inevitable then why should British politicians attempt to deal with civil rights abuses in Northern Ireland and risk provoking the re-emergence of the 'Irish Question' in British politics?

The British attempted to insulate themselves from Northern Ireland by refusing to rule it directly and imposing the Stormont Parliament. In addition a 'Speaker's Convention' emerged at Westminster which forbade the discussion of affairs held to be the responsibility of the Northern Ireland Government. The British withheld royal assent for a Northern Ireland Bill abolishing proportional representation in local elections, because it threatened to entrench the domination of the Ulster Unionist Party. When the Unionist cabinet threatened to resign the British backed down.

Nationalists tended to assume Modernisation, and other 'historical forces', were inevitably bringing about Irish unity (O'Halloran 1987). From this perspective, unionist opposition to unification was an anachronism which would be worn down by the forces of 'progress'. Each episode of unionist resistance is interpreted as the last stand before unionists realise they are really Irish and succumb to the inevitable. If Irish unity is inevitable then this removes the need to persuade unionists of the advantages of Irish unity.

Ireland: Years of Polarisation 1921–58

During the 'Years of Polarisation' the South did little to try to win unionist support for unity. In 1920–22 Sinn Féin, angry at the expulsion of Catholics from employment in the North, organised a boycott of Belfast which seriously affected North/South trade. In 1922 a North/South pact was agreed which promised North–South co-operation and hoped to resolve controversy over the border on an inter-governmental basis. The pact quickly collapsed and in 1923 the Free State government set up its own tariffs and customs machinery on the border. In 1925 the British, Northern Irish and Irish Governments agreed to amend the Irish Treaty and transfer the powers of the Council of Ireland to the parliaments of the North and South. It provided for the meeting of the two governments to 'meet together as and when necessary for the purpose of considering matters of common interest arising out of or connected with the exercise and administration of the said powers'. These regular contacts did not take place and the Prime Ministers of Northern Ireland and the South did not meet for 40 years.

During the 1930s relations between Northern Ireland and the Irish Free State polarised. As Unionist leaders infamously declared Northern Ireland a Protestant state, Nationalists in the South underlined the Catholicism of the Irish Free State. James Craig, the Prime Minister of Northern Ireland (1921–40), declared: 'In the South they boasted of a Catholic State. They still boast of Southern Ireland being a Catholic State. All I boast of is that we are a Protestant Parliament and a Protestant State.' Northern Ireland had been set up during a period of crisis: there was IRA activity in the North and unionists feared an invasion from the South. Discrimination was justified against the Catholic minority on the grounds that they were a disloyal 'enemy within' who could not be trusted in positions of power. In 1933 Sir Basil Brooke, future Prime Minister of Northern Ireland, bragged that he did not have

> a Roman Catholic about his own place ... He would point out that the Roman Catholics were endeavouring to get in everywhere and were out with all their force and might to destroy the power and constitution of Ulster. There was a definite plot to overpower the vote of unionists in the North. He would appeal to loyalists therefore, wherever possible, to employ good protestant lads and lassies.

(For an assessment of discrimination, see Chapter 4.)

The victory of the anti-Treaty party, Fianna Fáil, in the 1932 Free State elections brought Eamonn de Valera, the leader of the anti-treaty forces, to power. De Valera's protectionism and the advent of a 'trade war' between Britain and the Free State resulted in a decline of cross-border trade. In 1933 de Valera argued that if British influence and financial contributions were withdrawn, 'the force of common interest, the natural interdependence of the two parts of the country and the sentiment of nationality would work irresistibly for the restoration of the unity destroyed by British policy in 1920' (Whyte 1990 p. 131). The Catholic priorities of the Free State were becoming more apparent in the 1930s. In 1931 Cardinal MacCrory told Catholics that the Protestant Church of Ireland was 'not even a part of the Church of Christ' (Kennedy 1988 p. 191). De Valera began 'openly to stress specifically Catholic priorities', British heritage was dismantled and Protestants in the South claimed persecution as their numbers dropped 32 per cent between 1911 and 1926. This culminated in the 1937 Constitution which enshrined the special position of the Catholic Church in the South. After 1956 de Valera argued that the choice for unionists was 'either assimilation or emigration with compensation' (Bowman 1982 pp. 318–19).

De Valera's confrontational approach to Britain and the creation of a more Catholic Ireland probably served to shore up the unionists' position within the UK. Craig claimed that the coming to power of the gunman 'forever destroyed any hopes of a united Ireland'. Lord Londonderry pointed out the benefit to unionism of a hostile administration in the South. With the 'doubtful friendship' of the more moderate Cosgrave governments in the South (1922–32), the Unionist government would be under 'continual pressure' to make concessions to keep him in power. The 'more or less open opposition of a de Valera government' removed this pressure (Harkness 1993 p. 33). While historians have rightly highlighted the sectarian nature of the Northern Ireland state in the 1930s, others have argued that it was the Southern shift to more sectarian positions which produced a Northern response (Kennedy 1988 p. 229).

'A Nation Once Again'?

The British Government handed back the Treaty Ports to de Valera's Government in 1938, mistakenly believing that in return the Free State would support Britain in the coming war and allow access to the ports. As in the First World War, British politicians hoped that Ireland might be reunited through the struggle of North and South against a common enemy. In 1940 when Britain 'stood alone' against the Nazis, an offer of unity was made to the Irish government by Neville Chamberlain. De Valera rejected the scheme because Britain looked likely to lose the war and there was no guarantee that a united Ireland would result from their proposals. Furthermore, he 'could not imagine how the British could ever obtain a firm grasp upon Craigavon [the Prime Minister of Northern Ireland], let alone thrust him toward Dublin' (Fisk 1983 p. 216). In the aftermath of Pearl Harbor Churchill telegraphed de Valera: 'Now is your chance. Now or never. "A nation once again."' Again, this was to be achieved out of common struggle, rather than British coercion of the unionists (Fisk 1983 pp. 324–5). Northern Ireland's loyalty to the Allies during Second World War won it international credit, particularly in the USA which had been traditionally sympathetic to the claims of Irish nationalism. The Free State's wartime neutrality weakened its international standing. De Valera sent his condolences to the German embassy on the news of Hitler's death, an incident which obscured the generally sympathetic position taken by the Free State government towards the Allies.

In the immediate post-war period the Irish Free State launched an anti-partition campaign, raised the question of discrimination in Northern Ireland and left the Commonwealth by declaring itself a Republic in 1948. There was plenty of sympathy in the newly-elected Labour Government for Irish unity, to come over time and through co-operation, but not for coercing Northern Ireland out of the Union. Herbert Morrison thought there was nothing to be lost by 'a policy of developing good co-operative relations in matters of common concern' between North and South but he did not want to raise the explosive issue of partition: 'If new circumstances arose, among them a change of view on the part of Northern Ireland (if it occurred) that would be another matter but to expect us to coerce Ulster was expecting too much' (Cabinet Papers (46) 381, 16 October 1946). Prime Minister Clement Attlee concluded 'that the Government of the Irish Free State considered the cutting of the last tie uniting them to the British Commonwealth as a more important objective than their policy for ending partition' (Harkness 1996 p. 82). The Labour Government gave Northern Ireland a guarantee that it would remain within the UK as long as its Parliament consented. Following the South's declaration of the Republic, a working party of officials concluded that 'So far as it can be foreseen, it will never be to Great Britain's advantage that Northern Ireland should continue to form part of a territory outside his majesty's jurisdiction' (PRO (Public Record Office) Gen 262/13 'Ireland – Report of Working Party Officials' CP (49) 4, 7 January 1949). The South's decision to leave the Commonwealth may have raised British strategic fears of a hostile, united, independent Ireland. Nevertheless, the Ireland Act 1949 permitted Irish unity with the consent of the Northern Ireland Parliament, and the Irish Free State consistently expressed its willingness to join NATO in return for an end to partition. The British Labour Government's willingness to contemplate Irish unity in the 1960s suggested there was no overriding British strategic interest in Ireland.

Autonomy under Threat: Northern Ireland and the UK

In the post-war period the autonomy of the Northern Ireland state was becoming undermined. First, the growth of the welfare state made Northern Ireland more economically dependent on Britain. Second, Stormont could not cope with its unemployment problem without the co-operation of Westminster. Third, the region's dependence on Westminster was underlined by the Conservative Government's application to join the European Economic Community in 1961 and its need to attract foreign investment. Fourth, the prospect of a Labour Government at Westminster alarmed unionists who feared this would make interference more likely.

The growth of the state

The election of the Labour Government in 1945 and its passage of welfare legislation presented the Unionist Government with three choices. First, it could implement the legislation 'step by step' with Westminster and accept that the cost of introducing this would leave Northern Ireland financially dependent on London. The problem, according to Northern Ireland's Minister for Commerce, was that 'Britain seemed to have shifted and significantly leftwards and governments, Labour or Conservative, would hereafter assume much tighter planning and control, irksome to Ulstermen used to semi-independence' (Harkness 1977 p. 179).

Second, following the logic of this financial dependence they could call for direct rule from London. However, this would remove the Stormont Parliament which had proved to be a useful tool for resisting British interference.

Third, they could reject the welfare legislation passed by the Labour Government and financial dependence on London and shift towards Dominion status, thus preserving Northern Ireland's autonomy. This would make the Unionist Government 'masters of our own house', having actual as well as nominal power and responsibility '. . . We would no longer be able to confess our inability to control our own destinies and we would be relieved from the constant anxiety as to what an unfriendly British Government might be tempted to do in the way of pressing us to end partition' (Harkness 1977 p. 183; see also Bew *et al.* 1995). Yet this might destroy Northern Ireland's economic security and undermine the greater independence the Government hoped to secure. The Northern Ireland Prime Minister, Basil Brooke, 'saw no alternative to carrying on as before, gaining as much as possible the benefits of Westminster social legislation, while diminishing, or at least packaging as acceptably as possible, the less pleasing socialist measures, trusting to pragmatic, ad hoc responses to avoid major confrontation' (Harkness 1977 p. 186).

The decision of the Stormont Government to implement, more or less, British welfare legislation meant it was increasingly acting as an agent of the British state. Local government assumed a new importance as the distributor of state resources: 'elected local governments especially in urban areas, now pursued policies in the housing, highways and planning fields more likely to bring them into contact and conflict with local citizens' (Bulpitt 1983 p. 169). Unionist dominance of local government in Northern Ireland and its discriminatory practices exacerbated the disadvantages experienced by the Catholic minority (see Chapter 4).

The Unemployment Crisis

In the years following the Second World War, Northern Ireland became the most depressed region of the UK. It had a growing unemployment problem and was increasingly dependent on subsidies from the British Exchequer. By February 1961 around 8.1 per cent of the insured population were out of work. The Northern Ireland Government was under electoral pressure from the Northern Ireland Labour Party (NILP) to take effective action to solve the unemployment crisis, or else to persuade the British Government to do so. In the summer of 1962 the NILP collected 100000 signatures on a petition calling for the recall of Parliament: 'Years before the first Civil Rights march the Loyalist working class took to the streets in protest against social and economic conditions' (Arthur 1984 p. 82). The unemployment crisis revealed the extent of Northern Ireland's dependence on the UK. The Northern Irish Government complained of its powerlessness to meet the challenge which faced it on its own since all the major tools of economic management were in the hands of the British Government (C(61) Annex II 'Measures for the relief of unemployment in Northern Ireland – Proposals by the Northern Ireland Government', PRO).

Since partition successive British Governments had been extremely reluctant to risk re-opening the 'Irish Question' by interfering with Northern Ireland's affairs. So, in spite of Northern Ireland's financial dependence on Westminster, Stormont was relatively autonomous. However, unionists were alive to the possibility that some future, probably Labour, government in London might use its financial leverage to undermine Northern Ireland's constitutional position. During the early 1960s the impression was given that Britain would take a more active and interventionist role in Northern Irish affairs. The 'centre' was playing an increasing role in local politics throughout the UK as it attempted to modernise Britain through 'planned economic growth, more efficient public administration and a more democratic political process' (Bulpitt 1983 pp. 171–2). Both Conservative and Labour parties adopted policies which *appeared* to involve British politicians taking decisions on the economy of Northern Ireland (House of Commons, vol. 640, col. 872, 12 May 1961). The Ulster Unionists required an increased role for Westminster in the affairs of Northern Ireland and yet, at the same time, feared that this would lead to opportunities for nationalists to raise questions of civil rights abuse and partition.

Northern Ireland, the EEC and the World

The British Conservative Government's application to the European Economic Community (EEC) in 1961 underlined Northern Ireland's growing subjection to UK and international influences which it was beyond the Stormont Parliament's ability to control. The decision to enter was taken by the British Parliament without the need for the consent of the Northern Ireland Parliament. The Euro-enthusiasts' Modernising assumptions were largely accepted and echoed in Northern Ireland by politicians across the communal divide, regardless of whether or not the implications of those assumptions were welcome. Nationalists favoured European integration since for them the logical corollary of a united Europe seemed to be a united Ireland, while unionists feared that if the Republic had direct representation in the EEC Northern Ireland's position may be viewed in an unsympathetic light (Dixon 1994a). The first British and Irish attempt at EEC membership failed. The second attempt in 1967 also failed but was marked by growing unionist opposition to European integration. While Terence O'Neill, the Northern Ireland Prime Minister, favoured entry, six out of eleven Ulster Unionist MPs at Westminster opposed it. O'Neill turned the logic of Modernisation against the Nationalists by arguing that joining the EEC might result in Irish unity but it would also result in the Republic rejoining the Union. Ulster would remain British 'because that is the freely expressed political will of its people'.

The European question heightened unionist constitutional uncertainties at a time when they feared that the processes of Modernisation were shifting power away from Northern Ireland and undermining Stormont's ability to control the future of the region. Attempts to attract foreign investment may have been a further factor in raising unionist insecurities. During the 1950s and 1960s external investment from Britain, the USA and other foreign-owned companies was responsible for the bulk of employment growth. In order to attract foreign investment the Northern Ireland Government had to project a positive image internationally. Since world (and particularly US) opinion had never been sympathetic to the unionist cause – except, perhaps after the Second World War – there may have been concern that increased dependence on foreign investment could be used as a lever to undermine Northern Ireland's place in the Union.

Prospect of Labour

The bipartisan accord which had kept Northern Ireland out of British politics for so long was showing signs of weakening under the impact of the need for 'national' economic planning and politicians pressing to raise civil rights issues at Westminster. In Opposition, the British Labour Party used the plight of Northern Ireland's economy as an example of the Conservative Government's poor economy management and drew up proposals for the introduction of a UK-wide economic plan. The 'Speaker's Convention', ruling discussion of Northern Ireland affairs at Westminster out of order, was relaxed in order to permit discussion of the UK economy as a whole. Stormont was *potentially* vulnerable to political manipulation by Westminster because of growing integration into Britain's economic policy-making and the region's financial dependence on Westminster. In spite of the 'unionist' record of the 1945–51 Labour Government, the Party was popularly associated with the cause of Irish nationalism, an association kept alive by periodic pro-nationalist interventions by Labour MPs.

At the 1964 Westminster General Election there was considerable disquiet at the prospect of a Labour Government. On the eve of polling, a headline in the *Belfast Telegraph* read: 'Craig Slams Labour Plan – Disregard of Constitution alleged'. The Labour Party's plan to set up a regional planning board in Northern Ireland was criticised by the Unionist Minister, William Craig, on the grounds that regional planning was the prerogative of Stormont. According to Craig, Labour's proposal 'looks like a disregard of Ulster's constitutional position, or at best an impertinence' (*Belfast Telegraph*, 14 October 1964).

Unionist insecurity was further raised by Harold Wilson's comments on civil rights. He promised the Campaign for Social Justice (CSJ) 'that a Labour Government would do everything in its power to see that the infringements of justice to which you are so rightly drawing attention are effectively dealt with'. The unionist *Newsletter* splashed across its front page 'WILSON BOMBSHELL', claiming Wilson's response to the CSJ 'cut across the Government of Ireland

Act, which reserves certain powers to the Northern Ireland Government. It would also be a contradiction of recent assurances by Mr Wilson that he will consult with the Ulster Government, but will not interfere in the internal affairs of Northern Ireland.' Wilson probably had not intended to raise communal passions in Northern Ireland. He was reported to have remarked during the 1964 campaign: 'Any politician who wants to get involved with Ulster ought to have his head examined.' (*The Sunday Times*, Insight Team, 1972 p. 80) However, the unintentional effect of Wilson's intervention, coupled with his party's 'national' planning policy and traditional sympathy for Irish nationalism, was probably to exacerbate unionist insecurity and sense of vulnerability to Labour's power.

Labour's narrow majority at the 1964 Westminster General Election focused the party's resentment on the 12 Ulster Unionist MPs at Westminster who were voting with the Conservative Opposition. This resentment fuelled the interest of the Labour Party in civil rights in Northern Ireland, leading to the formation of the Campaign for Democracy in Ulster in 1965. Even among the Conservatives, the Unionist Party's traditional allies, there was some interest in Northern Ireland, and the party's 1966 manifesto described the need for counties West of the Bann (where discrimination was most intense) to share in the North's increasing prosperity.

O'Neill, Modernisation and modernisation

The emergence of O'Neill as Prime Minister of Northern Ireland in 1963 led to a modernisation of at least the rhetoric of unionism if not the substance. O'Neill's speeches were permeated with the assumptions of Modernisation Theory, reflecting an awareness of the 'new economic and political realities' facing Northern Ireland in what appeared to be an increasingly integrated and interdependent world. The old antagonisms between unionists and nationalists had been worn away and appeared a 'ludicrous anachronism' which, O'Neill's supporters claimed, he was trying to replace with 'normal twentieth-century politics, based on a division between Right and Left' (O'Neill 1969 p. 11). O'Neill's modernising rhetoric mirrored that of the British political elite and alleviated their pressure to intervene (Dixon 1993).

Four themes stand out in O'Neill's speeches: first, *the economic and political dependence of Northern Ireland on Britain*, and the consequent need to win the support of British public opinion. In an increasingly integrated and interdependent world Northern Ireland could no longer afford the 'luxury of insularity'. Northern Ireland was 'utterly dependent on London', 'the great powers of control of the economy, the ultimate purse string, the final instruments of fiscal and economic policy – these are in London, not in Belfast'. Furthermore, Northen Ireland's place in the Union was dependent on a 'substantial proportion of the British people' being 'convinced of the justice of our cause' (O'Neill 1969 pp. 38, 52–3). O'Neill and Heath both agreed that Northern Ireland's 'surest shield is our good name in Great Britain: if we have ever to lose this, our position could be perilous indeed' (O'Neill in *Ulster Unionist Council Yearbook* 1967, Heath in *Belfast Telegraph*, 3 October 1967). This highlighted the vulnerability of the region's place in the UK to the whims and prejudice of British political and public opinion which appeared to know or care little about Northern Ireland (Loughlin 1995).

Second, O'Neill emphasised *Northern Ireland's need to maintain a good name in order to win external investment from the rest of the UK and further afield.* Poor relations with the Republic could cause embarrassment in the USA. In 1945 there was not a single American company with a plant in Northern Ireland but by 1964 this situation had 'been completely transformed' (O'Neill 1969 p. 180, Bew, Patterson and Teague 1997 p. 26).

Third, O'Neill hoped *the improvement of relations with the Republic of Ireland and Catholics in Northern Ireland could increase prosperity and develop understanding of the unionist position* (as well as appease British pressure). He hoped that 'if relationships can be conducted on a sane and reasonable level, policies of hatred and violence will make less and less appeal'. This in turn would promote understanding of Northern Ireland's constitutional position in the South, if not support for it (O'Neill 1969 p. 159).

The fourth theme in O'Neill's speeches was his Modernising belief that *economic interests and increased contact would and should win out over communal allegiances, resulting in a strengthening of the Union rather than its weakening.* O'Neill saw both economic and emotional underpinnings in unionism and communal identity (O'Neill 1969 pp. 47, 114). However, implicit in O'Neill's unionism is an assumption that economic interests should override communal ones, and since unionism was more economically rational than nationalism it would therefore ultimately win out. O'Neill's famous Crossroads speech in December 1968 asked, 'Is a freedom to pursue the un-Christian path of communal strife and sectarian bitterness really more important to you than all the benefits of the British Welfare State?' (O'Neill 1969 p. 142, Faulkner 1978 p. 41). He hoped to rally 'the moderates', in particular the churches, against 'the raucous sound of extremism [which] is often heard much more loudly than the steady ground-swell of moderation', and urged the community as a whole in the 'complex of activities in which its members are engaged' to 'reach out . . . across denominational barriers'. Cross-community contact would lead to 'mutual benefits in terms of greater knowledge and respect' (O'Neill 1969 pp. 115, 130–1).

During the 1960s both 'moderate unionists' and nationalists took comfort from an apparent acceleration of the Modernising process, believing developments heralded the triumph of their ideology over the other. O'Neill's modernising regime was met with opposition both inside and outside his party, as he attempted to reassure unionists that his more conciliatory approach towards Catholics did not mean that the Union was in danger (O'Neill 1969 p. 51). However, leading figures in the Labour Government did interpret O'Neill's modernising approach as indicating unionism's weakness on partition (a perennial danger for reforming unionists).

North–South Co-operation and Wilson's 'Surrogate Nationalism'

During the 1950s Dublin–Belfast relations were at a low ebb. In the North, de Valera's republican rhetoric was perceived as fuelling the IRA's violent 'Border Campaign' of 1956–62. The replacement of de Valera with Sean Lemass in 1959 was welcomed by the British since Lemass wanted closer co-operation with the UK, 'partly for its own sake and partly in the hope of creating a more friendly climate of opinion between Northern Ireland and the Republic' (Bew, Patterson and Teague 1997 p. 25). By the 1950s North/South trade was very limited and economic integration was an unlikely motor for Irish unity. However, in 1958 the Republic emerged from its state of relative economic isolation and introduced its 'First Programme for Economic Expansion', which recommended the opening up of the country to foreign investment and an industrial export drive as a means for generating economic growth. In 1961 the Republic applied to join the EEC with the UK. The Republic of Ireland was also emerging from diplomatic isolation and using international platforms to raise the question of partition. Although the Republic refused to join NATO it joined the Organisation for European Economic Co-operation in 1948, the Council of Europe in 1949, the United Nations in 1955, and the International Monetary Fund and World Bank in 1957. The Republic was able to use these international platforms to raise the question of partition.

Sean Lemass, the Irish Taoiseach, successfully justified this radically new direction in the Republic's economic policy by claiming that it would undermine partition. De Valera agreed, and argued in November 1957 that the proper way to end partition was for the South to have as close relations as they could with those in the Six Counties by combining on matters and interests common to them both (Bowman 1982 p. 308). Politicians in the South from both major parties seized on movement towards European co-operation as a means to unite Ireland (Dixon 1994a). Unionists and republicans were both fearful of the implications of the opening up of the Southern economy. Unionists feared new tactics were being deployed to end partition through social, economic and cultural co-operation (*Newsletter*, 30 January 1958). For republicans, Sean Lemass' break with the economic protectionism of the 1930s represented the final capitulation of Fianna Fáil to Britain, whose strategy was now 'to snare Lemass back into the United Kingdom' through the economic imperialism of free trade (Patterson 1997).

The Republic's more conciliatory position represented a shift from regarding Britain as the principal barrier to ending partition towards addressing the opposition of unionists to Irish unity. In July 1963 Lemass recognised that 'the Government and Parliament [of Northern Ireland] exist with the support of the majority' and that 'the solution of the problem of partition is one to be found in Ireland by Irishmen' (Patterson 1999 pp. 152–3). In April 1964, after a visit to London where he met Sir Alec Douglas-Home and Harold Wilson, Sean Lemass declared:

> I do not believe that there now exists in Britain either amongst its political leaders or the mass of its people any desire to maintain partition or any belief that it serves British interests... I am sure there would be a general and sincere welcome for any move to bring it to an end by agreement amongst Irishmen. This sentiment has not yet found clear political expression from British leaders – as I have urged of them – but this I believe to be now only a matter of time. (*Newsletter*, 14 April 1964)

In response to Lemass' overtures, O'Neill demanded the full constitutional recognition of Northern Ireland by the South and appealed for a concentration on more immediately relevant issues. The meeting of Lemass and O'Neill at Stormont in January 1965 was the first meeting between the prime ministers of Northern Ireland and the South since 1925. O'Neill had not consulted his cabinet or party over the surprise invitation to Lemass, which was bound to raise concerns over the North's constitutional status in some quarters. When O'Neill addressed Stormont to explain the reasons for inviting Lemass to the North, he felt the need to reassure the assembly and his backbenchers that 'Our Constitution . . . is not in doubt' (O'Neill 1969 p. 157). He argued that the Government of Ireland Act 'never intended that . . . there should be anything but a purely *political* boundary between North and South'. The unionist *Newsletter* welcomed the Lemass/O'Neill meeting but also carried published quotes from Lemass which could be read as suggesting the Southern Premier saw the talks as a means to Irish unity (*Newsletter*, 15 January 1965). Desmond Boal, MP for the Shankhill, opposed the meeting, calling for the Southern Government to recognise the existence of Northern Ireland (*Irish Times*, 19 March 1965). The maverick Protestant Unionist, the Reverend Ian Paisley, demonstrated outside the gates of Stormont, throwing snowballs at Lemass' car and protesting that O'Neill was undermining Northern Ireland's position in the Union.

There is contemporary evidence that Harold Wilson favoured Irish unity, or at least did not oppose it ('surrogate nationalism' is Bew et al's description 1979). This suggested that Britain had no overriding strategic interest in Northern Ireland. The O'Neill–Lemass cross-border talks complemented Wilson's desire to improve Anglo–Irish relations, with a view to creating a free-trade area with the South. Among the Labour Government's contributions to improving Anglo–Irish relations was the return to Ireland of the flag which flew over the General Post Office in 1916 and the remains of the Republican hero, Roger Casement, for burial. In March 1965 Wilson made a speech which Ulster Unionists interpreted as hinting at a political or constitutional initiative by the Labour Government on Ireland. Wilson told a St Patrick's Day Banquet at the Irish Club in London that he represented more Irish people in the British Parliament than Charles Haughey did in the Dáil: 'All of us recognise that even before your next St Patrick's Day banquet, if we maintain this momentum things can be better. If we can turn our backs on the past and our faces to the future, I believe, speaking of the two islands, that there is nothing we cannot do together' (*The Times*, 18 March 1965). Wilson also proposed a meeting of the three Prime Ministers of the British Isles. He had not consulted O'Neill who rebuffed this suggestion, and told Stormont that the Union 'is our most precious possession and will be maintained by all means at our disposal' (*Irish Times*, 19 March 1965).

In May 1965 Sean Lemass declared that he was convinced the British would not oppose any solution approved by the peoples of both parts of Ireland. He shared Wilson's apparent belief that the two parts of Ireland would gradually grow together through a process of fruitful co-operation. Conventional patriotism was dying out and he suggested that some kind of 'Council of Ireland' might deliberate and advise on cultural affairs (*The Guardian*, 31 May 1965, *Irish Times*, 19 March 1965). *The Daily Telegraph* reported Wilson as favouring Irish unity within the Commonwealth (six years later, in November 1971, Wilson publicly came out in favour of this position: see Bew, Patterson and Teague 1997 p. 37). One press report claimed that Wilson wanted to be the Prime Minister who solved the Irish Question and that he believed that increased trade, by helping to reduce tension between North and South, would promote this (*The Sunday Times*, 12 December 1965). At the Council of Europe in 1967 Wilson echoed Lemass' formula that the Irish Question should be resolved by the Irish themselves (*Irish Times*, 24 January 1967). Patrick Gordon-Walker, Labour's Foreign Secretary, announced that Britain was not maintaining partition and accepted that Ireland's problems should be solved by Irishmen in Ireland (*Irish Times*, 3 February 1965). In February 1968 the Deputy Secretary for Commonwealth Relations claimed that the British remained benevolent 'towards any solution that might be agreed upon in Ireland between Irishmen' (*Irish Times*, 1–2 January 1999). In December 1965, the Anglo–Irish Free Trade Agreement was signed between Britain and the Republic of Ireland. It was welcomed by Stormont, although *The Sunday Times* had noted a suspicion surrounding the Anglo–Irish talks that Northern Ireland's 'birthright is being willfully sold' (*The Sunday Times*, 12 December 1965).

The impact of Modernisation Theory and the 'surrogate nationalism' of Harold Wilson may help to explain the growing concerns amongst unionists that Northern Ireland's autonomy and its constitutional position was becoming eroded. The British political elite, above all, wanted to avoid re-opening the 'Irish Question' in British politics. The process of Modernisation appeared to be accelerating with the O'Neill–Lemass meeting, and this held out the prospect of resolving the border issue alongside a profitable improvement in Anglo–Irish relations. Unionists had substantial reason for their perception that events were running against them and it is against this background of heightened unionist insecurity that their response to the emerging civil rights movement should be considered. Paradoxically, poor Anglo–Irish and North–South relations probably helped to reassure unionists of their constitutional position within the UK. Apart from the moment of crisis in 1940, the British Government was unlikely to take steps to pressure unionists into a united Ireland when the South appeared so hostile and increasingly Catholic in ethos.

Conclusion

A review of the history of Britain and Ireland since partition casts doubt on the credibility of Modernisation Theory. The principal patterns of trade are much more East to West than they are North to South. The dependence of the Republic of Ireland on Britain was such that, in 1952, a firm of American economists concluded that this dependence was incompatible with the status of political sovereignty. The South's economic dependence on Britain did not prevent it asserting and extending its independence from Britain through neutrality during the Second World War and the declaration of the Republic afterwards. Neither does there seem to be any strong evidence that the process of Modernisation has made unionists more sympathetic to a united Ireland or northern nationalists any more sympathetic to remaining in the Union. While the Republic has become less economically dependent on Britain, Northern Ireland's dependence on the British subvention has grown. The South continues to be more economically dependent on the UK than the North has ever been on the South. What emerges from this review of the post-partition period is the importance of politics over economics. The economic fortunes of Ireland, North and South, have ebbed and flowed, but the strength of the adherence of Southern nationalists to their independence and Ulster unionists to the Union has been solid.

Modernisation Theory is 'structure' oriented and leaves little scope for 'agency'. It is objective historic forces such as economic integration that make Irish (or British Isles) unity inevitable. Agents (for example, politicians, governments) can only delay the inevitable working out of these forces. *This neglects the impact of the Theory itself in shaping the perceptions and therefore actions of politicians, governments and people.* Modernisation Theory could be deployed in the 'propaganda war'. While moderate unionists such as O'Neill attempted to turn it to his advantage by arguing that it would lead to British Isles unity, nationalists had more success in persuading British politicians that the inevitable result of Modernisation was Irish unity and that unionist resistance flew in the face of history. Paradoxically, too, O'Neill's reformist efforts may have undermined the Union, not because these reforms were intended to achieve this but because British politicians interpreted this reformism as unionist weakness on the border issue: reformism sent out the wrong message to the British.

British politicians could, conveniently, ignore the abuse of civil rights in Northern Ireland since, according to Modernisation Theory, these were likely to be resolved in the longer term by the development of closer links between the North and South of Ireland which would inevitably result in unity. Politicians in the South failed to take steps to win the support of unionists by assuming that Irish unity was inevitable and unionism an outdated anachronism. In Northern Ireland unionist fears of Irish unity were stoked and nationalist hopes raised by the process of economic integration, particularly during the 1960s when 'the Troubles' erupted. At the same time, the more conciliatory stance towards Catholics taken by the Unionist Prime Minister, Terence O'Neill, was underpinned by an interpretation of Modernisation which suggested that the Union would be bolstered. For Republicans, a belief in the inevitability of Irish unity could encourage and legitimise the use of violence, but it could also encourage the IRA to lay down arms and leave unity to inexorable, historic forces.

Since the 1960s the assumptions of Modernisation Theory – although they appear to be contradicted by 'reality' – have continued to pervade the thinking of politicians in Britain and Ireland. They were strongly apparent in the 1960s and in the British Government's reaction to the conflict when 'the Troubles' erupted in 1968–69 (see Chapter 6). They received a boost after Britain and Ireland's entry into the EEC in 1973 and have since informed the various attempts at constructing a settlement in Northern Ireland (particularly Sunningdale 1973, the Anglo–Irish Agreement 1985, the Downing

Street Declaration 1993, the Joint Framework Documents 1995 and the Good Friday Agreement 1998). It is against the background of this belief that North–South trade and co-operation will ultimately lead to Irish unity that various constitutional initiatives during 'the Troubles', and unionist hostility to them, should be understood.

4

The Civil Rights Movement

This chapter presents an account of, and three key perspectives on, the origins and development of the civil rights movement. Leading unionists alleged that it was a republican/Communist tactic to bring about a united Ireland. Nationalists claimed it was an attempt to win 'British rights for British citizens' and not about the border question. The civil rights *campaign* originated in the early 1960s and became a mass *movement* when the second civil rights march was attacked by the RUC on 5 October 1968. An attempt is made to review the motivation of the individuals and organisations involved in the civil rights campaign, plot its development, and the problems that faced it in achieving its objectives. What inspired the civil rights movement: a quest for civil rights, discrimination and deprivation, or Irish unity? Why did the civil rights movement emerge in the 1960s and not before? Did it develop from the emergence of 'a new Catholic middle class', the republican movement or traditional Catholic activists? Why did the Unionist Government not concede to the demands of the civil rights movement?

How Much Discrimination was there?

The question of discrimination is still highly politically charged and deployed in the propaganda war between the competing parties. Unionist politicians seldom acknowledge that discrimination occurred during the Stormont period, perhaps fearing that to do so would concede legitimacy to the IRA's violence. Some unionists attempt to minimise the extent of discrimination in order to vindicate Stormont, reject nationalist grievances and strengthen their arguments for a return to majority rule local and regional government. Nationalists tend to exaggerate the extent of discrimination in order to claim the moral high ground and put pressure on unionists to shift their position.

There is little doubt that there was discrimination against Catholics during the Stormont period; the academic debate revolves around the *extent* of discrimination against Catholics (Whyte 1990 p. 64). Crude statistics are often misleading and there is complex debate over how to measure discrimination. There have been reasons advanced for disparities between Catholics and Protestants, other than overt discrimination, and these include: lower Catholic educational standards; Catholics discouraging their co-religionists from serving the state (in the RUC or civil service); differences in attitudes to work; inadequate knowledge of job opportunities; concentration of Catholics in peripheral areas and the uneven development of capitalism; the larger size of Catholic families; and the legacy of past discrimination (Teague 1993). The most authoritative survey of discrimination during the Stormont period ordered the different fields of overt discrimination in order of demerit (Whyte 1983), as shown below:

1. *Electoral practices*: local government boundaries were in some cases 'gerrymandered' to produce unionist majorities in Catholic majority areas. The abolition of proportional representation for local government elections in 1922 shifted the control of some authorities to unionist control and prevented Catholic majorities from winning control. In 1967 the UUP secured 60 per cent of the seats on Londonderry Corporation with just 32.1 per cent of the vote.
2. *Public employment*: there was discrimination against Catholics who tended not to reach the upper levels in public employment.
3. *Policing*: the composition of the police force, the Royal Ulster Constabulary, was disproportionately Protestant and biased against Catholics. The part-time Ulster Special Constabulary was found to be a 'Protestant militia'. The Northern Ireland Special Powers Act gave the Minister of Home Affairs draconian powers to 'take all such steps and issue all such orders as may be necessary for preserving the peace and maintaining order'.
4. *Private employment*: discrimination against Catholics, particularly since a majority of employers were Protestant.
5. *Public housing*: allocation unfairly favoured Protestants.
6. *Regional policy*: evidence that development was concentrated in the more Protestant East of the province rather than the Catholic West.

Discrimination against Catholics was particularly severe at the local authority level and in the predominantly nationalist area west of the River Bann, where it was needed to secure unionist domin-ance. The area '... had less than a quarter of the total population of Northern Ireland yet generated not far short of three-quarters of the complaints of discrimination' (Whyte 1983 pp. 30–1). Hous-ing was a key issue in the emergence of the civil rights movement and it was in these gerrymandered councils in the West that conflict was 'particularly intense' (Purdie 1990 p. 86). While local government has a poor record, the Stormont Government did 'put through the original gerrymander which underpinned so many of the subsequent malpractices, and then, despite repeated pro-tests, did nothing to stop those malpractices continuing' (Whyte 1983 p. 31). The problem of unequal life chances for Catholics persists; the Good Friday Agreement 1998 has established an Equality Commission to develop further strategies to deal with this problem.

There is some evidence that Catholics have also discriminated against Protestants. According to Barritt and Carter, 'Many local councillors take it for granted that they are dispensers of patronage to their own side; and the exercise of this patronage is made easier by the custom of expecting personal canvassing of the Council or of its committee before appointments are made' (Barritt and Carter 1962 p. 99). In nationalist Newry in 1962 only 22 out of 765 coun-cil houses were occupied by Protestants, and no Protestants at all were employed by the council (Barritt and Carter 1962 p. 67, Gudgin 1999). Since local government was dominated by unionists, anti-Protestant discrimination would not have had the same impact as Protestant discrimination against Catholics. The Socialist and civil rights activist, Bernadette Devlin, argued that:

> Both the Protestant Unionists and the Catholic Nationalists deny they discriminate against each other, but both use religion to divide and rule the working class. It is only less serious on the Catholic side because there are fewer Catholic bosses and fewer Catholic local authorities in a position to practise discrimination. (Devlin 1969 p. 57; see also Smith and Chambers 1991 p. 369, Boyle and Hadden 1994 p. 46)

She condemned the hypocrisy of 'Catholic slum landlords marching virtuously beside the tenants they exploited, Catholic employers marching in protest against the Protestants they excluded from their factories' (Devlin 1969 p. 155).

Unionists have responded in three ways to charges of discrimination:

(a) by saying that there was no discrimination;
(b) by saying that there was no discrimination but you could not expect the Northern Ireland state to give nationalists who questioned the very existence of the state positions of influence within it (however, for much of the Stormont period, Northern Ireland was not in a state of war or siege, yet Catholics continued to be excluded);
(c) by saying that there was some discrimination during the Stormont period but that it has been exaggerated. Few unionist politicians will admit privately, or indicate publicly, that discrimination occurred.

The 1960s: Polarisation or Reconciliation?

There is debate over the climate of opinion in Northern Ireland during the 1960s. There is simultaneously evidence both of a thawing in community relations and polarisation. Optimists contrast the dismal 1950s with the modernising 1960s, portraying it as a period in which Catholics were shifting their allegiances away from a united Ireland and towards the pursuit of full participation and equality in the Northern Ireland state, while O'Neill was holding out the prospect of reconciliation with the Catholic minority. Between 1955 and 1959 the vote for republican candidates slumped from 23.7 per cent to 11 per cent. The IRA's Border Campaign of 1956–62 was called off because of 'the attitude of the general public whose minds have been deliberately distracted from the supreme issue facing the Irish people – the unity and freedom of Ireland'. The IRA subsequently began to pursue a more political path. The emergence of a new, moderate, nationalist opposition at Stormont also encouraged hopes for reconciliation. Other signs of reconciliation included the growth of ecumenism; the 'Orange–Green talks' between the Orange Order and the Ancient Order of Hibernians; and the confidence of Catholics resulting from the election of the first Irish–American Catholic President of the United States, John F. Kennedy. O'Neill's more conciliatory approach to community relations and his rhetoric of modernisation was also taken as evidence for optimism.

The pessimists about the 1960s emphasise growing conflict over expanding state resources, the impoverishment of the Catholic working class and evidence of continuing sectarianism and rising nationalist sentiment. The deployment of British troops was threatened by tensions surrounding the Divis Street Riots of 1964 and the commemorations of the Battle of the Somme and the Easter Rising in 1966. Loyalists were being mobilised against O'Neill by Ian Paisley's Ulster Protestant Volunteers and the Ulster Committee for the Defence of the Constitution. In 1966 the Ulster Volunteer Force was established, murdered two Catholics and was banned by the Stormont Government. Meanwhile recruitment to the IRA was growing, perhaps stimulated by conflict over the flying of nationalist flags and the Easter Rising commemoration. While the emphasis of the organisation had shifted towards political struggle, it still continued to organise and prepare for a military campaign. Moreover, there were still numerous incidents involving republicans and the IRA was having difficulty controlling its activists (Purdie 1990 pp. 10, 31, 44–6). With the benefit of hindsight, the surge of antagonism and violence which followed the civil rights march of October 1968 might suggest that the optimistic view of community relations in the 1960s was rather superficial.

The Campaign for Civil Rights

Why did the civil rights movement occur in the 1960s and not before? The election of a Labour Government, a party traditionally sympathetic to Irish nationalism, in 1945 aroused nationalist expectations. The Anti-Partition League (APL) was formed in 1945 to press nationalist demands and in the Irish Free State the government also launched an anti-partition campaign (Purdie 1986 p. 67). The APL attempted to combine a campaign to highlight discrimination with anti-partitionism. To the British 'it stated its case moderately and supported it with facts and figures which were likely to raise doubts about Unionist rule', while the APL spoke to nationalists 'in terms of the ideas and beliefs of Irish nationalism' (Purdie 1986 p. 73). 'The prominent people in the APL...were also prominent in the economic life of the community – small businessmen and professionals who were a natural focus of communications and leadership' (Purdie 1986 p. 74). The APL was rurally based, traditionally nationalist and deeply Catholic. After maximising the APL's vote 'there was little to do beyond going through the motions again and again' and the campaign fizzled out (Purdie 1988 p. 75). The APL had used discrimination 'not as an issue demanding reforms within Northern Ireland but as a means of exposing unionism and of justifying their denial of the legitimacy of the Northern Ireland government' (Purdie 1990 p. 40). There was some limited sympathy for the APL among the Friends of Ireland group at Westminster which was largely composed of Labour MPs, but there was a reluctance to re-open the Irish Question (Purdie 1983). The Connolly Association's (see below) campaign to release republican prisoners after the end of the IRA's border campaign 1956–62 suggested that Labour MPs could be mobilised around issues of civil rights more easily than partition.

The civil rights campaign of the 1960s included groups and individuals with very different political agendas and class backgrounds.

The Northern Ireland Labour Party

In the early 1960s and up until 1965 the strong performance of the NILP at the polls raised the possibility that an anti-UUP grand coalition that included nationalists could defeat the Unionist Government at Stormont (Purdie 1990 p. 64). The NILP attempted to build from its base among Protestants to attract more Catholics to the party. Between 1958 and 1962 the party doubled its total vote at Stormont elections. Charles Brett, the NILP Chairperson, told his party at its 1963 conference, 'I believe that the time has come when we must challenge the Catholic vested interests as well as the Protestant ones' (Brett 1978 p. 85). The NILP probably benefited electorally during this period both from its new liberal appeal to Catholics and its continued perception in the unionist community as a Protestant labour party (Dixon 1993 p. 78).

The contribution of the NILP to the civil rights movement has been airbrushed from history by some nationalist writers who were perhaps too keen to draw a simple 'black and white' story of the civil rights period (Dixon 1996c). However, 'Throughout the 1960s, while concentrating on economic matters, the NILP plugged away at many of the issues that were taken up by the civil rights movement' (Purdie 1990 p. 69). The NILP annual conference overwhelmingly approved of the cross-communal direction in which the party was moving. It endorsed, by 18300 votes to 900, the chairman's three-point action plan to combat religious discrimination in the region: first, to set up a Joint Tribunal to examine allegations of religious discrimination; second, to establish a joint working party to develop a points system for the allocation of housing; and finally, to appeal to employers to allocate jobs to applicants on merit alone (Dixon 1993 pp. 79–80).

The NILP, with its Protestant base of support, was sensitive to the communal interpretations that could be placed on the demand for civil rights. The party couched its appeal for civil rights demands in unionist terms, suggesting, for example, that civil rights reforms would give Stormont a greater degree of legitimacy. Reforms which could be interpreted as nationalist-inspired were advocated, such as measures against discrimination and on electoral law, but so too was a 'unionist' proposal to increase Northern Ireland's representation at Westminster by three more seats to bring it into line with the region's population (Dixon 1993 p. 79). Its 'Electoral Reform Now' document avoided the more sensitive issue of discrimination in employment and housing, and the repeal of the Special Powers Act. Brett opposed open interference by the British Government in Northern Ireland because it would 'arouse deep resentment', and might force Stormont into a defensive position from which 'it could not with honour retreat'. A Royal Commission would only 'stir up old issues and hatreds'. Reform was more likely to be secured by 'private and discreet' pressure by the Labour Government on the Unionist Government, making the granting of financial or economic aid dependent on progress with reforms. However, although 'Private representations of the strongest possible nature' had been made to the Labour Government to have religious discrimination included in anti-race discrimination legislation, the Government 'did not find it possible to accede to this pressure' ('Notes on Resolutions for the British Labour Party Annual Conference 1965' 11 August 1965, LPA, quoted in Dixon 1993 p. 104). In spite of the NILP's proclaimed loyalty, at the 1965 Stormont elections O'Neill claimed that Harold Wilson controlled the NILP and attacked it as an anti-partitionist party; pamphlets were circulated with the slogan, 'If you want a Catholic for your neighbour vote Labour' (Purdie 1990 p. 64).

The Nationalist Party

During the 1960s the Nationalist Party was coming under fire from nationalists who criticised the party's failure to contest elections, its lack of a modern regional party organisation, failure to unite nation-alists and provide leadership, ineffectiveness in winning redress for Catholic grievances and emphasis on partition to the exclusion of social and economic issues (Purdie 1990, Lynn 1997 pp. 232–3). A nationalist pressure group, dominated by teachers and intellectuals, called National Unity, which later transformed itself into the National Democratic Party, urged the Nationalist Party to unite the opposition and recognise that Irish unity could only come about by consent (Lynn 1997 p. 184). In response the Nationalist Party did attempt to transform itself into an orthodox, modern, democratic political party with an individual membership and national confer-ence. In January 1964 the party launched 'Operation Truth and Justice' to bring to the attention of the British political parties 'the disabilities operating against Catholics in the Six Counties' (Lynn 1997 p. 171). The party became the official opposition at Stormont in 1965, after encouragement from the Irish Taoiseach, and con-tinued to use constitutional methods in an unsuccessful bid to convince O'Neill and the British Government to introduce reform into Northern Ireland. Austin Currie, a radical member of the Nationalist Party, wanted the party to use extra-parliamentary methods to raise civil rights issues, but the party leadership feared that this would result in violence (Lynn 1997 p. 202). In November 1967 the Nation-alist Party leader, Eddie McAteer, appealed to O'Neill 'to try to find some basis of progress without either of us playing to the gallery' but he was rebuffed (Lynn 1997 p. 203).

The Connolly Association and the Republican Movement

The role of the republican movement and the Connolly Association in the origins of the civil rights movement has been underestimated. The British-based Marxist Connolly Association campaigned for Irish unity among the Irish in Britain, and had strong links with the Communist Party of Great Britain. During the 1950s the organisa-tion argued that 'the way to a peaceful solution of the Irish problem was to discredit Ulster Unionism in Britain through exposing the dis-criminatory practices which occurred under the Stormont regime, in the process winning sympathetic allies for the cause of Irish reunifi-cation' (Coughlan 1990). The Association had won the support of half the Parliamentary Labour Party for the release of republican internees during the Border Campaign and now hoped to perform a similar role with civil rights. In the early 1960s the Association organised a series of civil rights marches across England and the campaign was taken up by the National Council for Civil Liberties, the Movement for Colonial Freedom and later by the Campaign for Democracy in Ulster.

During the 1960s the Connolly Association's civil rights approach influenced the republican movement in a more political direction. However, IRA membership was also expanding from 657 members in 1962 to 1039 members in October 1966 (*The Independent on Sunday*, 4 January 1998) with the hope of participating in a military campaign (Patterson 1997 pp. 107, 111). In October 1966 the General Army Convention decided that IRA GHQ should 'concentrate more on training the "Army" for a military campaign and that only men who are prepared to carry out this policy be elected to the Army Executive'. The Convention also decided to infiltrate the trade union movement by identifying with civil rights and job discrimination issues, and:

> fostering especially such few areas and actions as involve both Catholics and Protestants with a view to undermining the basis of support for Unionism among the Protestant population, keeping intact however the basic principle of training of key people in the Movement in the use of weapons so that when the time comes the movement will be prepared to back up its political and economic advances with such force and popular support as will ensure complete and rapid victory. ('Review of Unlawful and Allied Organisations' prepared by Garda Commissioner, 1966, quoted in *The Independent on Sunday*, 4 January 1998)

The leadership's approach appears to have been to pursue the politicisation of the republican movement while containing the pressure for military action by engaging in limited military activities. The hope was that popular Catholic agitation for civil rights would squeeze the Unionist regime. The republican movement would break through to Protestants and a united movement of Catholics and Protestants would bring down the Northern Ireland state (Patterson 1997 pp. 107, 111–12). However, as events unfolded it became clear that the civil rights movement had unleashed communal violence which divided rather than united Protestants and Catholics. The republican movement played the driving role in the establishment of the Northern Ireland Civil Rights Association and was active in stewarding marches.

The Campaign for Social Justice

This was founded in Dungannon, Co. Tyrone, on 17 January 1964 by Mrs Patricia McCluskey and her husband, Dr Conn McCluskey. The CSJ grew out of the Homeless Citizens League (HCL) which they had also founded. The HCL was established after 40 young Catholic housewives petitioned and 67 picketed Dungannon Urban District Council over poor housing conditions and discrimination in housing allocation (Purdie 1990 p. 83). Nevertheless the HCL's activities forced the council to make concessions by making representations to Stormont. It also revealed a 'gentleman's agreement' between Unionists and Nationalists to allocate housing on a sectarian basis, so that Catholics would become the tenants of 'Catholic houses' and Protestants the tenants of 'Protestant houses' (Purdie 1990 pp. 90–1). The success of the HCL demonstrated the effectiveness of direct action and contrasted with the failure of the Nationalist Party's parliamentary approach.

The CSJ was formed to oppose the policies of 'apartheid and discrimination' implemented by the Stormont Government, and its first objective was 'to collect comprehensive and accurate data on all injustices done . . . and to bring them to the attention of as many socially minded people as possible'. The CSJ was composed of 'educated people' drawn from the Catholic, professional, university-educated, middle classes. The 13-strong committee contained no Protestants but included two consultant surgeons, two GPs, an architect and a science professor. The objectives of the group were equal rights within the UK, although most in the CSJ aspired towards Irish unity (Purdie 1990 pp. 94–5). Dr Conn McCluskey called on the Nationalist Party to shift its strategy and to 'concentrate on getting our rights and trying to overcome gerrymandering. I feel that to mention the border just puts the Unionists backs up and some other poor devils lose their chance of a house or job' (Dr C. McCluskey to McAteer, 1 July 1963, quoted in Lynn 1997 p. 165; see also *Irish Times*, 1–2 January 1999). The CSJ hoped to go over the head of the Stormont Government and appeal to Westminster by breaking the 'Speaker's Convention' which prohibited discussion of Northern Ireland so that the government could legislate to protect minority rights (Purdie 1990 p. 96). The CSJ did succeed in drawing Harold Wilson into saying that a Labour Government would intervene to deal with discrimination, throwing unionism into a panic.

The Labour Government 1964–66 and the Campaign for Democracy in Ulster

The slender four-seat majority which Labour won at the 1964 General Election focused attention on the 12 Ulster Unionist MPs at Westminster who held the balance of power and voted with the Conservatives. Labour MPs, incensed at the sight of Ulster Unionists loyally trooping into the Opposition lobby at Westminster to vote on issues which did not relate to Northern Ireland, took a new interest in the region (Dixon 1993 pp. 96–8, 112). The Campaign for Democracy in Ulster (CDU) was founded as an all-party pressure group for the reform of Northern Ireland (Purdie 1990). The use of 'Ulster' in the name of the pressure group was deliberate; the border question was deemed to be irrelevant to the CDU and the objective was to obtain 'full British rights for the people of Northern Ireland, to which they are entitled as British subjects'. However, at least two of its founding members were members of the socialist republican Connolly Association. The leading parliamentary advocate for the CDU, the Labour MP Paul Rose, had become interested in civil rights after attending a Connolly Association meeting and reading one of its pamphlets. The CDU and Gerry Fitt sought an investigation into the workings of the Government of Ireland Act, something which could be seen by unionists to strike at the very heart of partition. By early 1966 approximately 40 Labour MPs tabled a motion calling for the establishment of a Royal Commission to inquire into the working of the Government of Ireland Act 1920 (P. Rose 1981 pp. 135–6, Dixon 1993 pp. 98–9, 125, Lynn 1997 p. 195).

The CSJ and CDU were comprised predominantly of people who aspired towards Irish unity and were probably seen by many Protestants as anti-unionist and interventionist. Mrs McCluskey, of the CSJ, said it was not possible for her to join the NILP because it was regarded as 'the poor man's Unionist party' and 'if we joined the NI Labour at this stage whoops of rage would go up from "patriot" Nationalists and we would be engulfed in a wave of emotionalism and resentment' (letter from P. McCluskey to 'various' 9 April 1965, Labour Party Archive). The CSJ was all-Catholic in composition and 'did not want to be "contaminated" by any Northern Ireland politicians, except Gerry Fitt' (Purdie 1990 pp. 93–5). The CDU also gravitated more towards anti-partitionist civil rights supporters such as Fitt, elected MP for West Belfast in 1966, than the unionist NILP. Gerry Fitt told a Connolly Association conference that he was asking for 'British standards as they apply in the island of Great Britain', but he coupled this with a claim that unionists were in Northern Ireland 'by no right'. 'He is not there by his right of being an Irishman, because he disclaims any Irish nationality...He is there because he wants to maintain this little oasis of fascism in Northern Ireland' ('The Irish Question – Challenge to Democratic Britain', Report of Conference 25 February 1967).

The simultaneous advocacy of civil rights, 'British rights for British citizens', with anti-partitionism and the overwhelmingly Catholic/ nationalist membership of the civil rights movement led unsurprisingly to a perception that the two demands were linked. It was not just unionists who interpreted the attempt to raise civil rights as an anti-partitionist tactic. An editorial in the nationalist *Irish News* claimed, 'A big campaign to focus public attention on the question of partition in Ireland is at the moment going on quietly but effectively in Britain. In recent months the CSJ in Northern Ireland has been active with meetings and the various injustices imposed on the minority in the six counties' (*Irish News*, 8 September 1965). The NILP maintained its support for civil rights but, after its poor performance at the 1967 corporation elections, the Party's Secretary reported that 'A platform of civil rights will not win us any more votes' (Secretary's report on corporation elections, May 1967, quoted in Graham 1982 p. 248). The Executive of the NILP was generally critical of the interfering and pro-nationalist stance of the CDU and pulled back from the civil rights platform which appeared increasingly identified with nationalism (Purdie 1990, Dixon 1993 pp. 135–6). The 1966 Westminster General Election produced a Labour Government with almost a 100-seat majority. It removed the irritant of the influence of Ulster Unionist MPs and the salience of the civil rights issue at Westminster declined.

O'Neill: Bridging the Gap?

The Divis Street Riots of 1964 and the violence surrounding the 1966 commemorations of the Battle of the Somme and the Easter Rising were reminders that communal tensions in Northern Ireland could require the deployment of British troops on the streets and precipitate the re-opening of the 'Irish Question' (*The Sunday Times*, 1972 p. 82). In 1966 the British Government feared a campaign of IRA violence to mark the Easter Rising and was anxious that (Rose

1999 pp. 18–20) if the troops were deployed then any clashes between soldiers and the IRA should not be publicised as 'a people's uprising against the excesses of the Crown forces' (*Irish Times*, 1–2 January 1997). The loyalist paramilitary Ulster Volunteer Force was formed to defend and uphold the Protestant North against the IRA. The UVF carried out a number of petrol bomb attacks on Catholic shops, homes and schools in February–April 1966 and in June 1966 was responsible for the murder of three Catholics. Wilson denounced the ultra unionists as 'quasi fascist' and O'Neill banned the UVF. Brian Faulkner, a minister in O'Neill's cabinet and later Prime Minister, wrote of the fears

> which Ian Paisley was beginning to exploit: fears that better North/South relations might undermine Ulster's position as part of the United Kingdom; fears that the South was only trying to find a new way of effecting its claim on our territory; fears aroused by the massive republican celebrations of the fiftieth anniversary of the 1916 Rising and the accompanying riots; and fears that the ecumenical movement was in Northern Ireland designed to reduce opposition to a takeover by the Catholic Irish Republic. (Faulkner 1978 pp. 42–3)

The Labour Government put some pressure on O'Neill to reform Northern Ireland, but did not want to push him 'too far' in case he was removed from office by hardliners within his own party. Initially, Labour's new Home Secretary, Frank Soskice, had wanted to intervene in Northern Ireland but 'reluctantly' concluded that it would be constitutionally wrong and unwise in practice, 'at least for the present'. In April 1965, Soskice visited Northern Ireland and claimed 'substantial progress' had been made by the Unionist Government: 'From England we watch it, we admire it and we rejoice in it' (*Irish Times*, 3 February 1995). At a meeting with O'Neill in August 1966, Wilson and Roy Jenkins, Labour's Home Secretary, agreed to 'a period of consolidation' to stem 'a dangerous tide of reaction' (*Sunday Times* Insight Team 1972 p. 81, H. Wilson 1974 p. 843). In a meeting with the Irish Government in December 1966, Harold Wilson cited O'Neill's 'difficulties with the Rev Ian Paisley' as a reason not to push him further; he also argued that O'Neill's position 'within his own party and cabinet was none too secure' (*Irish Times*, 1–2 January 1997). That month O'Neill announced a package of reforms: abolition of the university constituency and creating four additional territorial constituencies instead; abolishing the business vote for Stormont elections; and setting up a statutory boundary commission. Roy Jenkins, the Home Secretary and historian, warned against direct British intervention. He argued that history showed, the English did not have a talent for solving Irish problems, and that: 'Few issues in the past have shown a greater capacity to divert and dissipate the reforming energy of left-wing British Governments than deep embroilment in Irish affairs' (Hansard, vol. 751, col. 1687, 25 October 1967). In May 1968, shortly before the civil rights movement took to the streets, Wilson told the House of Commons, 'in the last two or three years considerable advances have been made under the present Premier of Northern Ireland. Not enough, I agree, but what has been achieved has been remarkable in view of the prejudice he has to meet in that particular area of the UK' (Hansard, vol. 768, col. 732, 21 May 1968).

There was hardline pressure against O'Neill's largely symbolic gestures towards Catholics from within his cabinet, unionist back-benchers, the largely autonomous constituency parties and outside his party from the maverick Protestant Unionist, Ian Paisley. This symbolism is usually derided, but it may have paved the way towards a more substantive, material and political accommodation with nationalists (Loughlin 1995 p. 177, Cash 1996 p. 129). The *Belfast Telegraph* explained the constraints on O'Neill thus:

> The calmer approach to the problem is that of Captain O'Neill and his Government, as accepted by Mr Wilson [the British Prime Minister], who have adopted a liberalising policy, and the question is now one of judging at what pace this can be implemented having regard to the feeling not only of the Unionist Party but of those Roman Catholics who are waiting and with patience, to benefit from it. (*Belfast Telegraph* editorial, 4 October 1967)

On the principle of Catholics joining the UUP there was also concern among unionist politicians at how this may be received among their electorate, since 'most unionist politicians supported the principle of Catholic membership while believing the change was better introduced gradually and quietly, and not made a public issue' (Gailey 1995 p. 86).

O'Neill's leadership skills are certainly open to question. He had an autocratic style and failed to consult with his party, most famously over his ground-breaking meeting with the Irish

Taoiseach in 1965. O'Neill placed considerable hope in the ordinary decency and common sense of the people of Ulster (and civil society) to see the sense of his 'moderate' and modernising way forward. At times O'Neill considered himself to be English and 'was sufficiently removed from traditional unionism to be quite happy to ignore its symbols and its sacred history in favour of elements of an instrumental and rational view of politics' (Bruce 1989 p. 71) but this tended towards the abandonment of all that was distinctive about unionist politics. His more middle-class, liberal unionist circle was insulated from the world of the Protestant working class, who were concerned at the direction of O'Neillism and receptive to Ian Paisley's 'traditionalist' message (Bruce 1989 pp. 70–1, Gailey 1995).

Ian Paisley led the opposition to O'Neill outside the UUP. This 'prophet in the wilderness' appeared to be increasingly justified in his critique of O'Neill by the turn of events. Paisley's populist appeal was effective: 'A traitor and a bridge are very much alike for they both go over to the other side.' He helped to establish the Ulster Constitutional Defence Committee in April 1966 and the Ulster Protestant Volunteers to defend the Union. He opposed ecumenism and a march of his through 'republican territory' to the Presbyterian Assembly, in June 1966, resulted in a riot (Bruce 1989 p. 81).

Politicians operate under constraints and whether even a skilful unionist leader could have delivered sufficient support for civil rights reforms to meet Catholic demands without undermining his or her position is open to question (Bruce 1989 p. 70, *Irish Times* 1–2 January 1999). By April 1965, just a few months after the O'Neill-Lemass meeting, O'Neill asked for a vote of confidence in his leadership. During 1966 and 1967 there were two revolts against him which ended in the Prime Minister broadcasting to the people and further votes of confidence. O'Neill demoted one rival, William Craig in 1966, and sacked another, Harry West, in 1967. The NILP chairman told Roy Jenkins that the government should support the 'extremist' Faulkner against O'Neill

> as a man capable of carrying his party with him...Roy Jenkins appeared to be fascinated at the suggestion that reforms were most likely to be secured, and bloodshed avoided, by supporting the 'bigot' against the 'moderate'. Plainly, the proposition intrigued him intellectually, and we discussed it up and down at great length. (Brett 1978 p. 135)

During the period 1966–68, both the NILP and the CDU tried and failed to persuade the Labour Government and the wider labour movement of the importance of swift civil rights reform in Northern Ireland. The CDU almost collapsed due to lack of interest. Between August 1966, when the use of the army in Northern Ireland was first mooted, and October 1968, the Labour Government had taken no steps to improve its supervision of the region and there was little information available when the conflict erupted.

Politics in the Streets

The formation of the Northern Ireland Civil Rights Association (NICRA) on 29 January 1967 originated with a decision taken by the republican Wolfe Tone Society in August 1966. A 13-person steering committee was drawn from the Amalgamated Union of Engineering Workers, the CSJ, the Communist Party of Northern Ireland, the Belfast Wolfe Tone Society, the Belfast Trades Council, the Republican Clubs, the Ulster Liberal Party, the National Democratic Party, the Republican Labour Party, the Ardoyne Tenants Association and the NILP; later on, a liberal Young Unionist was co-opted on to the committee. NICRA was based on the National Council for Civil Liberties and its constitution 'emphasised the association's character as a body which would make representations on the broad issues of civil liberties and would also take up individual cases of discrimination and ill-treatment' rather than reflecting a commitment to militant protest (Purdie 1990 p. 133). But it did little between its founding and the proposal for the first civil rights march which came to it in June 1968 from Austin Currie (Purdie 1990 pp. 134–5, Lynn 1997 p. 206).

During 1967 the Nationalist MP, Austin Currie, had been campaigning on the failure of Catholics to be allocated council housing by Unionist-controlled councils. In October 1967 Currie drew attention to squatting by homeless Catholic families as an example of 'growing desperation and frustration' and he predicted 'more squatting, more acts of civil disobedience, more emphasis on the "other means" and less on traditional parliamentary methods'. He advocated direct action as the only means by which the nationalist population could improve their conditions (quoted in Lynn 1997 pp. 205–6). Currie also shared nationalist Modernising assumptions that Irish unity was inevitable and that the religious and economic barriers to it were crumbling (*Irish Independent*, 18 September 1964).

The Nationalist Party rejected Currie's direct action tactic, feeling this had not been 'properly thought through' and could lead to widespread violence (Lynn 1997 pp. 205, 208, 234). Some of Currie's Derry Nationalist Party colleagues had been involved in the street protests of 1951 and 1952 which had resulted in serious public disturbances. After these experiences they were reluctant to take politics into the streets. Eddie McAteer, the Nationalist Party leader, urged party members to think carefully before 'going home and taking up the pike...We must not allow ourselves to be goaded into precipitate action.' McAteer continued to pursue the parliamentary path and persuade Stormont or Westminster to act, 'aware of the growing frustration and anger amongst many in the Catholic community'. Rejecting direct action, the Nationalist Party failed to put itself at the head of the civil rights movement and was subsequently marginalised when that movement took to the streets. Direct action swiftly won a reform package 'which far exceeded anything that the Nationalist Party had been able to gain in over 40 years'. The historian of the Nationalist Party concludes, 'What happened in Derry on 5 October 1968, and the subsequent events in the weeks and months ahead seemed to indicate that only direct action appeared to bring about the desired results' (Lynn 1997 pp. 207, 213, 234).

Austin Currie pressed on with his direct action approach. After failing to get Stormont to intervene, in June 1968 Currie joined a Catholic family which was squatting in a house in Caledon and was about to be evicted. The new tenant was to be a 19-year-old unmarried Protestant woman who was the secretary to a solicitor and Unionist parliamentary candidate. Currie then proposed and NICRA agreed to, a protest march from Coalisland to Dungannon. The march, organised by republicans, took place on 24 August 1968 to the accompaniment of nationalist bands (Devlin 1969 p. 91). NICRA refused to accept the re-routing of the march to the Catholic area of the town, since it would have implied that it was a sectarian march. Paisley's Ulster Protestant Volunteers counter-demonstrated and the police kept the two marches apart. When some of the marchers tried to attack the counter-demonstrators they were beaten back by the RUC.

The platform called for restraint and the chairperson reminded the crowd that they were demonstrating for civil rights, jobs and houses (Purdie 1990 p. 136). Gerry Fitt declared 'We want civil rights and a 32-county Republic' (Gordon 1989 pp. 118–19). The NILP spokesperson argued that many Protestants, like himself, favoured civil rights. One participant, Bernadette Devlin, contrasted the republicanism of the marchers with the civil rights creed of the politicians and organisers: 'it was hilarious to see how out of touch they were with the people they supposedly respresented' (Devlin 1969 pp. 93–4).

The second civil rights march took place on 5 October 1968 and was again a response by NICRA to a local initiative, this time from the left-wing Derry Housing Action Committee (DHAC) which was composed of left wingers in the NILP and the republican movement. In Derry/Londonderry there had been the most flagrant case of gerrymandering, and while deprivation was distributed among both Catholics and Protestants, Catholics disproportionately bore the brunt. The failure of a joint nationalist–unionist campaign to bring the second university to Derry rather than Protestant-dominated Coleraine, led by John Hume, heightened a sense of grievance. The republicans denounced the City Corporation's housing record and took direct action against evictions. Housing was 'an issue which was the central and most widely felt grievance of Derry Catholics' (Purdie 1990 p. 174). Catholics suspected that Derry's dismal record on housing was because it would upset the balance of political power on the council by shifting the distribution of Catholics and their votes within the City. The DHAC's direct action tactics appeared to be an effective form of protest in a gerrymandered, Unionist-dominated City council. By the summer of 1968, a leading member argued:

> [their] conscious, if unspoken, strategy was to provoke the police into over-reaction and thus spark off a mass reaction against the authorities. We assumed that we would be in control of the reaction, that we were strong enough to channel it. The one certain way to ensure a head-on clash...was to organise a non-Unionist march through the city centre. (McCann in Purdie 1990 p. 184)

The march was banned but an estimated 400–600 marchers defied the ban and were brutally attacked by the police. This then descended into a general violent confrontation between the RUC and young Catholics in the adjoining Bogside, who had not been involved in the march (Purdie 1990 pp. 143–6). According to one of the organisers of the march the 'effect seemed to be out of all proportion' to the issues raised by the march (Ó Dochartaigh 1997 p. 21). The violence which met the 5 October march was captured by the television cameras and evoked attacks by the US police on Blacks in the Deep South. Its broadcast outraged British and world opinion and finally forced Ireland back on to the British political agenda. O'Neill told his cabinet that they were under pressure from Wilson to 'justify some of our practices' and that 'we have now become the focus of world opinion' (*Irish Independent*, 7 January 2000). The US Government was putting pressure on the British Government. Some unionist politicians responded to the march by claiming that the civil rights movement was a republican/Communist front but, according to Purdie, 'the whole affair was a series of blunders and the violence resulted from a breakdown of control by the leaders of the march and the controllers of the police, and not from any pre-existing plan' (Purdie 1990 p. 146).

The 5 October march transformed the civil rights campaign from a collection of groups and activists to a movement with branches all over Northern Ireland where 'there was a significant Catholic population' (Purdie 1990 p. 156). As Catholics clambered aboard the civil rights bandwagon the radicals of the DHAC were marginalised. The more 'respectable' and 'moderate' members of the Catholic community – 'mainly business and professional people, clergy, trade unionists and political leaders' – established the Derry Citizens Action Committee (DCAC) 'to harness the energies and enthusiasm of the people in a disciplined manner' (Frank Curran, former editor of the *Derry Journal*, quoted in Purdie 1990 p. 189). Its demands were modest and confined to 'civil rights': a two-year crash house building programme in Derry; 'some form of legal control in the renting of furnished accommodation'; and a fair points system for the allocation of housing (O Dochartaigh 1997 p. 25). The DCAC organised and carefully stewarded demonstrations, 'the DCAC, unlike the DHAC, took seriously the likely outcome of its actions and prepared carefully in order to give effect to its determination to avoid violence. This further increased its authority and enabled it to keep control over events, at least for the next few months' (Purdie 1990 p. 191).

The RUC did not have the strength to control the big marches (over 15000) now being organised without the co-operation of the DCAC (O Dochartaigh 1997 p. 29). As time went on the DCAC had increasing difficulty restraining and controlling their supporters, 'particularly young Catholics living in ghetto areas', who wanted to respond to loyalist provocation (Purdie 1990 pp. 193–4). On 22

November O'Neill, under pressure from the publicity surrounding the October march, announced a reform programme which included proroguing the Londonderry Corporation; a Development Commission was appointed to run the City. In December O'Neill successfully appealed for calm (see Chapter 5) and was supported by the Nationalist Party, the DCAC and other 'moderates' in the civil rights movement. At the end of 1968 the DCAC had been largely successful in policing and organising demonstrations, but in 1969 its grip weakened as the conflict took on a more sectarian tone.

In January 1969 a small left-wing student group, the People's Democracy, defied a NICRA moratorium and organised a march from Belfast to Derry. The march was attacked repeatedly and at Burntollet was ambushed by loyalists with clubs; approximately half of these were off-duty members of the B Specials (a part-time overwhelming Protestant force with a reputation for sectarianism). The violence which met the Burntollet marchers in January 1969 reinforced the shifting focus of debate in Northern Ireland from political and economic issues to the more sensitive issue of reform of the state's security apparatus (Bew and Patterson 1985 pp. 16–18). Following police violence republicans established 'Free Derry' by organising local vigilante committees and barricades to keep out the RUC. The DCAC were appalled by this, 'But blood was up and there was nothing they could do about it' (McCann 1974 p. 53). By early 1969 republicans could see the advantage of Catholic mobilisation for achieving Irish unity (Ó Dochartaigh 1997 pp. 46–7).

Marches were continuing but were provoking serious confrontations with the RUC and getting out of control of the DCAC. In April 1969 Samuel Devenney was beaten by police and later died. After April it was difficult 'to organize a demonstration which did not end in riot', but 'by ending the demonstrations the moderates took away from the youth any channel for expression other than riot. The rage and frustration which lay just beneath the surface of life in the Bogside could no longer be contained within the thin shell of the [D]CAC's timid respectability' (McCann 1974 pp. 57–8). The agenda was shifting away from civil rights towards RUC brutality and the need to defend nationalist areas. Young rioters now ignored the persuasion of moderates or republicans to desist from attacks on the RUC (McCann 1974, Ó Dochartaigh 1997 pp. 40–1, 53, 115).

The hope of republicans and socialists that confrontation with the Stormont Government would produce a united working-class movement of Protestants and Catholics quickly appeared to be misplaced. By Easter 1969 'There had been a distinct resurgence of basic nationalist feeling in Derry' (Ó Dochartaigh 1997 p. 45). The socialist activist Eamonn McCann commented in early 1969 on the sectarian tone of some of the civil rights initiatives:

> the cry 'get the Protestants' is still very much on the lips of the Catholic working-class. Everyone applauds loudly when one says in a speech that we are not sectarian, we are fighting for the rights of all Irish workers, but really that's because they see this as the new way of getting at the Protestants.

In August 1969 Orange Order parades in Derry were the occasion for fierce rioting which the RUC could no longer contain. NICRA organised demonstrations across Northern Ireland to relieve RUC pressure on the rioters in Derry. In Belfast republicans laid siege to an RUC station and the ensuing rioting resulted in the deaths of five Catholics (four killed by RUC gunfire) and two Protestants. On 14 August the British Army was finally deployed on the streets. Lord Scarman later commented:

> While the Catholic minority was developing confidence in its power, a feeling of insecurity was affecting the Protestants. They became the more determined to hold their traditional summer parades, particularly those in Londonderry and Belfast. In these circumstances sectarian conflict was to be expected, unless the police were strong enough to prevent it. (Scarman 1972 vol. 1, para. 1.8, p. 6)

Republicans did not make strenuous efforts to avoid conflict between loyalists, the RUC and nationalist youths. Ó Dochartaigh argues, 'It does not seem unreasonable to suggest that they saw 12 August as an opportunity to bring the very existence of Northern Ireland into question' (Ó Dochartaigh 1997 p. 116). In this they were encouraged by Jack Lynch, the Irish Prime Minister, who made anti-partitionist remarks, raising fears among unionists of a nationalist agenda behind the civil rights movement and of an Irish invasion from the Republic. The day before British troops were deployed, Jack Lynch called for a UN peace-keeping force and said 'that the Irish Government can no longer stand by and see innocent people injured and perhaps worse'. 'Recognising ... that the reunification of the national territory can provide the only permanent solution for the problem, it is our intention to request the British Government to enter into early negotiations with the Irish Government to review the present constitutional position of the six counties of Northern Ireland' (*Irish Times*, 14 August 1969). Irish troops were moved to the border to set up field hospitals for the injured. In the Republic, members of the Fianna Fáil government were attempting to influence the character of Catholic insurgency and were involved in supplying arms to the emerging Provisional IRA in the North (Patterson 1997 pp. 130–4). The Scarman report later criticised Lynch's speech: 'There is no doubt that this broadcast strengthened the will of the Bogsiders to obstruct any attempt by the police to enter their area, and to harass them by missile and petrol bomb attacks, whenever they appeared on the perimeter.' There were real concerns among unionists, including senior unionist ministers, that the Irish Army might invade (*Irish Times*, 3 January 2000). For nationalists, 'This put new heart into the fight. News that "the Free State soldiers are coming" spread rapidly', and they 'believed themselves within a whisker of a united Ireland' (McCann 1974 p. 60, Ó Dochartaigh 1997).

Debating the Origins of the Civil Rights Movement

A Republican/Communist Conspiracy?

The Unionist response to the civil rights movement was to brand it a republican/Communist conspiracy to overthrow the Northern Ireland state and bring about a united Ireland. Christopher Hewitt has argued that the emergence of the civil rights movement and the subsequent violence was due 'to nationalist indoctrination and foreign involvement rather than socio-economic disadvantage', which he argues was exaggerated (Hewitt 1991 p. 17). During the 1960s Catholic nationalism was as strong as ever, with the vote for the Nationalist Party buoyant. Catholics involved in the civil rights movement were often nationalists and, Hewitt argues, were not genuine in their demand for civil rights but used civil rights as a tactic to raise the question of partition and overthrow the Northern Ireland state (Hewitt 1991 pp. 28–9, 37). The failure of civil rights leaders to endorse the constitutional position of Northern Ireland, condemn Catholic discrimination against Protestants and the fact that many civil rights leaders went on to found the nationalist SDLP is cited as proof of the anti-partitionist intent of the civil rights movement.

Nationalists and republicans did play a prominent role in the civil rights campaign. The socialist republican Connolly Association was influential on the IRA, the Campaign for Democracy in Ulster and the Labour Party in raising civil rights issues. The IRA were active in establishing NICRA, active in the DHAC (which called the Derry march) and in organising and stewarding marches. While the IRA leadership may not have predicted the immediate consequences of the political, civil rights strategy, most republicans would probably have shared the primary objective of raising partition. Given close Republican involvement in the campaign and that of other prominent anti-partitionists, as well as the past record of nationalists in using allegations of discrimination to raise the issue of partition, it is not so surprising that some unionists perceived that the civil rights campaign's goal was anti-partitionist (a view shared by the nationalist *Irish News*) or even a republican front, particularly in the context of growing unionist insecurity (see Chapter 3). 'Even some of the most "moderate" elements in the [civil rights] campaign regarded the re-unification of Ireland as an ideal outcome. Many moderates such as John Hume saw the reform of Northern Ireland "as a necessary prerequisite to the eventual and inevitable marriage of the two parts of Ireland"' (*Derry Journal*, 13 March 1969, quoted in Ó Dochartaigh 1997 p. 60). It could be argued that the formal commitment of some elements in the campaign to 'British rights for British citizens' was a tactical move to win support in Britain among politicians who did not want to re-open the 'Irish Question'. Through civil rights Stormont could be delegitimised and the existence of the Northern Ireland state questioned. Appeals for an investigation into the workings of the 1920 Government of Ireland Act could easily be interpreted as raising the border question. It seems reasonable to conclude that *some* of those involved in the civil rights movement did see it as a tactic to undermine Stormont and bring about a united Ireland, while others saw it as a shift away from the traditional mix of civil rights and anti-partitionism towards a primary focus on civil rights (and working-class unity), with unity further down the road. Of course, there were some liberal and socialist unionists who believed that civil rights reform would strengthen the Union.

This unionist view of the civil rights movement can be questioned on several counts.

First, *by underestimating discrimination and Catholic grievance it is unable to explain the kind of mass violence that was provoked by the civil rights campaign and does not explain why the civil rights movement emerged and achieved success in the 1960s.* The increase in vote for the Nationalist Party can be interpreted as a shift away from republicanism and towards participation in the Northern State rather than as evidence of increased national feeling. When violence erupted it correlated with the nationalist vote but also with deprivation.

Second, *it does not recognise that at least for some of those nationalists in the civil rights campaign there was a shift towards an emphasis on civil rights rather than the border question during the 1960s.* That many, but not all, of those involved in the civil rights campaign were Catholics and nationalists does not detract from the justice of their cause. Indeed, given the disproportionate impact of discrimination on the nationalist community it is not surprising that nationalists were more likely to be involved in the civil rights movement and affect its character

Third, *while accepting the key role played by republicans in the civil rights campaign, the evidence suggests that republicans and communists were not in effective control of NICRA* (Purdie 1988 pp. 33, 39). The thinking behind the IRA's civil rights strategy did not anticipate the resurgence of communal conflict which followed and the opportunities which might later flow from that. After 5 October the republicans in NICRA urged restraint and a moratorium on demonstrations and marches (Purdie 1988 p. 39, Purdie 1990 pp. 157–8).

The New Catholic Middle-Class Thesis (Top-Down)

The 'new Catholic middle-class' thesis has been the 'orthodox' explanation for the emergence of the civil rights movement. The Cameron Commission which reported on the background to the October 1968 violence was an early authoritative source for this account, which has subsequently found widespread support. This thesis, echoing Modernising assumptions, argues that the civil rights movement was led and founded by a new, expanded Catholic middle class which emerged in the 1960s. This new middle class was the product of two developments.

First, it was a product of the expansion and extension of the British welfare state to Northern Ireland. The universal benefits provided by the welfare state brought benefits to both Catholics and

Protestants. The 1947 Education Act in particular is singled out for its role in facilitating the emergence of a new, educated Catholic middle class.

Second, economic modernisation and an influx of international capital opened up new opportunities to middle-class Catholics and raised their expectations because it recruited personnel on a non-discriminatory basis. The extension of the welfare state to Northern Ireland demonstrated the material benefits of British citizenship to the 'new Catholic middle class', opening up a disparity in the standard of living between North and South. The benefits of British citizenship made Catholics more British and weakened their enthusiasm for Irish unity. They encouraged Catholics to participate in and seek a fairer deal from the expanding British state. 'The Catholic middle class, while not abandoning their nationalist sentiments, began to seek the reform of Northern Ireland as their first goal; and before long for many it became the overriding goal' (O'Leary and McGarry 1996 pp. 158, 160) The motivation of most of those in the civil rights movement is not Irish unity but civil rights (O'Leary and McGarry 1996 p. 168). According to Cameron:

> A much larger Catholic middle-class has emerged, which is less ready to acquiesce in the acceptance of a situation of assumed (or established) inferiority and discrimination than was the case in the past. This is, we think, an important and new element in the political and social climate of Northern Ireland and has played its part in the events which led to the setting up of this Enquiry. (Cameron 1969 para. 11)

The civil rights movement is seen as a highly organised, disciplined, mass protest movement, under the strong control and leadership of the 'new Catholic middle class' located in NICRA. The replacement of the old rural, anti-partitionist Nationalist Party by the SDLP is seen as symbolic of this new emergent elite 'wholly different and separate in outlook, purpose and social background'; 'with urban as well as rural support, they (the SDLP) more closely resemble an urban middle class, a social group fundamentally different from the traditional hierarchic structure from which the Nationalists were drawn' (Morgan 1987 p. 103).

The 'new Catholic middle class' thesis is favoured by nationalists since it is useful in the propaganda war for emphasising the failings of unionists and the British who rebuffed the increasingly

British-oriented 'respectable Catholic middle classes' which led the civil rights movement. It underlines the sincerity of the civil rights movement in seeking redress and in not raising the question of the border, contrasting with the unionist 'republican conspiracy' argument. The Unionists and the British Government appear all the more reprehensible in their failure to meet reasonable civil rights demands. The escalation of the conflict from demonstrations to anti-partitionism and the 'armed struggle' appears all the more understandable, if not excusable.

The 'new Catholic middle class' thesis has been subjected to withering criticism, principally by those who advance a more 'bottom-up' perspective on the civil rights movement. There are four main points of criticism.

First, *while there was an expansion in the Catholic middle class this took place before 1961 and therefore before the establishment of the CSJ or NICRA*. There was 'virtually no change in the social structure of the male Catholic population' between 1961 and 1971 (Bew, Gibbon and Patterson 1995 p. 151).

Second, *there is little evidence to link the expansion in higher education to activism in the civil rights movement*. Morgan argues that it was only in the mid-1960s after the civil rights movement began to emerge that the student population in Northern Ireland as a whole began to expand and many Catholic and working-class students started to go through university. From the available evidence there was a gradual increase in Catholic university education in the 1950s and 1960s but the most dramatic increases came in the 1970s (Morgan 1987 p. 108, McKeown 1997). Against this it could be argued that it is the absolute increase in the number of Catholics in higher education which is relevant here but it would have to be shown how this affected the civil rights movement.

Third, *the impetus for the civil rights campaign and movement was a result of pressure from below and the locality, rather than any central organisation (such as NICRA) or the Catholic middle-class*. This propelled the CSJ, NICRA and Catholic middle-class activists into action. The HCL and CSJ were formed after direct action by Dungannon housewives. Austin Currie's support for direct action followed from squatting by Catholics in his area and it was he who proposed the first civil rights march from Coalisland to Dungannon. While NICRA was divided on the issue, an important factor in winning over NICRA was the support of the republican movement and the locally-based CSJ. The impetus for the 5 October march in Derry came from the DHAC, composed of republicans and left-wing members of the NILP, who had already launched a number of direct actions to draw attention to bad conditions and discrimination in housing. The moderate organisations of the civil rights campaign, including NICRA, the CSJ, the DCAC and others, attempted to manage and restrain rather than lead developments in the civil rights movement, and their attempts to lead, steward and control marches appeared to have a diminishing effect. Even the republicans struggled to control nationalist youths from rioting. The 'new Catholic middle-class thesis' 'fails to show why such a narrow impulse should have generated such broad appeal and impact'; 'it hardly shows why the movement was to acquire an irreversible momentum among the Catholic population at large' (Bew, Gibbon and Patterson 1995 p. 149). As one activist put it, 'I am not sure how many of our speakers mesmerised the masses. Certainly the masses mesmerised the speakers' (Eamonn McCann quoted in O'Clery 1986 p. 140).

Fourth, *the role of the Catholic middle class in the civil rights campaign was limited; it is questionable as to whether NICRA could be described as a 'middle class' organisation and whether any other civil rights body apart from the CSJ could be considered middle class*. Multinational investment did not disrupt traditional employment patterns and few Catholics were employed in the newer financial and managerial sectors of the economy. Those from the middle class involved in the civil rights movement were largely not members of a 'new' middle class but members of the old, traditional middle class which serviced its own community. Teachers continued to dominate the Catholic middle class and political activism (Morgan 1987 pp. 62, 109). The initiative for the founding of NICRA came from the republican movement and the 13-person steering committee was drawn mainly from traditional organisations which showed little evidence of the impact of a new Catholic middle class (Purdie 1990 p. 133).

Finally, *the 'new Catholic middle class' thesis ignores the communal context into which the civil rights campaign marched*. It loses sight of why unionists were so sceptical of its non-sectarianism and had real grounds for suspecting it of anti-partitionism.

Growth of State Explanation (Bottom-Up)

The 'growth of the state' approach sees the rise of 'ethnic' politics since the Second World War as related to the expansion of the state and political and economic competition for state resources. The segregated, communal division of labour is broken down by competition for state resources – public housing, public employment, public invest-ment – which brings the communal groups into contact, competition and therefore conflict (this contrasts with Modernisation Theory).

Since partition a Catholic 'quasi-state within a state' has existed which, together with its own social infrastructure (Church, sporting activities, Ancient Order of Hibernians, newspapers, businesses), provided an extensive network of communally-based services (edu-cation, welfare, social and health services) to the Catholic com-munity. The 'quasi-state', dominated by the Catholic Church and staffed by the Catholic middle class, was involved in extensive informal negotiation between the Church and the state (Morgan 1987). The welfare reforms of the Labour Government, largely adopted by Stormont, dramatically increased the state resources available for distribution, and increasingly Catholics looked beyond the Catholic quasi-state to the Northern Ireland state where it could achieve much higher levels of welfare provision and opportunities for employment. Morgan and Taylor point out:

> Practically all of the civil rights issues concerned aspects of state expansion: the allocation of *public* housing, discrimination in *pub-lic* employment, the siting of *public* institutions. As local govern-ment became the chief interface between Catholics and the newly enlarged state, so also it became an area of increasingly bitter controversy...at base, the movement represented an attempt to define a new relation between state and society in Northern Ireland. (Morgan and Taylor 1988)

It was only after the Second World War that public authorities sought to remedy the appalling state of housing in Northern Ireland:

> There were few allegations of discrimination in the allocation of public housing because there was little public housing to allocate. All this changed after 1945, however, when a large-scale public housing drive was launched. By 1961, 21 per cent of all housing in the province was public-rented; by 1971 the proportion was 35 per cent. As public housing became more plentiful, so complaints about its allocation multiplied. (Whyte 1983 p. 18)

The thrust of the civil rights campaign and movement was from below, drawing its strength from growing conflict over discrimination, access to state resources and the impoverishment of the Catholic working class (Morgan 1987, Bew, Gibbon and Patterson 1995). Between 1911 and 1961 the position of the Catholic working class deteriorated, providing the conditions of alienation out of which the civil rights movement could quickly mobilise significant support. The civil rights movement

> was only ever loosely organised, often spontaneous. It was an immense wave of anger that had been nursed through decades of frustration and resentment, suddenly released in one collective surge. It bypassed 'normal' political channels [the elite of middle class Catholics and unquestioned bishops] because these could not express what people felt. Street marches were the tactic that made the connection between political action and the pressure from below, and gave it voice. (Morgan and Taylor 1988)

The civil rights movement, having exhausted the constitutional methods for the redress of its grievances, finally took to the streets. This tactic 'utilised the tensions produced by the threat that violence might rise from their activities, either because they had lost control of some of their supporters or because they had provoked their opponents' (Purdie 1990 p. 3). Some leading members of the civil rights movement may have been sincere in their view of the civil rights march as 'non-sectarian' but this was a 'perception which was not widely shared' (Purdie 1990 p. 244; see also Purdie 1990 p. 186 on DHAC). The march upset the 'tacit understanding between the two communities about territorial divisions' and provoked a dispro-portionate and brutal response from the police. The advocates of direct action had been warned of the danger that taking politics into the streets would provoke communal clashes but they may have felt that this was the only way civil rights demands would be met. This sparked off a sectarian response which spiralled beyond the control, or probably intentions, of civil rights leaders (Purdie 1990 pp. 247–8). The spontaneous mobilisation of large sections of the Catholic com-munity after the 5 October 1968 march and the difficulty leaders of the civil rights movement had in controlling this explosion is suggest-ive of the discontent of the Catholic community and the 'bottom-up' thrust of the movement. The reappearance after 1969 of the repub-lican movement 'amplified the effect of Catholic political mobilisa-tion while simultaneously reducing the ability of its formal leadership to "deliver" support for any particular political compromise it was offered' (Bew, Gibbon and Patterson 1995 p. 156).

Growing conflict over state resources and the impoverishment of the Catholic working class help to explain why the civil rights movement erupted in the 1960s, but there were possibly three further triggers. First, the Labour Party raised the spectre of intervention in Northern Ireland affairs without any real desire to become involved, which left it reliant on O'Neill 'to drag Northern Ireland into the twentieth century'. Catholic expectations, and unionist fears, had been heightened by the election of a Labour Government in 1964 and this was a strong incentive for civil rights mobilisation (e.g., the CSJ and the CDU).

Second, Catholics were disgruntled with the ineptitude of the Nationalist Party and were finding that direct action was a more effective means for redressing grievances. After the Labour Government's failure to intervene and O'Neill's limited reformism, the only apparent option for the civil rights campaign was to take to the streets. This proved an effective tactic and produced swift results.

Third, heightened unionist insecurity and division (Chapter 3) constrained O'Neill's ability to deliver reform. He was both unable to persuade unionism of the necessity of reform or to deliver sufficient concessions to the civil rights campaign. Given the involvement of nationalists and republicans in the civil rights movement it was not surprising that unionists inaccurately saw the civil rights movement as *solely* an attempt to force Northern Ireland out of the Union. As O'Neill told his cabinet in October 1968, 'Of course, there are anti-Partition agitators prominently at work but can any of us truthfully say in the confines of this room, that the minority has no grievance calling for remedy?' (*Irish Times*, 1–2 January 1999).

Conclusion

Different accounts of the civil rights movement are used to promote different political agendas in the propaganda war for British, Irish and international opinion. The Labour Government tried to avoid blame by claiming that it had not been warned about civil rights and the impending crisis. Nationalists argued that the civil rights movement was inspired solely by civil rights in order to win external sympathy for intervention. Republicans claim that their political violence after 1969 was reactive, the result of the violence and repression which met the peaceful civil rights campaign. Unionists and loyalists claimed that the civil rights movement was a republican/Communist conspiracy designed to bring about a united Ireland. There is a degree of 'truth' in all these explanations, which is what makes them such effective 'myths' in the propaganda war.

The great problem is trying to discern the *intentions* of the various parties and organisations in the conflict. Certainly the civil rights movement's claims were largely just (if exaggerated for impact) and deserved to be met regardless of whether they were raised tactically or not. Undoubtedly, some nationalists and probably more republicans believed that the end of partition could be brought nearer by advancing civil rights demands which were more effective in winning external support and intervention than traditional anti-partitionist campaigns had been. But there is no evidence that the subsequent violence and 'armed struggle' by the IRA was planned in advance. After October 1968 the republican movement may have increasingly felt, encouraged by the actions of the Irish Government and the mobilisation of the Catholic masses, that its opportunity to end the partition of Ireland had finally arrived. It had every incentive to provoke further conflict with the state.

The Unionist Government's refusal to meet peaceful demands for reform was both unjust and counter-productive, allowing the republicans to plant the question of partition firmly on the political agenda. O'Neill, in spite of his personal commitment to reform and the backing of the British Government and important elements of the media (see Conclusion), faced considerable opposition within his cabinet, on the backbenches and his wider party to a modernising reform programme. It has to be doubted whether even a more skilful leader or unionist government might have been able to deliver reform in the face of such structural constraints. Unionists were completely outmanoeuvred and unprepared for the civil rights explosion. They lost the subsequent propaganda war hands down. By January 1969 O'Neill was telling his cabinet that 'As things stand it [is] all too widely accepted throughout the UK that a sectarian Government, directing a partisan force, is confronting a movement of idealists' (*Irish Times*, 3 January 2000). Even a report of British Home Office civil servants argued 'There are legitimate grievances in Northern Ireland and it is entirely legitimate that they should be ventilated by demonstration' (*The Independent on Sunday*, 1 January 2000). In Britain public and political (Labour *and Conservative*) opinion was sympathetic to the civil rights movement and hostile to the 'un-British', sectarian practices of the 'backward' Stormont administration.

5

The Crisis of British Policy over Northern Ireland 1968–73

The British Government had tried to minimise their involvement in the Northern Ireland conflict. As they were drawn into deeper involvement they drew on the assumptions shaped by the experience of British and colonial politics. At first the British attempted to resolve the conflict by reforming Northern Ireland and bringing it up to 'British standards' of democracy in an attempt to undermine the material basis for communal division and replace nationalist/unionist divisions with 'normal' left/right politics based on economic interests. When violence failed to subside the conflict was increasingly seen in 'colonial' terms and the use of repression was justified to subdue 'sinister forces'. The increasingly repressive nature of the Unionist Government's security policy in Northern Ireland by alienating nationalists made the task of finding a political accommodation between nationalism and unionism more difficult. The key questions facing the British Government were: how could the British avoid direct rule without supporting a Unionist Government which was polarising opinion in Northern Ireland? How could the British reconcile the tension between the army's counter-insurgency strategy, which demanded political determination to defeat the IRA, and the government's political strategy which negotiated with nationalists and republicans in order to draw them into a 'peace process'? How could the British conciliate nationalists without provoking a backlash from loyalists who feared that the Union was being sold out? This period saw the height of 'the Troubles' and exposes the limits on the British Government's power to impose its will on the conflict.

Bipartisanship

There were three principal reasons behind the rapid establishment of a bipartisan approach by the Conservative and Labour parties to Northern Ireland in 1968 (Dixon 1995a). First, perhaps the fundamental reason for the operation of bipartisanship is that an accord between the British political parties can help to promote a consistent British policy towards Northern Ireland and facilitate a resolution to the conflict, or at least help to contain the situation and stop it 'infecting' British politics. In the context of Northern Ireland, bipartisanship works by the two principal British parties broadly agreeing on the constitutional principles of their approach to the issue. They can then present a united, British, front to the contending communal groups. This prevents those groups from exploiting the political differences between the British parties and playing one off against the other and holding out on the agreement. For example, if the British political parties were divided in their approach and became aligned with different factions in Northern Ireland (the most obvious case would be an alignment of Labour with the nationalists and the Conservatives with the unionists), each change of government at Westminster could result in the reversal of the previous government's Irish policy and the imposition of one more favourable to their respective allies in Northern Ireland. If this was to occur, the chances of reaching a permanent and stable solution to the conflict would be diminished. If Westminster maintains a sufficiently broad agreement on its approach, then it reduces the likelihood of the contending groups in Ireland refusing to reach a settlement in the hope of the return of a British Government more sympathetic to its cause.

The nature of issues such as Northern Ireland means that the opposition party, whether as part of a bipartisan approach or not, is potentially in a position to wield considerable influence on government policy. Outside a bipartisan relationship, the posture of the opposition can disrupt the government's attempts at accommodation by offering a more favourable settlement to one of the parties. This induces that party to hold out on any settlement with the government of the day in the hope that the next election will return a government more favourably disposed to its demands. If the political parties operate a bipartisan approach, then the government's policy has to be framed broadly enough to take the opposition with it.

In 1968 bipartisanship was used to bolster O'Neill against his 'hardline' rivals. Both the Conservative leader, Edward Heath, and the Prime Minister, Harold Wilson, were agreed that for progress to be made in Northern Ireland support must be given to those who were pursuing a 'moderate policy' against the 'extremists'. Wilson noted the importance of bipartisanship in presenting a united front to dampen the expectations of 'bigots' or 'zealots' who might have led the fight against O'Neill (House of Commons Debates, vol. 775, col. 582, 12 December 1968). O'Neill sold the Five Point Reform Plan to his own community by pointing to Conservative/Labour unity and arguing that there was no alternative but to accept it (*Newsletter*, 10 December 1968, quoted in Gordon 1989 p. 135). Unionists attempted to pressure the Conservative Party to take a firmly pro-Unionist stand but the Conservative Shadow Home Secretary, Quintin Hogg, 'flatly rejected this'. For Hogg, the bipartisan approach was based on agreement on two fundamental points: first, that the Labour Party was 'not less committed than we' to the constitutional guarantees, 'so together we speak for the whole of the people of this island' and, second, that 'discrimination was wholly indefensible' (Conservative Party 1969 pp. 48, 50).

A second reason for the establishment of bipartisanship is to insulate the issue from British domestic opinion. The deaths of British soldiers in Palestine sparked off a populist revolt among British public opinion in favour of withdrawal, and the threat of another public revolt hung over politicians as they contemplated subsequent decolonisations. By presenting a united front to the contending parties in Northern Ireland, the British bipartisan approach could minimise inter-party conflict which might stimulate the demand for withdrawal amongst domestic British public opinion (Dixon 1995a, 2000a).

Third, the 'legacy of the Irish Question' had left a scar on the collective memory of British politicians and it was hoped that a cross-party approach would help to contain the impact of the conflict and not necessarily promote any particular constitutional outcome. Both Quintin Hogg and James Callaghan expressed an awareness of the 'lessons of history' and a determination not to polarise the country over Ireland to the extent that it had been in 1914, when Britain approached civil war.

British Nationalism and Irish Unity

The violent events of 5 October 1968 were an affront to British national pride and shocked public opinion which had been led to believe that its political system was a model for the rest of the world. This judgement appeared to have been vindicated by the absence of violent confrontations between 'violent students' and 'sadistic police' which had shaken every other major western country during 1968. The media had not prepared the British public for the sudden confrontation with the 'political slum' in its own back yard. Press reaction was 'virtually unanimous' in its support for the Catholics' demands for civil rights, since these 'were seen to accord with what were considered British standards' (Kirkaldy 1984 p. 175).

British nationalism became the hallmark of the response of the British political parties to the conflict. It underpinned the bipartisan (or two-party) approach of the parties to the crisis and informed the nature of its attempts to resolve the conflict through reform on the British model. As Harold Wilson pointed out on television, this was not just 'on our doorstep...it is in our house' (Wilson 1974 p. 871). British politicians tended to see the conflict in Northern Ireland as a 'backward', 'religious' 'throwback' to the seventeenth century. By contrast, the 'British model' of liberal democracy had international respect for producing consensus and stability. The civil rights movement's demand for 'British rights for British citizens' appealed to British patriotic sentiment, and it was hoped that these civil rights demands could be satisfied while avoiding the re-opening of the 'Irish Question'. The key to resolving sectarian divisions was therefore modernisation, bringing Northern Ireland up to date and into line with the British model which was at the forefront of the 'modernised' world. In short, Northern Ireland had to be made 'more British'; once Northern Ireland, its people and institutions, were 'more like us' their outdated conflict would be consigned to history. By undermining the economic basis of sectarianism the anachronistic bonds of religion are severed and the unity of Protestant and Catholic workers forged around modern, 'real' economic and social issues. The 'British model' was the standard for most of the reforms introduced into Northern Ireland, including the creation of 'normal', two-party, 'class' politics; a British 'bobby on the beat' police force; an ombudsman; 'one man one vote'; and revision of the Special Powers Act.

Northern Ireland appeared increasingly 'un-British' as the reform strategy failed and violence and sectarianism persisted. A British nationalism was emerging which regarded England, Wales and Scotland as the 'nation', excluding Northern Ireland. British Labour and Conservative politicians increasingly contemplated more radical action, including Irish unity. The Labour Party in particular combined support for reform with a traditional sympathy for Irish unity as a natural, inevitable and just outcome of Modernising forces. Some believed that reform would undermine the material basis of sectarianism and lead to Protestant support for Irish unity. The interests of British and Irish nationalism coincided, the 'British' arguing that Northern Ireland was certainly not part of the British nation and the Irish claiming it as part of their own nation.

British Influence, Unionist Disaffection

British politicians had avoided direct intervention by leaving reform to O'Neill, and the 'hardline' opposition to his premiership cautioned the Labour cabinet from pushing him 'too hard' to deliver substantive reform. In private meetings with O'Neill, representatives of the Labour Government urged further reform in the local government franchise, housing allocations and in the appointment of a Parliamentary Commissioner. There was concern for Britain's international image which the Special Powers Act and 'some aspects of the Londonderry outbreak' had tarnished (Wilson 1974 p. 845). The outcome of the O'Neill–Wilson meeting was a five-point plan, announced by O'Neill in November 1968. This plan consisted of a points system for public housing allocation; the creation of a Parliamentary Commissioner for Administration; reform of local government; revision of the Special Powers Act; and the abolition of Londonderry Borough Council and its replacement by a non-elected Development Commission (Cunningham 1991 p. 19). This package dealt with most of the demands of the civil rights movement, except 'one man one vote' in local government elections. In December 1968 O'Neill declared 'Ulster [is] at the crossroads' in a speech which resulted in 150 000 letters or telegrams of support and the return of a further 120 000 newspaper coupons.

Unionist hardliners urged O'Neill to resist British pressure to reform. Wilson exacerbated O'Neill's problems by claiming credit for pressurising the Northern Ireland Government to reform (Callaghan 1973 p. 93). Those unionists who had long suspected British behind-the-scenes interference in Northern Ireland's affairs were now finding evidence to substantiate their concerns. The joint statement released at the end of the Wilson–O'Neill talks repeated the constitutional guarantee contained in the Ireland Act. However,

Wilson warned O'Neill's unionist opponents that if the Northern Ireland Prime Minister was overthrown he would 'need to consider a fundamental appraisal of our relations with Northern Ireland' (House of Commons Debates, vol. 772, col. 690, 5 November 1968). This was a none-too-subtle threat to raise the question of Northern Ireland's constitutional position within the UK which contradicted Labour's reassurances that the constitutional position of Northern Ireland was secure and that the border was not an issue. Although the British prepared for the introduction of direct rule, they probably wanted to avoid this option at all costs (*The Independent on Sunday*, 2 January 2000).

These threats of intervention were a bluff (Bloomfield 1994 p. 108), designed to bolster O'Neill's arguments for reform (i.e., unless we reform the British will takeover) against hardliners. Perversely, these kind of threats from British politicians seemed to undermine rather than bolster O'Neill's position within unionism. Rather than pulling the UUP behind O'Neill's 'trust the British' position, these threats suggested that the British could not be trusted with the security of the Union. The implications of this for unionist strategy were that power should therefore be kept, as far as possible, within Northern Ireland and the hands of unionists. A tougher line should be taken in dealings with a British Government which – against its reassurances – appeared prepared to sell the Union out. Brian Faulkner resigned as Minister for Commerce in January 1969 over O'Neill's capitulation to British pressure and rejected the media's division of unionists into pro- and anti-O'Neill with 'the latter represented as reactionaries, bigots and hard-liners' (Faulkner 1978 p. 53). The 'hardliner' William Craig, who was sacked by O'Neill in December 1968, claimed that he was not opposed to the reforms, but did object to the supine response of O'Neill to the Labour Government's demands rather than protecting the rights and privileges of the Ulster Parliament and Government (Gordon 1989 pp. 142–3).

Indirect Rule

The Labour Government attempted to strike a *balance* between the claims of nationalists and unionists to avoid becoming more deeply involved in Northern Ireland. According to Callaghan, 'my short-term aim was to try to restore a sense of self-confidence in the Ulster

Unionist Cabinet ... and to calm the fears of the Catholic community without awakening those of Protestants' (Callaghan 1973 p. 70; Crossman 1977 p. 622). The Secretary to the Northern Ireland cabinet warned the British against introducing direct rule, arguing that it might lead to a Protestant backlash, sectarian civil war and the establishment of a provisional government headed by extremists (*Irish Times*, 3 January 1999). The Labour Government had had its fingers burnt over Rhodesia, and Northern Ireland threatened to repeat that scenario.

By encouraging O'Neill to pursue a programme of reform, the Labour Government could use its influence to maintain 'indirect rule' through Stormont and so avoid becoming too directly involved in the conflict. However, the extension of civil and economic rights for Catholics was not necessarily compatible with non-intervention if these reforms resulted in the defeat of O'Neill. If Wilson pushed O'Neill too hard, then 'hardline' unionists might gain the upper hand within the UUP and oust the Northern Ireland prime minister. Such a course of events could then force the Labour Government to become more involved in Irish affairs to secure reforms, and perhaps ultimately lead to the suspension of Stormont and the introduction of direct rule from Westminster. There was concern that the intro-duction of direct rule would be met with considerable resistance from within Northern Ireland, not least from the unionist-dominated police and civil service, therefore resulting in British military rule (*The Sunday Times* 1972 pp. 103–4). The alienation of unionists as well as republicans might well result in the Army's 'nightmare scenario' of fighting an unsustainable 'war on two fronts'. So, although Wilson was talking about getting tough with Stormont, he did not take measures to follow through with his threats if he was defied by the unionists.

On 3 February 1969 12 Unionist backbenchers called for O'Neill's resignation and in retaliation he called the 'Crossroads' election. The 1969 election underlined the rifts within the unionist bloc: unofficial pro-O'Neill unionists stood against official anti-O'Neill unionists. O'Neill himself was only returned with a 1414 majority over the Reverend Ian Paisley. The result was also a blow to the modernising hopes of the British Government which had been built up by the media. The Labour cabinet minister, Richard Crossman, wrote that: 'O'Neill was the man we were relying on in Northern Ireland to do our job of dragging Ulster out of its eighteenth-century Catholic-Protestant conflict but he had "totally failed" to win a liberalising mandate' (Crossman 1977 pp. 381–2). Following UVF bombing attacks on public buildings and utilities, which were wrongly blamed on the IRA, O'Neill resigned in April 1969 to be succeeded by his cousin, James Chichester-Clark. The Labour Government had prepared for the collapse of the Northern Ireland Government in the winter of 1968–69. Following serious rioting in Derry and several bombings, British troops were posted to guard electricity, water and other public service installations in remote areas in April 1969. James Callaghan told the cabinet that 'the Northern Ireland Government was genuinely going ahead with reforms. Our aim must be to influence while getting embroiled as little as possible' (Castle 1984 p. 640). By May 1969 he was able to tell the cabinet that four out of the five demands the Government had put to O'Neill had been met and the review of local government franchise had been accepted in principle. According to Chichester-Clark, James Callaghan found the content and pace of reform 'entirely acceptable' (letter from Chichester-Clark to Callaghan, 6 August 1969, PREM 13/2843). Richard Crossman expressed his concern that such a policy might lead the Government to prop up whatever the 'Protestant Orangemen' of the RUC define as law and order. The cabinet agreed that intervention was to be avoided if at all possible (Crossman 1977 pp. 453, 458).

The loyalist marching season during the summer of 1969 provided an opportunity for both Protestants and Catholics to vent their frustrations with political developments in Northern Ireland. After violence following the marches on 12 July, Wilson and Healey favoured the banning of all further parades in Northern Ireland. Callaghan was advised by the Northern Ireland Home Affairs Minister that the RUC had neither the resources nor the resolution to impose a parade ban, while Chichester-Clark told him he would fall from power if the marches were banned (*The Sunday Times* 1972 p. 102). The marches went ahead and the subsequent rioting led to the deployment of the British Army on the streets of Northern Ireland.

The Army: In and Out?

The British Army was not deployed on the streets of Northern Ireland on 14 August 1969 to protect Catholics against the largely Protestant RUC and rampaging loyalist mobs. James Callaghan had been advised 'from all sides...on no account to get sucked into the Irish bog'. Such was the Government's desire not to become embroiled in the 'Irish Question' again that Callaghan suggested that giving Northern Ireland independence might be preferable to the introduction of direct rule, but this was dismissed on the grounds that it would lead to civil war (*Irish Times*, 3 January 2000). The Labour Government warned the Stormont Government that the deployment of troops might result in direct rule, and this was also leaked to the newspapers. This was probably a bluff designed to ensure that the Unionist Government did not call for the use of troops until all its resources had been exhausted (Callaghan 1973 pp. 15, 42–3). These resources included the deployment of the infamous B Specials and the use of CS gas, an indiscriminate weapon which affected innocent and guilty alike. This was used only days before British troops were finally deployed and calmed the rioting. On 11 August ministers agreed that as the overriding consideration was to avoid the use of troops, top priority should be given to the strengthening of the RUC and the deployment of the Ulster Special Constabulary (*Irish Times*, 3 January 1999). The Scarman Report later 'concluded that if Peacocke [Inspector-General of the RUC] had correctly appreciated the hopelessness of the police position... and not been so sensitive to the political pressures against calling the army, then Londonderry and Belfast might have been spared much of the ensuing tragedy' (Ryder 1997 p. 116). In this way the British Government were able to force Stormont to exhaust its resources, regardless of the consequences for inflaming communal tensions, and then avoid responsibility for the resulting deterioration. Chichester-Clark argued that the Labour Government's threat to suspend Stormont was an incentive to rioters to keep up the pressure (letter from Chichester-Clark to Callaghan, 6 August 1969, PREM 13/2843).

The army was to be borrowed by Stormont for a short holding operation, so that reforms could be introduced to bring Northern Ireland up to 'British standards' of democracy and modernity. There was a precedent for military intervention and swift withdrawal from Northern Ireland. In 1935, following rioting in Belfast, the army was called out for just eleven days in aid of the civil power and then withdrawn once order had been restored. In August 1969 the army were welcomed by nationalists and operated in a non-confrontational way, facilitating a quick withdrawal. An indication of the Government's desire to limit the involvement of the army was the reduction of troop numbers there in the first days of August 1969, at a time when General Freeland was pleading for reinforcements. The General Officer Commanding (GOC) suspected that the 'honeymoon period' would not last and had 'strong misgivings' about the consequences of becoming involved in an urban guerrilla war (*Irish Times*, 3 January 2000). If Protestants resisted and Stormont collapsed, the Ministry of Defence projected that direct rule would require the deployment of 20–30 000 troops. In practice, according to one minister, Labour's policy was 'to do anything which would avoid direct rule' (*The Sunday Times* 1972 p. 103). Meanwhile, Callaghan considered drafting in British police officers to relieve the army of the burden of police duties (CC(69) 43rd Conclusions, Minute 3 Thursday, 11 September 1969, CAB 128/46).

The army had been introduced on to the streets because of the breakdown of the local police force. A priority for the British, therefore, was the restoration of order and the strengthening of the local security forces so that the troops could be withdrawn. The strategy of 'Ulsterisation' – the replacement of British Army personnel by locally-recruited forces – is conventionally seen to have begun in the mid-1970s. Yet Ulsterisation seems to have been the strategy of the British from the moment troops were deployed on the streets in August 1969. The failure of the army to implement this policy until the mid-1970s was due to the weakness of the local security forces and the ferocity of the IRA campaign. The mid-1970s did not represent a strategic switch but the opportunity to realise the goal of police primacy which had been pursued since 1969 (Rees 1985 p. 51, Urban 1992 p. 15).

Reform: Modern British Standards

On 19 August 1969 Callaghan put five recommendations to the cabinet: first, for the 12 000 B Specials to be disarmed; second, the transfer of some authority to Westminster; third, for advisers to be attached to the Northern Ireland Government; fourth, that a coalition of more elements should be brought into the Stormont Government; and finally, for the establishment of a community relations organisation and possibly a minister for Northern Ireland (Callaghan 1973 p. 66, *The Times*, 27 August 1969). Callaghan also considered proportional representation as a means of building cross-sectarian consensus, boosting such moderate forces as the NILP. The cabinet agreed that their negotiators should bargain for as much of Callaghan's recommendations as possible. Barbara Castle underlined the Government's dilemma: 'Nobody wants us to have to takeover political control, with all the trouble that implies – indefinite embroilment in Northern Ireland. Equally we have minimum demands that must be met' (Castle 1984 p. 700). Denis Healey, the Minister of Defence, was sympathetic to the plight of the Catholics but wanted to avoid the army's nightmare scenario of a war on two fronts. He argued that 'we must keep the Protestants quiet' (Benn 1988 pp. 196, 198).

Following negotiations 'The Downing Street Communiqué' was published on the 19 August 1969 setting out 'the principles which should govern their future actions'. There were four main points:

(a) 'the border is not an issue' and Northern Ireland would remain part of the UK so long as that was the will of the people and Government;
(b) Northern Ireland was a domestic issue not an international one;
(c) 'troops have been provided on a temporary basis';
(d) 'the momentum of internal reform should be maintained'; everyone was entitled to equality of treatment and freedom, and the restoration of normality would accelerate economic development and promote social stability.

In addition to this, there was an undertaking that the Northern Ireland Government would 'take into the fullest account' the views of the Labour Government, particularly in the field of equal rights. The Communiqué also stated that the GOC Northern Ireland 'will with immediate effect assume overall responsibility for security operations'. After a triumphant trip to Northern Ireland Callaghan established two inquiries, one under Lord Scarman into the disorders of August 1969 and another under Lord Hunt into the police. The Unionist Government declared its intention to establish machinery for investigating citizens' grievances, a Community Relations Board and joint working parties of the officials of Westminster and Stormont to ensure fair allocation of housing, avoidance of discrimination in public employment and promotion of good community relations. Callaghan was pleased with the result of his negotiations with Stormont: 'the principal achievement, without doubt, was to have secured by agreement a very great extension of Westminster influence without facing the crisis that would have arisen if the Ulster Unionist Government had resigned' (Callaghan 1973 p. 99).

The border, as the Downing Street Declaration made clear, was still officially 'not an issue' but there were signs that it was already creeping on to the political agenda. The causes of 'the Troubles' were widely seen as at root economic. The Cameron Report on the disturbances June 1968 to January 1969 concluded that the causes of the trouble were both material (including housing provision and allocation, discrimination in local government appointments) and security-related ('resentment' among Catholics against the B Specials and the Special Powers Act). The assumption was that once these grievances had been dealt with peace would be established and 'normal British style class politics' would develop.

James Callaghan, while subscribing to the materialist analysis of the Northern Ireland conflict and keen to bring Northern Ireland up to British standards of democracy, also appeared to hint at the possibility of Irish unity by talking of raising the problem on to 'a new plane' (Labour Party Conference Report 1969 p. 184, Callaghan 1973 p. 107). The Home Secretary complained to the cabinet of the 'world-wide propaganda campaign' directed by the Irish Government against the UK and Northern Ireland Governments. He argued that if the Irish Prime Minister

> really wanted a united Ireland, he must conciliate Protestant opinion: but so far his tactics had done nothing but alarm it. Nevertheless, if there were to be any prospect of a final solution, relations between the North and South of Ireland and between the South and the United Kingdom must be lifted to a different plane. As things stood at present this was likely to take a long time. (CC (69) 43rd Conclusions, Minute 3 Thursday, 11 September, 1969, CAB 128/46)

When Callaghan published his reflections on Northern Ireland, in *A House Divided* (1973), the former home secretary publicly came out in favour of eventual Irish unity. The Irish minister, Charles Haughey, met the UK ambassador to Dublin and offered him Irish entry into the Commonwealth, and British or NATO access to Irish bases in return for Irish unity. The ambassador told Haughey that there would be a Protestant backlash in the North caused by British 'open dickering with the South' over the border. Haughey more or less accepted this (*Irish Times*, 7 January 2000).

The logical extension of Labour's strategy to extend the British model of democracy to Northern Ireland was to introduce a British class-based, two-party system. While the Labour Party undertook to revitalise the NILP as a non-sectarian party of labour, the Conservatives attempted to transform the UUP into a non-sectarian, conservative party (Hogg 1975 p. 242, Dixon 1993). An alternative strategy was to unite the predominantly Catholic opposition forces with the NILP to at least offer Catholics some prospect of a share in governmental power. The success with which the NILP and the wider labour movement had managed to combine Catholics and Protestants within its organisations impressed both Conservative and Labour observers. The Northern Irish labour movement appeared a familiar haven of 'British normality' in a communal political culture which British politicians found disorienting. A proposal to merge the NILP with the British Labour Party collapsed under pressure from a number of civil rights activists who later formed the SDLP. One report claimed that the Government did not want to alienate the civil rights leaders on whom they depended 'not to let the civil rights movement get out of hand' (*Private Eye*, 13 February 1970).

Ulsterisation

The British Army was deployed on the streets of Northern Ireland because of the weakness of the RUC. Harold Wilson was keen that the size of the RUC was increased so that the conflict could be 'Ulsterised' and the army could be withdrawn or its role reduced. This would lower the chances of a conflict between either the forces of 'British imperialism and Irish nationalism' or even disaffected loyalists who resented British intervention. The police had become discredited within the nationalist community so the British favoured steps to see that the RUC and B Specials were reformed in such a way as to make them acceptable to nationalists. Unionists, however, tended to see the police not only as a force for law and order but also as a powerful bulwark against untrustworthy British politicians who might manipulate unionists into a united Ireland. Chichester-Clark told Wilson at the 19 August meeting that British troops could not be withdrawn because the police were now discredited among a section of the people (Callaghan 1973 p. 59). The Northern Irish Prime Minister suggested that rather than disband the B Specials, which would sign his political death warrant, they be put under army command. Wilson agreed but emphasised his hope that confidence would be restored in the RUC as soon as possible so that the army could relinquish overall control of the security situation and the troops could be withdrawn. Denis Healey, Minister of Defence, was mindful of recreating a 1914-style confrontation between the British Government and the security forces, and expressed doubts over disbanding the B Specials. He preferred instead to disarm them and limit their activities to guarding key points, frontier work and the defence of police stations.

The Hunt Report, published on 10 October, proposed an unarmed, civil police force 'which will be in principle and in normal practice an unarmed force'. The paramilitary B Specials were to be disbanded and replaced by an RUC reserve and a locally recruited part-time military force of 4000 (this became the Ulster Defence Regiment, or UDR, with a strength much less than the 8481 of the Ulster Special Constabulary, USC) under the control of the British Army. There was also to be a large increase in recruitment to the RUC since, according to the Hunt Report, it was 'seriously below effective strength'. In particular 'vigorous efforts' were to be made to recruit Catholics, who made up only 11 per cent of the RUC (Hunt pp. 29–30, 43). The RUC was to be brought nearer the British model through closer links with British forces, and the adoption of the British rank and promotion structure. It was even proposed that the RUC's uniform be changed to blue. An English Inspector-General, Arthur Young, who had much experience of colonial policing, was appointed head of the RUC. As Callaghan wrote: 'The underlying theme of the Report was that policing in Northern Ireland should become more akin to policing in the UK' (Callaghan 1973 p. 113).

On 10 October 1969 James Callaghan endorsed the Hunt Report. There followed two nights of rioting by loyalists on the Shankhill Road during which Constable Victor Arbuckle became the first policeman to be killed during 'the Troubles'. Three people were killed during the rioting and 66 injured, including 14 soldiers and three policemen with shotgun wounds. Even before the Hunt Report there had been considerable conflict between the army and loyalists, resentful at British interference in Northern Ireland. Craig criticised Chichester-Clark for allowing the army to takeover control of security. Paisley threatened a general strike if Protestant demands were not met. He presented Chichester-Clark with a petition signed by nearly 100 000 expressing opposition to the disarmament of the B Specials. Shots were fired at the army on the

Shankhill, and 54 RUC and 48 soldiers were hurt in the rioting. Callaghan reacted to the continuing rioting, warning that the attainment of civil rights coupled with the proper structure of the police force 'has got to put an end to this nonsense in the streets. It has got to end' (*The Times*, 10 October 1969). Callaghan told Parliament that Protestant violence was 'based on a false appreciation of the situation and on rumours which have no relevance at all and no truth'. He completely failed to appreciate the importance of the police force to the unionist community in Northern Ireland and was puzzled by the sensitivity of the Unionist cabinet to the Hunt Report (House of Commons Debates, vol. 788, col. 56, 13 October 1969, Callaghan 1973 pp. 110–11).

There were some misgivings within the cabinet about establishing the UDR. But as Barbara Castle recalled, '[we] were persuaded by the argument that this was the only way to prevent the "B" Specials from going underground' (Castle 1984 p. 716). This has been a perennial security argument in Northern Ireland. The theory is that it is better to channel the frustrations of militant Protestants and their desire to defend the Union by bringing them into the official state security organisations, where a degree of control and discipline can be exerted, than to allow these disaffected people to express their frustration through non-state, paramilitary organisations, where the state has no control. By replacing the B Specials with the UDR, the members of this notorious force might be watered down with new (particularly Catholic) blood, but also disciplined through the control of the British Army and its officers. The rapid establishment of the UDR, which became operational on 1 April 1970 (with 18 per cent Catholic membership), again reflected the urgency with which the Labour Government wanted to withdraw British troops. By February 1970, three out of the eight additional army units deployed in Northern Ireland had returned to Britain (Cunningham 1991 p. 32).

The False Dawn and 'Sinister Forces'

Towards the end of 1969 Northern Ireland had quietened down and the Labour Government dared hope that the programme of reform was beginning to take effect and was sufficient to meet Catholic grievances (Dixon 1993 pp. 214–16). By October 1969 John Hume's Independent Organisation was claiming that when the proposed reforms were fully implemented, 'the civil rights movement in this country can be considered to have drawn to a hitherto unbelievably successful conclusion' (quoted in Ó Dochartaigh 1997 p. 141). Prime Minister O'Neill recalled in his memoirs, 'Any liberal-minded person must admit that the Civil Rights movements brought about reforms which would otherwise have taken years to wring from a reluctant Government' (O'Neill 1972 p. 111). Significantly, Callaghan's meeting with Chichester-Clark in January 1970 was concerned mainly with economic matters. The result of Labour's concern to tackle the economic basis of the violence was the 'Northern Ireland Development Programme 1970–75' which 'drew a direct link between improving employment prospects and housing, and reducing violence' (Cunningham 1991 p. 32).

Violence in Northern Ireland persisted in spite of the implementation of the reform programme. British definitions of the conflict began to shift; less and less was the conflict seen in optimistic 'liberal' terms of rational social, economic and security problems which were amenable to British reform. A more 'conservative' approach became apparent which increasingly identified 'sinister' and 'irrational forces' to explain the continuing conflict and justify a more hardline security stance. The 'conservative' explanation had the added benefit for British political and military elites of passing off blame for the continuing violence on the Northern Irish rather than any British failing.

From its initial non-confrontational stance the army began to patrol nationalist areas to enforce law and order. In Derry, 'relations between the army and sections of the Catholic community began to break down within weeks of the army's arrival' (Ó Dochartaigh 1997 p. 154). The 'heavy handedness' of the army's operation diminished nationalist toleration for their presence and by January 1970 there were already clashes with the British Army 'which it appears some Republicans helped to provoke' (Ó Dochartaigh 1997 p. 167, ch. 4). It seems reasonable to suggest that repressive army tactics helped to alienate nationalists, but at the same time some republicans were attempting to provoke just such a reaction. At the beginning of 1970 republicans were already preparing for military action, some for defence but others for offensive action to bring about a united Ireland (Ó Dochartaigh 1997 p. 195). On 1 April 1970, the first conflict between British troops and Irish Catholic civilians for two generations broke out at the Ballymurphy housing estate on the western edge of Belfast. The troops were now being attacked by the people it was thought they were there to defend. The victory of Ian

Paisley and a fellow Protestant Unionist at two Stormont by-elections in April 1970 indicated the growing polarisation of Northern Ireland politics and the deepening of the crisis. General Freeland issued a warning that anyone carrying or throwing petrol bombs was liable to be shot dead after a warning. He also spoke of 'sinister people' who were behind the youth gangs attacking the troops (*The Times*, 4 April 1970). Roy Hattersley, a Minister of Defence, also blamed the violence on 'sinister elements' stirring up the Catholic masses. Conservative politicians were also impatient with the failure of the reform programme to end the violence. A Conservative minister later wrote, 'Seldom can a protest movement anywhere have so rapidly achieved so many of its initial objectives' (Windlesham 1975 p. 92). Enoch Powell argued that grievances had been exaggerated out of proportion to serve the purposes of anarchy and Irish unity. Quintin Hogg believed the riots reflected 'sinister influences', people 'who seem to hate humanity as such'. This was a rude awakening for the Labour Government, particularly with a General Election approaching. The Ballymurphy Riots undermined the optimistic belief that the reform programme introduced by the Labour Government had met Catholic grievances and set the region on the road to 'normality'. Callaghan's initial optimism turned towards despair; he was fed up with Catholics 'stringing the British government along, making fresh demands as soon as old ones were met', and he felt that only the people of Northern Ireland, not Britain, could not solve the problems of Northern Ireland (*The Sunday Times* 1972 p. 222).

Security Policy and British Counter-Insurgency Strategy

In dealing with the Northern Ireland conflict the army was able to draw on its colonial experience of counter-insurgency (Dixon 1997b). The prescriptions of British counter-insurgency doctrine in the 1960s emphasised above all *the determination of the political elite to defeat insurgents*. This required the political and military elite to be unequivocal in their resolve to defeat insurgents. Political concessions to insurgents suggested that the state was weak and encouraged them and the civilian population to believe that the insurgents would win.

There were four principal inter-related requirements of British counter-insurgency strategy during this period. *First, and most important, the primary factor for victory is the determination of the political elite to defeat the insurgents.* The military accepted that neither side could win militarily and that the army could only 'hold the ring' while a political solution was found (Heath 1998 p. 423; see also Hamill 1986, Dixon 1997c). However, if the insurgents won the battle for the 'hearts and minds' of the local population then all was lost. An unswerving determination by the government to defeat the insurgents would help win over the 'neutral mass' of the population to the government's side. This would end the prospect of success on which the insurgents depended to mobilise popular support. Bipartisanship demonstrated the determination of the British political parties to defeat insurgents and, by limiting party conflict, reduced divisions among public opinion. The media would play a complementary role in this propaganda war by maintaining the support of domestic public opinion and demonstrating British determination to defeat the insurgents. According to the head of British Army information services in Northern Ireland 1971–73, Maurice Tugwell, 'The first essential in defeating insurgents (and almost the only essential) is an open-ended determination on behalf of the government and its supporters to defeat the insurrection.' This would counter republican expectations of the inevitability of their victory captured in the slogan *Tiocfaidh ar la*! ('Our day will come').

The second requirement of British counter-insurgency strategy emphasised the importance of winning 'the battle for hearts and minds' of the affected population. The government, by showing its political determination to win, is more likely to win the 'battle for hearts and minds' by discouraging the public from supporting the insurgents. If, on the other hand, the local population think the government will lose they may well throw in their lot with their future masters, the insurgents. Success for the government in the battle for 'hearts and minds' not only robs the insurgents of the popular support which sustains their campaign, but it also means that intelligence – a vital component of counter-insurgency operations – is more likely to be passed on by the public.

There were three principal means by which 'the battle for hearts and minds' could be won:

1. By good government and nation-building, to induce the population away from the insurgents' cause. The military also had a role to play by engaging in civil projects which would benefit the local population, including youth clubs, dances, sport and even a meals-on-wheels service.

2. Through 'psychological operations' to persuade the local population that the government side would win and was also on the side of 'the people' against an enemy which used terror. Enemy propaganda had to be countered and a positive image of the government forces promoted. The army also used 'black propaganda' against loyalists and republicans, including false stories planted in the media which were designed to undermine and disorientate the enemy.

3. Through the doctrine of 'minimum force'. To win 'the battle for hearts and minds' the army would have to be sensitive to the political implications of its actions and therefore the use of 'minimum force' would help to avoid the alienation of the local population. The term 'minimum force' is open to widely differing interpretations. Some of the more disastrous security operations and tactics deployed in Northern Ireland – collective punishments such as curfews and detention of suspects – fell within some experts' definitions of 'minimum force'. These caused severe reversals for the army in the battle for 'hearts and minds'.

The third requirement of British counter-insurgency theory stressed the importance of police primacy and civil–military co-operation for providing the intelligence to track down insurgents. The gathering of such intelligence is, in turn, facilitated by the government winning the 'battle for hearts and minds' which results in the local population passing intelligence to the army or police. British counter-insurgency doctrine tended to favour the primacy of the police in fighting insurgents and a more restricted role for the army, for several reasons. The police were more effective intelligence gatherers; more likely to be sensitive to local opinion, and therefore more effective at winning 'hearts and minds'; helped to create an image of normality; could be cheaper than the army; and were better trained for a 'peacekeeping' role. Police primacy also reduced the chances of British soldiers being killed and leading to domestic calls for the troops to be brought home (Dixon 2000a). The weak state of the locally recruited security forces meant that police primacy could not be implemented until the mid-1970s, by which time the RUC had been considerably strengthened.

Fourth, the centralised co-ordination of effort on all fronts – political, economic, military, psychological – was required to bring the full force of the state to bear against insurgents. Under 'indirect rule' in Northern

Ireland the army was answerable both to Stormont and London, and the need for centralised co-ordination was not fulfilled. Furthermore, even under 'direct rule' the Secretary of State for Northern Ireland did not combine command of the armed forces and political initiatives in a way that counter-insurgency doctrine would demand.

What was remarkable about British counter-insurgency strategy was its dependence on political rather than military action. This dependence and the need to co-operate so closely with the civil authority was not something which came naturally to the army. The stress on the role of the politicians in British counter-insurgency doctrine also provided a convenient excuse for military failure. The army's failure to defeat insurgents could be blamed on the lack of resolve of the politicians or the 'restrictive' framework of law which prevented it from doing its job properly. The higher profile of 'the Troubles' in domestic British politics, compared with counter-insurgency campaigns in the far-flung Empire, resulted in greater political involvement in security operations. This exacerbated tensions in civil–military relations.

Northern Ireland: 'Minimum Force' and Escalation

The replacement of a Labour Government by a Conservative Government (seen as traditionally pro-unionist), in June 1970, prepared the way for a more repressive security policy in Northern Ireland. The Falls Road Curfew, 3–5 July 1970, following closely after the Conservatives' June election victory, confirmed in the minds of some the new trajectory of British policy. The Curfew ranks alongside the introduction of internment as one of the most disastrous army operations. Significant supplies of arms were found but five civilians were killed and 60 injured. Sixteen hundred canisters of CS gas were fired into the Lower Falls area. The army later admitted that 58 allegations of looting and other misconduct 'were of such a nature as to suggest that an offence might have been committed, but there was no evidence on which action could be taken' (*The Times*, 18 September 1970). As a result of the Curfew, many Catholics became alienated from the army. Recruitment to the IRA accelerated and by the autumn of 1970 it was able to take offensive action against the British Army (*The Sunday Times* 1972 p. 221). By early 1971 both the Official IRA and the Provisional IRA were involved in offensive operations against the British Army (Smith 1995 p. 95), and in

February 1971 the first British soldier was killed. In May 1971 off-duty soldiers could visit friends in nationalist parts of Derry, but after the introduction of internment in August 1971 this was no longer possible (Ò Dochartaigh 1997 p. 16).

The Northern Ireland Prime Minister, James Chichester-Clark, called on Edward Heath to take more repressive security measures to reassure unionists. When this was refused he resigned in March 1971 and was replaced by Brian Faulkner, who was perceived to be more 'hardline' on security issues and who favoured 'a strategic shift to a short-run policy of aggression' (Bew, Gibbon and Patterson 1995 p. 167). The British Government was caught between its anxiety to avoid direct rule, thereby increasing its entanglement in the conflict, and opposition to Stormont's requests for a harsher security policy, which might escalate the conflict and precipitate direct rule anyway.

John Hume announced that the army's 'impartial role has now clearly ended' after the British Army killed two Catholics in Derry. The government's failure to hold an inquiry into the deaths resulted in the SDLP's withdrawal from Stormont. The introduction of internment in August 1971 ended what remaining hopes there were that the nationalists would co-operate with the Stormont regime. The British were reluctant to reject Faulkner's request for internment, fearing this would precipitate direct rule. Internment was a response to the growing intensification of the IRA's offensive and, while it was welcomed widely in Britain at the time, it was a serious blunder. Internment was directed solely at the nationalist community: to have picked up Protestants might have compounded Faulkner's political problems. Not only did it prevent any political accommodation with nationalists in Stormont but it also resulted in a massive escalation of violence. In the two years prior to internment 66 people were killed, including 11 soldiers. In the first 17 months after internment 610 were killed, including 146 soldiers. The use of 'interrogation in depth' techniques by the army against some internees led to substantiated allegations of torture. The escalation of violence following internment led to increased pressure on Faulkner from 'hardliners' to crack down even harder on terrorism. On 'Bloody Sunday', in January 1972, 13 innocent Catholic civilians were killed by the British Army, further escalating the conflict. In March 1972 Heath demanded the transfer of security powers from Stormont to Westminster. Faulkner resigned and, finally, the British Government was forced to take direct responsibility for Northern Ireland.

Army practice in Northern Ireland appears neither to have employed 'minimum force' nor to have been designed to win 'hearts and minds', in spite of the prescriptions of counter-insurgency. The use of CS gas, the Falls Road Curfew and internment constituted communal punishment. Following internment, in August 1971, the army's operations were designed primarily to facilitate the collection of intelligence on IRA activity in the main centres of Catholic population and thus to enable IRA activists to be arrested and put behind bars. The army set out to compile intelligence dossiers on all the inhabitants of a suspect area so that the IRA could be rooted out. These were compiled by regular house searches, person stop and searches, arrests and 'the interrogation in depth' (torture) of selected suspects. Paddy Hillyard has argued: 'It has not been simply a matter of the widespread curtailment of basic rights through the widespread abuse of the powers of stop, arrest and search, but the constant and systematic harassment of thousands of people within clearly defined areas.' The number of house searches escalated as shown below:

1970	3 107
1971	17 262
1973	74 556
1974	74 914
1975	30 002

He estimated that the impact of such tactics on the Catholic community resulted in one in four Catholic men between the ages of 16 and 44 being arrested at least once between 1972 and 1977. On average every Catholic household in Northern Ireland had been searched twice, but since many homes would not be under suspicion some houses in certain districts would have been searched 'perhaps as many as ten or more times' (Hillyard 1988 pp. 169, 197). Robin Evelegh, Commanding Officer of the 3rd Battalion Royal Green Jackets in Belfast, complained that the army's 'widespread search, arrest and screening operations' 'strongly alienated' the non-terrorist population: 'Nothing could have been more calculated to drive the non-committed part of the population into the arms of the terrorists from a sense of personal outrage and humiliation' (Evelegh 1978 p. 29). The employment of such tactics, by alienating the local population, was likely to lead to a more restricted flow of vital intelligence to the security forces.

Political Will? The Protestant Backlash and Army Discontent

British counter-insurgency strategy required the political elite to be determined and uncompromising in their resolve to defeat insurgency. Following internment, however, bipartisanship appeared to be weakening, and leading politicians both in the Conservative Government and the Labour Opposition were becoming more sympathetic to the goal of Irish unity (Patterson 1986, Dixon 1993, Bew, Gibbon and Patterson 1995 pp. 168–9). In his Guildhall Speech to the City of London, Heath declared that the nationalists' aspiration for Irish unity by democratic and constitutional means was legitimate and that if a majority in Northern Ireland wanted Irish unity 'I do not believe any British Government would stand in the way.' There were also reports of an emerging bipartisan consensus in favour of Irish unity (*The Guardian*, 29 November 1971, *The Economist*, 11 December 1971, Heath 1998 pp. 432, 436). At a cabinet meeting on 4 February 1972 the Conservative Government considered repartition and population exchange with the South to resolve the conflict. As Eamonn McCann points out, 'The minutes suggest that the British Government was far from dogmatic about the constitutional future of the North. None of the ministers is recorded expressing a straightforward defence-of-the-realm position' ('Post-Bloody Sunday, it was all to play for', *Sunday Tribune*, 26 September 1999). The Minister of Defence, Lord Carrington, even argued that expecting nationalists to wait 20 years for a united Ireland was asking too much, which suggested that there was no overriding defence objection to Irish unity (Bew, Gibbon and Patterson 1995 p. 169).

The conflict, particularly on the left, was seen increasingly by the political elite as a colonial one rather than an internal UK problem. The logical corollary of this position was British withdrawal and Irish unity. In November 1971 Harold Wilson put Irish unity, albeit by consent, on the agenda in his 15-point plan. In March 1971 James Callaghan had raised the proposal for an all-Ireland council. The Labour Party began to discuss British withdrawal under the code-name 'Algeria'. The alternative party of government – and a credible one at that – was not displaying the political will and determination required by British counter-insurgency doctrine. The response to Wilson's plan from the Conservative Government was not hostile (Dixon 1993 p. 292). In March 1972 Wilson went to Dublin to meet the IRA. This was followed by the introduction of direct rule, a key IRA demand which alienated unionists. Following the introduction of direct rule, Willie Whitelaw, the newly-appointed Secretary of State for Northern Ireland ordered the army to take a 'low profile' approach in nationalist areas to create the political space for a constitutional initiative. In June 1972 the Provisional announced a ceasefire and in July Gerry Adams was among the IRA leaders who were flown to London to take part in talks.

British 'determination' was further undermined by an apparent shift in British public opinion. An NOP poll published by the *Daily Mail* in September 1971 suggested 59 per cent of people in Britain wanted the immediate withdrawal of the army from Northern Ireland. The British media found itself under attack from Conservative politicians who felt their reporting of Northern Ireland was undermining the morale of the British people and their army (Dixon 2000a). Even before internment the Home Secretary warned of the danger of a populist movement for British withdrawal gaining momentum if soldiers continued to be killed. After Bloody Sunday, ministers in the Conservative Cabinet expressed their concerns about the rise of 'troops out' sentiment in Britain. Heath argued that 'there was a growing feeling that they could not go on indefinitely doing a horrible job with no sign of an improvement' (*Sunday Tribune*, 26 September 1999). There was a belief in the IRA that if sufficient British soldiers were killed this would precipitate withdrawal. From the IRA's perspective they were riding a post-war tide of victories for 'liberation movements' and, even by the end of 1971, the IRA was sufficiently encouraged for its paper to declare 1972 'The Year of Victory' (Hamill 1985 p. 22, Smith 1995 p. 101).

The apparent gains of the IRA and the ambiguity of British policy towards Northern Ireland provoked unease among loyalists who feared their position within the Union was becoming undermined and mobilised to defend it. In late 1971 and early 1972 the DUP, the UDA and Vanguard were established. (Vanguard was a hardline faction principally within the UUP which later, in 1973, established itself as the Vanguard Unionist Party.) A vicious loyalist murder campaign got under way, which was probably partly a response to increasing republican violence and directed towards pushing the state to adopt a more repressive security policy (Patterson 1986, Loughlin 1995 ch. 9, Bruce 1999 p. 191). During 1971–73 a loyalist backlash developed, raising the prospect of the British Army facing its 'nightmare scenario' of a war against both loyalist and republican paramilitaries.

Whitelaw's new 'hearts and minds' approach to security involved the adoption by the army of a 'low profile', no re-occupation of republican 'no-go' areas, the introduction of 'special category' (i.e., political) status for republican prisoners, and the release of detainees. In March 1972, 913 republican detainees had been interned; by June 1972 this was down to 372 and by August 1972 to 243. The government's general policy was 'to exploit the introduction of direct rule in the hope of creating a better "hearts and minds" climate among the Catholics without thereby provoking Protestant reaction'. (Carver 1989 pp. 421–2) These concessions and the subsequent negotiations with the IRA recognised the political nature of the republican struggle and contradicted the message that was being promoted in the propaganda war, where the IRA were portrayed as mindless psychopaths, thugs and criminals.

In reaching out to republicans, Whitelaw risked upsetting the 'balance' and provoking unionists. By June 1972 an opinion poll found that 74 per cent of Catholics but just 21 per cent of Protestants thought Whitelaw was doing a good job (McAllister 1977b p. 116). Loyalists, fearing the truce with the IRA was the prelude to a sell-out by the British Government, began to establish their own barricades. On 3 July a stand-off between 8000 members of the UDA and the outnumbered army threatened to lead to heavy bloodshed if soldiers were forced to fire on the advancing loyalists. The IRA was also escalating its campaign after the end of the ceasefire. The Army negotiated and averted a clash with the UDA which could have resulted in the army fighting a war on two fronts: 'an unenviable and probably impossible position' (Hamill 1986 p. 110).

The army was unhappy with the government's new strategy as it was felt that the release of detainees led to greater violence and the 'low profile' approach of the army gave the IRA a chance to regroup (Hamill 1986 p. 103, Carver 1989 p. 427). The 'weakness' being displayed by the army, it was argued, resulted in the drying-up of intelligence. Army morale suffered and officers complained 'that the low profile restrictions were causing casualties and [they] felt that the policy had nothing to do with their jobs' (Hamill 1986 pp. 106–7). There was also dissatisfaction that the politicians, by negotiating with the IRA and being ambiguous on the constitutional future of Northern Ireland, were not demonstrating the determination necessary to win and were thus provoking a backlash among the loyalists. The army suffered rising casualties and the 'nightmare scenario' of a 'war on two fronts' appeared to be approaching. Army officers were 'convinced that the army had a better understanding of what was going on and they rated the Government as being politically naive' (Hamill 1986 p. 107). The former Chief of General Staff, Michael Carver, described the army's dilemma:

> if the situation was allowed to continue unchanged, we should be faced with the choice between fighting the UDA directly, in order to prevent them from fighting the IRA, or taking the general offensive against the IRA as an indirect method of preventing the UDA from fighting them. If we did neither, we should be failing to prevent inter-sectarian strife and to show that violence did not pay. There would be repercussions outside Northern Ireland; the authority of government, and respect for the forces of law and order would be gravely undermined. We should be prepared to declare a state of grave emergency in Northern Ireland and resort to the same sort of measures that a government would be prepared to take in war. (Carver 1989 pp. 424–5)

Lord Carver concluded:

> This period was marked by the difficulty of balancing the political and military factors. The Government achieved some success in detaching support from the IRA both in the Republic and in Northern Ireland, but at the cost of building up a Protestant reaction, indirectly encouraging the formation of Protestant armed bodies, on the excuse that the army was neither protecting the Protestants nor pursuing the IRA vigorously enough, and also at the expense of some loss of control over and suppression of the activities of the IRA. (Carver 1989 p. 423; see also Dixon 1997c)

Since 1969 the British political and military elite had striven to avoided confrontation with Protestants (Bew, Gibbon and Patterson 1995 p. 167). By concentrating their efforts against the republicans the security forces were dealing with their principal threat but also soothing unionist discontent, probably running with the grain of the locally recruited security forces' attitudes and preventing a 'war on two fronts' (Urban 1992 pp. 238–9).

The decision of the British, on 31 July 1972, to launch 'Operation Motorman' to remove the republican 'no-go' areas was in keeping with the structural, anti-republican, bias of British policy. It was a massive and successful operation, employing 12 000 troops, and marked a 'decisive blow' against the IRA and a major step in the reduction of violence (Smith 1995 p. 110). Advocates of a more repressive, 'militarist' strategy of counter-insurgency might argue that signs of political concessions by the British political elite aggravated the conflict in Ireland to the heights of the summer of 1972, and that it took the biggest British military operation since Suez to clear the no-go areas, a 'tough' measure which was long overdue. Consequently, this produced the desired decrease in violence. Those with a more 'political approach' to counter-insurgency would tend to argue that Motorman succeeded because the government had created the political space in which it could be successful. The introduction of direct rule and Whitelaw's 'softly, softly' security policy had divided the nationalist community. The IRA's 'Bloody Friday' bombing atrocity (killing 11 and injuring 130) and war-weariness were also taking its toll on republican support for violence (Smith 1995 p. 104).

The loyalists were not pacified by Operation Motorman. In October 1972 the UDA briefly declared war on the British Army and unionist politicians adopted a more militant rhetoric. Former Unionist minister John Taylor said: 'Enjoy this Christmas, it may well be your last in peace. After New Year you will probably have to organise to resist an imposed solution by the British Government.' William Craig, leader of Vanguard, declared his willingness 'to come out and shoot and kill'. In late 1972 and early 1973 the army did crack down on loyalist areas. In February 1973 the first loyalists were interned and in response loyalists called a strike which brought Northern Ireland to a standstill and resulted in widespread violence. One of the loyalist leaders of the strike claimed that 'the power of the grass roots' can no longer be ignored (Bew and Gillespie 1993 p. 59).

The Security Dilemma

The events of the summer of 1972 illustrate Britain's security dilemma in Northern Ireland and the constraints operating on its power. The British had two principal objectives as far as the local security forces were concerned.

1. To create forces which implemented the law impartially and which enjoyed the confidence and consent of the people of

Northern Ireland. This was seen to require that the personnel of such forces be drawn widely from across all communities in Northern Ireland.

2. To create such forces swiftly and in sufficient strength to control and bear the brunt of the conflict so that the British Army could be either withdrawn or its commitment significantly reduced.

Catholic recruitment to the part-time UDR was, initially, favourable. Moderate nationalist politicians (including the SDLP) and church leaders encouraged their followers to join. By March 1970 Catholics constituted 39 per cent of the recruits for the new organisation (Ryder 1992 p. 39). However, the murder by the IRA of Catholic members of the security forces and the repressive policy of Stormont, which alienated many in the Catholic community, and perhaps also sectarianism within the force contributed towards a decline in Catholic recruitment to the UDR and RUC. The apparent shift in British policy during 1972 and the resulting 'Protestant backlash' began to undermine Protestant recruitment to the local forces and therefore also to undermine British hopes of extricating the army from the conflict. The RUC was still weak, its intelligence and morale were poor and it could not hope to take on the burden of primacy in the struggle against the IRA.

The dependence of the British Government and military on the Protestant community for the recruitment of the local security forces in effect constrained the ability of the British to police that community. If the army 'took on' the Protestants too forcefully then they ran the risk that Protestants would not join the UDR and the RUC. The consequences for British security policy were dire: the advantages of police primacy would be lost and the British army would be unable to give up the burden of policing. Although General Tuzo, the GOC 1971–73, denied that the army dealt more leniently with loyalist extremists than the IRA, he 'made it clear that he was reluctant to find himself fighting two different wars at the same time' (Carver 1989 p. 428). Similar dilemmas of policing a communally divided society such as Northern Ireland had also been apparent in Britain's withdrawal from the Empire (Dixon 1997c pp. 199–200). The Ulster Defence Regiment's relationship with the loyalist paramilitary Ulster Defence Association was also problematic. Here there may have been a problem over whether UDA members should be allowed to join the UDR and therefore subjected to some state control and also improving Britain's chances of

Ulsterising the conflict by increasing the strength of the local security forces, or whether to forbid UDA/UDR joint membership and
send these men out into the streets (Fitzgerald 1991 p. 279). There
were suspicions in British political and military circles that the loyal-
ties of the RUC and UDR were to Ulster unionism rather than the
British state and that there were limits to which the RUC could be
pushed in order to police its own community (Donoughue 1987
p. 129, Urban 1992 pp. 51–2).

The army's reliance on the local security forces was compounded
during the years 1972–74 by a crisis within its own ranks. In 1972 no
fewer than 103 soldiers were killed, and the following year the army
experienced a recruitment crisis which was attributed to its role
in Northern Ireland. The recruitment of men into the army from
civilian life was:

1969–70	21 411
1970–71	24 337
1971–72	31 298
1972–73	26 484
1973–74	15 310
1974–75	22 041
1975–76	27 238	(Dixon 2000a p. 111)

Lord Carrington, Minister of Defence, commented in June 1973:
'Northern Ireland has had some effect, not among serving soldiers so
much, but parents who may have discouraged their sons from going
into the Service' (*The Times*, 20 June 1973). An army survey found
that: 'After four years of trying to keep the peace in Ulster, however,
there is no little doubt that the army's role there is bad for recruiting.
Surveys among potential recruits show that early in 1973, although
the overwhelming majority thought it should remain there, 46 per
cent of them were put off joining by the prospect of serving there.'
The problems of recruitment and the retention of currently serving
soldiers was compounded by the widespread opposition of many army
relatives to their sons serving in Northern Ireland and their agitation
for withdrawal. British politicians feared a populist campaign to
'bring our boys home' which had developed in Britain over Palestine
in the late 1940s (Dixon 2000a). The army was overstretched by its
involvement in Northern Ireland and this threatened its ability to
contribute fully to NATO. The recruitment crisis underscored the
importance of police primacy in Northern Ireland and the need to

increase recruitment to the local, and by now overwhelmingly Protestant, security forces. Antagonising unionism was unlikely to produce the necessary flow of recruits to implement police primacy and also threatened the army with a 'war on two fronts' (Hamill 1986 p. 149). The dependence of security policy on the need to recruit Protestants into the security forces is the context against which the British Government's failure to order the army to take stronger action against the Protestant community can be more fully comprehended, and in particular its reluctance to take on the loyalist Ulster Workers' Council (UWC) strike in May 1974 which brought down the British-backed power-sharing executive (Chapter 6).

Conclusion

The 'structuralist' argument that the outbreak of conflict in Northern Ireland was inevitable has been deployed by Labour politicians and civil servants to absolve themselves from responsibility for the crisis in Northern Ireland. Just as structuralist Modernisation Theory let politicians off the hook by predicting the inevitability of Irish unity, the assumption that the English had failed, and always would fail, to do anything positive in Ireland was a self-fulfilling prophecy. Nevertheless, considerable constraints do seem to have operated on the Labour Government's room for manoeuvre and the fear that British 'interference' might provoke a civil war was a real one. The assumptions of British political ideology were inadequate for understanding the communal pattern of politics in Northern Ireland. The 'modern', 'progressive' British political model was imposed through a programme of reform, but there was little understanding of the impact of these reforms and the fears they aroused. When reform failed to stop the violence it was 'the natives' (nationalists and unionists) and 'irrational, sinister forces' who were increasingly blamed for their own plight, with little responsibility becoming attached to British political or military elites. The emphasis of policy shifted from reform to security, resulting in the disaster of internment. In both the Labour and the Conservative parties; increasingly Northern Ireland was no longer seen as 'British', and the easiest way out appeared to be Irish unity.

The lack of determination displayed by British politicians in the propaganda war was undermining the army in its fight with the IRA, and threatening to involve it in a 'war' with loyalists also. This was apparent in the failure to introduce direct rule earlier; the premature introduction of internment; the negotiations and truce with the IRA; the release of detainees and 'disastrous' low profile approach of Whitelaw; and Labour's support and Conservative sympathy for Irish unity. From the perspective of the British counter – insurgery strategy, by raising uncertainty about the constitutional future of Northern Ireland, the politicians were losing the propaganda war and encouraging the IRA to believe they were winning and that they should continue to intensify their 'armed struggle'. In addition this approach also raised the hackles of unionists who, believing they were to be driven into a united Ireland, mobilised to put pressure on the British to act against the IRA. The imperative to Ulsterise security was only likely to be realised by recruiting from among unionists who might not join the security forces if they felt they were implementing a policy which was destroying the Union. This resulted in a bias against confrontation with unionists, and towards confrontation with republicans, which is perceptible throughout 'the Troubles'. If the Government alienated both republicans and loyalists then this might lead to the army's 'nightmare scenario' of an unwinnable 'war on two fronts', against both the IRA and loyalist paramilitaries, in which their position could become untenable. From this counter-insurgency perspective, the consequence of the politicians' weakness was the heavy casualties and recruitment crisis suffered by the army, as well as the growing disillusionment and support for withdrawal among British public opinion. The strain this produced on civil–military relations manifested itself in calls from some quarters for a stronger military role in British politics and raises questions about the extent of political control over security policy (Foot 1989, Dixon 1997b pp. 201–3).

6

The First Peace Process 1972–74: The Power-Sharing Experiment and its Failure

After the introduction of direct rule in 1972 the British Government tried again to construct an accommodation on the moderate, centre ground of Northern Irish politics where, it was assumed, there existed a 'moderate silent majority' for peace. The 'power-sharing experiment' attempted to balance unionist and nationalist claims and find a compromise to which the Northern Irish political elites could bring their parties and voters. If a deal was struck which was 'too favourable' to either nationalism or unionism then it was less likely that the party leaders who had the rough end of the deal would be able to persuade their supporters and voters to endorse that agreement. Furthermore, the ability of political leaders to lead their parties and voters was likely to vary from party to party and be influenced by the wider political environment. Power-sharing with some kind of Irish dimension was always likely to be the only settlement which could attract significant cross-community support. After the violence of the previous four years, was it possible for nationalist and unionist political elites to reach a settlement which could bridge the gap between their parties and voters? What kind of power-sharing and what kind of Irish dimension could maximise support for accommodation? How could the governments, if not the parties themselves, create the conditions in which support for a centrist settlement would be maximised? Alternatively, what constitutional arrangement might minimise nationalist and unionist alienation and contain the conflict?

British Colonial Policy: Building up the Moderates

British attempts to build up a 'moderate centre' in Northern Ireland were reminiscent of its imperial policy. In Empire the British had intervened and attempted to engineer constitutional settlements based on the 'centre', 'an amorphous mass of responsible, tolerant, silent and simple people ready to be mobilized in defence of compromise. The aim was to elicit and organize this "centre"' (Utley 1975 p. 25, Darwin 1988 p. 168, Furedi 1994).

Frank Furedi's discussion of Malaya, Kenya and British Guiana in *Colonial Wars and the Politics of Third World Nationalism* bears comparison with British policy towards Northern Ireland. He argues that in these cases 'radical nationalists' were susceptible to influence from the 'grassroots' which made it difficult for them to cut deals with the British colonial power. The British attempted 'to restore order' which was in effect 'about curbing or deactivating mass politics' (Furedi 1994 p. 189).

> By the middle of the emergencies, it was clear to imperial officials that they could do little to influence popular aspirations for change. The response to this insight was to fight a rearguard action and attempt to shape the manner in which change could be achieved by constructing an environment which restrained mass participation and created a political framework that was insulated from popular pressure. Thus, whatever their starting point, gradually the emergencies became a kind of controlled experiment in change. (Furedi 1994 p. 189)

British imperial officials attempted to establish political structures which distanced nationalist politicians from mass pressure. The British became adept at detaching and strengthening moderates from anti-colonial movements and isolating the extremists, who tended to be more popular and plebeian (Furedi 1994 p. 240). British administrators could not influence the masses directly but could do so by influencing their political leaders. However, those moderate nationalists who wished to 'collaborate' with the British faced the difficulty of doing so while at the same time retaining credibility and popularity with the masses (Furedi 1994 pp. 247, 250). Nationalist, anti-colonial leaders had to be responsive to their own activists and the masses or face being outflanked by rival elites. Simultaneously, they had to try to lead their movement towards what appeared to be a 'realistic' settlement.

Experts in Whitehall looked upon anti-colonial leaders as never totally reliable because under mass pressure they could go beyond the permissable. In a sense, even the most co-operative leader was to some extent a prisoner of the masses. The more astute colonial administrators understood that leaders had to keep their activists in check and that quite often they had to take radical steps to retain their credibility. Through the activists, mass pressure could be exerted on leaders, thereby ensuring that relations with the colonial authorities would be tense. (Furedi 1994 p. 250)

Extreme activists would put pressure on anti-colonial leaders and so 'London was sensitive to the need of anti-colonial leaders to retain a radical public image' (Furedi 1994 p. 255). Furedi suggests there is some limited evidence that the British would manufacture martyrs out of their nationalist 'collaborators'/moderates, by arresting them, in order to bolster their image among the masses (Furedi 1994 p. 251).

The Moderate Silent Majority?

British strategy combined elements of both a top-down and a bottom-up approach to conflict resolution (Dixon 1997a, 1997c, 1997d). On the one hand the political elites were to be coerced and cajoled into agreement (top-down), while on the other initiatives were taken to promote reconciliation at the grassroots level (bottom-up). The initial tranche of reforms instituted after troops were deployed on the streets of Northern Ireland in August 1969, for example, were aimed at dealing with what were perceived to be the roots of the conflict: economic, social and security reforms were implemented. The Community Relations Commission was among proposals to encourage 'harmonious community relations'. Politicians of both major British parties publicly subscribed to the assumption that the electorate was more 'moderate' than its political representatives, either because this belief was genuine or else as part of the propaganda war to encourage and mobilise moderation.

The faith of both major British political parties in the moderates appeared to be borne out by the success of the trade union movement, the women's peace movement and moderate political parties in challenging communal polarisation. The revitalisation of the NILP was seen, particularly in Labour circles, as an important step for uniting Catholic and Protestant workers along class rather than sectarian lines. The NILP's apparently strong showing at the June 1970 General Election (98 194 votes) suggested it was a major player in the conflict and demonstrated a potential to transcend communal divisions (its strong showing was probably due partly to the absence of a nationalist alternative as the SDLP was only established in August 1970). The apparent success of the trade union movement in uniting Protestant and Catholic workers within their ranks also reinforced the moderate assumptions of *both* British Labour and Conservative politicians. During 'the Troubles' the trade union movement has been largely successful in preventing violence spilling over on to the shop floor. Its leaders, both Protestant and Catholic, were leading figures calling for calm and 'moderation'.

Following the introduction of direct rule in March 1972, a peace movement developed and took to the streets in nationalist West Belfast, which was 'assiduously cultivated by both Whitelaw and the SDLP' (McAllister 1977b p. 116). Some Catholics called for a cease-fire, since many were tired of the conflict and levels of violence. In April 1972 the Official IRA murdered Catholic Ranger William Best of the Royal Irish Rangers, home on leave in Derry. There followed angry protests from the women of the Bogside and the Creggan and calls for the OIRA to leave these areas. In May 1972 the OIRA declared a ceasefire, recognising that 'the overwhelming desire of the great majority of all the people ... is for an end to military actions by all sides'. In June 1972 the Provisional IRA called a short truce while secret talks were held with the British Govern-ment. Willie Whitelaw attempted to build on the opportunity opened up by the introduction of direct rule to win over nationalists to an accommodation with unionism (see Chapter 5).

During this period the Provisionals believed they were on the verge of defeating the British and so their uncompromising stance in talks with the British Government and Opposition is not so surpris-ing. From the IRA's anti-colonial perspective they were riding the tide of post-war decolonisation, for if the British had retreated from the rest of the Empire why not Northern Ireland? They hoped to kill as many British soldiers as were killed in Aden believing, with some reason, that this might precipitate a withdrawal (Dixon 2000a). The republicans' unwillingness to negotiate ruled them out of any peace process although the British continued to try to draw them into democratic politics. Sinn Féin was encouraged to contest the British General Election of 1974 and after that election Sinn Féin and the loyalist UVF were legalised (Taylor 1997 p. 170). The PIRA worked to undermine any power-sharing settlement: in September 1973 it bombed a London hotel to coincide with power-sharing negotiations, and during the period of the power-sharing executive it stepped up its bombing campaign to bring the executive down (Smith 1995 p. 125). The PIRA's intransigence left the government little alternative but to build peace on the moderate centre ground of Northern Irish politics, attempting to boost moderates while marginalising the PIRA and loyalist extremists. A security crackdown could be implemented with the support and endorsement of constitutional nationalism from both North and South.

The success of 'moderates' fuelled hopes that it was these members of civil society who were more representative of the people than 'intransigent' and 'bigoted' politicians. 'Moderates' claimed the existence of 'a silent moderate majority' and some favoured a referendum to test this sentiment. The *Belfast Telegraph* was an influential propagandist for the moderate cause, applauding 'the triumph of commonsense from below' (Bromley 1989 p. 218). David Bleakley, of the NILP, and former Minister for Community Relations, claimed in his book *Peace in Ulster* (1972): 'Fortunately the evidence indicates that the mass of Ulster people are on the side of reconciliation.' Their presence is not often obvious because 'they speak a language which too often goes unnoticed in an age which gives pride of place to news framed in a context of violence' (Bleakley 1972 p. 67). At British Army Headquarters in Lisburn, briefing officers spoke of the 'mass of moderate opinion about to be mobilised', and 'the great white snowball of peace' that was rolling out of Derry (Hamill 1985 p. 106). Opinion polls seemed to bear out the optimism of the Government and 'moderates'. In August 1972 *Fortnight* magazine published opinion poll results concluding that 'after four years of violence in Northern Ireland there has been a substantial swing towards non-sectarian voting'.

The 'moderate centre' of Northern Ireland politics, except for the SDLP, met at the Darlington Conference in September 1972. Whitelaw hoped to split off the liberal wing of the Ulster Unionist Party, and shepherd the hardliner Brian Faulkner from centre stage (*The Times*, 2 June 1973), in order to build up the moderate middle ground of the SDLP, NILP and APNI. The inclusion of the SDLP among the 'moderate' parties was open to question. It drew its support more or less exclusively from Catholics, supported Irish unity and refused to participate at Darlington because of the continuation of internment. Including the SDLP in a 'moderate' coalition with unionists was likely to test its stability severely. A less diverse coalition of moderates might have a greater chance of success, and hence the British Conservative Government's hope that the 'socialist' NILP would perform well at forthcoming elections and prove to be 'a more compromising representative of moderate opinion', or perhaps put pressure on the SDLP to adopt a more accommodating stance.

The British Government's problem was that it was two years since elections had been held in Northern Ireland and it was difficult to assess what kind of support each of the parties commanded. The violence of the intervening period had allowed the people to look into the abyss of communal violence and, it was argued, they would surely not vote for those 'extremists' who had generated that violence and stood in the way of fair compromise. Opinion polls reinforced the government's hopes of a strong 'centre'. British politicians, from both major parties, attempted to shore up the centre ground by threatening the people of Northern Ireland with the 'consequences' of rejecting Britain's power-sharing approach. Again there were overtones of chauvinistic British nationalism, as 'we' the British people demanded that 'they', the people of Northern Ireland, accept the settlement 'we' were developing to settle 'their' conflict. Heath warned that people would 'get very fed up' if the people in Northern Ireland did not take this opportunity to get together (*The Times*, 24 March 1973). Supporting the government's 1972 Green Paper (see below), Merlyn Rees argued:

> If we were rejected, that of itself would mean that there was no moderate majority in both communities, in both camps, which is the basis on which we have been working for four years. If it were proved wrong, it would mean needing to face up to a complete reappraisal of policy by any British Government, because the basis on which that Government had been working would have been shown to be false. (House of Commons Debates, vol. 846, col. 57, 13 November 1972)

Since it was felt that the current political elites did not represent the moderate majority, Harold Wilson spoke of the election of 'genuinely representative' politicians at the polls. British threats against the people of Northern Ireland proved to be counter-productive; rather than boosting moderates they helped to produce precisely those conditions of constitutional insecurity which had historically undermined moderate forces (Lawrence, Elliott and Laver 1975 pp. 68, 85).

The Settlement: Power-Sharing and an Irish Dimension

The British Government's wooing of the nationalist community after direct rule and the PIRA's 'Bloody Friday' outrage opened up the political space for the SDLP, urged on by the Irish Government, to lift its ban on discussions with Whitelaw. Although the SDLP did not take part in the Darlington Conference it did produce a policy document, *Towards a United Ireland*, which reflected the assumptions of Modernisation and adopted a greener stance than any of the nationalist parties in the Republic. Northern Ireland, it argued, was 'inherently unstable' and any settlement would have to take place in an all-Ireland context. The British Government was urged to declare itself in favour of Irish unity and a power-sharing executive was proposed, but with control of security policy remaining at Westminster. A National Senate of Ireland would integrate the whole island 'by preparing the harmonisation of the structures, laws and services of both parts of Ireland and ... agree[ing] on an acceptable constitution for a New Ireland and Its relationships with Britain'. The British and Irish Governments should accept joint sovereignty as an interim system of government. The SDLP's policy document was ambiguous on consent and did not specifically state that Irish unity required the consent of a majority in Northern Ireland, unlike the party's constitution.

The British Government's Green (discussion) Paper was published on 31 October 1972 against a background of continuing violence from loyalist and republican paramilitaries. The Green Paper laid down minimum requirements and parameters for a political settlement and introduced the idea of power-sharing, suggesting that any devolved assembly would have to receive cross-community support and that there were strong arguments for the minority to exercise a share of executive power. The constitutional guarantee was emphasised and would be tested by periodic border plebiscites. It was hoped that clear-cut constitutional guarantees might calm unionist fears and help pull Northern Ireland back from the brink of civil war (*The Guardian*, 11 October 1972). The Border Poll, held in March 1973, produced a 57.5 per cent vote of the electorate for the Union, with 0.6 per cent against (nationalists and republicans boycotted the poll).

Disconcertingly for unionists, British guarantees came with threats. While the Green Paper guaranteed the position of unionists within the UK there was also a veiled threat that membership of the UK carried obligations as well as rights, and it was not for Northern

Ireland alone to decide how it was to be governed as part of the UK. Furthermore the British also claimed 'neutrality' on the constitutional future of Northern Ireland: 'No UK Government for many years has had any wish to impede the realisation of Irish unity, if it were to come about by genuine and freely given mutual agreement and on conditions acceptable to the distinctive communities.' Britain would not impede Irish unity but its priorities in Northern Ireland were, first, peace and stability; second, prosperity; and, third, that the region should not offer a base for any external threat to the UK (Northern Ireland Office *The Future of NI: A Paper for Discussion*, Belfast 1972, para. 52, 74). The legitimacy of the Republic's interest in the North was recognised; economic and security interdependence, along with Ireland's membership of the EEC, pointed towards a closer relationship between the North and South of Ireland; and it was 'clearly desirable that any new arrangements for Northern Ireland should, whilst meeting the wishes of Northern Ireland and Great Britain, be, so far as possible, acceptable to and accepted by the Republic of Ireland'. But it was for the people of Northern Ireland to decide what their relationship should be to the UK and the Republic (para. 78).

The government's White Paper, *Northern Ireland Constitutional Proposals*, was published in March 1973 and closely resembled the Green Paper. After consultations the government had found four 'very significant areas of agreement' concerning: a devolved assembly; a single-chamber elected legisative assembly of 80–100 members; a structure of powerful committees within the assembly; and the protection of fundamental human rights and freedoms. The Northern Ireland Assembly and its power-sharing executive would have responsibility for social security, education, industry, agriculture and planning, with the prospect of security being devolved at a future date. The White Paper recognised that the problems in Northern Ireland required bottom-up community initiatives, economic prosperity and reconciliation as well as constitutional structures. The UK favoured the establishment of a Council of Ireland which would cover areas of mutual interest such as tourism, regional development, electricity and transport (para. 110). If the Council was to be 'a useful working mechanism in North–South relations, it must operate with the consent of both majority and minority opinion in Northern Ireland, who have a right to prior consultation and involvement in the process of determining its form, functions and procedures' (para. 111). After elections to a new Assembly the British Government would consult with the representatives of

Northern Ireland opinion and the government of the Republic to discuss three inter-related objectives: the principle of consent and acceptance of the status of Northern Ireland; 'effective consultation and co-operation in Ireland'; and security co-operation against terrorists (para. 116).

The recognition of the importance of the Irish dimension by the British Government accompanied a growing acknowledgement of the legitimacy of the Republic's role in resolving the conflict in Northern Ireland. By mid-1971 Heath could not accept that 'anyone from outside the UK can participate in meetings to promote political development of any part of the United Kingdom' (*Irish Times*, 6 April 1998). After the introduction of internment Heath criticised the Irish PM's call for an end to internment 'as unwarranted interference in the internal affairs of the UK'. But on 6–7 September 1971 Heath met Lynch in a meeting which symbolised Britain's recognition that the Republic had a legitimate interest in northern affairs (Fitzgerald 1991 p. 99). Consultation with the Irish Government, according to Heath, 'was essential if we were to convince moderate opinion in Northern Ireland that we were acting in good faith', because 'Until we could establish a productive working relationship with the Irish Government, the political deadlock could not be broken' (Heath 1998 p. 424).

During 1972 the nature of the Protestant backlash was becoming apparent and also the impatience of British politicians was beginning to concern Irish politicians. The emphasis of Irish policy correspondingly shifted from the rhetoric of Irish unity towards the prerequisite of reconciliation, and the Irish Government encouraged the SDLP to enter talks with the British. On 24 November 1972 Heath and Lynch met, and the Irish Taoiseach described 'a closer meeting of minds than he had ever experienced before'. The London correspondent of the *Irish Times* reported that the Irish 'entered enthusiastically into negotiatons, and from this point onwards the British kept them very closely informed, usually in advance, of their proposals. Relations, recently so chilly, soon became warm, even excessively cosy' (Downey 1983 p. 125). The importance of the Anglo–Irish process was indicated by Heath's visit to Dublin in September 1973, the first visit by a British Prime Minister since 1921. The advantages to the British of a closer relationship with the Irish Government were that it increased the likelihood of achieving a settlement with nationalist support; it held out the prospect of more effective cross-border security co-operation against the IRA (which, for some, was the key to defeating the IRA); and it also helped reduce any international pressure, particularly from the USA.

The White Paper warned the people of Northern Ireland of their obligations (para. 12b) but also looked to the 'law-abiding' majority 'to stand together against those small but dangerous minorities which would seek to impose their views by violence and coercion, and which cannot, therefore, be allowed to participate in working institutions they wish to destroy' (para. 118). The Paper concluded, 'The Government believes ... that the majority of the people of Northern Ireland have an overwhelming desire for peace and that they will accept the opportunity which these proposals offer' (para. 122).

The problem for the British of pushing the Irish dimension and courting the Irish Government was that it tended to further alienate unionists who were already highly suspicious of British intentions. The ruling Ulster Unionist Council (UUC) voted not to reject the government's White Paper on 27 March 1973 by 381 votes to 231. On 30 March a faction broke away from the UUP to found the Vanguard Unionist Progressive Party (VUPP), a party with overt paramilitary connections, which opposed the White Paper proposals along with Paisley's DUP (which then favoured direct rule). The VUPP was relatively ambivalent about the Union and favoured a powerful Northern Ireland assembly, but there were those who also supported independence. A coalition of loyalists opposed to the White Paper (including the DUP, VUPP, anti-White Paper UUP, representatives of loyalist workers, the Orange Order and the UDA) agreed on four points: the defeat of the IRA; the utter rejection of the Council of Ireland; full parliamentary representation (at Westminster); and control of the RUC by Northern Ireland's elected representatives.

The Failure of Moderates

The illusion of a 'moderate silent majority' was shattered by the result of elections to the local councils in May and to the Assembly in June 1973 (see Table 6.1). A *Fortnight/Sunday Times* poll had predicted success for moderate parties and purported to show 'a clear shift to the centre parties and almost total support for making the White Paper proposals work'. The polls' prediction of the number of Assembly seats to be won by the 'moderate parties' are followed by the number actually won: NILP predicted 9 seats (actual 1); the APNI 11 (8); and the SDLP 12 (19). The NILP was

Table 6.1   The June 1973 Assembly election results

Party	% vote (no. of seats)
pro-White Paper UUP	29.3 (24)
SDLP	22.1 (19)
APNI	9.2 (8)
NILP	2.6 (1)
Total	63.2 (52)
anti- White Paper UUP	8.5 (8)
DUP	10.8 (8)
VUPP	10.5 (7)
West Belfast Loyalists	2.3 (3)
Total	32.1 (26)

almost obliterated, winning just 2.5 per cent of the first preference votes, while the APNI took only 14 per cent of the vote, well short of the 19 per cent predicted by the *Fortnight* poll. It was estimated that less than 0.25 per cent of the transferred vote crossed the sectarian divide and lower preferences votes were transferred away from moderates (Cunningham 1991 p. 53). The 'unofficial view' from Whitelaw's office hoped for substantial Alliance success and agreed with the *Fortnight* poll in its assessment of APNI support (*The Guardian*, 31 May 1973). The Assembly elections had produced the very outcome the British had tried to prevent, namely a dramatic upsurge for loyalist and anti-White Paper unionists resulting in a 'tribal confrontation' (*Sunday Telegraph*, 1 July 1973). The contrast between opinion poll predictions and electoral outcomes in this election lends credence to the generalisation that opinion polls tend to overestimate moderate opinion in Northern Ireland (Whyte 1990 p. 82).

The outcome of the Assembly elections in June 1973 dashed British hopes of a moderate power-sharing executive composed of the NILP, APNI and liberal Unionists. Any power-sharing executive would have to include both the 'hardline' UUP leader Brian Faulkner and the nationalist SDLP in order to achieve sufficient Catholic representation on an executive. This relative diversity of parties meant that Unionists would have to be part of an executive with people who favoured Irish unity. Faulkner only had the support of a minority of unionist seats in the assembly if the 'centrist' NILP and APNI were not counted as unionist. The strong showing of the hardline VUPP and the DUP was likely to constrain Faulkner's room for manoeuvre.

Crucially, Faulkner did not have a clear mandate for entering a power-sharing executive with the SDLP. The UUP's manifesto had stated: 'We are not opposed to power-sharing in government, but we will not be prepared to participate in government with those whose *primary aim* is to break the union with Great Britain' (my emphasis). According to McAllister, 'the Protestant electorate interpreted the manifesto as explicitly excluding the possibility of powersharing with the SDLP, while Faulkner's shrewd use of words included it' (McAllister 1977b p. 129). Two of Faulkner's power-sharing assembly members opposed the White Paper, another supporter was killed in a car crash, while a further was elected to be speaker of the assembly. When the Assembly met Faulkner enjoyed only the support of only a minority of unionists, 21 votes, compared to 27 opposed to the White Paper proposals. Faulkner's problem was to attempt to lead the UUP into an accommodation with nationalism without further splitting his party or losing support to the 'hardline' unionist parties which lurked on his flank. British politicians had already attempted to coerce the Northern Ireland electorate to vote for moderate politicians; with elections out of the way the government now attempted to coerce the parties towards the centre ground.

Bipartisanship and Agreement over Northern Ireland

The British Labour Party had used its influence on behalf of nationalists to delay the introduction of a border poll in 1973 and to oppose the Conservative Government's proposals to increase Northern Ireland's representation at Westminster by bringing it into line with the region's population (Dixon 1995a p. 166). After the Assembly elections the British parties united to drive unionists and nationalists swiftly towards a settlement. The unity of the British parties would help to persuade the political parties in Northern Ireland, particularly the SDLP, that there was no advantage to be had by holding out on a power-sharing settlement with the Conservative Government since this was also supported by the Labour Party. The Conservative Prime Minister, Edward Heath, threatened Northern Ireland with integration into the UK if agreement was not reached. Heath's threat of integration may have undermined Faulkner's position, since many unionists would have preferred integration with the rest of the UK to power-sharing with an Irish dimension. Whatever

Heath's intentions, this outburst helped to propel the SDLP towards talks (Dixon 1995a p. 168).

The Irish Government had also moved into line with the British to impress on nationalists in the North the importance of a settlement. The Irish Taoiseach, Liam Cosgrave, told a meeting of British Conservatives that although he wanted a united Ireland, to press for this goal in the prevailing climate (of loyalist unrest) would 'dangerously exacerbate tensions and fears' (*The Times*, 3 July 1973). Nevertheless, the SDLP went to work on the Irish coalition government and over the summer of 1973 succeeded in winning its support for a strong Irish dimension. It could be that 'the irredentism of the Republic's official ideology made it difficult for a southern government to be in open disagreement with the elected representatives of the "beleaguered minority" in the north' (Bew and Patterson 1985 p. 58). The hardening of the SDLP's position occurred in spite of that party's success in being elected the representatives of the overwhelming majority of Catholic opinion which voted. Although the party leadership may have had difficulties maintaining party unity, 'the other anti-partitionist groups posed no serious challenge to them' (White 1984 p. 141; see also McAllister 1977b p. 126) and, following direct rule and Operation Motorman, the IRA's campaign appeared to be waning in popularity among nationalists (Kelley 1988 pp. 199–200).

On 5 October 1973 representatives of the APNI, UUP and SDLP met at Stormont for talks on the formation of a power-sharing executive. They agreed an economic and social programme but came into conflict over whether the RUC should change its name. On 21 November the SDLP agreed with the UUP and APNI on the principle of a Council of Ireland and the composition of a power-sharing executive. The UUP was to receive a majority of the seats, six, with the SDLP taking four and the APNI one. Four non-voting members were also included: two SDLP, one Unionist and one APNI. This allowed Brian Faulkner to claim a UUP majority on the executive which was an important concession if the UUP leader was to fight off growing dissent within his party. On 23 October the UUP's Standing Committee supported the policy of allowing UUP Assembly members to join a power-sharing executive by 132 votes to 105 (Gillespie 1998 p. 103). On 20 November, the day before agreement on the composition of the power-sharing executive, the UUC voted only narrowly against a proposal to reject power-sharing by 379 votes to 369, and supported the party leadership in a further vote by 374 votes to 362.

Sunningdale: The Deal

Agreement on the executive opened the way for talks between the three Northern Irish pro-power-sharing parties and the British and Irish Governments at Sunningdale, in Berkshire, on 6–9 December. Holding the conference outside Northern Ireland insulated the party leaders from their party and electoral grassroots. The loyalist parties were excluded from participation in spite of their substantial representation for fear that they would disrupt negotiations. The Sunningdale Conference represented a high point in Anglo–Irish relations: it was largely an 'intergovernmental conference' (White 1984 p. 150) and the Irish Government 'had the feeling that they were "working in parallel" with the British Government' (Kyle 1975 p. 439). The talks were held to decide the nature of the Irish dimension which had been outlined in the White Paper and establish the political framework in which power-sharing would operate. The unionists were looking for: recognition of Northern Ireland's constitutional position within the UK; improved security co-operation with the Republic against terrorism, including moves on extradition; and a weak cross-border body. The nationalists by contrast wanted a strong all-Ireland body with executive and harmonising functions; reform of the RUC; and movement on the release of detainees. The negotiations and controversy revolved around three main areas.

1.   *Articles 2 and 3 and majority consent.*   Faulkner needed concessions from nationalists on Articles 2 and 3 of the Irish constitution and recognition of Northern Ireland's place within the Union if he was to be able to deliver a settlement to northern unionists. The Irish Government felt it would not be able to deliver support for a referendum, required by the Irish Constitution, to change Articles 2 and 3 in the face of strong opposition by the more republican Fianna Fáil party. On only one occasion has an amendment to the Constitution been passed without the support of the principal Opposition party and that was on the establishment of the Constitution itself. The Irish Government offered a solemn declaration 'that there could be no change in the status of Northern Ireland until a majority of the people of Northern Ireland desired a change in that status'. The British Government declared that it would support the wishes of the majority of the people in Northern Ireland and that the present status of Northern Ireland was as part of the UK. If in the future the majority of people indicated a wish to become part of a united Ireland, the British Government would support that wish.

John Hume saw this 'as an important weapon to use against his republican opponents. If it could be established that the British interest was to ensure that there was peace and stability, it would mean that the solution relied totally on a process of persuasion, undermining the argument for violence' (White 1984 p. 149). The Irish Government did not endorse Britain's interpretation of the present status of Northern Ireland since this would have conflicted with the territorial claim.

2. *The Council of Ireland*. The Council of Ireland was to comprise a Council of Ministers and a Consultative Assembly. The Council of Ministers would have 14 members, seven from the Northern Ireland executive and seven members of the Irish Government, but would only be able to take decisions by a unanimous vote (thus giving unionists a veto). It was to enjoy 'executive and harmonising functions and a consultative role'. The executive functions of the Council of Ireland were not defined; instead 'studies would at once be set in hand to identify and, prior to the formal stage of the conference, report on areas of common interest in relation to which a Council of Ireland would take executive decisions and, in appropriate cases, be responsible for carrying those decisions into effect'. The studies would investigate areas of policy suitable for executive action by the Council of Ireland in the fields of: exploitation, conservation and development of natural resources and the environment; agricultural matters; co-operative ventures in the fields of trade and industry; electricity generation; tourism; roads and transport; advisory services connected with public health; sport; culture and the arts. There was no limit to the array of functions which could be devolved to the Council of Ireland with the agreement of the NI Assembly and the Oireachtas (Irish Parliament). In the New Year a conference would be held between the executive and the two governments to consider reports on the studies commissioned and to sign the agreement reached. Alongside the Council of Ministers was to be a Consultative Assembly of 60 members, half to be elected by proportional representation from the North and half from the Republic, which was to have 'advisory and review' functions. A Secretariat to the Council would 'service the institutions of the Council and ... supervise the carrying out of the executive and harmonising functions and the consultative role of the Council'.

3. *Security and extradition*. 'It was broadly accepted that the two parts of Ireland are to a considerable extent inter-dependent in the whole field of law and order, and that the problems of political

violence and identification with the police service cannot be solved without taking account of that fact.' A Joint Law Commission was established to look into the legal issues. The unionists wanted the Republic to deliver on extradition even though the Irish constitution did not allow extradition for political offences; by 1975 none had taken place. It was agreed that people committing crimes of violence in Ireland, however motivated, should be brought to trial wherever they were arrested, allowing members of the IRA to be tried in the Republic for offences committed in the North. The British Government indicated a willingness to devolve responsibility for policing to the executive and to end internment as soon as the security situation permitted. There was also a vague hint in the Sunningdale Communiqué that policing might become the responsibility of the Council of Ireland.

The Unionists pushed too far?

With the benefit of hindsight, it is clear that the unionists were out-maneouvred at Sunningdale and pushed 'too far' towards a settlement. Garret Fitzgerald, the Irish Foreign Affairs Minister, noted at the time, 'On any objective assessment the Irish Government and the SDLP have gained most and the Unionists least' (Fitzgerald 1991 p. 220). The Irish Government and the SDLP, after the event, 'began to confess ruefully that they had had too easy a victory. But after all, they had fought their own corner and had expected others to do likewise' (Kyle 1975 p. 441). It should have been clear to the participants at Sunningdale that Faulkner was already coming under serious pressure both from within his own party and from loyalist rivals to the UUP over his participation in power-sharing. His ability to deliver sufficient unionists to an accommodation was therefore highly constrained. The Irish Government threw its weight behind the SDLP at Sunningdale, whereas the British Government attempted to play the role of 'honest broker' between nationalists and unionists. The UUP delegation appeared ill-prepared for the talks and came under considerable pressure not only from national-ists but also from Edward Heath, the British Prime Minister. The *Irish Times'* correspondent later commented that Heath's 'desire to rid himself of his Irish incubus' led him to bully Faulkner. He 'sided, again and again, with the SDLP; he ensured that the outcome was precisely what was sought by the representatives of the Northern

Ireland Catholics' (*Irish Times*, 13 August 1974, Faulkner 1978 p. 234, Downey 1983 p. 126, White 1984 pp. 145–6, 153, Bew and Patterson 1985 p. 64).

The contrast between the behaviour of the British and Irish Governments was a strong one. The Republic, together with the SDLP, declared its support for Irish unity while the British declared that it would implement the will of the majority, not favour the Union. This was a position Heath had taken up since at least 1971 and restated at Sunningdale. Both the British and Irish Governments assumed that if Faulkner accepted something then he could sell it (White 1984 pp. 146, 152). However, both Paddy Devlin of the SDLP, and Conor Cruise O'Brien of the Irish Government's delegation, were concerned that Faulkner was being pushed too hard. Paddy Devlin told O'Brien and the Alliance party delegates, 'Look, we've got to catch ourselves on here. Brian Faulkner is being nailed to a cross. There is no way Faulkner can sell this' (White 1984 p. 152). Garret Fitzgerald later recalled that Devlin 'was not going to have his friends... hung from lamp-posts on their return to Belfast, as they assuredly would be if the list of executive functions we had agreed were published' (Fitzgerald 1991 p. 215; see also White 1984 p. 159). The list of powers was subsequently reduced, but British and Irish Governments were dismissive of the dangers to Faulkner's position.

There was plenty of scope for loyalists to exploit the detail of Sunningdale to rally unionists against the agreement. The British position on the Council of Ireland had shifted from giving it 'some executive functions and a consultative role' to having 'executive and harmonisation' functions (Bew and Patterson 1985 p. 60). The Council of Ireland could be interpreted as having the makings of an all-Ireland Parliament. The Council of Ministers was to be a free-standing, executive body with what were likely to be extensive powers and without a need to have its decisions ratified by the NI Assembly. The Consultative Assembly also had the potential to develop from a consultative role into a legislative all-Ireland Parliament. The British failed to move significantly over internment or on reform of the RUC, in spite of strong pressure from the Irish Government. This probably led the SDLP to focus on and play up its gains on the Council of Ireland (Bew and Patterson 1985 p. 59, Bew and Gillespie 1993 p. 74).

If the British had conceded on the security agenda then Faulkner's position may have been undermined as much by changes in security policy as by the Council of Ireland. Some opinion polls indicate that security issues are probably more divisive in Northern Ireland than the constitutional question. Faulkner perhaps calculated that he could more easily deliver a *symbolic* Council of Ireland, on which unionists had a veto, than tamper with the RUC (a powerful guarantor of the Union and unionist power). In this Faulkner underestimated the symbolic importance of the Council to unionists (Faulkner 1978 pp. 229, 237). For many unionists the detail of the Sunningdale Agreement was likely to be obscured by the aim of Irish nationalists, through Modernisation, to bring about a united Ireland and widespread suspicion of British intentions and guarantees. For many unionists their perceptions of the track record of the parties and governments involved in Sunningdale was probably a better guide to their disposition and the outcome of any agreement than the rhetoric and ambiguity of the Sunningdale Communiqué. Loyalists were overwhelmingly opposed to Sunningdale. But even the moderate 'unionists' of the Alliance Party were concerned at the power of the Council of Ireland (White 1984 pp. 155–6).

The Irish Government largely failed to deliver its share of the Sunningdale Agreement to the Faulkner unionists. This may have been due to its vulnerability to nationalist pressure from the Opposition Fianna Fáil party. The Irish Government's recognition of Northern Ireland was one of the few gains for unionism, but this became devalued by the Boland case in the Republic which claimed that Sunningdale was contrary to the Irish Constitution. In defending itself against Boland's charges the Irish Government denied that any part of Ireland was part of the UK, denied that majority consent was necessary for Irish unity, and claimed that Sunningdale was merely a statement of policy and represented only *de facto* recognition of Northern Ireland. The Irish Government attempted to retrieve the situation by reassuring unionists and claiming that the factual position was that Northern Ireland was part of the UK and could not be changed without majority consent (Bew and Gillespie 1993 pp. 78–9, 81). The Irish Government also failed to deliver on extradition and the Joint Law Enforcement Commission later recommended that instead of extradition the courts in the Republic could try people for offences committed in the North (Gillespie 1998 pp. 104–5).

Leading figures in the SDLP clearly saw the Council of Ireland, modelled on the 'Modernising' institutions of the EEC, as a step down the road to a united Ireland (White 1984 p. 145; see also Chapter 3 above). Public declarations of this boosted the argument of the anti-power-sharing loyalists. Paddy Devlin described the SDLP's strategy at Sunningdale as being:

> to get all-Ireland institutions established which, with adequate safeguards, would produce the dynamic that could lead ultimately to an agreed single State for Ireland. That meant... that SDLP representatives would concentrate their entire efforts on building up a set of tangible executive powers for the Council which in the fullness of time would create and sustain an evolutionary process. All other issues were governed by that approach and were aimed generally at reducing loyalist resistance to the concepts of a Council of Ireland and a power-sharing Executive. (Devlin 1975 p. 32)

In December 1974 the SDLP's Austin Currie claimed that Sunningdale 'fulfilled Wolfe Tone's desires to break the connection with England and substitute the common name of Irishman for Catholic, Protestant and Dissenter' (*Irish Times*, 17 December 1973, quoted in Gillespie 1998 p. 107). The Irish Prime Minister, Liam Cosgrave, gave an interview, arguing that Sunningdale meant that a united Ireland was on the way (White 1984 p. 156). The following month, Hugh Logue of the SDLP infamously told a heckler in Dublin that the Council of Ireland was 'the vehicle which will trundle Unionists into a United Ireland'. This statement confirmed unionists' worst fears about Sunningdale and, coupled with the Boland case and the failure to deliver on extradition, severely damaged what chances Faulkner had of selling the settlement to unionism. The fragility of the power-sharing experiment was not apparent to the British public who were being led to assume that based on a 'moderate majority' the Northern Ireland conflict had been resolved, at least for a generation.

Selling Sunningdale

Power-sharing unionism's grip on the UUP was disintegrating and in December the United Ulster Unionist Council (UUUC) was founded to unite anti-Sunningdale unionism (Gillespie 1998 pp. 105–8). The power-sharing experiment got under way on 1 January 1974, but three days later the UUC voted against the Sunningdale settlement by 454 votes to 374 and Faulkner resigned as UUP leader. According to Gillespie, 'Faulkner's resignation as leader of the Ulster Unionists ended the moral legitimacy of the Sunningdale deal and killed Sunningdale as an effective political package.' Faulkner had been invited to participate in the executive as leader of the UUP but, since he was no longer leader, on what basis was he included in the executive (Gillespie 1998 p. 108)? Although the power-sharing parties had represented a majority of the people of Northern Ireland, Faulkner only represented a minority of the unionist population. The agreement reached by Faulkner on the composition of the executive and at Sunningdale was not to be submitted by the elites for the endorsement of the electorate. The insulation of the power-sharing executive until the next Assembly elections, in 1977, would, it was hoped, give power-sharing a chance to work and prove its worth to the people of Northern Ireland.

The British General Election of February 1974 was called for domestic reasons and gave opponents of power-sharing the opportunity to hold a referendum on Sunningdale. The result further dispelled hopes in the moderate silent majority as power-sharing unionists were decimated at the polls. The SDLP retained its share of the vote but the APNI share dropped from 9.2 per cent to 3.1 per cent and Faulkner's unionists (13.1 per cent) were heavily defeated. The anti-Sunningdale parties, who had joined together in the UUUC, won a majority (51.1 per cent) of the vote under the slogan 'Dublin is only a Sunningdale away'. The *Belfast Telegraph* revised its 'moderate' analysis and, after anti-Sunningdale unionism's 'sweeping victory' at the polls, dropped its criticism of 'loyalist populism' as unrepresentative and undemocratic. The executive lacked 'representation of the loyalist masses', and to save power-sharing loyalists would now have to be appeased (Bromley 1989 pp. 220–1).

The newly elected Labour Government refused to hold fresh elections to the Assembly to take account of the shift in mood of the unionist population, and announced that there would be no elections to the Assembly for four years. The new Secretary of State for Northern Ireland, Merlyn Rees, was pessimistic about the prospects for power-sharing and made contingency plans in the event of its collapse (Rees 1985 p. 60, Donoughue 1987 pp. 128–9, Whitelaw 1989 p. 122). He described power-sharing as 'a remarkable achievement' which was 'almost unbelievable' given the history and strong pressures on elected representatives in the region (Rees 1974). By April 1974 Rees did not believe the executive could last much longer and shared Faulkner's view that there should be a watering down or abandonment of the Council of Ireland, but he was overruled in the cabinet by Wilson and Callaghan (Devlin 1975 pp. 16–17, Downey 1983 p. 134, Bew and Patterson 1985 p. 66, Benn 1989 p. 137, Fitzgerald 1991 p. 232).

The Labour Government's announcement of a security strategy of normalisation reinforced unionist fears of a British withdrawal. *Normalisation* combined an attempt to *Ulsterise* the burden of security, putting the locally recruited UDR and RUC in the frontline as far as possible and reducing the exposure of the British Army, with *criminalisation*, treating paramilitary violence as a criminal rather than a political act (Hansard, vol. 871, col. 1466, 4 April 1974, Dixon 1997b). With fewer soldiers on the streets and paramilitaries treated like common criminals the conflict would appear to the outside world as a 'normal' issue of law and order. Complementing normalisation was the legalisation of Sinn Féin and the UVF to encourage their participation in the political process. The unionist *Newsletter* argued: 'Little wonder anger is growing. Little wonder the majority, particularly, are more convinced than ever that the real British design must be to scuttle, or ... get out at the earliest possible opportunity through the offices of the Council of Ireland' (*Newsletter*, 15 April 1974).

Unionists complained, with some substance, that the Sunningdale settlement was being imposed over the heads of the people of Northern Ireland (*Newsletter*, 25 and 28 February 1974). Following the election Faulkner attempted to shore up his diminishing support by taking a more hardline stance; he opposed the Council of Ireland unless the Republic repealed its territorial claim. Unionists and the Alliance preferred a gradual approach to the ratification of Sunningdale to allow unionism to become accustomed to the operation of the executive and to prevent further antagonism. Faulkner and the British Government heightened unionist insecurities by using the threat of British withdrawal in an attempt to scare unionists into supporting the executive as a least worst alternative. There was also some evidence of unrest among the SDLP. Paddy Duffy, the SDLP's Treasurer, spoke of the possibility of a reassessment of party policy in favour of joint British and Irish rule for 10–15 years before Irish unity if Sunningdale was not ratified (*Newsletter*, 7 May 1974).

Opinion polls continued to indicate considerable support for power-sharing and a Council of Ireland among Catholics, but much less so among Protestants. An NOP poll conducted between 31 March and 7 April 1974 found 69 per cent of the people of Northern Ireland favoured giving the executive and Sunningdale a chance.

However, while 72 per cent (against 4 per cent) of Catholics thought the Sunningdale proposal for a Council of Ireland was a good rather than a bad idea in principle, only 26 per cent of Protestants thought it was good in principle while 52 per cent thought the Council of Ireland was bad. Around 55 per cent of Catholics said power-sharing was their most favoured solution to the conflict but only 18 per cent of Protestants did (Rose *et al*. 1978). Reflecting on this period, Rees claims to have been less impressed by opinion polls than by a petition demonstrating the strength of loyalist opposition to Sunningdale (Rees 1985 p. 59).

The Ulster Workers' Council Strike: Politics in the Streets

The power-sharing executive came under pressure from both republicans and loyalists. The IRA escalated its bombing campaign in the spring of 1974 to undermine power-sharing and break the British Government's will to remain in Northern Ireland (*The Sunday Times*, 7 April 1974). The power-sharing executive was brought down in May 1974 by the 14–day long loyalist Ulster Workers' Council strike. This 'general' strike was precipitated by a decision to ratify Sunningdale in the Assembly, by 44 votes to 28. The strike paralysed Northern Ireland, in particular by a series of power-cuts, and brought the power-sharing executive to its knees.

There is considerable controversy over the nature of the UWC strike. There are two main schools of thought: first, a more 'nationalist' view sees the power-sharing experiment as a viable initiative which was beginning to reap dividends for the people of Northern Ireland. It stresses the importance of the loyalist paramilitaries and intimidation in the success of the UWC strike and argues that the Labour Government lacked the nerve to deploy troops early in the strike; if it had, the strike would have collapsed (Anderson 1994 pp. 29, 32). Second, a more 'unionist' perspective emphasises the spontaneity of the strike and the widespread support it quickly gained amongst unionist civil society and the masses, frustrated with an unrepresentative political elite. The role of intimidation is acknowledged, particularly at the start of the strike, but the strike's popular appeal among unionists is emphasised. The executive was 'effectively dead' by December 1973 (Gillespie 1998 p. 112), perhaps more apparently following Faulkner's loss of his party's support in January and the rout of power-sharing unionists at the February

1974 election. From this perspective the executive was likely to collapse in any case, whatever the Labour Government or participants in the executive did. In this context the British Government's failure to act against the UWC and risk confrontation with unionism is more understandable, particularly in light of the 'security dilemma' and fear of a war on two fronts.

The decision to call the UWC strike was taken by a new Protestant working-class leadership rather than solely by the traditional elected representatives of the loyalist community. It consisted of paramilitary leaders and factory workers, including several active trade unionists, and was seen by many as an important development in Protestant working-class consciousness (Fisk 1975 pp. 48, 64). The organisers of the strike were non-party loyalists who were suspicious of their political representatives. The loyalist politicians opposed the strike and only threw their full weight behind it once it was apparent that it was gaining increasing public support (Anderson 1994 pp. 71–2). 'The politicians seemed to have been a moderating influence inside the [UWC] Committee, constantly advising against pushing people too far' (Anderson 1994 p. 89, also p. 26). Harry West, a leading anti-power-sharing unionist, argued that the strike was not aimed at democratic government but an imposed government:

> The Executive is a group of people appointed by an English politician who is not answerable in any way to the assembly or to the Ulster electorate. It is the appointed Executive which is supposed to represent Northern Ireland in any Council of Ireland. The whole Sunningdale project is thus completely dissociated from any kind of control. (Anderson 1994 p. 137)

The *Newsletter* suggested that unionists had, in recent years, been herded by the British Government towards the edge of a cliff and had gone along with this until the point at which they were being asked to jump. During the UWC strike they were saying 'No' (*Newsletter* editorial, 27 May 1974). Popular support for the strike gathered pace amongst unionists as it was seen as the only means by which an imposed system of government could be removed. The *Belfast Telegraph* 'miscalculated the strength of loyalist opposition to the arrangements proposed at Sunningdale and showed little appreciation of the underlying fears of British withdrawal which drew many loyalists into supporting alternative constitutional schemes' (Bromley 1989 p. 228).

The Labour Government appealed to the 'moderate silent majority' to assert themselves against these 'Protestant fascists' who were an 'intimidating, bullying minority'. The Northern Ireland labour movement failed to live up to the hopes invested in it as a 'Back to Work' march failed and the NILP's vote declined. The official trade union movement had to fight off challenges to its authority from loyalist workers' organisations who felt that it was politically unrepresentative of their workers' views. The apparent success of the Northern Ireland trade union movement in keeping violence off the shop floor may have misled observers into believing they had more of a 'moderating' influence over their members than was the case. Although unions did contain both Catholic and Protestant members, 'The situation however has only been reached by carefully avoiding many of the contentious issues which divided Northern Ireland society, and indeed almost any hint of political controversy' (Darby 1976 pp. 150–1, Whyte 1990 p. 39). Belatedly the SDLP realised Faulkner's failing popular support and attempted to shore up his position and reassure unionism by phasing in the Council of Ireland. Backbench SDLP Assembly members rejected the compromise package and a Labour Minister of State warned them that if they did not support it they would lose the support of the Labour Party which had been so important in giving the SDLP influence at Westminster (Dixon 1995a p. 169). The SDLP took a further vote, narrowly endorsing the package.

The executive did not have any security powers and was reliant on the Labour Government taking a security initiative to break the strike. The government was reluctant to send the army in against the strikers, risking a violent confrontation with unionism, but it was also unable to run essential services. There were real concerns that deploying the British Army, which Rees felt was his 'only firm base' in Northern Ireland, to break the UWC strike would have precipitated a violent confrontation with loyalists and a 'war on two fronts' (Fisk 1975 p. 203; see also Chapter 5 above). Rees believed that 'in their hearts' the RUC supported the UWC strike and an adviser to the Labour Government claimed that there were limits to what the RUC would do against their religious brethren. Rees argued: 'It is one thing to fight the IRA and quite another to fight a whole community' (Rees 1985 p. 90; see also Fisk 1975 pp. 203–4, Donoughue 1987 p. 129). Wilson's 'Spongers Speech' sealed the fate of the executive: the British Prime Minister attacked 'people who spend their lives sponging on Westminster and British democracy and then systematically assault democratic methods'. Faulkner recalled the 'immense damage' done by Wilson's insulting speech which 'brought out Provincial feeling against him and vastly increased popular support for the strike' (Faulkner 1978 p. 276). In his resignation statement Faulkner finally accepted that 'from the extent of support for the present stoppage ... the degree of consent needed to sustain the Executive does not at present exist' (McAllister 1977b p. 145). British policy towards Northern Ireland since 1972 collapsed with the power-sharing executive.

Blaming 'Them' not 'Us'

The Labour Government's explanation of the UWC strike reversed following the executive's collapse. Initially, Labour had taken the 'nationalist' line that the loyalist strikers were 'Protestant fascists', bullies who had succeeded through intimidation. After the triumph of the strike Labour shifted towards a more unionist position, suggesting the inevitability of power-sharing's failure and so distancing the Labour Government from responsibility for its collapse. In his British nationalist 'Spongers Speech', Wilson had rallied 'us', the 'British' people, against 'them', the people of Northern Ireland, tapping into chauvinist, populist sentiment which manifested itself in opinion polls supporting withdrawal (Dixon 1996a).

> The people on this side of the water, British parents, British taxpayers, have seen their sons vilified and spat upon and murdered. They have seen the taxes they have poured out almost without regard to cost ... going into Northern Ireland. They see property destroyed by evil violence and are asked to pick up the bill for re-building it. Yet people who benefit from this now viciously defy Westminster, purporting to act as though they were an elected government, people who spend their lives sponging on Westminster and British democracy and then systematically assaulting democratic methods. Who do these people think they are?

The Labour Government turned its back on the 'moderates' and talked up the importance of a new Protestant nationalism displayed during the strike, which it viewed as a new class awareness that might form the basis for an accommodation among working-class Protestants and Catholics. For a while the UWC was seen, along with the loyalist paramilitary groups (the UVF and UDA), as perhaps a more accommodating, and representative, alternative to the sterility and intransigence of unionist politicians. The UVF launched the Volunteer Political Party which rather unsuccessfully contested elections (Nelson 1984, ch. 14). In the Westminster election of October 1974 and the Convention election of May 1975 the 'hardline' trajectory of unionist opinion was confirmed and power-sharing unionists were decimated. However, the nationalist SDLP was not punished by their electorate for their involvement in the power-sharing experiment. Garret Fitzgerald reported that Rees told him: 'much of the trouble in Northern Ireland in the previous five years had derived from taking advice too often from moderates' (Fitzgerald 1991 pp. 244–5).

Lessons?

The power-sharing experiment probably came closer than any other initiative during 'the Troubles' until the second peace process (1994–) to resolving the conflict in Northern Ireland. Competing interpretations of its collapse can be coupled with different prescriptions for resolving the conflict.

'Power-Sharing Collapsed because Unionists Opposed Power-Sharing and the Irish Dimension'

This bleak interpretation suggests that unionists were unwilling to share power with Catholics and dressed up their opposition to power-sharing by focusing on the Council of Ireland. This is indicated by Faulkner's lack of a mandate for entering into power-sharing with the SDLP and therefore his eroding support even before the negotiations at Sunningdale. For republicans this interpretation underlines the fact that no partitionist accommodation was possible with intransigent unionism; a resolution to the conflict could only come through a military campaign to bring about a united Ireland. For nationalists, however, this argument might imply the need to impose a settlement over the heads of the unionists, such as the Anglo–Irish Agreement 1985. For unionists, the lack of support for power-sharing might imply either a more integrationist settlement treating Northern Ireland like any other part of the UK, or even independence. Some of those unionists who worked to bring down power-sharing, David Trimble and John Taylor, later emerged as champions of the Good Friday Agreement in 1998.

'Power-Sharing Collapsed because of the Irish Dimension'

This interpretation suggests that Sunningdale was 'a bridge too far'. Faulkner was pushed too hard in the negotiations at Sunningdale, the Irish Government did not deliver its share of the settlement and as a result the Northern Ireland Prime Minister was unable to sell the package to the unionist community. Evidence is provided – from opinion polls, unionist opinion, newspapers and politicians – which suggests that unionists might well have accepted power-sharing with nationalists if this had not included an Irish dimension or such a strong Irish dimension. The close result on the UUC in favour of power-sharing, but before Sunningdale, indicates at the least a party finely balanced on the issue and perhaps anxious at the prospect of negotiating the Irish dimension. The implication from this interpretation is that power-sharing is a viable settlement to the conflict in Northern Ireland as long as it is not encumbered with an Irish dimension, or at least with a weaker Irish dimension than that outlined at Sunningdale.

'Power-Sharing and the Irish Dimension Collapsed due to the Weakness of the Labour Government'

This view is held by nationalists but also by some power-sharing unionists who blame the British rather than the executive for the collapse of power-sharing. This nationalist interpretation blames the Conservatives for calling the February 1974 election at a vulnerable time for the executive, and the Labour Government for not using force to nip the UWC strike in the bud and prevent the paramilitary intimidation which was the key to its success. It suggests that what is required in the future is for the British Government to face down any unionist resistance, if necessary by force. This breaking of the 'unionist veto' on constitutional developments would provoke a reassessment within that community of its relationship with Britain and make it more amenable to accommodation. However, the British had attempted and failed to coerce the mass of unionists into the Sunningdale settlement, indicating the weakness of this approach. Neither did the confrontation between the British Government and unionism after the Anglo–Irish Agreement 1985 (AIA) provoke the reassessment among unionism which nationalists had predicted. If anything confrontation over Sunningdale and the AIA appeared, at least initially, to harden attitudes among unionists.

'Power-Sharing Failed because the Political Environment was too Polarised to Sustain it'

This argument suggests that the power-sharing experiment was too far ahead of its time. The intensity of the violence and the rapidly changing and uncertain political environment was not conducive to building an accommodation between unionists and nationalists. The non-participation in the 'peace process' of loyalist and republican paramilitaries and their determination to destabilise the executive, along with the ambiguity of British Government policy, were significant factors in the failure of the experiment. The structural constraints were such that it was simply beyond the power of the various agents (politicians, parties, governments) to bridge the gap.

Conclusion

The British Government's policy towards Northern Ireland has combined elements of both a bottom-up approach, focusing on reform and reconciliation from below, and a top-down approach, focusing on an elite settlement. The government favoured reconciliation through the promotion of non-sectarian parties, 'integration' and grassroots 'reconciliation' work; and, at least initially, had faith in 'the people' or civil society as a 'moderating' influence. The elections of June 1973 were a severe setback to the hopes of a more voluntary power-sharing accommodation and the British Government took an increasingly coercive and elitist (top-down) approach, as pressure was exerted on the constitutional parties towards the centre ground. With hindsight, it is clear that Faulkner and power-sharing unionists were out-negotiated at Sunningdale by nationalists and pushed 'too far' by the British. The February 1974 General Election demonstrated that unionism was strongly opposed to the deal. The British and Irish Governments took little action to shore up power-sharing unionism and it eventually succumbed to the power of unionist civil society and mass protest during the UWC strike.

The British Government has to share responsibility for creating the climate of constitutional uncertainty and grievance in which the unbalanced Sunningdale settlement failed. Unionist fears that power-sharing and Sunningdale represented an attempt to manipulate Northern Ireland out of the Union were 'reasonable' (rather than paranoid) given British policy during this period. The British parties were impatient at their inability to resolve the conflict in Northern Ireland and appeared ready to off-load the problem if possible. At this point the easiest route to British extrication appeared to be through Irish unity, with which there was considerable sympathy at Westminster among both the Labour *and Conservative* parties. Harold Wilson later argued in his memoirs that the continuation of Sunningdale and power-sharing was a more radical and speedy way of uniting Ireland than his 15-point plan (Wilson 1979 p. 70; see also Haines 1977 p. 114).

By pushing pro-power-sharing unionists 'too far' the chances of reaching a compromise – whether 'just' or not – that all parties could sell to their supporters were not maximised. The failure of the SDLP to be punished by its electorate for its involvement in power-sharing, in spite of its concessions during the UWC strike, and its lack of an electoral rival, indicates that the SDLP might have been able to move further towards Faulkner's position without jeopardising its electoral support (although there were problems in managing the party: see Dixon 1997c, 1997d). Yet even if a deal had been more 'evenly' cut between nationalists and unionists there is still doubt as to whether the pro-power-sharing forces had sufficient support or a sufficiently favourable political environment in which to make such a deal work.

At the beginning of the second peace process in 1994 the Conservative ex-Minister of State for Northern Ireland, Michael Mates, stated that any settlement would be 'Sunningdale Plus'. This begged the question of why, if Sunningdale failed in 1974, should it be more successful in 1994? Shortly before the signing of the Good Friday Agreement an adviser to the UUP leader referred to power-sharing and the importance of keeping the grassroots on board in any process: 'We are concerned that we don't become isolated from our own support. That is why we are holed up here [in Northern Ireland], and not on top of a mountain. We can see the ghosts of the past in the corridors' (*Irish Times*, 3 April 1998).

7

The Limits of British Policy 1974–81: From Withdrawal to Integration

The UWC strike and the two Westminster elections of 1974 destroyed the assumption on which British bipartisan policy had rested since at least the introduction of direct rule in 1972. This was that there existed a 'moderate majority' for compromise and that unionist and nationalist 'extremists' had little popular support within their communities, but relied on intimidation to impose their will. The sweeping success of the loyalist coalition in the February 1974 General Election and the popular support for the UWC strike exploded the myth that, on the loyalist side at least, the 'moderate silent majority' were coerced by a small group of 'extremists' who had no popular support. It was not until the Hunger Strikes of 1981 that the extent of the Provisionals' popular support became obvious. Having defied Britain's attempts to 'impose' a settlement, there was now a widespread expectation in Northern Ireland that the Labour Government would live up to its threats and withdraw. This period established the parameters of British policy towards Northern Ireland. Why did Britain not withdraw after the collapse of power-sharing? Why was British policy so 'unionist' from 1974 to 1979? Why did Mrs Thatcher abandon the unionism of the Conservatives' 1979 manifesto and sign the Anglo–Irish Agreement in 1985? To what extent has British policy towards Northern Ireland been constrained and therefore characterised by continuity?

The Withdrawal Option

Opinion polls suggested that withdrawal from Northern Ireland would have been a popular option amongst British public opinion.

Merlyn Rees had been preoccupied with the effect that the collapse of the executive might have on British public opinion and its support for withdrawal, particularly since it was those who proclaimed loyalty to the British Crown who had defied the British Parliament and its policy (Rees 1985 pp. 92–3, Fitzgerald 1991 pp. 237–8). In the early 1970s, Labour spokespersons had made public threats of 'consequences' if power-sharing was brought down. Privately, the Labour leadership referred to the option of withdrawal from Northern Ireland by the codename 'Algeria' (Haines 1977 p. 114, Donoughue 1987 p. 128). In April 1974 an Irish Government delegation met Wilson and were unhappy with his talk of an 'agonising reappraisal' on the issue of British troops serving in Northern Ireland if the executive fell (Fitzgerald 1991 pp. 233–4). Following the collapse of power-sharing, withdrawal was seriously considered by a cabinet sub-committe of the Labour Government. The other main possibilities considered were repartition and the creation of a 'no-man's land' along the border with the Republic. 'The committee ended up rejecting all three possibilities, arguing that all of them would probably aggravate the problem still further' (Bew and Patterson 1985 p. 77).

The British Labour Government rejected the withdrawal option above all because it would have destabilised Britain and Ireland. According to Rees, 'A declaration of intent to withdraw was not on; the position of the Army would become untenable immediately such a declaration was made, irrespective of the time-scale given' (Rees, quoted in 'Minutes of meeting between the Secretary of State at the NIO [Northern Ireland Office] and a Conservative Deputation led by Mr Neave', 12 December 1975). Following a British withdrawal it was expected that sectarian conflict between loyalists and republicans would have led to an irresistible demand in the Republic for it to send its army North to protect nationalists. Civil war in Ireland could have destabilised the Southern government and British trade with a key partner. According to a British 'secret military analysis' the regular Irish Army 'would not necessarily be decisive, either militarily or politically' against northern unionists (Donoughue 1987 p. 133). It was also feared that the civil war would spill over into Britain, particularly those cities in which there was a large Irish community (*The Sunday Times*, 26 May 1974). The civil service advised Rees that a unilateral withdrawal would be followed by a 'catastrophic breakdown of control...accompanied by major violence'. A gradual withdrawal without power-sharing would result in a loyalist government which would receive no support from the South against republican violence (Rees 1985 p. 99). The pressure of international opinion and the destabilisation created by the conflict may have resulted in Britain re-intervening, but this would probably have required the deployment of even greater force.

The debate on Northern Ireland within the higher echelons of the Conservative Party gives a sense of the constraints operating on British policy regardless of which party was in power. In September 1975 Margaret Thatcher's 'Leader's Steering Committee' considered the options on Northern Ireland.

> It was agreed that withdrawal was not a solution to violence in either Northern Ireland or in Britain. It was agreed that a United Ireland was not feasible. Repartition was discussed, and views expressed for and against. The difficulties of a large-scale population movement and of agreeing a new boundary with the Dublin Government were referred to, though it was felt that the idea needed careful examination. Direct Rule was thought inevitable, at least in the short term, if the Convention broke down. ('Leader's Steering Committee', LSC (75) 41 minutes, 10 September 1975)

A draft paper by Airey Neave, 'Debate on Northern Ireland', considered the long-term options for Northern Ireland. Direct rule had value 'only as a medium-term measure' and 'was not attractive as a medium-term solution'. Integration would end uncertainty over Northern Ireland's constitutional position but 'it would increase the burden at Westminster at a time when devolution for Scotland and Wales is contemplated. It would worsen relations with the minority and the Republic'. Repartition 'is impractical except in a civil war situation, when fear rather than policy would lead to de facto repartition'. A federal Ireland 'has drawn no significant support'. As for independence, 'It can be argued that Northern Ireland is a financial and military burden; that local politicians remain unco-operative; and that the British public are fed up with Northern Ireland.' However, without the British Army there would be all-Ireland civil war. 'National Army morale would suffer a blow from an apparent defeat by terrorists. Britain would face international opprobrium for creating a "Congo" situation, and a militant extremist state could appear on our doorstep, with serious consequences for our social order.' Withdrawal would also conflict with successive pledges made by the British Government ('Debate on NI: January 12th, LCC/76/ 95, Draft 4, 22 December 1975).

Some leading British politicians may have felt or hoped that Sunningdale would gradually lead to a united Ireland and remove the issue from British politics. After the power of unionism had been demonstrated during the UWC strike, Irish unity was no longer the most convincing means by which the British could extricate themselves from Ireland without leaving a power vacuum, instability and civil war. The transfer of power to an independent, unionist-dominated, Ulster – bolstered by the overwhelmingly Protestant RUC and UDR – was now likely to be a more effective means of complete British withdrawal (Donoughue 1987 p. 128; for NIO officials on independence, see Fitzgerald 1991 p. 279).

This adaption to the newly apparent 'realities of power' was indicated by the shifting perspectives of Harold Wilson, James Callaghan and Merlyn Rees, who felt Britain had done its best to impose a settlement but now it was up to the Irish to sort out their own mess (also Reginald Maudling, Rees 1985 pp. 94–5). Wilson, who had declared in favour of Irish unity in 1971, developed a 'Doomsday Scenario' which involved the announcement of dominion status for Northern Ireland and the transfer of sovereignty to a new constitutional authority which would permit a British withdrawal (Donoughue 1987 p. 129). As Home Secretary in 1969, Callaghan had argued that independence might be preferable to direct rule. In 1973 Callaghan published *A House Divided* in which he came out in favour of Irish unity; he had also told Fitzgerald that Irish unity would only require the 'acquiescence' of the people in the North (Fitzgerald 1991 p. 131). By 1981 Callaghan had come out for an independent Ulster, arguing 'that Britain was incapable of ever offering a settlement that would satisfy both sides' (House of Commons, vol. 7, col. 1046–53, 2 July 1981). Merlyn Rees also shifted his ground, detecting and encouraging a new Ulster nationalism, particularly among 'extremists', which would transcend sectarian divisions in an independent Ulster. Significantly, integration was felt by both Labour and Conservatives to lead to Westminster being even more dominated by Northern Ireland affairs (Hansard, vol. 874, col. 1066–8, 4 June 1974, Wilson 1979, p. 128). The government's White Paper described 'a new awareness in the Protestant and Catholic working class of their real interests' (White Paper, para. 53) and some journalists also detected hope in a new common Northern Ireland identity. The UDA, with its New Ulster Political Research Group, unsuccessfully took up the idea of an independent Ulster. There was also a flirtation among some members of the SDLP with independence.

The parameters of British policy were being tested. Irish unity or Ulster independence appeared to be unrealistic options, although the British Government may have encouraged the latter in the hope of winning significant nationalist support. The contemplation of these options by the two principal parties in British politics, and their reasons for rejection, suggests that there was little overriding British interest in Northern Ireland beyond stability. The belief among some in the IRA leadership that the British were about to withdraw was not compatible with an analysis which suggested its interests were inextricably bound up with a military presence in the North.

The British Government were faced with three 'hard realities':

(a)   there could be no solely military victory to the conflict, as British counter-insurgency strategy made clear (see Chapter 5);
(b)   unionists could not be coerced into a united Ireland (this had been demonstrated during the power-sharing experiment: see Chapter 6);
(c)   there could be no stable and peaceful Northern Ireland unless there was some accommodation to the legitimate demands of nationalists, probably involving power-sharing, if not also an Irish dimension. This was tested during the 1974–79 period when British policy drifted towards integration.

Stalemate: The Constitutional Convention

Following the collapse of power-sharing the British Government proposed a Constitutional Convention of the parties in Northern Ireland to negotiate a settlement. The responsibility for a solution was placed on the people and politicians of Northern Ireland. If they failed, Rees later argued, 'it would at least show the world, and give a message to the South of Ireland, that the blame did not all lie with the British' (Rees 1985 p. 107). According to its White Paper, *The Northern Ireland Constitution* (Cmnd 5675), the government continued:

to believe that the best and most desirable basis for political progress in Northern Ireland would be the establishment of local institutions enjoying broadly-based support throughout the community... It has always been recognised that there is no means to impose such a system upon Northern Ireland if substantial sections of its population are determined to oppose it. (para. 48)

Although it was acknowledged that there 'is an Irish dimension' it was only vaguely defined and there was no mention, as there had been in Wilson's 15-point plan, of the goal of Irish unity.

The collapse of power-sharing and subsequent elections made it painfully apparent that the centre ground in Northern Ireland had diminished and the likelihood of a new accommodation was a distant one. The October 1974 British General Election results confirmed the dominance of anti-power-sharing unionists as the UUUC increased its share of the poll from 51 per cent to 58 per cent. The Constitutional Convention elections in May 1975 again produced an anti-power-sharing majority, 54.8 per cent of the vote and 47 out of 78 seats. Between the Assembly elections of June 1973 and the Constitutional Convention elections in May 1975 the vote for the centre parties fell from 38.3 per cent to 17.5 per cent, while the loyalist vote rose from 35.4 per cent to 54.8 per cent. A review of opinion polls found that 'British Government policy is vulnerable because the settlement it recommends – power-sharing – is now a minority taste among all four communities within the British Isles... The concurring majority accepting direct rule appears to do so by default, because there is nothing else that the two communities can agree about' (R. Rose *et al.* 1978 pp. 45, 47, 52). Even supposing the SDLP was prepared to accept power-sharing without an Irish dimension, there was no guarantee that this would be acceptable to unionist political leaders. The ground on which an acceptable compromise might be achievable had shifted towards unionism (Fitzgerald 1991 p. 256).

While an Irish dimension appeared no longer to represent practical politics – since unionists had so strongly opposed it – there remained a possibility that power-sharing could be resurrected. In September 1975 William Craig, the notoriously hardline leader of the VUPP, proposed an emergency voluntary coalition government with nationalists. Craig claimed that coalition government in times of national emergencies, such as war, was part of the British political tradition and he proposed giving the SDLP representatives three seats in a voluntary coalition, backed by a strong committee system, which would last for no longer than five years. Ian Paisley initially favoured Craig's emergency coalition proposals but then reversed his position under grassroots pressure and to avoid a split within the

DUP (Moloney and Pollak 1986 pp. 332–5, Smyth 1987, pp. 101–2). Denounced by other loyalist parties, the one hopeful initiative during the Constitutional Convention collapsed, taking with it Craig's political career and the VUPP. Craig's fate was a reminder of the difficulties unionist leaders faced in bringing unionism towards an accommodation.

The UUUC used its majority in the Convention to monopolise the Convention's report to the Secretary of State. It proposed a virtual return to Stormont except for a committee system that would 'give real and substantial influence to an opposition and to make Parliament more effective', a privy council in which some places would be offered to leading members of opposition parties, and a 'Bill of Rights and Duties to protect the rights of the individual citizen'. The representation of the minority in the executive should not be compulsory and an institutionalised Irish dimension was rejected in favour of good neighbourly relations. Rees told the Commons that the Convention report did not 'command sufficiently widespread acceptance throughout the community to provide stable and effective government' (*Irish Times*, 13 January 1976). The Convention reconvened but failed to find a wider and more acceptable framework. In March 1976 the Convention was wound up. Rees declared there would be a new form of 'positive' home rule in Northern Ireland. Ministers would begin to govern as if direct rule was permanent, or at least indefinite, rather than acting in a stop-gap capacity, being unwilling to take major decisions which might later be taken by a local parliament (*The Guardian*, 5 March 1976). On 5 March 1976 Merlyn Rees said that the government 'does not contemplate any major new initiative for some time to come'.

The Labour Government ruled out the options of Ulster independence and Irish unity. With little prospect of a compromise power-sharing settlement, the government fell back on direct rule, insulation and containment. Harold Wilson's senior policy adviser said that after the 'humiliating capitulation' in May 1974 the British Prime Minister tried not to get too deeply involved in Northern Ireland. 'Our policy became one of consolidation, trying to contain terrorism and just to get through from year to year' (Donoughue 1987 p. 132, see also Haines 1977 p. 112). Northern Ireland no longer appeared as a routine item on the cabinet agenda (Wilson 1977 pp. 65–6). The Prevention of Terrorism Act (PTA) was introduced by the Labour Government in response to the IRA's Birmingham pub bombings in November 1974 (killing 19, injuring 182). The debate on the PTA was characterised by 'the passionate desire of a British Parliament to batten down the hatches, to shut out the ugly, dangerous infection which threatens us from outside' (*New Statesman*, 6 December 1974). The Act made provision for the exclusion of people entering Britain from Northern Ireland and for their exile to that region without any requirement to inform the victim of the reasons for their exclusion. The Labour Government continued to pursue 'Ulsterisation', heightening concerns that the British were withdrawing but also further insulating the conflict from British politics.

The IRA Ceasefire 1975–76 and the Fear of British Withdrawal

After the collapse of the executive the Labour Government did not keep the Irish Government informed of its Northern Ireland policy (perhaps for fear of further alienating unionists) and appeared to be deliberately cultivating a belief that it was about to withdraw. The Irish Government was concerned that British withdrawal would destabilise Ireland and pose a threat to democratic government in the Republic (Fitzgerald 1991 p. 271). When the British Government became engaged in 'contacts' with the IRA the Irish Government opposed these on the grounds that they lent the republicans legitimacy and undermined constitutional nationalism (Fitzgerald 1991 p. 262). This fear was probably sharpened by the impressive displays of unionist violence and power demonstrated by the Protestant backlash in 1972, the loyalist mobilisation around the UWC strike and the loyalist atrocity in Dublin and Monaghan in May 1974 (which killed 27 people and injured 120). The Irish Government accepted that unionism had been pushed too far at Sunningdale and hoped for some kind of devolved settlement. There were reports that the Irish coalition government feared that in the event of a British withdrawal the loyalty of the Irish Army could not be counted on and a coup might result in a right-wing Fianna Fáil takeover (Kyle 1975). The Irish Government campaigned in the USA and Europe against withdrawal from Northern Ireland and sought reassurances from the British Government on the matter (*Irish Times*, 20 July 1983, 21 July 1983). In January 1975 Garret Fitzgerald, the Irish Minister for Foreign Affairs, asked Henry Kissinger to intervene if the British Government decided to withdraw since it would endanger Ireland and even lead to Communist influence, an argument which was likely to draw US interest (Fitzgerald 1991 p. 259). The Irish Government also warned its EEC partners that most of the solutions being mooted for Northern Ireland would have violent consequences which would sweep across Ireland (*New Statesman*, 22 November 1974). It also refused the SDLP's request to draw up contingency plans for British withdrawal since this might give the British an excuse to withdraw (Fitzgerald 1991 p. 255). According to a leaked policy document, the Irish Government's policy following the UWC strike was to adopt a low profile and avoid any reference to the Irish dimension (seen as an idea in advance of its day) which might reduce the chances of power-sharing by increasing loyalist strength (*Irish Times*, 26 September 1974, Murray 1998 p. 55). The negotiations and truce between the British Government and the IRA, in late 1974 and early 1975, were seen as further evidence of British intent to withdraw.

Both major British parties had warned the people of Northern Ireland of the 'consequences' of rejecting the power-sharing experiment, so it was not surprising that after the UWC strike there was a widespread expectation that the British were about to withdraw, leaving behind an independent Northern Ireland. While the Irish Government, the SDLP and unionists feared the consequences of British withdrawal, the republican movement thought their time had finally come. The collapse of power-sharing, the establishment of the Constitutional Convention and acceleration of Ulsterisation raised expectations within the IRA that they were on the brink of victory, having 'long since forsaken the notion that Britain had any desire to stay in Ireland' (Bew and Patterson 1985 p. 80). Republican expectations of a British withdrawal had reached such a height that Ó Bráidaigh warned the British not to withdraw and leave behind a 'Congo situation' (that is, a bloody civil war).

The Labour Government exploited republican expectations by entering into a truce with the IRA and using this pretext to further Ulsterise the conflict and demoralise and defeat the republican movement. Successive British Governments had attempted to bring the IRA into the political process in 1972. Rees' legalisation of Sinn Féin and the UVF (the UDA had not been banned) and his announcement of the end of internment also represented an attempt to encourage the Provisionals down a political path and a hope that they might contest the Convention elections. He mentioned that given 'a genuine and sustained cessation of violence' anything might be possible, hinting at withdrawal (Smith 1995 p. 130, Taylor 1997 pp. 170–1).

On 10 December 1974 Protestant clergymen met the IRA at Feakle in the Republic of Ireland. The clergymen had drafted a document which they hoped to clear with the Provisionals and the British Government. The IRA leader Ruairí Ó'Brádaigh maintains that he received a letter from the British Government which requested a meeting to devise structures of British withdrawal from Northern Ireland (Taylor 1997 p. 177). William Arlow, one of the Protestant clergymen at Feakle, claimed that the British had given an undertaking to the IRA that if the Convention collapsed the British would begin the process of withdrawal. This is probably the impression that the British Government deliberately attempted to convey to the IRA in an attempt to split and demoralise the movement (*Irish Times*, 9 June 1978, *The Sunday Times*, 18 June 1978, Bew and Patterson 1985 pp. 82–3). During the truce the British Government refused to give a public undertaking to withdraw because of the impact this was likely to have on the unionist population, leading to 'a Congo-type situation which both Brits and the Republican Movement wish to avoid. Grave statements lead to the opposite happening' (Republican Minutes, quoted in Taylor 1997 p. 190). The IRA demanded British withdrawal and self-determination, an amnesty for all 'political' prisoners and an end to detention without trial. The IRA leadership demonstrated their control over their movement by calling an unannounced ceasefire on 27 January 1975 which became official on 9 February.

The truce was to be monitored through a number of 'incident centres' manned by Sinn Féin, to avoid the misunderstandings and confrontations which destroyed the 1972 truce. These incident centres, with their 'hot lines' to the government, 'were a watershed in the public perception of Sinn Féin, giving it a political standing in the nationalist community and, more importantly, a physical presence' (Taylor 1997 p. 186). The clear recognition of the political nature of the republican movement and hope that it would contest elections contrasted starkly with the attempt of the government to criminalise the IRA and normalise the conflict. The SDLP and the Irish Government were concerned at the boost these centres gave to Sinn Féin's credibility among nationalists in the North. The loyalists saw them as further evidence to confirm the widespread expectation that the British were withdrawing. In this context the loyalist paramilitaries declared their support for an independent Ulster. The result of this constitutional insecurity was an upsurge in sectarian killings by loyalist and republican paramilitaries as the fight for post-British ascendancy intensified. Between 1974 and 1976 loyalist paramilitaries killed 452 people, 40 per cent of all their victims throughout the conflict (Fay *et al.* 1999 p. 138). The victims of republican paramilitaries were increasingly sectarian, being Protestant civilians and the locally recruited security forces (Sutton 1994 p. 198, 202). The republican leadership, split between moderate and hardline factions, had severe difficulties in maintaining the unity of the IRA during the truce (Bew and Patterson 1985 pp. 84–6, Smith 1995 pp. 122, 130). According to Ruairí Ó Brádaigh, the bilateral truce broke down in September 1975 because of an unprecedented assassination campaign by loyalists; the failure of the British to give a public declaration of intent to leave Ireland; and the attitude of the Irish Government in sabotaging the process by hunting down Ó Conaill and making representations to the British (Ó Brádaigh, *Sunday Tribune*, letters, 17 October 1993, *Irish Times*, 30 April 1992).

By July 1975 the Provisionals felt they had little to show for their ceasefire. On 4 November 1975 Rees announced the abolition of special category status: all those convicted after 1 March 1976 would be treated as 'ordinary criminals'. The criminalisation of republican prisoners marked a further step in Britain's strategy of normalisation, and republican resistance to this led to the Hunger Strikes of 1981. On 12 November Rees announced the closure of the incident centres. IRA hopes of a British withdrawal received a further setback when Harold Wilson declared, on 12 January 1976, that a united Ireland was neither a practical proposition nor a solution which any British party would wish to impose, and announced a raft of security measures (Bew and Gillespie 1993 p. 109). Nevertheless, speculation about British withdrawal continued into 1977 (*Irish Times*, 15 January 1977). The last meeting between the Provisionals and representatives of the British Government took place on 10 February 1976 (although one account suggests talks 'persisted intermittently until July 1976': *The Sunday Times*, 18 June 1978). The British used the truce 'to increase their surveillance and infiltrate the IRA's ranks, and in the first five months of 1976 over 400 people were charged with violent offences' (Smith 1995 p. 133).

British deception during the 1972 and 1975 ceasefires (and later during the Hunger Strikes of 1980–81) led republicans to be suspicious of declaring any future extended ceasefires. In March 1993 the British Government representative cited a letter from Rees to Wilson which stated, 'We set out to con them and we did' (Sinn Féin 1993, pp. 28, 31). The old Provisional leadership now made way for the new, younger, more militant, 'northern leadership' of Adams and McGuinness, who attempted to restore unity and morale to a shattered organisation (Patterson 1997 p. 181). Since 1972 the IRA had believed it was on the brink of victory over the British and regularly declared each year to be the 'Year of Victory'. Even in 1977 the IRA continued to declare that victory was close (Smith 1995 pp. 135, 137), but this may have been seen as necessary 'propaganda' to sustain the morale of the organisation. During 1977, the IRA finally accepted that their offensive against the British had failed to produce a withdrawal and that the Southern leadership's 'Truce' strategy had collapsed. The IRA reorganised itself into a cellular structure to minimise the chances of penetration by the security forces and settled down for the 'Long War'. Simultaneously, there was an attempt to 'broaden the battlefield' beyond the 'armed struggle' to involve republicans in a political struggle in the 'war' against the British presence. According to a captured IRA document on the reorganisation of the republican movement, Sinn Féin was to be radicalised 'under army [IRA] direction...and should agitate about social and economic issues which attack the welfare of the people' (Clarke 1987 pp. 251–3, Patterson 1997 p. 180).

The British Government, in the meantime, continued to develop their strategy of *normalisation*. This involved *criminalising* the paramilitaries and creating the appearance of a more 'normal' society by *Ulsterising* security and putting the police rather than the army in the front line of the fight against terrorism/criminality. The truce and the increasingly communal nature of the violence reduced the pressure on the British Army and this finally allowed the government to implement its policy of Ulsterisation and police primacy. The army resisted its loss of power and there was considerable counter-productive rivalry with the RUC. According to some reports, the army was also running its own propaganda war against Merlyn Rees, unhappy with the Government's 'contacts' with the IRA and its policy for the release of detainees. At the end of March 1975 the Labour Government asserted its control over the army's 'black propaganda' operation (Curtis 1984 pp. 241–3, Hamill 1985 pp. 177–83, Rees 1985 pp. 225–8, 302, Foot 1989, Mason 1999 p. 166). There has been continuing concern about the lack of political control over the security forces (Urban 1992, Dixon 1997b, Needham 1998).

Between 1976 and 1977 over 2500 people, mostly IRA, were convicted of murder, attempted murder, and arms and explosives offences. The RUC was having success in breaking down IRA members during interrogation, an internal IRA document admitted: 'The three-day and seven-day detention orders are breaking volunteers, and it is the Irish Republican Army's fault for not indoctrinating volunteers with the psychological strength to resist interrogation' (Clarke 1987 p. 251). A Provisional leader admitted, 'We were almost defeated' (Moloney 1980, Kelley 1988 pp. 284–5). In August 1978 Amnesty International found that suspects detained in Castlereagh RUC detention centre had been 'ill-treated'. This was confirmed in the subsequent Bennett Report, commissioned by the British Government.

The Truce saw a period of rising inter-communal violence in Northern Ireland which peaked in 1976. In the expectation that the British were about to withdraw, loyalist and republican paramilitaries attempted to assert their predominance by turning to sectarian assassination. During 1975–76 the IRA killed 85 Protestant civilians, while loyalists and loyalist paramilitaries killed at least 171 Catholic civilians (Sutton 1994 p. 198). The strength of the loyalist backlash 'tied up IRA resource and questioned long-held Republican assumptions about the Loyalist community' (Moloney 1980). As it became clear that the British Government was not going to withdraw, loyalist paramilitary killings and support for independence declined. In September 1977 the Secretary of State for Northern Ireland, Roy Mason, declared that 'The myth of British withdrawal is dead forever' (*Irish Times*, 17 September 1977) and the Orange Order was also dismissing unionist fears of a British withdrawal. According to Loughlin, 'the Queen's Silver Jubilee visit to Northen Ireland in August 1977 was seen as marking the end of a period when it was widely believed that Westminster had been seriously considering withdrawal from the province' (Loughlin 1995 p. 205). The decline in loyalist paramilitary violence between 1977 and 1985 has been attributed to: the effectiveness and increased strength of the RUC against the IRA, reducing the need for paramilitary organisation; the effectiveness of the RUC against the loyalist paramilitaries; and 'the low incidence of dramatic initiatives and the calming effect this had on unionist perceptions of their precarious position' (Bruce 1999 pp. 191–2).

The VUPP had been the third largest unionist party at the 1975 Convention elections, but by the 1977 local elections its share of the vote was just 1.5 per cent. The UUP managed to establish its dominance in the unionist bloc, increasing its share of the vote from 25.8 per cent in the Convention elections, to 29.6 per cent in the

1977 local elections, to 36.6 per cent in the 1979 Westminster elections. Ian Paisley's DUP suffered: its share of the vote fell from 14.8 per cent in 1975, to 12.7 per cent in 1977 and to just 10.2 per cent in 1979. In 1977 Paisley entered into a United Unionist Action Council with anti-Craig Vanguard elements, the remnants of the UWC and the UDA. They called a loyalist strike for May 1977 to force the British Government to adopt the loyalist Convention Report and more repressive security measures. Roy Mason described the strike as the most dangerous threat to Northern Ireland during his tenure as Secretary of State: 'If Paisley succeeded in unleashing the worst instincts of Ulster loyalism, we probably wouldn't be able to hold the line.' He was concerned that 'civil disobedience could easily spill into open insurrection' (Mason 1999 pp. 173, 185, 190). The UUP opposed the strike, the RUC stood firm and the 10-day strike collapsed. Although Paisley had staked his credibility on a successful outcome, the DUP made significant gains in Council seats in the elections which followed shortly after.

The British Parties and the Ulster Unionists

The close result of the October 1974 Westminster General Election created a strong incentive for both British parties to court Ulster Unionist support in the House of Commons. The Labour Government's need to avoid alienating the Ulster Unionists and the pressure from the Conservative Opposition to take a more repressive stand on law and order succeeded in making the period 1976–79 that most fondly remembered by unionists since the outbreak of 'the Troubles' (Dixon 1994b). The election of Mrs Thatcher to the leadership of the Conservative Party in February 1975 led to the appointment of two right-wing, unionist Conservative MPs, Airey Neave and John Biggs-Davison, as respectively opposition Conservative spokesperson and deputy on Northern Ireland. The rhetoric of bipartisanship was broken (if not its substance) as the Conservative front bench became very critical of the Labour Government's security policy. Labour's less authoritarian inclinations on security issues did not reflect public opinion and therefore left it vulnerable to Conservative attack. In January 1976 the Labour Government united with the Conservative Opposition behind a package of security measures which included: increased surveillance operations; more checkpoints; more extensive use of personal identity checks; and the official introduction of the

Special Air Service (SAS) into Northern Ireland (*Irish Times*, 13 January 1976). On 15 January 1976, Harold Wilson chaired the first all-party security meeting on Northern Ireland. Bipartisanship remained intact because of the parallel shifts in the policy of the Labour Government and Conservative Opposition, but also because of the strength of 'moderate' or 'wet' Conservatives who favoured the approach of the Heath government's Irish policy and acted as a check on Neave's unionism. They were resistant to any shift in party policy which abandoned power-sharing and broke the bipartisan approach with the Labour Party (Dixon 1995a p. 170).

The Labour Government, under pressure from the Conservatives and competing with them for the support of the UUP at Westminster, took a more unionist stance on constitutional and security issues. By the end of 1977, Airey Neave had threatened to break bipartisanship on four occasions but claimed that Labour had now taken over the security policy of the Conservative party (Dixon 1995a p. 170). The replacement of Rees by the hardliner Roy Mason in September 1976, long demanded by the Conservatives, bolstered bipartisanship and facilitated Labour's attempts to win the support of the Ulster Unionists at Westminster (*The Daily Telegraph*, 3 December 1976). The new Labour Secretary of State, accepting the impasse on the constitutional question, took a low key approach to the constitutional question, emphasising instead economic and security reforms and concentrating on making direct rule work. But even Mason did not believe a purely military solution was possible (Mason 1999 p. 224). British governments continued to see the promotion of economic prosperity and reducing inequalities as the means by which the conflict could be ameliorated and a climate created in Northern Ireland which would be more conducive to a political settlement. The minority Labour Government reached an 'understanding' with the Ulster Unionists in 1977. The Labour Government's constitutional approach became more unionist, as did the Conservative Opposition, moving away from power-sharing and promising to increase Northern Ireland's representation at Westminster in line with its population (Dixon 1994b).

Constitutional Irish Nationalism: The SDLP and the Republic

From the SDLP's perspective, the Labour Government had failed to save power-sharing through its inactivity and was now undermining constitutional nationalism by negotiating with the IRA and making concessions to the 'integrationist' unionist agenda. There was debate within the SDLP between, on the one hand, the supporters of the party leadership who favoured partnership and a strong Irish dimension and, on the other, dissidents in favour of working with loyalists towards British withdrawal and accommodation in an independent Ulster. At its 1976 party conference there was significant support for independence and a complementary motion calling for 'the British Government to declare its intentions of withdrawing to give the divided people of Northern Ireland the opportunity to negotiate a final political solution and a lasting peace'. This motion was only defeated by 153 votes to 111, with 12 abstentions and 10 out of 16 of the party's former Convention members voting in favour of a British declaration of intent to withdraw (a key IRA demand). Opponents of a declaration of intent feared this would result in a violent grab for power by republican and loyalist paramilitaries, resulting in civil war and a bloodbath. Ben Caraher, vice chairman of the SDLP, argued, 'The only people who could possibly be considered realistic negotiators would be the paramilitary groups because they would have the power. The SDLP would have no power and little relevance because only those who could enforce their voice would have power.' A British declaration of intent would lead to a collapse of its power and a swift withdrawal: 'The urge to clear out lock, stock and barrel would be overwhelming.' The independence lobby argued that the British were withdrawing anyway and that the party should be looking to independence as a compromise which could allow loyalists and republican paramilitaries to give up violence and work out alternative constitutional arrangements (*Irish Times*, 6 and 11 December 1976).

The SDLP warned the Labour Government that its drift towards integration would result in the alienation of constitutional nationalism to the benefit of the IRA. In September 1977 James Callaghan reassured the SDLP and the Irish Government that he was determined to bring about some form of power-sharing (*Irish Times*, 21 September 1977). In October 1977 the Irish Independence Party was founded; it sought British withdrawal from Northern Ireland following which the people of Northern Ireland might choose independence or a united Ireland (*The Guardian*, 8 October 1977). This further increased pressure on the SDLP to adopt a more radically nationalist approach. In 1978 the SDLP party conference passed a carefully worded withdrawal motion with only two dissenters. It called for British disengagement 'as part of an overall political solution' and for a conference of the two governments and the 'two traditions' in the North 'with a view to finding a permanent solution to the Irish problem'. The motion expressed SDLP disaffection without demanding a precipitate or unconditional British withdrawal, which would lend legitimacy to the IRA's political position. This represented an attempt by party leaders to pressurise the British into coercing unionists to deal with nationalists (*Irish Times*, 6 April 1978).

As the prospect of a British withdrawal receded and the Labour Government took a more unionist approach to Northern Ireland, so nationalists in the Republic also adopted a more militant stance. In June 1977 the 'greener' Fianna Fáil party replaced the Fine Gael/Labour Coalition as the Government of the Republic of Ireland. In 1975 Fianna Fáil published a policy statement arguing for the British Government to encourage the unity of Ireland and declare its commitment to implement an ordered withdrawal from Northern Ireland. The Fianna Fáil leader, Jack Lynch, retreated from his party's policy statement. He argued that 'in the present, unstable and emotional atmosphere such a declaration [of intent by the British to withdraw] would be highly dangerous' (Fitzgerald 1991 p. 271). Fianna Fáil's call for a British declaration of intent to withdraw was seen by some as influential in winning the 1977 election. On 11 January 1978 Jack Lynch, the new Taoiseach, called for a British declaration of intent to withdraw, but no date to be set. Also in that year the Irish Government stated that it would not renew the Sunningdale guarantee given to unionists. Public opinion in the Republic was increasingly supportive of Irish unity: in 1973, 37 per cent indicated that a united Ireland was their preferred solution, and this increased to 42 per cent in 1977, 54 per cent in 1978 and 56 per cent in 1980 (Mair 1987 p. 90). A 1978 survey of opinion in the Republic found 75 per cent of respondents endorsed this position (Rose *et al.* 1978 p. 48).

The shift in the position of the SDLP and the Irish Government towards a 'greener' withdrawal position may well have been a tactical move to check the unionist drift of British policy. Between 1974 and 1977, for both nationalists and unionists, there was a heightened expectation that the British would pull out. By 1978 withdrawal could be advocated, safe in the knowledge that this policy would not be implemented. This 'greener' stance appeared to provoke a bipartisan British response, with both the Labour Government and Conservative Opposition moving to reassure the SDLP on their continuing commitment to power-sharing (Fitzgerald 1991 p. 288).

After the Conservative Party's 1979 Westminster election victory the British Government rejected integration and shifted towards devolution. This allowed the SDLP to soften its withdrawal position and, by November 1979, it was calling only for the British to withdraw their constitutional guarantee from unionists (*The Guardian*, 5 November 1979). The Irish Government also appeared to be shifting its position on the North towards some locally elected devolved administration at Stormont (*The Guardian*, 22 November 1979, *Irish Times*, 25 August 1982). However, the election of Charles Haughey to the leadership of Fianna Fáil in December 1979 ended cross-party co-operation in the Republic on the North as Haughey took up a more militantly republican stance. He insisted on a British declaration of intent to withdraw, while Fine Gael and Labour preferred Irish unity by consent (Mair 1987a pp. 98–9).

The US Dimension

During the early 1970s, the US executive did not exert much pressure on the British Government over its Irish policy (Wilson 1995, Heath 1998 p. 435). Britain's power-sharing experiment and co-operation with the Republic probably reassured the US Government. In 1976 a British junior minister in Northern Ireland reported that the US Government would co-operate to stem the flow of funds to republicans so long as the British Government acted in an 'even-handed manner': 'there is no alternative to partnership and co-operation in Northern Ireland' (House of Commons, vol. 903, col. 160, 12 January 1976). During the mid-1970s the SDLP and the Irish Government looked to the USA to bring pressure to bear on the British Government. The collapse of power-sharing, the truce between the IRA and the British Government, the emergence of the 'Peace People' (a cross-community peace movement) and the descent of Northern Ireland into sectarian violence undermined the republican 'anti-imperialist' view of the conflict. This suggested that the British and the IRA were the main protagonists in the conflict and paid little attention to unionist opposition to Irish unity. The process of normalisation (criminalisation and Ulsterisation) allowed the British Government to present the violence in Northern Ireland as criminal, anti-terrorist and (even) anti-Communist, arguments which were likely to resonate strongly in the 'West'. The British Government and constitutional Irish nationalism were united, however, in their attempts to counter Irish-American support for the IRA (Wilson 1995 pp. 109, 119). The rumours about a British withdrawal may have galvanised the Irish Government into action against the IRA, which represented a significant threat to the Irish state. The advantage of the Irish Government's anti-IRA campaigning in the USA is that it was likely to have more credibility and make a greater impact on an Irish-American audience than the British Government. The Irish Government was also not shy about playing the anti-Marxist and Western security interest cards in the USA (Prior 1986 pp. 219–20).

Jimmy Carter, running for the US presidency in 1976, raised the issue of Northern Ireland in his pursuit of the Irish-American vote. Irish republican groups in the USA capitalised on human rights violations in Northern Ireland to galvanise support against the British Government. Supporters of constitutional nationalism mobilised to counter republican influence and speak out against the IRA. According to A. J. Wilson, 'Irish-American political leaders had traditionally been reluctant to issue outright condemnations of the republican tradition because they typically supported Irish unity and strategically adopted an ambiguous position on the use of violence.' The 'Four Horsemen' – leading Irish-American figures: Thomas 'Tip' O'Neill, Speaker of the House of Representatives, Senator Ted Kennedy, Senator Daniel Moynihan, and Governor Hugh Carey of New York – issued a statement on 16 March 1977 opposing the use of violence in Northern Ireland. Governor Carey attacked the Provisionals as 'Irish killers' and the OIRA as 'Irish Marxists', and these sentiments were echoed by the liberal Democrat, Senator George McGovern (Wilson 1995 pp. 130, 133). This may have had an effect on the flow of funds to the US-based Irish Northern Aid Committee (NORAID), which is pro-republican, from hard-core republicans which reached its low point in the second half of 1977 after the Carter initiative and the statement of the 'Four Horsemen' (Guelke 1988 p. 132, Wilson 1995 p. 139). US politicians may have reassessed their attitude to Northern Ireland as the more communal nature of the conflict became apparent after the collapse of power-sharing and the Irish Government lobbied to avoid a British withdrawal. The US ambassador to Ireland, William Shannon, explained in 1977:

Senator Kennedy is typical of most Irish Americans, and myself, in his change of views about the problem in Northern Ireland. When it started in 1969 the civil rights issue burst into flames, and Irish Americans tended to think of it as the final act of the drama which began in 1916. There was an instinctive desire to rally behind the Irish, kick the British out, and reunite the country...But as the guerrilla war dragged on, people have become much more conversant with the realities and complexities of the situation. Now Irish Americans realise that if the British withdraw it would be nothing like the withdrawal from Dublin in 1922. On the contrary, if Britain was to withdraw now, there would be more violence. (*The Times*, 27 September 1977, quoted in Wilson 1995 p. 140)

The 'Four Horsemen' later called on the British Government to launch a new political initiative, envisaging talks between the UUP and the SDLP. They pressured President Carter to issue a statement on Northern Ireland, a draft of which, it was reported, 'stressed that the Irish Government would have to be represented at any political discussions' (Wilson 1995 p. 135). A statement on Northern Ireland was issued by President Carter on 30 August 1977, signalling a significant departure in US policy and establishing a precedent for future interventions. It attacked republican supporters in the USA and offered economic aid in the event of a solution to the conflict.

There is a strong argument that constitutional Irish nationalism succeeded in bringing US pressure to bear on the British Government to shift its policy on Northern Ireland. The involvement of the Foreign Office in Northern Ireland affairs from the late 1970s onwards suggests a recognition of the importance of the international dimension of the conflict (Donoughue 1987 p. 135). The British Government was attacked for human rights abuses and political inactivity by US politicians (Wilson 1995 pp. 156–7), and in 1979 the US State Department suspended the sale of arms to the RUC after pressure in Congress. The British Government's 'Atkins Initiative' on 25 October 1979 is often attributed to pressure from the USA (Guelke 1988 p. 117, Wilson 1995 pp. 164–5). When the initiative did not make much progress, 'The Four Horsemen were somewhat disappointed that the British did not force the unionists into some form of cooperation' (Wilson 1995 p. 164).

Undoubtedly US pressure has been a significant constraint on British policy during 'the Troubles'; the difficulty lies in attempting to assess the extent of US influence. The shift of British policy from integrationism to the 1972–74 policy of power-sharing with an Irish dimension could be attributable to pressures other than US influence. After all, the Sunningdale settlement of 1973 had been agreed at a time when US influence was not thought to be particularly significant.

The impact of US pressure on the Atkins Initiative is largely circumstantial, as there is evidence that British policy was likely to shift away from the integrationism of the Conservative Party's 1979 manifesto even before the British General Election and before the US ban on the sale of guns to the RUC (see below). In any case, the Initiative was not such a departure in British policy since Mason had held talks with the parties. US influence may have been exaggerated; with or without US pressure there were strong, long-term structural constraints operating on British policy which explain the pursuit of power-sharing and an Irish dimension in 1979–80.

Back on Track: The Atkins Talks 1979 and the Dublin Summit 1980

The Conservative Party's 'unionist' 1979 General Election manifesto promised on Northern Ireland that 'In the absence of devolved government we seek to establish one or more elected regional councils with a wide range of powers over local services.' The election of a Conservative Government with a large majority freed both Labour and Conservative parties from the need to win the support of Ulster Unionist MPs at Westminster and therefore gave the British Government more room to manoeuvre. The Conservatives disappointed unionists by failing to implement its 'integrationist' manifesto promise and instead launched an initiative to promote power-sharing devolution and in 1980 an Anglo–Irish process. Humphrey Atkins told the Northern Ireland Committee (NIC) of the Conservative Parliamentary Party 'that he did not intend to go ahead with it [the regional council scheme] at present since its only supporters in Northern Ireland were the Official Unionists' (NIC, 31 October 1979). The rapid retreat of Labour and Conservatives from their more unionist stance after the 1979 election suggests that their previous attitude was a tactical adjustment to win UUP support at Westminster, as well as a reaction to the polarisation of politics in Northern Ireland.

Airey Neave seems to have been shifting from his integrationist stance *before* the 1979 election and the Conservatives were unlikely to implement their integrationist manifesto (*The Guardian*, 27 March 1979, 31 March 1979, *The Daily Telegraph*, 31 March 1979, Prior 1986 p. 193, Dixon 1998). The integrationism of the Conservative Party's 1979 election manifesto was soon jettisoned and the Conservative Government picked up from where the power-sharing experiment left off in 1974, pursuing a twin-track strategy. First, power-sharing and devolution were promoted through the 'Atkins Talks' of 1979–80 and subsequently through Prior's 1982 'Rolling Devolution' initiative. Second, an Irish dimension was considered by the Atkins Initiative and promoted through the Anglo–Irish process from 1980 onwards. Originally, the Atkins Initiative ruled out discussion of the 'Irish Dimension' but this was forced on to the agenda by the SDLP who refused to participate without its inclusion (Bew and Patterson 1985 p. 114). Gerry Fitt resigned from the SDLP over its refusal to engage in the Atkins Initiative without discussing the Irish dimension when, he argued, the British had significantly qualified the unionists' consitutional guarantee (*The Guardian*, 22 November 1979). Like Paddy Devlin, who had been expelled in 1977, Fitt was on the more socialist wing of the SDLP and prioritised an accommodation with unionism over the all-Ireland dimension.

The relative continuity of British constitutional policy – in spite of Thatcher's personal unionist sympathies – can be explained in terms of the internal and external constraints operating on it rather than, as O'Leary has argued, 'painfully slow ethno-national policy learning' (O'Leary 1997; see also Dixon 2000b). During the 1975–79 period Thatcher was constrained in her attitude towards Northern Ireland by the threat of intra-party opposition from 'moderate' Conservatives and the importance of bipartisanship. After 1979, Margaret Thatcher argues, she realised that to defeat terrorism she had to undermine support for republicanism. This would not be achieved by implementing the Conservative manifesto's integrationist policy since this would alienate nationalists in the North, the government of the Republic of Ireland (who Thatcher hoped would co-operate in fighting the IRA and pacifying the region) and international opinion (Thatcher 1993 pp. 384–7; Goodall 1993 p. 128 and Prior 1986 p. 194 make similar points). The Conservative Government did not, therefore, have to take 'two decades to learn what Edward Heath mostly understood in 1973' (O'Leary 1997) because there were ministers in the cabinet and civil servants who had been intimately involved with the 1973 policy. Mrs Thatcher's ignorance of Northern Ireland affairs may suggest a heightened vulnerability to the influence of such experience (Prior 1986 p. 239).

Margaret Thatcher warned, in a *New York Times* interview, 'We will listen for a while. We hope we will get agreement. But then the government will have to make some decisions and say, having listened to everyone, we are going to try this or that, whichever we get most support for' (Bew and Patterson 1985 p. 112). This was hardly the statement of a politician with strong convictions over Northern Ireland. On 21 May 1980 Thatcher and the Irish Taoiseach, Charles Haughey, met and recorded the importance of the 'unique relationship between the peoples of the United Kingdom of Great Britain and Northern Ireland and the Republic and ... the need to further this relationship in the interests of peace and reconciliation'. There were reports that the Irish Government was prepared to enter a defence agreement with the UK in return for Irish unity (*The Sunday Times*, 18 May 1980). In November 1980 the 'Atkins talks' collapsed without agreement. The following month, the British Prime Minister led an impressive delegation of British politicians to Dublin for an Anglo–Irish Summit. The two governments agreed to establish 'joint studies to consider citizens' rights, security matters, economic co-operation and possible new institutional arrangements'. These studies 'explored possible forms for new Anglo–Irish institutions at various levels', were pursued at an official level during 1981 and presented to both Parliaments on 11 November 1981. This co-operation was cemented in the Anglo–Irish Intergovernmental Council which was established in November 1981 and heralded regular meetings at ministerial and official level between the two governments.

At the Dublin summit Thatcher acknowledged Britain's unique relationship with Ireland and said that at future meetings there would be 'special consideration of the totality of relationships within these islands'. Don Concannon, who had been a Labour Minister of State at the NIO for five years, commented on the study groups set up by the Dublin Summit 1980: 'My own view of the study groups is that they represent the old, unofficial governmental co-operation on a formalised basis and improved status' (Don Concannon, 'Report on the Visit to the Irish Republic 31/3/81 to 2/4/81 presented to M. Foot', Labour Party Archive). The Irish Taoiseach, Charles Haughey, claimed that the December Summit had significance for the unity of Ireland. This angered Thatcher and alienated unionism. Paisley took to the 'Carson Trail' to prevent the betrayal of the Union by perfidious Albion through the extension of the Anglo–Irish process.

The Propaganda War and the Hunger Strikes 1980–81

As the IRA's hopes of a quick victory against the British evaporated, the 'Long War' between the British Government and the IRA was likely to place an even greater premium on the 'propaganda war'. Publicly the British condemned the IRA as criminal 'godfathers', terrorists or even Marxists who prevailed only through intimidation. It was a propaganda strategy deployed in the withdrawal from the Empire (Carruthers 1995). The process of 'normalisation' was designed by the British (and followed to some extent by the Irish Government) partly to win the propaganda war in Britain, Ireland and internationally. Privately, successive British Labour and Conservative Governments treated the republican movement as politically motivated and continued to have 'contacts' with the IRA and had granted their prisoners 'Special Category' status.

A secret report by Brigadier Glover, 'Northern Ireland Future Terrorist Trends' (1978), implied that the IRA's violence was 'politically inspired' by 'an inward looking Celtic nationalism' rather than Marxism, and there were no indications of a 'substantial link' between these organisations and the Soviet Union. Glover argued that 'Our evidence of the calibre of rank and file terrorists does not support the view that they are merely mindless hooligans drawn from the unemployed and unemployable.' The report noted a recent trend away from 'cowboy' shootings and sectarian attacks 'which, by alienating public opinion, both within the Catholic community and outside the Province, is politically damaging'. Propaganda was important to the IRA and the leadership was becoming 'increasingly sensitive of the need to avoid alienating support not only in the Roman Catholic areas of the Province but also in the Republic and among those of Irish extraction'. Glover went on to become Commander-in-Chief UK Land Forces, and after his retirement in 1987 stated publicly that 'In no way can or will the Provisional IRA ever be defeated militarily. The army's role has been now for some time...to help create the conditions whereby a full democratic, peaceful, political solution can be achieved' (*The Times*, 6 June 2000).

The Hunger Strikes were the site of a 'propaganda battle' fought between the British Government and the republican movement. The British Government wanted to portray the paramilitary prisoners as criminals and/or terrorists instead of granting them political, 'prisoner of war', status which might legitimise their 'armed struggle' in the eyes of the world. Roy Mason was particularly sensitive to the importance of the propaganda war against the IRA (Mason 1999). The Catholic Primate of All-Ireland, Tomas Ó Fiaich, claimed that conditions in the Maze Prison were 'unfit for animals' and that the paramilitaries were not ordinary prisoners. According to Mason:

> In a few emotive and grossly biased sentences he seemed to be undermining the legitimacy of our entire struggle against terrorism...His partisan words had far more impact than I could possibly say. From that point on, publicity began to move decisively against us, particularly in the United States. As John Hume of the SDLP told us in September, the Provisional IRA was 'winning the propaganda battle hands down'. (Mason 1999 pp. 210–11)

According to Mason, an intercepted message from a republican prisoner argued: 'It is no longer a status issue. Whoever wins this has the war won' (Mason 1999 p. 212).

The republicans resisted Britain's criminalisation strategy and sought 'political status' for their 'prisoners of war'. Both prisoners and the British Government 'chose terms that would have the most appeal to the broader public they were trying to manipulate, that would appear to make them more reasonable and their positions more tenable'. The 'truth' of these statements mattered less than their effectiveness in the propaganda war. The Sinn Féin spokesperson argued: 'Balanced statements...which seek to temper criticism of one side with criticisms of the other help no one.' While the British 'won the contest of wills' with the prisoners over political status they 'lost the propaganda war, resuscitated an ailing IRA, and politicized militant Republicanism' (O'Malley 1990 pp. 206–8, 211).

The Hunger Strikes were the result of the British policy of criminalisation. In June 1972 those interned or imprisoned were granted 'Special Category' status which gave certain privileges to those convicted of scheduled offences, but this was phased out from 1 March 1976. The republican movement resisted criminalisation, and at first republican prisoners refused to wear prison uniforms and instead wrapped themselves in blankets. The no-wash protest became the dirty protest in April 1978 when prisoners were denied permission to use toilets unless they wore prison uniform and refused buckets to slop out (O'Malley 1990 p. 22). Prisoners smeared excrement over their cells and refused to shave or bath. The IRA began a campaign of assassination against prison officers and 18 were killed by the end of the dispute. In 1980 the prisoners resorted to a traditional form of republican protest, the hunger strike. They made five demands:

(a) to wear their own clothes;
(b) to refrain from prison work;
(c) to associate freely with one another;
(d) to organise recreational facilities and have one letter, visit and parcel a week;
(e) to have lost remission fully restored.

The British Government felt that these demands amounted to granting the prisoners political status. James Prior told Conservative backbenchers:

> The central demand of the hunger strikers – for political status – could not be conceded for three reasons: (a) it would be morally wrong to accept that crimes committed for political reasons were different from other crimes; (b) the claim for political status had been rejected by the European Commission on Human Rights in June; and (c) because it would produce a violent Protestant backlash, and give encouragement to terrorists everywhere. (NIC, 6 November 1980)

Mrs Thatcher later argued,

> The purpose of the privileges they claimed was not to improve prisoners' conditions but to take power away from the prison authorities. They were also keen to establish once again, as they felt they had in 1972, that their crimes were 'political', thus giving the perpetrators a kind of respectability, even nobility. This we could not allow. (Thatcher 1993 pp. 389–90)

The IRA sought, in the words of Bobby Sands, the leader of the Provisionals in the H-Blocks, to 'broaden the battlefield' of the prison campaign beyond friends and relatives of the prisoners. In order to 'stir people's emotions[,] to arouse ... and activate them'. Sands argued for an 'army of propagandists' to put their views across:

> Now to tackle this broad spectrum of people in which we'll be plunging we must create our own mass media. The Brit mass

media being unreliable but we can use it wherever possible and through time they'll be forced to cover us, through what we are going to stir up . . . personally I envisage creating an atmosphere of mass emotion trying to use it as best we can and as soon as we can. To assert pressure from all angles on the Brits. (Smuggled prison communication from Bobby Sands, August 1980, quoted in Clarke 1987 pp. 242–3, 245)

The IRA's 'Long War' strategy, developed in the late 1970s, had advocated such a political mobilisation.

The first Hunger Strike fizzled out in December 1980 when the strikers believed that the British Government had made concessions on the substance of their demands. Publicly, Thatcher took a resolute stand against the Hunger Strikers; privately the government 'encouraged dialogue' inside the prison and urged the Foreign Office to make contact with the prisoners (O'Malley 1990 pp. 30, 31–5). When British concessions were not forthcoming, the Provisionals thought they had been duped by the British Government and this experience was to inform their handling of the second Hunger Strike.

A second Hunger Strike was launched in March 1981 and led by Bobby Sands. He was unexpectedly elected to Westminster at a by-election on 9 April 1981 which brought the Hunger Strikers great publicity. During the campaign voters were urged to vote for Sands to save his life. Controversially, the SDLP withdrew from the by-election contest to avoid splitting the nationalist vote and this allowed Sands to defeat the UUP candidate by 30 492 votes to 29 046, on a very high turnout of 86.9 per cent. The DUP did not stand to avoid splitting the unionist vote. After 66 days on hunger strike, Sands died on 5 May 1981; over 100 000 people attended his funeral. Nine other republican prisoners followed Sands to their deaths. Both the British Government and the IRA leadership in the Maze 'were impervious to the pleas for compromise, obsessed with the manipulation of the propaganda war, determined to prevail no matter what the cost. Each mimicked the other's behaviour' (O'Malley 1990 p. 64). The diminishing publicity gained by the Hunger Strike and the apparent futility of further deaths increased pressure for the strike to be called off. On 3 October 1981 the Hunger Strike was ended, 217 days after it had started. By the end of 1981 'the prisoners had been granted the substance of their demands'. Concessions would only be granted once the hunger strikers had been defeated and 'the concessions had ceased to be non-negotiable demands' (O'Malley 1990 pp. 200, 211).

The British Government faced down the Hunger Strikers partly to prevent a backlash from among unionists and British public opinion, 92 per cent of whom opposed granting political status to the IRA (O'Malley 1990 pp. 198–9, 201, Prior, NIC, 6 November 1980). The effect of the Hunger Strikes on unionists was disastrous. Nationalists argued that the republican prisoners were political and this was indicated by the way in which they had been sentenced in non-jury courts, their non-criminal family background and the huge increase in the prison population. Unionists tended to interpret the election of Sands and the turnout at his funeral as implying widespread Catholic support for terrorists who had murdered members of their community. After the Hunger Strikes and Sinn Féin's subsequent success with the ballot box, it was no longer possible to argue convincingly that there was no substantial Catholic support for the IRA and their 'armed struggle' which had killed so many Protestants. For unionists the publicity and interest surrounding the deaths of hunger strikers contrasted painfully with the funerals of 22 UDR and RUC men who had been killed by the IRA during the Hunger Strikes (O'Malley 1990 pp. 181–2). The SDLP, which had contributed to Sands' victory by declining to stand in the by-election, was condemned by unionists who said that: 'its repeated denunciations of violence and the IRA were a charade concealing the murderous intent behind the conciliatory words of Catholics. All Catholics were Republicans, enemies of the state' (O'Malley 1990 p. 165).

The alienation of unionists was reflected in the electoral support given to the hardline DUP. In the local government elections of May 1981 the DUP narrowly out-polled the UUP by 26.6 per cent to 26.5 per cent, illustrating the polarisation of opinion in Northern Ireland engendered by the Dublin Summit and the Hunger Strikes. In the local government election of 1977 the UUP had established a 16.9 per cent lead over the DUP. The centrist Alliance Party also lost ground between 1977 and 1981: its vote fell from 14.4 per cent to 8.9 per cent. At the European election of 1979 the DUP's Ian Paisley had easily beaten the UUP candidate by 29.8 per cent to 21.9 per cent, and this pattern in European elections was to be repeated. The DUP challenge to the UUP only eased in 1985. There was even speculation that Paisley might adopt a more 'moderate' approach towards negotiations with nationalists now that he appeared· to be winning the battle for leadership of the unionist bloc. In this atmosphere of polarisation, a political accommodation between nationalists and unionists was less likely.

Publicly Mrs Thatcher and the Labour Opposition were resolute against the hunger strikers. Privately, the government was negotiating with them, prepared to show some flexibility but not lose face. The Foreign Office was more concerned than the NIO with the impact of the Hunger Strikes on international opinion and opened up direct contact with the prisoners. The NIO was in touch with the prisoners through priest intermediaries (O'Malley 1990 p. 197). Gerry Adams later commented on the public/private contrast in the British Government's position:

> The fact is...that the British Government in their general demeanour and general public position were telling lies because on the one hand while Margaret Thatcher was saying the hunger strikers were the IRA playing its last card, on the other hand [a governmental official] was relaying to the IRA prisoners involved exactly what Mrs Thatcher's position was...The private position was a considerable bit apart from their public position in terms of the content as well as in the substance of what they were saying. (O'Malley 1990 p. 100, also p. 197)

Publicly, the British Labour Party gave full, bipartisan support to Thatcher's non-concession policy and its spokesperson visited Bobby Sands in prison to express this position. Privately, the Labour Party leader, Michael Foot, urged Thatcher to make concessions (Thatcher 1993 p. 391). The Irish Government did not grant its IRA prisoners political status, and the political position adopted by the Irish parties towards the Hunger Strikers shifted depending on whether the party was in government or opposition. With the 'responsibility' of government, both major Irish parties pursued similar policies (O'Malley 1990 pp. 149, 152–3).

The republicans won a huge propaganda victory during the Hunger Strikes. They were able to portray the political nature of the conflict in Northern Ireland to the outside world (criminals tend not to kill themselves on hunger strike) and also demonstrate a significant base of popular support (*The Sunday Times*, 31 May 1981). This represented a blow to the British Government's attempts to normalise the conflict and criminalise the IRA. The Hunger Strikes of 1981 unexpectedly led Sinn Féin into electoral politics, although it may have been a logical next step in the IRA's 'Long War' strategy.

However, Sinn Féin's entry into the electoral arena was likely to place constraints on the IRA's violence: the Sinn Féin 'fish' needed a supportive nationalist 'sea' if they were to be electorally successful. The IRA curtailed its violence to maximise the mobilisation of support for the Hunger Strikers (Smith 1995 pp. 160–1). At Sinn Féin's Ard Fheis (conference) in 1981 Danny Morrison asked, 'Who here really believes we can win the war through the ballot box? But will anyone here object if, with a ballot paper in one hand and the Armalite in the other, we take power in Ireland?' The Ard Fheis voted to contest the local elections and to take their seats if they won. Sinn Féin performed strongly, electing two candidates to Westminster and two to the Dáil. They reached their electoral peak at the Westminster General Election in 1983, winning 13.4 per cent of the vote but failing to dislodge the SDLP (17.9 per cent) as the main nationalist party. There appeared to be a real danger that Sinn Féin might overtake the SDLP and become the dominant nationalist party. This threatened to reduce the chances of any accommodation between nationalism and unionism, worsening the security situation and destabilising Ireland. Although there was evidence in the European elections of 1984 and the local government elections of 1985 that Sinn Féin's vote had peaked, the Irish Government exploited the republican threat to put pressure on the British Government to sign the Anglo–Irish Agreement in 1985 (Fitzgerald 1991 p. 529). Fitzgerald argued, 'The Anglo–Irish Agreement is the result of the IRA's performance on the hunger strike' (O'Malley 1990 p. 221).

Conclusion

Since partition British Governments had attempted to avoid re-opening the 'Irish Question'. Troops were reluctantly deployed on the streets of Northern Ireland in 1969 and only when disaster threatened was direct rule finally introduced in 1972. Between 1972 and 1974 some movement towards Irish unity seemed to be the most promising way of extricating Britain from the conflict. The Protestant backlash and unionist resistance defeated power-sharing and closed off this option. The limit of the British Government's power to impose a solution on the conflict was exposed. The British Government's best chance of withdrawing from Northern Ireland now appeared to be an independent Ulster rather than Irish unity, this reflected a new awareness of unionist power. The British

Government deliberately encouraged withdrawal speculation in order to engage the IRA in a truce and demoralise the republican movement. Nationalists, and even republicans, in Ireland responded to the prospect of a British withdrawal with consternation since it was most likely to lead to a destabilising civil war. Anticipating a withdrawal, the violence became more communal between republican and loyalist paramilitaries. In the meantime the British Government was able to reduce the burden of the conflict on the army and finally implement a policy of Ulsterisation. Britain settled down for the 'Long War' with its strategy for both the 'real' and 'propaganda' war against the IRA in place. As unionist constitutional insecurity decreased and the security forces secured greater success against the IRA, loyalist paramilitary violence dropped away. The IRA reorganised itself into a cellular structure for the 'real' war and prepared its resistance to Britain in the propaganda war, resulting in the confrontation over the Hunger Strikes.

In the propaganda war between 1974 and 1981 the British attempted to underline the (not altogether compatible) image of the conflict as communal (unionists versus nationalists), terrorist (state versus international, possibly Marxist, subversion) or criminal (police versus psychopaths/godfathers), while the republicans countered with their view of the conflict as an historically resonant, colonial one between British 'imperialists' and the 'freedom fighters' of the IRA. The republican movement effectively resisted Britain's 'normalisation' strategy, scoring a 'victory' in the propaganda war over the Hunger Strikes. The confrontation between the British Government and the Hunger Strikers portrayed a simple, colonial picture of haughty British imperialism against brave 'freedom fighters' which had been so familiar in the British retreat from the Empire. The position of unionists is lost in this image of British–IRA confrontation although the views of unionists probably constrained the British response to the Hunger Strikes. The lack of an overriding British interest in Northern Ireland beyond stability and the autonomy of unionist resistance to Irish unity undermines the credibility of republican ideology.

The public, high profile, propaganda war played out between the parties to the conflict had disguised various political realities which are often only privately acknowledged. The British Government maintained its propaganda offensive against republicans through criminalisation and normalisation whilst privately (and implicitly during the Truce) accepting that the republicans were largely politically motivated. Publicly British Governments refused to deal with terrorists while privately they investigated the possibility of a negotiated settlement. The Irish Government publicly maintained its commitment to Irish unity while privately was anxious to prevent British withdrawal and also co-operated with its traditional enemy against the IRA.

British policy appeared to swing from one extreme (speculation about withdrawal) to another (proposals for integration). The prospects for power-sharing had plummeted after the electoral collapse of 'moderates' and the failure of the Constitutional Convention. The Labour Government and Conservative Opposition sought UUP support in a finely balanced House of Commons by offering a more unionist approach to policy. The Irish Government and the SDLP responded to the unionist drift of British policy by adopting a more militantly nationalist negotiating stance and attempting to bring international, mainly US, pressure to bear on the British Government. Integration, by further alienating nationalists and republicans, offered the British little prospect of a stable settlement. After 1979, when Unionist MPs did not occupy such a pivotal position in the House of Commons, both the Labour Party and the new Conservative Government swiftly retreated from their prior, more integrationist position. The Conservative Government rejected the integrationist promise of its election manifesto and pursued the twin-track approach of power-sharing and an Irish dimension. The constraints operating on British Governments of whatever political conviction have ensured a broad, underlying continuity of policy (Dixon 2000b). This explains why Mrs Thatcher – purportedly a champion of unionism – was to develop a process which resulted in the Anglo–Irish Agreement of 1985, seen by most unionists as a terrible betrayal of the Union.

8

The Anglo–Irish Agreement: Origins and Impact

The Anglo–Irish Agreement (AIA) was signed by the British and Irish Governments on 15 November 1985. The 'Conservative and Unionist' Prime Minister, Margaret Thatcher, stout defender of British sovereignty against the European Union, had signed an Agreement which gave a foreign government a consultative role in British policy towards Northern Ireland. What had brought about the shift in Conservative policy from the integrationism of its 1979 election manifesto to the Anglo–Irish Agreement? Did the AIA represent a 'remarkable *volte face*' in Anglo–Irish relations, or was there more evolution and continuity in British policy? Did the British sign the AIA primarily in order to improve the security situation in Northern Ireland, by addressing nationalist alienation and winning the Republic's co-operation in the fight against terrorism? Was the AIA designed to coerce unionists and nationalists into power-sharing? Or was it just a step towards accommodation?

Negotiating the Anglo–Irish Agreement 1981–85

By the end of 1981 Northern Ireland had been polarised by the experience of the Hunger Strike and the murder of the Unionist MP Robert Bradford by the IRA. James Prior, who succeeded Humphrey Atkins as Secretary of State for Northern Ireland in September 1981, said privately that 'the province was "closer to civil war than is generally recognised"' (NIC Minutes, 28 January 1982). In January 1982 Prior outlined his thinking on Northern Ireland to the important Conservative Backbench Northern Ireland Committee (Needham 1998 p. 27). 'The involvement of the minority was essential for the defeat of terrorism.' 'Mr Prior said political advance was the vital prerequisite for improved security: since it would lead the Roman Catholic community to give their firm support to the security forces' (NIC 28 January 1982). Integration was not a possibility since discussion with the local parties revealed 'a complete lack of interest'. Inactivity 'made it very difficult for the government to defend its Irish policy in times of grave crisis' (NIC 28 January 1982) and cope with the political burden of dealing with Northern Ireland (Goodall 1993 p. 127). The British Government was concerned both at the plight of the SDLP (Prior, NIC 24 May 1984) and the gains made by the DUP at the expense of the UUP. Prior had 'deliberately ignored' Paisley 'so as to strengthen the hands of the Official Unionists (though so far that tactic had not had the desired effect)' (NIC 28 January 1982). Prior also expressed concern at the size of the subsidy to Northern Ireland.

In 1982 Jim Prior launched his 'Rolling Devolution' initiative. Elections were held for a Northern Ireland Assembly. Powers would increasingly be devolved to the Assembly if it demonstrated its ability to win cross-community support by 70 per cent voting for the devolution of further powers. Although the 'vast majority' of the cabinet supported Prior's plan, Thatcher was opposed and encouraged Conservative backbench opposition (Prior 1986 p. 199). According to Prior, Thatcher watered down his proposals on the Irish dimension and 'was worried about any form of, or even any suggestion of, devolution, for fear that this would give an opportunity once more to the advocates of devolution in Scotland and Wales to revive their campaigns' (Prior 1986 p. 197). The SDLP and Sinn Féin (SF) took part in the elections to the Assembly but the SDLP – under electoral pressure from Sinn Féin – refused to participate on the grounds that it ignored the Irish dimension. Sinn Féin also boycotted the Assembly.

The Conservative triumph at the British General Election of 1983 and Fire Gael/Labour's victory in the December 1982 Irish election opened up a window of opportunity for a significant British–Irish initiative on Northern Ireland. The Irish had pushed for an initiative in the second part of 1983 and discussions were started between officials (Dermot Nally for the Irish, and David Goodall for the British). As Goodall pointed out, the two Prime Ministers were coming to the initiative with 'widely differing positions', although both related to the threat of Sinn Féin to security and political stability. Thatcher 'was determined not to compromise the Union' and 'was interested primarily in finding ways of improving the security situation, and in particular of improving cross border cooperation against terrorism between the British and Irish security forces' (Goodall 1993 p. 129). The 'acid test' of any British–Irish deal was security and particularly cross-border co-operation (Young 1989 pp. 472–4, Goodall 1993 p. 129, Thatcher 1993 pp. 385, 397, 415, ICBH 1997 pp. 51–3). Thatcher sought an agreement 'which would acknowledge in a public way the Republic's interest in the affairs of the North, while keeping decision-making out of its hands and firmly in ours' (Thatcher 1993 p. 398). Geoffrey Howe, the Foreign Secretary, later recalled that in return for 'more effective cross-border security co-operation from the Irish Government' (favoured particularly by Thatcher) the Irish had to be able to demonstrate an enhancement of their political role in Northern Ireland (Howe 1994 p. 417). The British Government proposed a Joint Security Commission to consider joint policing both sides of the border, and Thatcher also requested a study into the feasibility of repartition (which she had considered in the mid-1970s), as this might produce political and security gains (Fitzgerald 1991 pp. 517–18, Thatcher 1993 p. 398, Howe 1994 p. 420).

The Irish Government was alarmed at the growth in political support for Sinn Féin and feared this would spread to the Republic and undermine its stability (Goodall 1993 p. 129). An initiative which addressed nationalist alienation could demonstrate to nationalists the advantages of constitutional politics and cut off Sinn Féin's advance. Fitzgerald would 'drastically lower nationalist sights on Irish unification' in return for an institutionalised role for the Republic in Northern Ireland which would promote reform and address national-ist alienation. The Irish argued that a role for the Republic in law and order in Northern Ireland, perhaps a mixed British–Irish police force operating in nationalist areas and British and Irish judges sitting in the Northern Ireland courts, would make the Union more acceptable to nationalists. The Irish Government also hoped that the British Government would concede Joint Authority in return for the repeal of the territorial claim (Goodall 1993 p. 130, Howe 1994 p. 416).

The ambition of the AIA was toned down due to British misgivings. The British doubted the capacity of the Irish Government to deliver a referendum in the Republic on Articles 2 and 3, which was necessary to change the constitution. The British also feared the attempt might provoke a republican backlash in the South, wrecking the initiative (Fitzgerald 1991 p. 511). In addition, Thatcher also felt the price the Republic was asking for repeal of Articles 2 and 3 was too high (Thatcher 1993 pp. 395, 399). The option of Joint Authority, strongly opposed by unionists, was ruled out by the British Government, but the 'central concept' of the AIA was established:

> firm and formal Irish acceptance of the Union (though without the repeal of Articles 2 and 3 of the constitution) as a basis from which the Irish Government, on behalf of the nationalist minority in Northern Ireland, could be given a systematic and institution-alised influence on British decision-making there without any diminution of British sovereignty. (Goodall 1993 p. 130)

Jim Prior argued the case for a fresh Anglo–Irish initiative if the political and security situation was not to get out of hand. He told the Conservative Backbench Northern Ireland Committee in November 1983: 'The Irish Republic now had as stable a government as it was ever likely to get, and so a great opportunity existed to move for-ward; it should be taken during the next year (or two, at the outside)' (NIC 10 November 1983). Prior was frustrated by the negativity of the Ulster Unionists who 'were making no overtures whatsoever to the SDLP. The Unionists' "retraction of their commitment to the minority" – coming at a time of great SDLP weakness – had the most serious implications. It would be disastrous if Provisional Sinn Féin overtook the SDLP' (NIC, 10 November 1983). If this happened Prior could foresee the whole of Ireland being taken over by Sinn Féin, a Marxist organisation, and this could result in the whole of Ireland becoming 'a Cuba off our western coast' (*Irish Times*, 11 November 1983, Prior 1986 p. 235).

Constitutional Irish nationalism launched the New Ireland Forum 1983–84 to develop a common nationalist approach to Northern Ireland and bolster the SDLP against Sinn Féin. All the major parties in the Republic participated, along with the SDLP. The elect-oral challenge of Sinn Féin shifted Fitzgerald's priorities from attempting to reach out to unionists to bolstering constitutional nationalism in the north. There were differences among nationalists over whether Irish unity required the consent of a majority of people in Northern Ireland. Fine Gael accepted consent, while Fianna Fáil's leader, Charles Haughey argued that unionist consent could result from pressure and coercion (Kenny 1986 pp. 44–5, 67, 108). Nevertheless the New Ireland Forum Report was issued recom-mending three options: a unitary Irish state; a federal state; and joint authority. The latter implied a continuing role for the British in North-ern Ireland and represented a step away from the other traditional nationalist options, which Fitzgerald claims were necessary to defend his nationalist flank from Fianna Fáil.

Margaret Thatcher's 'dismissal' of the three recommendations in the Forum Report, in what became known as her 'Out! Out! Out!' statement in November 1984, may have disguised a privately more sympathetic approach. The press and Irish reaction suggested the British–Irish summit had not gone well. However, there had been 'a great deal of common ground' between the two governments and, according to the Secretary of State for Northern Ireland, Douglas Hurd, 'The importance of the [Forum] document was fully appreciated on our side: Garrett Fitzgerald was correct in saying that the analysis of the problem contained in the Report marked a step forward' (NIC, 22 November 1984, Fitzgerald in ICBH 1997 p. 18, Needham 1998 p. 39). Margaret Thatcher came under strong pressure from within the cabinet, her advisers and US opinion to modify what was publicly perceived to be her negative stance towards the Republic.

British ministers referred to the government's 'twin-track' strategy in Northern Ireland. This was 'designed on the one hand to involve the constitutional nationalists in the institutions of Northern Ireland, and on the other to make progress on the Anglo–Irish front' (Hurd quoted in *The Observer*, 31 March 1985, Scott in NIC, 28 March 1985). Chris Patten was investigating by shuttle diplomacy whether a model of internal government could be constructed 'capable of winning [the] "reluctant acquiescence" of both communities (it was unrealistic to expect enthusiastic approval)' (NIC, 28 March 1985). Nationalist alienation and the Sinn Féin threat to the SDLP could be offset by giving the Irish Government a say in the affairs of Northern Ireland. By June 1985 Patten announced that the Government was not going to be able 'to bring both the internal train and the Anglo–Irish train into the station at the same time' (NIC, 13 June 1985). The Anglo–Irish train was coming in and it was hoped the SDLP might be prepared to enter a devolved internal arrangement in its wake. Patten underestimated unionist reaction to this proposal: he thought there was only a 'risk' that unionists would be too alienated to talk about progress on devolution. According to Patten, 'The SDLP wanted as much influence in an internal arrangement as they received in 1974 or at the very least influence commensurate with their share of the total vote' (NIC, 13 June 1985). The British Government's overtures to the Irish Government may have been 'balanced' by a more repressive stance on security policy to reassure unionism (*The Observer*, 31 March 1985).

Moderating Unionists?

On the one hand unionists could be reassured by Thatcher's 'Iron Lady' resolution during the Hunger Strike and 'unionist' reputation. On the other, the Conservative Government's abandonment of its integrationist policy, the 1980 Dublin Summit, Rolling Devolution and suggestions of an Anglo–Irish initiative concerned unionists. The UUP's improved performance against the DUP in the British General Election of 1983 gave it some room for manoeuvre towards a more accommodating stance. In April 1984 the UUP launched *The Way Forward* policy document which proposed that the Northern Ireland Assembly should be given a greater administrative function, and committees composed in proportion to the parties in the Assembly would take responsibility for health and education from unelected area boards. Prior welcomed the document as 'a considerable step forward' (NIC, 24 May 1984). The DUP document, *The Future Assured,* was also relatively accommodating, proposing that any bill rejected by a proportionally representative departmental committee would require a weighted majority of 60 per cent in the assembly before it became law. In early 1985 the unionist leaders were trying to encourage the SDLP to participate in and shore up the Northern Ireland Assembly in the optimistic belief that the tide was going their way (Aughey 1989 pp. 67, 69).

Douglas Hurd found Northern Ireland politicians to be privately courteous but publicly aggressive, 'All the constitutional parties had constituencies to answer to, and were wary of breaking free from the tired old rhetoric' (Stuart 1998 p. 146). Shortly before the Anglo–Irish Agreement was signed, the Northern Ireland Assembly Devolution Report Committee published the 'Catherwood proposals' in September 1985, offering for discussion a proposal giving the minority some checks and balances in a devolved assembly. In correspondence between Thatcher and the leaders of the two unionist parties in August and September 1985, Molyneaux and Paisley 'accepted the need for a cooperative and formalised relationship between Dublin and London' but opposed an Anglo–Irish Secretariat which would give the Republic 'a direct influence in the internal affairs of Northern Ireland'. While unionists would accept protection for minority interests, they would not accept power-sharing 'as of right' at executive level (Aughey 1989 p. 187).

There is some question as to whether the UUP's apparently more accommodating stance in the run-up to the signing of the AIA in

November 1985 was a genuine shift of stance or a tactical manoeuvre to undermine the inter-governmental negotiations and capture the moral high ground in the wake of any agreement. Conservative ministers were sceptical of the more moderate developments in unionist thinking (Chris Patten, NIC, 13 June 1985). In November 1984 the Secretary of State for Northern Ireland, Douglas Hurd, said 'In private, political leaders are reasonably responsive to the government's ideas: but in public they were difficult. Therefore, the moderate elements in the Official Unionist documents had not been fully tested' (NIC, 22 November 1984). Even Conservative allies of the Ulster Unionists were frustrated by their apparent intransigence. John Biggs-Davison argued that if the Official Unionists continued to be difficult the logical thing might be for the Conservatives to organise in Northern Ireland (NIC, 20 June 1985). T. E. Utley, a leading Conservative unionist, confidante of Margaret Thatcher and leader writer for *The Daily Telegraph*, argued:

> Our interest lay in obtaining greater cross-border co-operation on security where huge scope existed for improvement. It was necessary to face the fact that although the Irish Republic regards the IRA as a great threat, co-operation with Britain will remain a sensitive political issue in the South. Thus gestures should be made towards them as long as they did not create panic among Unionists in the North. The gestures would not lead to unity, but should be designed to produce a more favourable disposition to increased co-operation on security. The attainment of that aim was surrounded by considerable difficulty. It must not be obtained at the price of an injudicious concession.

Utley favoured integration but argued that 'it would be difficult to restore efficient local government if Sinn Féin obtained a large representation, and thus received a degree of legitimacy which it could exploit in ways that would make security worse' (NIC, 21 February 1985).

Explaining the Anglo–Irish Agreement 1985

The Anglo–Irish Agreement was signed on 15 November 1985, giving the Republic a consultative role in the running of Northern Ireland. Both governments 'affirmed that any change in the status of

Northern Ireland would only come about with the consent of a majority of the people of Northern Ireland'. The Agreement set up a British–Irish Intergovernmental Conference (IGC) which would meet regularly and on which the Irish Government delegation would represent northern nationalist interests on issues of politics, security, legal/justice issues, cross-border co-operation, identities and cultural traditions, and discrimination. The British and Irish Governments would make 'determined efforts... to resolve any differences' between them. Cross-border co-operation was to be promoted in security, economic, social and cultural matters. Provision was also made for a devolved, power-sharing assembly to takeover some of the functions of the IGC. A permanent secretariat made up of British and Irish civil servants was established at Maryfield, outside Belfast. The International Fund for Ireland was established to promote economic and social advance and encourage contact, dialogue and reconciliation throughout Ireland.

There are contending explanations for the signing of the AIA which tend to place different weight on one or a combination of the following, often inter-related and overlapping, arguments.

Fear of Sinn Féin

Constitutional nationalists in Ireland and the British Government were fearful that Sinn Féin might overtake the SDLP and become the principal party of nationalists in the North. This would make the chances of accommodation within the North a more distant prospect, could worsen the security situation and threaten the stability of Ireland (Thatcher 1993 p. 401). The Irish Government attempted to shore up the SDLP against SF, while the British Government attempted to deal with the IRA's threat to security and simultaneously pacify unionism. The Irish and British Governments both had an interest in redressing nationalist alienation and improving security co-operation in order to deal with the republican electoral and security threat (Fitzgerald 1991 p. 475). In negotiations the Republic wanted northern nationalist alienation dealt with by reform of the security system. Proposals for this included: reform of the RUC (possibly a separate Catholic police force in nationalist areas); Irish judges involved in joint courts; three judge courts; and the police patrolling with the British Army. By the time it was realised that SF's vote had peaked a momentum had developed in the negotiations, 'and the joint fear of Sinn Féin electoral success had gradually been replaced on both sides by a positive hope of seriously undermining its existing support within the nationalist community' (Fitzgerald 1991 p. 532). For the British the AIA could address nationalist alienation, strike at the base of Sinn Féin's support and improve security co-operation with the Republic against the IRA.

Security Policy

Several key sources confirm that Margaret Thatcher's principal motivation for signing the Anglo–Irish Agreement was security (Young 1989 pp. 472–4, Lawson 1992 p. 670, Goodall 1993 p. 129, Thatcher 1993 pp. 385, 397–8, 413 Howe 1994 p. 415). Thatcher realised that unless she took a 'wider political approach' which dealt with nationalist alienation in Northern Ireland, she would not be able to improve the security situation. To defeat the IRA, first, they had to be rejected by the nationalist community; second, they had to be deprived of international support; and third, relations between Britain and the Republic had to be carefully managed (Thatcher 1993 pp. 383–4). David Goodall, who was in the Cabinet Office and who helped negotiate the AIA, emphasises the importance Thatcher placed on the importance of security. She had wanted an agreement limited to security co-operation:

> And one of the tasks, certainly of Geoffrey Howe and also of officials, was to try and convey to the Prime Minister, get her to understand, that it was suicide for an Irish Government to enter into a security arrangement with the British which had no political content, which would simply make the Irish Government in the eyes of their own electorate appear to be supporting British military and security activity in Northern Ireland, without any political benefit for it.

The Republic would accept the legitimacy of the Union while gaining an Irish dimension which would end nationalist alienation (ICBH 1997 pp. 51–3). Fitzgerald hoped that reduced nationalist alienation and reform of the security forces in Northern Ireland would undermine the minority's toleration of the IRA (Fitzgerald 1991 p. 496). Mrs Thatcher later complained about the Irish Government's failure to deliver security improvements. This did not necessarily relate to a rise in the statistics of violence but to 'the real danger that

Sinn Féin would replace the SDLP as the main voice of nationalist opinion – with the inevitable consequence that violence and terrorism would increase' (Howe 1994 p. 415). Thatcher claimed that the AIA failed to deliver any significant improvement in the security situation, and its alienation of unionism led her to regret signing the Agreement.

External Pressure

The Anglo–Irish Agreement was signed to contain external pressure from the Republic, the USA and Europe on the British Government (Fitzgerald pp. 468, 535). Irish Government sources claim that their lobbying for US pressure played a decisive role in persuading Thatcher to modify her position (Wilson 1995 p. 245) while Guelke argues that US pressure probably played a significant role (Guelke 1988 p. 147). Others play down US influence: the British Foreign Secretary during this period, Geoffrey Howe, wrote, 'Only rarely were we under direct pressure from the other side of the Atlantic specifically to change our policies' (Howe 1994 p. 422). However, Thatcher also mentions international opinion as a constraining factor on British policy and the advantages of the AIA in dealing with it (Thatcher 1993 pp. 403, 413).

Bureaucratic Conflict

It has been suggested that the AIA was driven by bureaucrats and that they actually sought to circumvent Thatcher's instinctive opposition to the Agreement (Fitzgerald 1991 p. 334, Howe 1994 p. 414). There is considerable evidence of bureaucratic conflict over the negotiation of the AIA between the Cabinet Office, Foreign Office and the Northern Ireland Office. Robert Armstrong and David Goodall were responsible for negotiating much of the AIA on behalf of the British Government and favoured a more ambitious settlement. The Foreign Office was concerned at the damage Northern Ireland did to the UK's international image, particularly in the USA. This contrasted with the 'narrow contributions' (Donoughue 1987 p. 135) from the 'traditionalists' (Howe 1994 p. 420) in the Northern Ireland Office. The NIO was closer to conditions on the ground and 'more realistic' than the English-based civil service about the impact of policy changes on Northern Ireland, particularly, perhaps, on how far the unionists could be pushed (see

Fitzgerald 1991 p. 510). Although they warned Thatcher of a back-lash against the AIA, even the NIO did not anticipate its extent (Howe 1994 p. 420, Stuart 1998 pp. 138–9, 150). Robert Andrew, the Permanent Secretary at the NIO from 1984 to 1988, argued: 'We were very conscious of what had happened at Sunningdale...and we were conscious that if this agreement was pushed too far and was too radical, there would be a very strong reaction from the Union-ist majority' (ICBH 1997 pp. 21, 40). Tom King, who succeeded Hurd as Secretary of State for Northern Ireland in September 1985, probably reflected the influence of the NIO when he raised 'serious concerns' about the AIA just after he came into office (Fitzgerald 1991 pp. 557–8, Howe 1994 p. 425).

British Withdrawal

Unionists argued that the Anglo–Irish Agreement was yet another turn of the ratchet in Britain's long-term goal of withdrawal from Northern Ireland in which the Union was by stages being destroyed. The British were being driven by the bombing campaign of the IRA and the Foreign Office's need to appease US opinion and bring the Republic into NATO. *The Times* commented that the three men primarily responsible for the AIA – Armstrong, Howe and Hurd – saw Northern Ireland as an encumbrance, 'a drain on the economy and an obstacle in foreign relations', and did not have any enthusiasm for the Union (*The Times*, 5 December 1985, quoted in Cochrane 1997 p. 16). This account is plausible but lacks evidence and underestimates the difficulties which would face the British Government in trying to manipulate Northern Ireland out of the Union, and which had emerged so starkly in the early to mid-1970s.

Coercive Power-Sharing

This argument suggests that unionists were blocking any progress towards power-sharing devolution in Northern Ireland. The Anglo–Irish Agreement was therefore a rational, Machiavellian masterplan which, by establishing a stronger Irish dimension, coerced the unionists into seriously negotiating a power-sharing settlement with nationalists (McGarry and O'Leary 1996 pp. 234, 238). David Goodall, who worked in the Cabinet Office and was involved with the negotiation of the AIA, argues that it was intended to introduce an Irish dimension without ending the Union but also contained an incentive designed 'to push the people of the Province in the direction of devolution and power-sharing' (Goodall 1993 pp. 129, 131). Yet the evidence overwhelmingly supports Goodall's view, along with all the other key sources, that *Thatcher's* primary motivation in negotiating the AIA was to undermine the IRA and win the co-operation of the Republic against terrorism.

The Irish Government may have felt that the AIA would shoe-horn the unionists into power-sharing, but there is little evidence and considerable doubt as to whether this loomed large in the calculations of Margaret Thatcher, although others in the government and bureaucracy may have nursed this hope. Thatcher's doubts about power-sharing devolution were apparent in her hostility to Prior's Rolling Devolution initiative which she felt was unrealistic and might set a dangerous precedent for devolution in Scotland and Wales (Thatcher 1993 p. 400, but see p. 387). One report suggests that Thatcher favoured an Irish dimension over devolution as a way of calming nationalist alienation (*Irish Times*, 2 March 1982). Nick Scott told Conservative backbenchers before the signing of the AIA that full power-sharing 'was ruled out by the opposition of some of the parties in the province' (NIC, 28 March 1985; Hurd was also pessimistic – see Fitzgerald 1991 p. 512). Neither was the coercive element in the AIA novel, as the British had brought considerable coercive pressure to bear on the parties during the power-sharing experiment.

Thatcher: English Unionist, English Nationalist?

Thatcher claims her 'own instincts are profoundly unionist' and felt that 'given my own known attitude towards Irish terrorism they [unionists] would have confidence in my intentions' (Thatcher 1993 p. 385; see also Prior 1986 p. 196). The British Prime Minister and other leading Conservatives were shocked and bewildered by the outraged reaction of Ulster unionism to the AIA, indicating a considerable gap in perception and understanding between Ulster unionists and their English or 'British' Conservative allies. Thatcher's sympathy for Ulster Unionism in Northern Ireland was highly qualified. She was 'an anti-Unionist Unionist' (Stuart 1998 p. 140) who supported the Union but found Unionists difficult to deal with and was critical of the Unionist record of discrimination against

Catholics (Fitzgerald 1991 p. 527, Thatcher 1993 p. 386, Loughlin 1995 p. 210). By contrast, she agreed that the SDLP 'were a moderate party in comparison with the Unionists, adding that they were very courageous' (Fitzgerald 1991 p. 381).

Mrs Thatcher's attitude towards the AIA is probably best understood as that of an English Unionist (or English Nationalist as she once argued: see *The Guardian*, 16 November 1985). Her sympathy for unionism, and unionism's enthusiasm for Thatcher, was based on her hardline security stance but this served to disguise her 'weakness' on the constitutional position of Northern Ireland. Her antipathy to multiculturalism and 'homogeneous' view of the English/ British nation may have spilled over into her sceptical view of the prospects for power-sharing and sympathy for repartition. Thatcher's English nationalism is illustrated by her concern for the plight of 'our boys' in the British Army and Northern Ireland's financial drain on the rest of the UK (Needham 1998 p. 217; see also Loughlin 1995 p. 210). Her sympathy for the soldiers can partly explain her determination to improve security through the negotiation of the AIA and acceleration of the policy of Ulsterisation which kept the British Army out of the front line against terrorism (Hamill 1986 p. 257). Robert Andrew, Permanent Secretary to the NIO, reported that the reason for the Government's initiative on Northern Ireland was the economic drain on the UK, and 'she was concerned about casualties among "our boys", and "our boys" actually meant the ones on the mainland rather than the RUC, but it was concern about "our boys"' (ICBH 1997 pp. 21–2). David Goodall reports Mrs Thatcher's determination to 'do something about Ireland', 'if only to stop the drain on British lives and treasure', by implication excluding Northern Ireland from the definition of 'British' (Goodall 1997 p. 127; see also Prior 1986 p. 204, Fitzgerald 1991, Howe 1994 p. 412, Andrew ICBH 1997 p. 22, Fitzgerald ICBH 1997 p. 61).

Why was the AIA Signed?

The Anglo–Irish Agreement was the product of competing agendas and priorities. The weight of evidence of politicians and civil servants involved in the negotiation of the Anglo–Irish Agreement is overwhelmingly supportive of the argument that the Agreement was signed *by Thatcher* to improve security co-operation with the Republic and contribute to the defeat of the IRA. The rise of Sinn Féin alarmed both governments and led to a political response designed to meet the republican challenge. The considerable bureaucratic rivalry, coupled with Thatcher's apparently poor English unionist understanding of Northern Ireland, resulted in an Agreement which was the product of differing agendas. For others within the British Government and bureaucracy it may have represented a step towards accommodation along the lines of Sunningdale, but they had to 'get around' Thatcher's misgivings (Fitzgerald 1991 p. 334). 'It took a gigantic struggle by many far-sighted people to persuade her [to sign the AIA]; but, although her head was persuaded, her heart was not' (Howe 1994 p. 427). Geoffrey Howe thought the Agreement was the start of an evolving situation of historic import-ance (Fitzgerald 1991 p. 542) and 'as much as could be achieved in one generation' (Goodall 1993 p. 131). For Goodall the AIA was not a definitive solution but 'a step in the right direction, improving mutual confidence and understanding of the problems of Northern Ireland between Dublin and London, and creating a new framework within which a solution might gradually evolve' (Goodall 1993 p. 131). The Irish Government was also motivated by concern at the rise of Sinn Féin and the continuing threat the republican movement posed to the stability of the Republic. The AIA would address nationalist alienation to stem the political success of Sinn Féin. Its pursuit of Joint Authority may have been an attempt at a final British–Irish settlement.

The AIA did not represent, as Brendan O'Leary has argued, a 'remarkable *volte face*' or 'a decisive turning point in Anglo–Irish relations' (O'Leary 1997). Many of the terms of Sunningdale 'may be seen as direct precedents for those of the 1985 Agreement' (Hadden and Boyle 1989 p. 20). The former Prime Minister, Ted Heath, said there was nothing in the AIA which was not in the Sunningdale Agreement 12 years earlier. Douglas Hurd, who served both Heath and Thatcher, also favoured a settlement along the lines of Sunningdale (Stuart 1998 p. 138). The former Cabinet Secretary, Robert Armstrong – who had also been involved with Irish policy under Heath, Wilson and Thatcher, and was a leading negotiator of the Anglo–Irish Agreement – argued that it was part of a process which could be traced back to the Sunningdale Agreement and the idea of a Council of Ireland (Armstrong 1993, p. 204). The Conser-vative Government's clear majorities at Westminster in 1979 and 1983 allowed it to revive the twin-track policy previously pursued by Heath's government. The advantage of the AIA was that by dealing only with the 'external track' it could not be brought down as easily as the Sunningdale Agreement had been.

The Reaction to the Anglo–Irish Agreement

Both Thatcher and Fitzgerald 'had the same problem in mirror-image. Each was worried that they had gone too far [in the negotiations] and would lose support' (Howe 1994 p. 423). Not surprisingly the two governments tailored their contrasting interpretation of the Agreement to reduce domestic opposition: Fitzgerald addressed his republican flank by arguing that the AIA was 'as near to Joint Authority as one can get', while Thatcher soothed unionists by claiming the Irish role was merely consultative and Northern Ireland's place in the Union was actually reinforced.

Nationalists generally welcomed the AIA. The SDLP had been a leading force behind the Agreement and welcomed the British Government's decision to face down the 'unionist veto' on political progress. The SDLP was not willing to suspend the AIA to enter serious talks with unionists, and John Hume predicted that the unionists would be forced to negotiate by the end of 1986. The Irish Dáil endorsed the Agreement by 88 votes to 75 and the Seanad (Irish Senate) by 37 to 16. All the parties except Fianna Fáil supported the AIA: its leader, Charles Haughey, argued that the deal was unconstitutional and copper-fastened partition, but was later forced to qualify his opposition to the Agreement and committed his party to making it work (Mair 1987a p. 108). The republican movement publicly opposed the AIA as a security-driven agreement designed to defeat the IRA, but there is evidence that privately leading members welcomed it (Mallie and McKittrick 1997 pp. 35–6, Patterson 1997 p. 198). In the USA, the House of Representatives supported the Anglo–Irish Agreement by 380 votes to 1. The British Government encountered fierce opposition from unionists in Northern Ireland, but little from British politicians who illustrated again their lack of sympathy for Ulster Unionism by passing the AIA by 473 votes to 47.

The Unionists Revolt: Violence and the Union

Unionists saw the AIA as a step towards a united Ireland and their reaction was overwhelmingly hostile, even threatening to split the moderate Alliance Party. There were three principal unionist objections to the Agreement.

1. *Although the Agreement recognised that there could be no change in the 'current status' of Northern Ireland without the consent of a majority, nowhere was the 'current status' defined.* In 1973 the Sunningdale Agreement the British Government had stated that 'The present status of Northern Ireland is that it is part of the United Kingdom.' To demonstrate the weakness of the Republic's guarantee, two unionist politicians took a case to the Irish High Court claiming the AIA contradicted Articles 2 and 3 of the Republic's constitution. Echoing the Boland case of 1974, the Irish High Court rejected this claim but ruled that the Articles were a 'claim of legal right', a 'constitutional imperative' and Northern Ireland was not recognised as part of the UK.

2. *The AIA represented a complete capitulation to the nationalist agenda and gave the SDLP no incentive to enter into a power-sharing administration with the unionists.* Even if an assembly had been set up, the British–Irish Intergovernmental Conference would still retain considerable powers. If the AIA was merely consultative, why did Article 2 state that 'determined efforts will be made through the conference to resolve any differences'?

3. *Unionists complained because they had not been consulted by the British over the Agreement.* By contrast the SDLP, through their close relationship with the Irish Government, had been kept informed of the negotiations.

The strength of unionist opposition to the AIA was underestimated by British and Irish politicians. On 23 November there was a huge demonstration against the AIA. Although the NIO claimed the demonstration numbered only 30 000, probably to discourage further protest, there were actually 250 000 demonstrators (out of a total unionist population of about a million), 'the biggest rally of the Protestant people since... 1912' (Needham 1998 pp. 76–7). On the anniversary of the signing of the AIA in 1986 there was a protest of 200 000 people and rioting in loyalist areas. A petition in January/February 1987 raised 400000 signatures. A *Sunday Times*/MORI opinion poll published on 24 November 1985 found 83 per cent of Protestants did not think the AIA would improve the prospects for peace, while just 7 per cent thought it would. The poll asked those opposed to the AIA to indicate their support for different ways of protesting: 53 per cent favoured signing a petition; 44 per cent a mini-General Election; 39 per cent mass demonstrations; 27 per cent strikes; 15 per cent rent and rate strikes; 14 per cent refusal to pay water/electricity charges; 14 per cent a declaration of independence; 10 per cent armed revolt (*The Sunday Times*, 24 November 1985). The unionist MPs at Westminster resigned their seats so that a poll could be taken in Northern Ireland on the Anglo–Irish Agreement. In the following by-elections 418 230 votes were cast for anti-AIA candidates, representing 43 per cent of the electorate as a whole, although one unionist lost his seat to Seamus Mallon of the SDLP. The vote for the centrist Alliance Party slumped. Unionist councils refused to set rates and were fined.

The British Government anticipated unionist violence and hostility but was surprised at its extent. Thatcher called for immediate progress on the security front to placate unionists and with Tom King 'agreed that the political priority was to win over the support of at least some Unionist leaders and that wider Unionist opinion which I [Thatcher] felt was probably more understanding of what we were trying to achieve' (Thatcher 1993 p. 403). The British Government's need to placate unionist opinion is the context in which Thatcher and King made inaccurate statements which exaggerated the advantages of the Agreement to unionists. The Secretary of State for Northern Ireland, Tom King, argued that the Irish Prime Minister 'has in fact accepted that for all practical purposes and unto perpetuity there will never be a united Ireland because he has accepted the principle of consent that the will of the majority in Northern Ireland must predominate and that Northern Ireland, which is our fervent wish, remains part of the United Kingdom' (*Irish Times*, 4 December 1985). Thatcher wrongly claimed that 'the people of Northern Ireland can get rid of the intergovernmental conference by agreeing to devolved government' (*Belfast Telegraph*, 17 December 1985).

The Conservative Government had demonstrated again to unionists their English nationalist 'weakness' on the Union. Without the threat of unionist violence and civil war, the British Government probably had no overriding interest in remaining in Northern Ireland. Constitutional politics could not guarantee the Union, the Unionist MPs could easily be outvoted in the House of Commons and, as the Anglo–Irish Agreement appeared again to demonstrate, the unionism of their Conservative allies was suspect. To prevent Northern Ireland being rolled out of the Union, constitutional unionists took politics into the streets and used the *threat* of violence to demonstrate to the British and Irish Governments (and perhaps the nationalists) the limits to which unionists could be pushed, thus underlining the parameters of British policy. Had constitutional unionists failed to mobilise and show the strength of their opposition to the Agreement then the two Governments might have taken that as a signal that the British–Irish process could be accelerated towards Joint Authority (Seldon 1997 p. 432). The unionist dilemma was that constitutional unionists, by *threatening* violence, could encourage and legitimise the position of those who *actually* used violence.

The leaders of the constitutional unionist parties, Molyneaux and Paisley, were operating in a grey area in which it was difficult to discern whether their intention was to incite or contain violence. Unionist politicians were not only expressing the outrage of unionist opinion but also attempting to mobilise unionist power and threatening violence in order to set limits on British policy. At the same time, unionists ran the risk of inciting and escalating violence which would split unionism, worsen relations with nationalists and further damage the Union. The uneasy relationship between constitutional politics and the threat of violence was something that the VUPP had attempted to straddle in the 1970s. Shortly before the AIA was signed the Ulster Clubs were formed and they occupied this political ground between constitutional politics and violence, including a place on the steering committee for John McMichael of the UDA (Bruce 1994 p. 104). David Trimble, future leader of the UUP, was a member of both organisations and he described the 'unionist dilemma'.

If you have a situation where there is a serious attack on your constitutional position and liberties – and I regard the Anglo–Irish Agreement as being just that – and where the Government tells you constitutional action is ineffective, you are left in a very awkward situation... do you sit back and do nothing, or move outside constitutional forms of protest? I don't think you can deal with the situation without the risk of an extra-parliamentary campaign... I would personally draw the line at terrorism and serious violence. But if we are talking about a campaign that involves demonstrations and so on, then a certain element of violence may be inescapable. (*Newsletter*, 6 November 1986, quoted in Cochrane 1997 pp. 157–8, see also Aughey 1989 p. 72)

Unionist Politicians: Leading or Following?

At the end of February 1986 Molyneaux and Paisley appeared willing to try to reach agreement with Thatcher. At a meeting in Downing Street the leaders of the DUP and UUP were assured that the AIA would be operated sensitively and were offered concessions on new arrangements for enabling unionists to make their views known to the government; on consultations about the handling of Northern Ireland business at Westminster; and on the need for discussions on devolved government. Molyneaux and Paisley agreed to reflect on the British Government's proposals and the UUP leader expressed the hope that a forthcoming loyalist strike might not go ahead. The unionist leaders had shifted from saying initially that they would accept no part of the AIA to agreeing to discuss devolution if the AIA was suspended. The British Government wanted to be seen to be meeting unionist demands and calming their misgivings about the AIA. Tom King claimed that after devolution only cross-border security and economic co-operation would be dealt with by the IGC. When the unionist leaders returned to Belfast they were forced to retreat by their supporters and subsequently announced that they would hold no further talks with the Prime Minister unless the AIA were scrapped. Thatcher continued to oppose suspending the AIA and it was 'a gap' in the meeting of the Intergovernmental Conference that allowed the all-party Brooke Talks to get under way in 1991 (*Irish Times*, 26 February 1986, 27 February 1986).

The significance of this episode is that it illustrates the constraints operating on the unionist political elites and the problems they were to have in managing unionist opposition to the AIA. Molyneaux and Paisley had worked hard to find a compromise with the government and 'This was almost their undoing' (Aughey 1989 p. 89, Bruce 1994 p. 113) According to *The Sunday Times* it was obvious that Molyneaux and Paisley had been 'running to keep up with the pace of events in Ulster' and it would require some effort for the constitutional politicians to reassert their leadership (*The Sunday Times*, 2 March 1986, quoted in Owen 1994 pp. 61 and 75–76). The British Prime Minister recognised the dilemma of unionist leaders: 'Ian Paisley was in the forefront of the campaign against the Agreement. But far more worrying was the fact that behind him stood harder and more sinister figures who might all too easily cross the line from civil disobedience to violence' (Thatcher 1993 p. 403).

The unionist party leaders struggled to contain and control unionist protest against the AIA. On 3 March 1986 the loyalist strike against the AIA was accompanied by intimidation and rioting in which police were shot at twenty times and 47 RUC officers were injured. Attacks followed on police homes. The UUP leader, James Molyneaux, roundly condemned the violence and declared that future strikes would not be supported by his party. He was criticised by the DUP for giving up at least the threat of another day of action and the leverage this gave unionists against the British Government. The DUP argued that the level of violence had been exaggerrated and that unconstitutional action had to be 'bold and unapologetic' if it was to be effective against the British. In April a young Protestant, Keith White, was killed by a plastic bullet during rioting in Portadown. In the wake of this incident, Paisley hardened his rhetorical stance against rioting, risking the opposition of radicals within his own party (Cochrane 1997 pp. 149–50, 153). Unionist leaders were concerned that protest might escalate beyond their ability to control it. Molyneaux commented, 'the reality is that Mr Paisley and I...have been overtaken by the people of Northern Ireland' (*The Times*, 11 April 1996, quoted in Owen 1994). On 23 April 1986 a programme of protest and civil disobedience was launched to assert the control of politicians rather than paramilitaries over the anti-Agreement campaign. On 10 November 1986 a paramilitary-style militant loyalist group, Ulster Resistance, was formed. Ian Paisley participated in this group, although it has been argued that he played a moderating role within the organisation by attempting to keep control of protest and ensure it did not turn into revolt (Aughey 1989 pp. 76–7; see also Cochrane 1997 pp. 159–60, 162).

Whether unionist leaders exerted a moderating influence over their parties or not depends on your assessment of whether the people they led within their party and their electorate tended to be more 'extreme' or 'moderate' than their party leaders. In other words, to what extent do the structures in which politicians operate constrain their ability to lead their parties? The 'orthodox nationalist view' would condemn the unionist party leaders for stirring up loyalist opposition to the Agreement and encouraging it on to the streets, with the resulting violence and intimidation. This view would suggest that the unionist people are more 'moderate' than their unrepresentative politicians and that, generally, it is the politicians who cynically stoke up and exploit communal sentiment to further their own political ambitions. The constitutional pretences of unionist politicians are contrasted with the violence which is incited by their political rhetoric.

An alternative perspective would recognise the role Paisley and Molyneaux played in attempting to avert confrontation in February 1986. Finding unionist party and (perhaps) also public opinion opposed to negotiation, the two party leaders attempted to restrain and control unionist protest by leading that protest and channelling it, to some extent, into non-violent tactics. This view would emphasise the importance of unionist leaders being seen to represent and articulate unionist grievance, in order to maintain their leadership positions, but at the same time attempting to control and restrain the political expression of that grievance. In this view the unionist electorate at this point were more 'extreme' than their political leaders. Molyneaux took 'the long view' that the existence of a united unionist front on the AIA was an end in itself, maintaining unionist morale and allowing the letting-off of steam 'which had it not been released, may have been used for more destructive purposes' (Cochrane 1997 p. 193). Protest would continue until the British realised the AIA was not working. An indication that there was more extreme loyalist opinion than that being expressed by DUP leaders is apparent in the emergence and relative electoral success of the 'extremist' Protestant Unionist, George Seawright. Seawright was expelled from the DUP for anti-Catholic remarks but subsequently succeeded in winning significant support as a 'Protestant Unionist' and was elected to Belfast City Council (Bruce 1994 pp. 143–5). It is difficult to assess the constraints operating on politicians who often have a particular interest in emphasising those constraints and their own powerlessness, but it is worth considering that at times they may act in ways which are either more 'extreme' or more 'moderate' than their supporters.

Security, Polarisation and Reform

The difficulty with which the RUC policed unionist demonstrations against the AIA illustrated again Northern Ireland's 'security dilemma': the limited ability of the RUC to police the community from which it was principally drawn. Demonstrating loyalists clashed repeatedly with the RUC during the long hot summer of 1986, and some police officers were driven from their homes in loyalist areas. Between March and December 1986 there were 600 reported incidents of intimidation of police and their families; 120 police families had had to abandon their homes and 111 families were attacked or threatened on one or more occasions. Meanwhile the IRA continued its campaign of violence against the RUC. This placed considerable pressure on the overwhelmingly Protestant RUC, many of whom may have sympathised with the unionist demonstrators they were deployed to police. An above-average number of applications from RUC officers for jobs outside the force suggests strain and unrest (Owen 1994, Ryder 1997).

The RUC's willingness and ability to police Northern Ireland was once again called into question. According to Ryder, British ministers and their officials demonstrated 'a dangerous complacency... about feelings within the RUC'; 'the integrity of the force was recklessly taken for granted and the strength of emotional turmoil inside the ranks was dangerously underestimated' (Ryder 1997 p. 328). In April 1986 RUC officers were discussing mutiny, and one was quoted as saying that 'many of his colleagues were considering mutiny and resignations on a large scale' (*Irish Times*, 7 April 1986, quoted in Owen 1994 p. 73). The leaders of the DUP and UUP had placed carefully worded advertisements calling on the RUC to stage a 'Curragh style revolt' (Ryder 1997 p. 330). The Police Federation's representative in Parliament, Sir Eldon Griffiths, claimed that 'intolerable burdens were being placed on the RUC' (*Newsletter*, 11 April 1986, quoted in Owen 1994 p. 74). In a letter to *The Times* he argued, 'I adhere to the view that it is impossible in a free society for a civilian police force to police for long against the majority' (Ryder 1997 p. 329, quoting *The Times*, 30 April 1986). According to Richard Needham, the Intergovernmental Conference:

> did start to give Southern politicians and Southern policy makers a much better feel for the intractable division between the two communities in the North. They began to appreciate the limits to British power in either coercing the unionists or defeating the IRA. However much Southern ministers complained about the abuses of the security forces, they began to acknowledge in private the limits of control that could be exercised on the young men and women who were fighting terror in the hedgerows of south Armagh and in the alleyways of the Ardoyne. (Needham 1998 p. 78)

The prospects for power-sharing, already poor, appeared to recede even further as public and political opinion polarised. According to the polls, nationalist alienation did not appear to have been substantially reduced, but the AIA may have had a more subtle, favourable impact on Catholic opinion (O'Connor 1993). Some have claimed that the Brooke Talks in 1991 were a product of the AIA (Goodall 1993 p. 133). Alternatively, it could be argued that there was already movement towards power-sharing within unionism before the AIA and that the Agreement, coupled with its subsequent polarising effects in Northern Ireland on public and political opinion, delayed rather than accelerated the start of meaningful inter-party talks on power-sharing. The all-party Brooke Talks followed the announcement of a ten-week gap in the meeting of the IGC. Such a compromise might have been reached in the wake of the AIA in February/March 1986 had the Conservative Government been serious about pursuing devolution and addressing unionist grievances.

Violence increased after the AIA. Thatcher was disappointed that her restraint in developing security policies which might alienate nationalist opinion had not produced better security co-operation from the Republic against the IRA (Thatcher 1993 p. 415), although Goodall argues that cross-border security co-operation had 'significantly improved' (Goodall 1993 p. 132, Needham 1998 p. 79).

It is difficult to assess the AIA's impact in accelerating a process of reform in Northern Ireland. The strength of unionist opposition to the AIA led to the British Government 'adopting an extremely cautious position' on implementing reforms which would improve equality of opportunity and esteem or the improvement of the administration and justice. A 'tacit agreement' between the British and Irish Governments to minimise the contribution of the AIA to reform and the British emphasis on its own policy 'was intended to minimise unionist reaction to the establishment and operation of the new arrangements' (Hadden and Boyle 1989 pp. 73, 77). Therefore, northern nationalists tended not to be aware of the benefits that the AIA had reaped for them (Fitzgerald ICBH 1997 p. 64). It is also possible that some of the post-Agreement reforms would have been implemented by the British Government in any case, and that the negotiation of the AIA delayed British reforms so that they could be used as a bargaining chip in negotiations. The reform of Northern Ireland became caught up in the British–Irish negotiations of the AIA. According to the Northern Ireland Minister, Nick Scott, 'it was difficult for the government to decide whether measures designed to reassure Catholics (such as the repeal of the Flags and Emblems Act) should be undertaken as a separate exercise or as part of the hoped for agreement with Dublin' (NIC, 28 March 1985). By 1989, a review of the AIA reported that 'disappointing progress' had been made and that 'it cannot seriously be argued that the Agreement has resulted in any marked improvement in the general security situation or in better intercommunal relations' (Boyle and Hadden 1989 pp. 77, 73).

By 1988 the unionist protest against the AIA was running out of steam and the third anniversary demonstration was marked by only minor unionist protests. The UUP performed well against the DUP in elections held after the AIA. But this was not necessarily a vote for a more accommodating party since unionist opinion was moving in an increasingly integrationist direction and the share of the unionist vote was down. Within the UUP there was a majority of integrationists against a minority in favour of power-sharing (Bew, Patterson and Teague 1997 p. 72). There was also some talk of movement towards independence in the DUP and the UDA after the signing of the AIA. The SDLP had been the big winner from the AIA but increasingly appeared to be turning its back on devolution and power-sharing with unionists, favouring instead the development of the AIA into Joint Authority. The SDLP also looked to build common ground with Sinn Féin in the 1988 SDLP/SF talks. This dialogue was part of a chain of events which resulted in the IRA ceasefire of August 1994 and the 'peace process'.

Conclusion: Balancing a Settlement?

The AIA was signed by Thatcher principally to improve security but others sought movement towards a historic accommodation between unionism and nationalism along the lines of the Sunningdale Agreement. As Goodall has argued:

> any system of government for Northern Ireland which is to command the level of acceptance from each community necessary for the system to be workable must have special features to take account of the 'Irishness' of the minority as well, of course, as of the unionism and legitimate rights of the majority. This is the balance which the 1985 Agreement sought to achieve. (Goodall 1993 p. 129; see also Needham 1998 p. 88).

The British were out-negotiated by the Irish Government over the AIA, as they had been at Sunningdale, and this was a cause of

concern for unionism. Thatcher's English unionism did not appreciate the impact the Agreement would have on Ulster Unionism.
Unionists mobilised and demonstrated again their power to bring
Northern Ireland to the brink of civil war. The thrust of this power
came from below and unionist politicians struggled to assert control
over it. Without such a strong unionist reaction the British and Irish
Governments may have calculated that they could push unionists
even further in the future.

The limits of British power and its ability to impose its will on the
conflicting parties to the conflict was once again exposed. Both
Margaret Thatcher and her successor, John Major, believed that the
AIA had been a failure. For Major, the AIA 'had provoked years of
Unionist disenchantment for meagre benefits' (Major 1999 p. 433).
The unionist veto on Irish unity lay not just in the democratic
principle of consent but also in the ability of unionism to make
Northern Ireland ungovernable. There could be no British imposed
settlement (Major 1999 pp. 433, 441–2, 492). The AIA may have
resulted in the Irish Government having a greater appreciation of
the limits of British power, in particular its ability to police unionism.

The AIA is possibly more significant for its unintended than its
intended consequences. An unintended consequence of the AIA
and the British Government's subsequent 'facing down' of unionism
is that it may have helped to further undermine the republican ideological position that unionism was just a tool of British imperialism.
This growing realisation may have contributed towards the opening-
up of debate between the SDLP and SF, the IRA ceasefire in 1994
and the subsequent 'peace process' (Mallie and McKittrick 1997).

9

Endgame? The Origins of the Second Peace Process 1988–94

There are strongly divergent ideological explanations of the 'peace process' from the contending parties and governments in Britain and Ireland. These competing explanations are deployed to win political support and sympathy in the propaganda war and put pressure on other parties to the conflict to make concessions or compromises. Nevertheless, *based on the evidence available* we can cast doubt on key partisan accounts of the peace process and its evolution. In particular two influential perspectives, one unionist and one nationalist, are singled out for criticism. A more convincing explanation of the peace process, it is argued, lies in understanding the problems of attempting to achieve a 'balanced' settlement which brings both republicans and unionists to a historic accommodation along the lines of the Sunningdale settlement. During the recent conflict both the 'real war' and the propaganda war resulted in the development of a considerable gap between public rhetoric and underlying, sometimes privately acknowledged, political 'realities'. The key problem of the peace process was to bridge the ideological gap between unionists and republicans and bring sufficient cross-community elites, parties and voters to an agreement that would be sustainable. Leading participants in the peace process have attempted to choreograph its public presentation and wind down the propaganda war in order to maximise the support of diverse constituencies of public and party opinion for the process. Privately, there has been at least some recognition even among 'enemies' of the problems and constraints facing the various parties to the conflict in building peace.

This chapter reviews the events and controversies leading up to the IRA ceasefire of 1994, while the following chapter covers 1994–2000. They should be read together, and an assessment and critique of the unionist and nationalist view can be found at the end of the next chapter while an analysis of the peace process is carried out in the Conclusion. Some of the key questions of the peace process include: what are the origins of the peace process? How has the peace process been managed? Did the British Government obstruct the peace process by artificially raising the issue of decommissioning? How has the Sinn Féin leadership managed to sign up to the Good Friday Agreement which falls short of Irish unity and includes a regional assembly? How has the UUP leadership sold an agreement that includes an Irish dimension and a place for 'terrorists' in government?

Two Perspectives on the Peace Process

A Nationalist View

Nationalist accounts tend to portray the *Irish* peace process as a unilateral Irish initiative coming from John Hume and Gerry Adams supported by nationalist politicians in Northern Ireland and the Republic (O'Leary and McGarry 1996, Mallie and McKittrick 1997, Ruane and Todd 1999). Gerry Adams and John Hume enter into dialogue in 1988 and attempts are made to find common ground among nationalists in Ireland. In 1993 a 'Hume–Adams' document emerges around which Hume, Adams and the Republic's Prime Minister, Albert Reynolds, are united and this opens the way for the IRA's ceasefire in August 1994.

The British Government fails to appreciate the importance of the Hume–Adams dialogue and has to be pushed, persuaded and cajoled by the 'pan-nationalist front' (the SDLP, SF, the Irish Government and the US Government) to shift its intransigent position on Northern Ireland. However, it remains wedded to the failed path of all-party talks among the constitutional political parties, building peace from the centre out and excluding Sinn Féin. The Irish succeed in provoking a reassessment in British policy which moves slowly and reluctantly to bring the republican movement into the political process. The IRA ceasefire represents a triumph rather than a defeat for nationalism and republicanism. The British Government refuses to accept the sincerity of the ceasefire and then erects decommissioning as a further artificial barrier to IRA participation in all-party talks. This impasse over decommissioning leads to the breakdown of the IRA ceasefire in February 1996. The obstructionism of British policy is explained as being due to the Conservative government's precarious majority at Westminster and its dependence on the Ulster Unionist MPs at Westminster; the ideological affinity between Conservatives and Unionists; the influence of the security establishment; and the stupidity and incompetence of the Conservative government.

The Labour Government elected in April 1997 with a clear majority in the House of Commons accelerates the Peace Process and brings Sinn Féin to the negotiating table in spite of unionist objections. Their bluff called, the UUP sits down in all-party talks with Sinn Féin in September 1997. The Good Friday Agreement (GFA) is signed in April 1998 and supported as paving the way to Irish unity. This trend is reinforced by the growing Catholic proportion of the population of Northern Ireland. Unionists fail to fulfil their commitment to the GFA and, along with the British, insist on an IRA surrender through decommissioning. When devolution does take place it is ended by the British Government taking sides with the unionists over their demand for decommissioning. When devolution is restored the British continue to support the unionist agenda.

This account allows the Sinn Féin leadership an honourable, face-saving explanation for its involvement in the peace process which could be used to persuade the republican movement to accept its peace strategy. They could argue that it was the power of pan-nationalism, of which they were now a part, which was the driving force behind the *Irish* peace process. The war had not reached stalemate and neither were the IRA defeated; rather, the 'struggle' had been taken on to a new unarmed level where the might of pan-nationalism had demonstrated its worth by forcing the British Government into a series of reversals. The Good Friday Agreement is presented as a further step towards the ultimate goal of Irish unity.

A Unionist View

An influential unionist view sees the peace process as a 'surrender process' which is just the latest British attempt to disengage from Northern Ireland since 1921. The end of the Cold War in 1989 removed Britain's strategic interest in Northern Ireland and the IRA's City bombings of 1992 and 1993 created a powerful economic incentive for Britain to withdraw. The IRA's 1994 ceasefire was merely a tactical move to exploit the opportunities that a peace process gave them. Suspicions that a secret deal had been done between the British Government and IRA/SF were reinforced when in November 1993 the government admitted having secret 'links' with Sinn Féin. During the 'surrender process' the British Government has capitulated again and again to the terrorism of IRA/SF, who bank any political advantage and keep their guns ready to restart their terrorist campaign. The peace process has corrupted democracy by appeasing the power of the gun and the terrorist rather than respecting the people and the verdict of the ballot box. The IRA demonstrated in February 1996 that their ceasefire, contrary to pan-nationalist assurances, was not permanent but tactical.

Since 1997 the new Labour Government has capitulated to republican demands and SF has been admitted to all-party talks without any IRA decommissioning. The UUP sold out unionists by negotiating with SF and then signing the Good Friday Agreement, which represents a further step in Britain's manipulation of Northern Ireland out of the Union. Since the GFA the British have continued to concede ground to the republicans. Terrorist prisoners have been released and the RUC destroyed, while the IRA seeks to re-arm and carry out punishment beatings and shootings. The IRA have not decommissioned a single weapon yet Sinn Féin terrorists sit as Ministers for Health and Education in the new government of Northern Ireland. This unionist perspective would tend to favour the exclusion of unreconstructed terrorists from all-party talks and government. It would see the way forward as devolution resulting from talks among the constitutional parties or (for others) the closer integration of Northern Ireland with the rest of the UK.

Paradoxically, some in the Sinn Féin leadership accept this unionist account in order to reassure republicans that the peace process leads inevitably to Irish unity. Some anti-Agreement unionists have taken at face value claims by the Sinn Féin leadership that the Agreement leads to Irish unity.

'Balancing' Unionism and Nationalism

The account of the peace process presented here underlines the difficulties that the British and Irish Governments had in bringing both republicans and unionists *simultaneously* to the negotiating table in order to achieve a 'balanced settlement'. As a 'senior British source' argued: 'It is the job of the British Government to push the Unionists to a line beyond which they will not go; it is the job of the Irish Government to pull the Republicans to a line beyond which they will not come. What was left in the middle, the limits of potential agreement, would be left for discussion between the parties' (*The Observer*, 5 February 1995). This explains many of the apparent contradictions and inconsistencies in British policy during this period and leads to a more convincing explanation of the peace process than that offered by the above nationalist or unionist views (but at the risk of presenting an over-benevolent view of British policy). The problems of bringing unionist and nationalist political elites to the negotiating table and delivering their constituencies to a deal were apparent during the negotiation and failure of power-sharing in 1973–74. Then the Sunningdale Agreement was 'overbalanced' against unionism and Brian Faulkner was unable to maintain the support of his party or its supporters, a recurrent problem among unionist politicians (Seldon 1997 p. 423; see also Chapter 6 above). During the second peace process the SF leadership experienced difficulties delivering the republican movement while the UUP leadership had problems with both its party and electorate.

After 25 years of violence and propaganda war in which opponents were demonised and expectations of victory raised, there had been a polarisation among the people of Northern Ireland. Those political elites who wanted a settlement were going to have to manage the winding down of the propaganda war and prepare their respective supporters and voters for the compromises necessary for peace. This was perceived to require some choreography between the participants of the peace process in order to reassure different constituencies and bring them towards a settlement. The British Government had to balance the claims of both republican and unionist political leaders in order to create an environment which would maximise the chances of their political elites bringing their parties, supporters and voters to the negotiating table simultaneously and selling an agreement to them. It found itself in the contradictory position of having to declare itself firstly a neutral arbiter between unionism and nationalism – in order to attract republicans into the process – and also a champion of unionism, in order to reassure unionists of their place in the Union (Dixon 1998, 2000b, Major 1999 pp. 435–6, 440–2).

The British Government's attempts to investigate, through secret talks and public overtures, whether Sinn Féin would or could end their 'armed struggle' and enter the political process threatened to upset the balance between nationalism and unionism, particularly as the IRA continued to bomb and kill in Britain and Northern Ireland.

The unionists who had been the victims of so much IRA violence were suspicious that the British Government's overtures to the republican movement involved a surrender to terrorism. The British Government's courting of republicanism risked alienating unionism to the extent where loyalist and republican violence was escalating uncontrollably and any prospect of an accommodation between nationalism and unionism, whether it included SF or not, was impossible. John Major was also operating under considerable domestic pressure since his governing majority was not secure and domestic opinion might not understand his dealings with terrorists (Duignan 1995 pp. 127, 147).

Ironically, while the British Government was publicly hostile to the republican movement, privately it had every interest in seeing that Gerry Adams and the Sinn Féin leadership, *if they were genuinely intent on ending the violence*, were supported in delivering a united republican movement into a democratic political process. The British Prime Minister did have information that at least a faction within the republican movement wanted to find a way out of the violence (Major 1999 pp. 433, 436). The Northern Ireland minister, Richard Needham, wrote as far back as April 1992:

> We have come a long way since 1985. I believe the IRA (Sinn Féin) now know they cannot win but they do not know how to lose. They are frightened of schism which has confronted them before. Frightened that if some lay down their arms others will not. Then all will have been in vain. Those who died will have died for nothing, those in the Maze will stay there to rot. (Needham 1998 p. 322)

He also observed that 'Adams needed a way out which would keep his organisation armed and intact while avoiding division and internal civil war. He had to show his followers that in some way the fight had been worthwhile and he had to prise his men and women out of the prisons' (Needham 1998 p. 126).

While the republican *leadership* may have been convinced of the futility of the 'armed struggle' there was likely to be a transition period during which the leadership would have to espouse the old, violent 'politics of illusion' while they gradually attempted to shift the wider republican movement towards democratic politics (Dixon 1997d pp. 14–15). To maximise the ability of the Sinn Féin leadership to commit the republican movement to an unarmed strategy, they would need an 'honourable' way out of the conflict. The republican grassroots would have to be convinced that through 'unarmed struggle' and the 'pan-nationalist front' (SF, SDLP, Republic of Ireland, USA), republicans could wield more power than continuing with the 'armed struggle'. The peace process would therefore have to be *presented* as a solely Irish (pan-nationalist) initiative which demonstrated its power by securing a series of apparent victories over the British Government. The Irish Government might publicly take a more hardline republican stance than it privately favoured in order to show the republican movement that it was part of a wider 'pan-nationalist' movement which would champion its cause, use its influence to achieve some republican goals and not leave the movement isolated. This presentation of the Irish peace process might have appeased republicans, but it also raised unionist anxieties for their future in the Union. The British Government's role was therefore to reassure unionists and champion their concerns, as well as to encourage republicans to enter a peace process.

Unionist and republican political leaders attempted simultaneously to represent their parties and electorates while at the same time leading them towards the centre ground. This could involve contradictory actions, with hardline statements disguising fractionally more accommodating positions. Along with the contradictory messages being sent out by the British and Irish Governments (and the USA), this makes interpreting the peace process difficult. An official at the Northern Ireland Office said: 'You have to remember ... in these negotiations no one says anything necessarily because they believe what they are saying, but because they know someone else on their side expects them to say it' (*The Observer*, 5 April 1998).

Rethinking the 'Armed Struggle'?

While the 'nationalist view' suggests that the peace process was brought about as a result of Irish pressure for a change in British policy, the Provisionals were already rethinking the 'armed struggle' by the mid- to late 1980s. The confrontation between the British state and unionism over the Anglo–Irish Agreement could not be easily reconciled with a republican ideology that considered the unionists to be the tools and dupes of British imperialism. Publicly republicans attacked the AIA; privately there is evidence that leading figures welcomed it (Chapter 8). A reassessment by republicans of both

British interests and Ulster unionism was a logical development (Mallie and McKittrick 1997 pp. 33–4). The problem for observers was that while there may have been some developments in republican thinking and in Sinn Féin rhetoric, the brutal reality of the IRA's continuing violence overshadowed this and seemed a better indication of the republican movement's intentions.

The Hume–Adams talks in 1988 brought out into the open the ideological gulf between republicanism and constitutional nationalism, a gulf that by 1993–94 had been bridged and paved the way for pan-nationalist unity. During these talks Sinn Féin declared there would be no end to IRA violence before its participation in talks. They argued that the British should relinquish sovereignty over Northern Ireland and persuade the unionists to accept Irish unity, although Republicans also began to take more seriously unionist fears and concerns about a united Ireland. Sinn Féin's 1987 document, *A Scenario for Peace*, indicated a persistent vein of republican thought which saw unionists as illegitimate, temporary settlers in Ireland, it declared that 'Anyone unwilling to accept a united Ireland and wishing to leave would be offered re-settlement grants to permit them to move to Britain' (Bean 1995 pp. 18–22).

The SDLP's principal argument was that far from having key strategic and economic interests in Northern Ireland, as the AIA demonstrated, British policy towards Ireland was '*now* neutral and agnostic' (*Irish Times*, 19 September 1988; in fact, it had deployed this argument since the early 1970s). The British had no military or economic interests in Ireland; it was the opposition of one million unionists that prevented Irish unity. The SDLP made clear its opposition to the IRA's armed struggle but conceded that it was a political rather than a criminal movement, although this was not to be interpreted as lending any legitimacy to IRA actions. The SDLP favoured a strategy which welded together a 'pan-nationalist front' which brought national and international pressure to bear on the British Government to persuade unionists into a united Ireland.

There is evidence to suggest by the mid- to late 1980s the republican movement had fought itself, both politically and militarily, into a stalemate with the British Government (O'Brien 1993 p. 198, Bean 1995, Smith 1995 p. 196, Patterson 1997). While the IRA escalated its campaign of violence in order to 'sicken the British', reports from British security sources suggested that there was a sense of war-weariness among the IRA leadership which was despairing of the futility of the 'armed struggle' (O'Brien 1993 ch. 8). The contradictions of the 'ballot box and armalite strategy' generated debate within the republican movement and ideological developments. In *The Politics of Irish Freedom* (1986), Gerry Adams argued that the armed struggle was still of 'primary importance because it provides a vital cutting edge', but there was a realisation in republican circles that violence 'on its own is inadequate and that non-armed forms of political struggle are at least as important'. The 'armed struggle becomes armed propaganda' (Adams 1987 p. 64). Sinn Féin's involvement in electoral politics drew to the party many of the republican move-ment's brightest activists: 'The elitist, conspiratorial assumptions of the armed struggle were constantly undermined by the changes in republican political culture necessitated by community activism' (Bean 1995 p. 8). Sinn Féin's document, *Towards a Lasting Peace in Ireland* (1992), recognised both Northern Ireland's economic dependence on Britain and the possibility of a Protestant backlash following British withdrawal. A leading member of SF told the annual Wolfe Tone commemoration in June 1992 that British withdrawal 'must be preceded by a sustained period of peace and will arise out of negoti-ations', and Adams started to indicate a sympathy for joint authority (Patterson 1997 p. 240). In hindsight, these ideological developments within republicanism may have helped 'educate' republicans and prepare them for the compromises of the peace process.

The key question about the republican movement is whether the Sinn Féin leadership's rhetorical shift during the late 1980s and 1990s was merely a device to maximise SF's electoral appeal, or did it represent a genuine, sincere movement in the attitudes of leading republicans to the 'armed struggle'? The clandestine nature of the republican movement makes this question difficult to resolve. Nationalists have tended to accept the sincerity of Sinn Féin's shift while unionists, who faced the brunt of republican violence, have been highly sceptical.

There is evidence that while the Sinn Féin leadership may have been convinced of a new unarmed struggle, the middle and lower ranks and South Armagh and Tyrone were less enthusiastic (O'Brien 1993 pp. 204–8, Dixon 1997d pp. 14–15). In February 1992 Gerry Adams reportedly said 'he feared the emergence of an undisciplined, breakaway group from the IRA if a premature ceasefire is called in Northern Ireland' after failing to win sufficient backing for his new strategy at SF's annual conference (*The Daily Telegraph*, 24 February 1992). Hugh Annesley, the Chief Constable of the RUC, later described the IRA ceasefire as 'a very considerable achievement for the leadership. I have no doubt that if Adams and Co had tried it in 1989, '90, '91, then they would have been unable to carry the leadership with them' (*The Guardian*, 6 September 1995). This struggle between the SF leadership and grassroots republicanism may help to explain the slow and contradictory shifts in SF rhetoric during this period as the Adams leadership strained to sell a new strategy to the wider movement. It was not only unionists who tended to see the shifts in republican ideology and the ceasefire as a *tactic* to maximise its effectiveness in the propaganda war and to destabilise Northern Ireland and pursue Irish unity. Rhetorical shifts were accompanied by an escalation of IRA violence and the reassertion of fundamentalist positions: 'The IRA leadership had their own perverted logic. For them, an offer of peace needed to be accompanied by violence to show their volunteers that they were not surrendering' (Major 1999 p. 433).

The Secularisation of the Republic?

During the early 1990s Irish politics appeared to be undergoing a process of secularisation in which old cleavages over nationalism and partition were being replaced by more 'modern' divisions over economics and class. The formation of the Progressive Democrats in 1985, a split from the traditionally nationalist Fianna Fáil, combined a free market ideology with liberalism on social issues and moderately nationalist views on the North. In 1990 Mary Robinson, a secularising, socialist feminist, was elected President of the Republic in spite of her sympathies for northern unionism. The McGimpsey case in March 1990 upheld the view that Articles 2 and 3 of the Irish Constitution constituted a claim of legal right over Northern Ireland and a constitutional imperative. Following this, in December 1990 a bill was introduced aimed at unilaterally amending Articles 2 and 3 and was supported by the Workers' Party, Labour and Fine Gael but defeated by 74 votes to 66 (Bew and Gillespie 1993 p. 242). Gerry Adams was alarmed that the Republic might trade Articles 2 and 3 for a settlement (Sharrock and Devenport 1997 p. 286). There were also strong movements for peace in the South, particularly after the Warrington bombing in March 1993, and unionists seemed to be receiving a more sympathetic hearing. It has been argued that the secularisation of politics in the South and an accompanying 'social and cultural transformation' 'have fundamentally blocked off the

militant Catholic communalism that underlies much of the republican movement's northern success from any substantial echo in the
south' (Hazelkorn and Patterson 1994, p. 60; see also Mair 1987b).
The apparent rise of secularisation and 26 county nationalism,
coupled with Sinn Féin's electoral marginalisation in both North and
South, 'propelled Adams towards a political alliance with the
greener elements' in the South (Patterson 1997 p. 279).

A Departure in British Policy?

In response to political developments within Sinn Féin Peter
Brooke, the Secretary of State for Northern Ireland (1989–92),
through public speeches and secret contacts attempted to investigate
the possibility of ending the stalemate and bringing the republican
movement into the political process. In November 1989 Brooke gave
an important interview which claimed that although the security
forces could contain the IRA he found it 'difficult to envisage' their
military defeat. Neither would devolved government or economic
development 'cause terrorism to falter'. If the terrorists decided
'that the game had ceased to be worth the candle' then it would be
possible that the British Government could sit down and talk with
Sinn Féin. Significantly Brooke also used the colonial Cyprus analogy when asked whether he would consider speaking to Sinn Féin:
'Let me remind you of the move towards independence in Cyprus
and a British minister stood up in the House of Commons and used
the word "never" in a way which within two years there had been a
retreat from that word.' Brooke said he hoped the government
would be 'flexible' and imaginative if the IRA stopped its violence
(*Irish Times*, 4 November 1989). On 9 November 1990, Brooke's
Whitbread speech argued that 'The British Government has no selfish strategic or economic interest in Northern Ireland, our role is to
help, enable and encourage.' Mrs Thatcher had approved Brooke's
speech (whereas before the end of the Cold War she had reserva-
tions) and also gave her personal approval to secret talks with Sinn
Féin in October 1990 in order to find out what was happening in the
republican movement (Seldon 1997, *The Guardian*, 16 October
1999). In addition to these public overtures the British Army
developed a 'peace plan' in 1992 and in 1993 and, for the first year of
'the Troubles', the security forces did not kill anyone (*Irish Times*,
31 December 1993, Bew and Gillespie 1996 p. 15).

The nationalist view presents Brooke's initiatives as a radical departure in British policy yet there are considerable continuities between British policy in the early to mid-1970s (see Chapters 5–7). Britain had made statements on British neutrality in the past; politicians had spoken of the possibility of Irish unity by consent, had a history of dealing with the IRA (in contrast to the Irish Government) and had long believed that there was no military solution. The British Government's rhetorical invitations to SF were reminiscent of previous overtures: 'It was almost as if Sir Patrick had dusted down and slightly rephrased what Merlyn Rees had said in the run-up to the 1975 truce. What was to follow had much in common with that process' (Taylor 1997 pp. 328–9).

The continuities in British policy towards Northern Ireland suggest that the international dimension was not as significant as some have suggested in creating the conditions for a peace process. Questions of British 'neutrality' and its strategic interests in Northern Ireland are raised by those who emphasise the importance of the changing international environment to explain the Northern Ireland peace process. It is argued that the changing international environment, particularly the end of the Cold War and the development of peace processes in South Africa and the Middle East, made an IRA ceasefire 'far more likely' (Cox 1997 p. 676). No doubt the changing international environment was conducive to Sinn Féin's already shifting position: republicans like to see themselves fighting a war of national liberation alongside the PLO and ANC. The SF leadership could use the changing international environment as part of their ideological justification for shifting the republican movement from armed to unarmed struggle. However, the international dimension appears limited in its importance. The origins of the peace process probably pre-dated the end of the Cold War (1989 collapse of communism in Eastern Europe, 1991 end of Soviet Union) if your starting point is any of the following: the AIA 1985, the Haughey republican 'contacts' 1987, Hume–Adams 1988, developments in SF ideology (*A Scenario for Peace*, 1987), or the stalemate in the political and military struggle between the republican movement and the British Government.

While British overtures to Sinn Féin did coincide with the beginning of the end of the 'Cold War', the British claim it was prompted by an interest in exploring ideological shifts within the republican movement. In the early to mid-1970s, the British Government's willingness to contemplate withdrawal (and Irish unity or independence) suggests that it is unlikely that Britain had vital strategic, 'Cold War' interests in Northern Ireland which could only be preserved by military occupation. The 'Cold War' argument misses the continuities of British policy and exaggerates the significance of developments in British policy in 1989–90. The British had long accepted there was no purely military solution and that Britain had 'no selfish strategic or economic interest' in Northern Ireland. This had been argued by the SDLP since the early 1970s and was accepted by some leading Provisionals in the mid-1970s (see Chapters 6 and 7). The end of the Cold War and the restatement by Brooke of British policy in 1989–90 may have been more important for precipitating an ideological rethink among republican activists. The later development of peace processes in South Africa (1990) and Israel/Palestine (1993) were also, no doubt, useful to the SF leadership for legitimising the unarmed strategy, by pointing to the example of other liberation movements. The apparent upsurge of 'ethnic conflict' following the end of the 'Cold War' provided an alternative explanation of the conflict in Northern Ireland, although it was less flattering to the republican movement since comparisons with the former Yugoslavia and other 'ethnic conflicts' suggested SF/IRA were engaged in a communal conflict rather than a war for national liberation.

All-Party Talks versus 'Irish Peace Initiative'?

The attempt to reach an all-party agreement among the constitutional parties proceeded – through the Brooke (1991) and then Mayhew (1992) talks – while the British Government publicly and privately investigated the possibilities of an IRA ceasefire and negotiations. The two processes, the Brooke/Mayhew talks and the IRA ceasefire initiative, were proceeding in parallel. These are not necessarily contradictory or competing processes, as the nationalist view suggests, but complementary (Duignan 1995 pp. 103, 119). The prospect of an agreement among the constitutional parties at the centre could further marginalise the republican movement in Britain and Ireland and continue to undermine its violent campaign. Sinn Féin leaders were concerned at the progress of the Brooke/Mayhew talks and feared that they might succeed (Smith 1995 p. 197, Patterson 1997 pp. 231–2, 234). The prospect of bringing Sinn Féin into the political process may have acted as an incentive to unionists, but not the SDLP, to negotiate more earnestly in the Brooke/Mayhew talks. The establishment of an accommodation with the SDLP would allow unionists to avoid the distasteful prospect of having to negotiate with Sinn Féin.

If the British Government had solely pursued the Irish peace process it would have had no fall-back position if it turned out that the Sinn Féin leadership was not sincere in its desire to enter the political process. The unionists could be pacified by continuing with the talks process. If agreement was reached among the constitutional parties, Sinn Féin could always join the political process after a ceasefire. Periodically through 1993 and 1994, both British and Irish Governments were able to threaten to revive the talks process with the implicit threat to SF that if it did not play ball they would go off down the talks route (Major 1999 p. 463). Most famously this threat of the talks process was made by Reynolds shortly before the IRA ceasefire in 1994. The IRA were threatening not to call a permanent cessation of violence and reserved the right to defend nationalist communities. The Irish Taoiseach said:

> I've told them if they don't do this right, they can shag off; I don't want to hear anything about a six-month or six-year ceasefire; no temporary, indefinite or conditional stuff; no defending or retaliating against anyone; just that it's over ... period ... full stop. Otherwise, I'll walk away. I'll go off down the three-strand talks/ framework document road with John Major, and they can detour away for another 25 years of killing and being killed – for what? Because, at the end of that 25 years, they'll be back where they are right now, with damn all to show for it, except thousands more dead, and all for nothing. (Duignan 1995 p. 147)

The SDLP was in a position to play a pivotal role in influencing which process, the 'talks' or 'ceasefire initiative', was to be advanced. It could opt to push the talks process through enthusiastic and active engagement in the Brooke/Mayhew talks, or the SDLP could push the 'Irish peace process', pursuing its talks with SF and the Irish Government, and play a blocking role in all-party talks. The strength of the British and Irish Governments' threats to SF that they would push the talks process were in part dependent on the willingness of the SDLP to actively participate in that alternative. Without the SDLP, any settlement emerging from the 'talks process' would not have sufficient nationalist support.

The British Government, Irish Government and the SDLP were all crossing the line from attempting to marginalise Sinn Féin in the propaganda war to attempting to bring them into the democratic political process. In crossing the line from marginalisation to engagement there was a real risk of lending legitimacy and credibility to the republican movement. Engagement suggested that republicanism was a political movement with legitimate grievances and concerns that would have to be accommodated. For republicans engagement would allow their position to be seen as 'reasonable' and one which the electorate might consider voting for (Mallie and McKittrick 1997 p. 422). A further by-product of attempting to bring republicans into the political process was that it appeared to increase their influence and this risked upsetting the 'balance' and destabilising unionism. The British Government's public overtures to Sinn Féin and later revelations of private contacts intensified unionist fears that 'perfidious Albion' was again doing a deal behind their backs to force Northern Ireland out of the Union.

The Brooke–Mayhew Talks: Worth a 'Penny Candle'?

The polarisation following the AIA in 1985 prevented attempts to bring all parties into talks. In 1988, implicitly accepting the failure of their anti-Agreement campaign, the unionist leaders requested that the Secretary of State, Tom King, begin a process of 'talks about talks' to end the deadlock. In February 1989 representatives of the constitutional parties met in Duisberg; 'Discussion centred on ways of accommodating the Unionist demand that the workings of the AIA should first be suspended and the insistence of the SDLP that there should be no suspension and that discussions should be held outside the agreement' (Flackes and Elliott 1999 p. 241). In a speech on 9 January 1990 Brooke referred to the 'three relationships': relationships within Northern Ireland; the North/South dimension; and the East–West Anglo–Irish relationship. These relationships were to be considered during the Brooke/Mayhew talks with nothing being 'finally agreed in any strand until everything is agreed in the talks as a whole'. The acceptance by unionists of the three strands implied that a wholly internal settlement was not possible. In March 1991 a ten-week gap in the meetings of the IGC was announced which allowed the all-party 'Brooke' talks to proceed the following month. The talks ended on 3 July 1991 having not moved beyond the procedural level or reached strands two and three. The unionists generally took the blame for the talks' collapse from leader writers in Britain and Ireland. The talks were reconvened by the new Secretary of State, Patrick Mayhew, after the 1992 General Election.

Sinn Féin's hopes for the election of a more sympathetic Labour government at the 1992 election were shattered by the Conservatives' fourth victory in a row (Bew and Dixon 1995). However, John Major's majority in the House of Commons was reduced to 21 and was likely to be eroded through by-election defeat. One actuary predicted that 10.73 Conservative MPs could be expected to die in the course of a full five-year term of Parliament. This enhanced the leverage of the nine Ulster Unionist MPs and their sympathisers on the Conservative backbenches. In Northern Ireland Gerry Adams lost his seat in West Belfast to Joe Hendron of the SDLP. Shortly after the election, the IRA bombed the Baltic Exchange in the City of London, killing three and inflicting damage worth £800 million, thus causing more damage with one bomb than all the IRA's other bombings since 1969. Further City bombings were carried out in the years that followed, posing an economic cost to the British Government and a significant threat to the City of London as the world's financial centre. This prompted unionist claims that Britain's 7promotion of the peace process was driven by IRA bombs.

All-party talks among the constitutional political parties were reconvened under the new Secretary of State for Northern Ireland, Sir Patrick Mayhew, in April 1992. The pro-Union parties (APNI, UUP, DUP) entered the talks to devolve power to Northern Ireland and limit the impact of the AIA and the role of the Republic in Northern Ireland's affairs. The SDLP, on the other hand, wanted to extend the AIA and the role of the Republic. Strand Two of the talks on the North/South dimension took place in London in July 1992 and remarkably included both the participation of the Irish Government and the loyalist DUP. This was the first time in 70 years that all the constitutional parties had reached the negotiating table. However the DUP leadership was coming under some internal party pressure over its decision to go to London and negotiate with the Irish Government (*The Times*, 8 July 1992, *Irish News* editorial, 1 October 1992). Paisley and Robinson later stormed out of the talks since Articles 2 and 3 were not to be discussed, although significantly they did leave behind 'observers'. James Molyneaux led his team to Dublin, in an important symbolic move, to discuss the North–South dimension. Shortly before the Mayhew talks were suspended, on

10 November 1992, the UUP tabled important new proposals for the future of Northern Ireland. These:

(a)   proposed a Bill of Rights;
(b)   gave nationalists a 'meaningful role' in the Northern Ireland administration;
(c)   proposed a North–South 'Inter-Irish Relations Committee', operating within the context of a Council of the British Isles, which would, where there is common interest, facilitate business and better understanding between the Belfast and Dublin administrations;
(d)   proposed the removal of Articles 2 and 3 of the Republic's constitution.

The unionists found themselves blamed for the lack of progress during the Brooke talks but came out of the Mayhew talks with credit. Unionist flexibility later came back to haunt the party when the Northern Ireland Office used the documents submitted by the Unionist Party as its benchmark for drawing up the Framework Documents of February 1995 (this was supposed to summarise the area of agreement between nationalism and unionism). This resulted in a document which, arguably, was overbalanced towards the nationalist position.

Loyalists and Republicans: Striking a Balance?

In the early 1990s loyalist paramilitary violence escalated to the point where they were killing more people than the IRA. Two factors are usually cited to explain this: first, increases in loyalist violence have been linked to unionist insecurity about their constitutional future. The second factor was the removal of a generation of UDA leaders and their replacement by a younger, more violent leadership (Bruce 1999). The UDA was banned in August 1992. Some argue that the increasing 'effectiveness' of loyalist terrorism in nationalist areas was putting pressure on the republican movement to go for a settlement (Rowan 1995 p. 100).

The British Government's attempt simultaneously to pursue all-party talks whilst encouraging the republican movement into the political process probably exacerbated unionist insecurities and increased loyalist violence. Mayhew attempted to balance overtures to republicans with reassurances for unionists. On 16 December 1992 Mayhew criticised Britain's historical record in Ireland and argued that the government would not stand in the way of a united Ireland if that was the will of the majority and pursued by democratic and peaceful means. Any new structures for Northern Ireland would have to be acceptable to both major traditions and have an all-Ireland dimension. But there was no question of dealings with the IRA while they espoused violence (*The Guardian*, 17 December 1992). Unionists reacted with outrage to the speech, and even the moderate Alliance Party leader, John Alderdice, implied that the British Government was extricating itself gradually from Northern Ireland (*Irish Times*, 18 January 1993). On 2 March 1993 Mayhew attempted to reassure unionism by expressing his desire to restart all-party talks and denying that the Government was neutral on Northern Ireland (*The Guardian*, 3 March 1993). Alderdice was not convinced and insisted that the Conservatives were looking to take Northern Ireland out of the union 'through the back door' (*Newsletter*, 4 March 1993, *Irish Times*, 11 March 1993).

In April 1993 it was revealed that Hume had been engaged in secret talks with Gerry Adams. In June 1993 the Sinn Féin leader shook hands with the Irish President. This outraged unionists since it appeared to lend the republican movement legitimacy and represented a retreat in the propaganda war. Furthermore, the Secretary of State for Northern Ireland told a German newspaper, *Die Zeit*, in April 1993, 'Many people believe that we would not want to release Northern Ireland from the United Kingdom. To be entirely honest, we would, with pleasure. No, not with pleasure. I take that back. But we would not stand in the way of Northern Ireland, if that were the will of the majority' (*The Guardian*, 1 May 1993). In April Mayhew again attempted to reassure unionists and shore up support for the UUP against the DUP by raising key unionist demands; he declared there would be no joint authority, proposed a Northern Ireland select committee, suggested devolution to local councils and made no mention of the Irish dimension. The rising tide of loyalist terrorism caused great concern among nationalists. The nationalist *Irish News* commented, 'The British Government has succeeded in alienating nationalists and unionists alike. Sir Patrick Mayhew has achieved the remarkable feat of having simultaneously stoked unionist fears without having placated nationalists' (*Irish News*, 26 March 1993, quoted in Bew and Gillespie 1993 p. 294). In the summer of 1993 *The Shankhill People*, a local unionist newspaper, described 'A community in retreat which feels itself being squeezed physically, territorially and culturally'.

Hume–Adams

Following the collapse of the Mayhew talks in 1992, the British stepped up their secret contacts with Sinn Féin and investigated the possibility of a face-to-face meeting to persuade them that there was no longer any need for the armed struggle (Sinn Féin 1993 p. 13). On 24 April the IRA detonated a bomb at the NatWest tower in the City of London. The British Government subsequently sent a message to SF: 'Events on the ground are crucial, as we have consistently made clear. We cannot conceivably disregard them. We gave advice in good faith taking what we were told at face value. It is difficult to reconcile that with recent events' (Sinn Féin 1993 p. 30). There were IRA bombings on 20 May in Belfast, 22 May in Portadown, 23 May in Belfast and Magherafelt and on 26 May a soldier was shot and injured (*The Daily Telegraph*, 30 November 1993). On 3 June the British Government representative gave a coded account to Sinn Féin of the British cabinet's deliberations. Translated, this message suggested that recent bombings by the IRA had made a meeting with Sinn Féin much more politically risky for John Major and gave support to those in the cabinet who opposed the initiative (Sinn Féin 1993 p. 36).

Contacts between Hume and Adams were publicly acknowledged during the SDLP/SF talks of 1988 but have probably continued off and on since then (Mallie and McKittrick 1997 p. 118). On 6 October 1991 Hume sketched out a draft joint declaration to be made by the British and Irish Governments which, it was hoped, would succeed in winning an IRA ceasefire. On 10 April 1993 it was publicly revealed that John Hume and Gerry Adams had been engaging in secret talks. This revelation ruled out further progress in the Mayhew talks since the unionists would not sit down with John Hume while he was involved in talks with Gerry Adams. In June 1993 a 'Hume–Adams' document was agreed by Hume, Adams and the Irish Government which, along with the British Labour Party, appeared to be part of an emerging consensus around the notion of joint authority. The Irish Foreign Minister, Dick Spring, argued that the British and Irish Governments might have to consider an agreement over the heads of the Northern Ireland politicians and put it directly to the people in a referendum, if the unionists refused to reconvene the Mayhew talks (*The Guardian*, 8 July 1993). Hume and Adams, by publicly linking their report to a joint British–Irish initiative, made it more difficult for the governments to consider the Hume–Adams document. The British Government particularly needed to avoid pursuing an initiative which, because it had the fingerprints of Gerry Adams all over it, risked further alienating unionists.

In October 1993 loyalists carried out their 'most sustained assault on the nationalist community in Belfast since the early Seventies'. They carried out nearly 30 attacks in nationalist areas of Belfast, killing three Catholics (*The Observer*, 24 October 1993). On 23 October the IRA attempted to bomb a meeting of loyalist paramilitaries on the Shankhill Road, the heart of loyalist West Belfast, but the bomb exploded prematurely killing the bomber, Thomas Begley, and nine Protestant civilians. In retaliation for the Shankhill bombing, on 30 October loyalist gunmen burst into a pub in Greysteel and murdered five Catholics and injured eight.

In these conditions of heightened insecurity and increased violence, elements in both the British and Irish Governments acknowledged the importance of choreography and of balancing initiatives to bring republicans into the political process, while at the same time reassuring unionists. The British Government was interested in the Hume–Adams initiative but it could not bring the unionists into negotiations if it was seen to be on republican terms. For this reason, Hume was advised to *say publicly* that the Hume–Adams document would not be sent to London. An adviser to Dick Spring recounted that the publicity drawn by Hume to his initiative necessitated taking Adams' 'fingerprints' off the joint declaration in order to keep that process alive (Mallie and McKittrick 1997 pp. 189, 192, 210, 211; see also Duignan 1995 p. 99). Privately Major stressed to Reynolds that although Hume–Adams was still 'alive' he 'just couldn't publicly wear it' (Duignan 1995 p. 106); a British–Irish joint declaration would have 'to be seen to be utterly divorced from the Hume–Adams dialogue'. Major's biographer explained: 'Anger in the Loyalist community, too, made it even more imperative for him to distance himself from any suggestion of being influenced by the Hume–Adams initiative' (Seldon 1997 p. 421; see also Mallie and McKittrick 1997 pp. 226–7, Major 1999 pp. 449–50). Major and Reynolds reasoned, 'Hume–Adams was being declared dead, in order to keep it alive' (Duignan 1995 p. 106).

Both the British and Irish Governments were unhappy with the high-profile nature of Hume's dialogue with Gerry Adams. The Irish Government attempted twice to put distance between itself and Hume–Adams but was forced to retreat on both occasions. The SDLP leader had considerable influence on public opinion in the South and this constrained the Irish Government's ability to distance itself from

Hume. Unionists did not have a comparable influence on the British (Dixon 1995b p. 500, Duignan 1995 p. 120). John Major was also experiencing problems managing domestic public opinion over the IRA's bombing campaign in England. Following the Shankhill bombing Major told Reynolds of the political constraints operating on him:

> It's fine coming from where you are coming from over there, but I have to contend with the British public that doesn't understand what you are saying, nor have any appreciation of it, but sees the bald facts in front of them as they are and it's extremely difficult to continue on, to try and do something in those circumstances. (Mallie and McKittrick 1997 p. 203)

In addition, John Major had problems with his diminishing majority at Westminster (particularly with Conservative 'Eurosceptics') and unrest among unionist (or 'law and order') inclined Conservative backbenchers who could exploit anti-terrorist sentiment amongst public opinion (these MPs often turned out to be the same people). Since the 1992 British General Election, the Ulster Unionists had increased pressure on the Conservatives by abstaining or voting against the government in the Commons.

In July 1993 the Conservative government, facing a problem with its own rebels over the Maastricht Treaty, arrived at an 'understanding' with the Ulster Unionist MPs at Westminster. Both Unionists and the Government insisted no deal had been done, while reports emerged in the papers of unionist demands for more accountable and better governance. The Conservative government's need for UUP support in the Commons increased that party's influence, and Molyneaux was regularly consulted by the government. This gave the UUP leader the confidence not to oppose the Downing Street Declaration in December 1993, and forced the British Government to play something more like the supporting role for Ulster Unionists that the Irish Government has traditionally played for Northern Ireland nationalists (Dixon 1994b pp. 36–9).

Talking to Terrorists

Irish Governments have been unhappy about talking with the IRA for fear that this would lend them legitimacy. British Governments, by contrast, have a history of 'contact' and negotiation. While publicly the British Government was trying to reassure unionists, privately its contacts with Sinn Féin were intensifying. Up until February 1993 London actively courted the republicans by sending 19 messages, receiving only one reply. This suggests the British, contrary to the nationalist view, were keen to explore the republican movement's willingness to declare a ceasefire. The government kept the republicans informed of the Mayhew talks, passing on a detailed government report and assessment of the discussions in October 1992. This document also provided an outline of what kind of agreement the British thought it was 'possible to achieve, rather than its own sense of priorities in individual areas' (Sinn Féin 1993 p. 20). It anticipated closely proposals later published in the Framework Documents in 1995 and also states that the two governments were contemplating imposing a settlement over the heads of the parties.

The British and Irish Governments' statement in Brussels on 29 October had specifically ruled out talks with 'those who threaten or support political violence', and claimed there 'can be no secret agreements or understandings between the governments and organisations that support violence "as a price for its cessation"'. On 28 November 1993 the British Government's 'back-channel' links with Sinn Féin were revealed in *The Observer* newspaper. Only a week earlier John Major had told the House of Commons that '[If he thinks] we should sit down and talk with Mr Adams and the Provisional IRA, I can say only that that would turn my stomach. We will not do it'. After leaving government Major justified his deceit: 'When I was certain that someone was genuinely seeking a peace I'd have spoken to Beelzebub, if it would have delivered peace, because that was my objective.'

The British Government and Sinn Féin published differing accounts of their contacts. This is not surprising since they each had differing constituencies to reassure. The British Government needed to convince unionists that its 'contacts' with Sinn Féin were not intended to secretly sell out the Union. The Sinn Féin leadership had to reassure the republican rank and file that it had not been 'colluding' with the British Government or betraying the struggle. Both Sinn Féin and the British Government released documents giving their account of the 'back-channel' contacts. The British version issued by Mayhew contained 22 errors. It was withdrawn and revised in a way which brought it closer into line with Sinn Féin's version. The British version claimed contacts had been initiated in 1993, although Peter Brooke subsequently confirmed Sinn Féin's version that the 'contacts' dated back to 1990 and this has been confirmed by other well-placed sources (Mallie and McKittrick 1997 p. 244, Seldon 1997 p. 415; Major also casts doubt on Mayhew's account in Major 1999 p. 442). For these reasons Sinn Féin's account of the back-channel contacts (although incomplete) is thought to be a more accurate account of events.

Sinn Féin's account of the contacts allowed it to claim that all the running was made by the British and avoid charges from republican hardliners that there had been any surrender. The Sinn Féin leadership was operating to its own agenda which appeared to be advanced by British willingness to talk face-to-face with only a temporary ceasefire and the British representatives' talk of the inevitability of Irish unity through European integration. In SF's account the British had initiated contact in 1990 and had driven the process by sending representatives, messages, advanced copies of speeches, confidential documents and ultimately initiated a proposal for face-to-face meetings. The British Government was to attempt to persuade the republican movement that there was 'no longer' any need for the armed struggle, which implied recent developments had changed the situation in Northern Ireland, and that it was not Sinn Féin which had changed its position or principles, but external conditions. This account, however, which stressed the active role played by the British Government in the contacts, did not fit with the nationalist account of the peace process which suggested that it was a unilateral Irish initiative.

The British Government's incentive was to produce an account of its dealings with Sinn Féin which limited the effects of the revelations on the unionist community and to some extent British public opinion. Increased loyalist insecurity might result in a further escalation of loyalist violence: 'What concerned the RUC was the possible reaction of the North's loyalist paramilitaries if they thought a deal was being done between the British Government and the IRA. All hell could break loose' (Holland and Phoenix 1997 p. 8). Mayhew also expressed concern that revelations of British–republican contacts would boost the more 'hardline' DUP at the cost of its more accommodating UUP rival (Mallie and McKittrick 1997 p. 250). The British also wanted to avoid bringing the republicans into a 'peace process' only to lose the unionists.

In Northern Ireland opinions on talks with paramilitaries were polarised along communal lines. Protestants tended to oppose British talks with the IRA or even loyalist paramilitaries, while Catholics were in favour. Before the revelation of contacts in July 1993 a poll found 74 per cent of Protestants opposed to the opening of informal channels of communication with SF, while 70 per cent of Catholics were in favour (*Irish Political Studies* 1994 p. 221).

The British account of the contacts claimed that they had been initiated by Sinn Féin in February 1993 with a message claiming the war was over. Unionists were more likely to accept that the British Government should enter into contacts in this context. The British account of the contacts was altered to conceal the fact that the British had initiated contact in 1990 and sustained it over the years. Such prolonged, secret contacts were likely to fuel unionist suspicions over British motivation and lead to questions as to why these contacts continued while IRA violence had not stopped. The tone of the Sinn Féin account also suggests a closer and warmer relationship between the British representatives and republicans than the British version.

There is some evidence of an attempt by the British Government and Sinn Féin to choreograph the Provisionals' ceasefire and its entry into a peace process during the 'back-channel contacts'. The use of intermediaries allowed both sides to blame these for 'misunderstandings' and to distance themselves from hostile interpretations of their actions (*The Observer*, 5 December 1993). According to Miller and McLaughlin:

> It was important for them to maintain an attitude of 'business as usual' and to prepare the ground for a potential settlement... Both sides tailored their overtures for public and private consumption and exchanged advance copies of keynote speeches. This public limbering-up was accompanied by other behind-the-scenes exchanges. (Miller and McLaughlin 1996 pp. 125–6)

In 1975 the British had offered the IRA advice on media issues (O'Brien 1993 p. 171). In 1993 again the British Government offered Sinn Féin advice on how best to manage public opinion and criticise the British Government. Sinn Féin should emphasise that the British Government was foot-dragging on the peace process: 'Sinn Féin should comment in as major a way as possible on the PLO/Rabin deal; ... Sinn Féin should be saying "If they can come to an agreement in Israel, why not here? We are standing at the altar, why won't you come and join us".' It also said that a full frontal publicity offensive from Sinn Féin is expected, pointing out that various contingencies and defensive positions are already in place (Sinn Féin 1993 p. 41).

The Downing Street Declaration

The British and Irish Governments were working on a joint declaration which, drawing on Hume–Adams, it was hoped would lead to an IRA ceasefire. However, the British Government sought to rewrite the Irish Government's draft because Major judged that it was too closely associated with Hume–Adams and therefore 'had no chance of being accepted by Unionist opinion' (Mallie and McKittrick 1997 pp. 228, 264). On 25 November John Major wrote to Reynolds stating, with regard to the Joint Declaration:

> In the current political atmosphere there is clearly no hope of securing even tacit acceptance by the Unionist mainstream of a joint declaration along the lines of your draft. The text would be seen as deriving from Hume–Adams and thus would be assumed to be the product of negotiation with Sinn Féin. This is an impression which successive statements from Hume–Adams have done nothing to dispel.
>
> As we've agreed all along, association with Hume–Adams is a kiss of death for any text intended to secure acceptance on both sides of the community. (Mallie and McKittrick 1997 p. 229)

Importantly, if the IRA ceasefire failed to materialise the British Government needed to ensure that there was no vacuum in which violence could escalate. Alienate mainstream unionist opinion too much, and there would be little prospect for the reconstruction and development of the Mayhew talks. The British offered to rewrite the Irish document retaining the substance but putting it in a different framework. Emphasising the British need to pacify unionism, Major wrote that the British document 'goes as far as in my judgement the market will bear' (Mallie and McKittrick 1997 p. 229).

The Joint Declaration (also known as the Downing Street Declaration or DSD) published on 15 December 1993 attempted to attract SF into a 'peace process' without alienating unionism. It was therefore studiously ambiguous, capable of being favourably or unfavourably interpreted by both nationalists and unionists. The rhetoric of the document was nationalist, acknowledging the importance of overcoming the 'legacy of history', promising to promote co-operation at all levels between North and South and seeking 'to create institutions and structures which, while respecting the diversity of the people of Ireland, would enable them to work together in all areas of common interest. This will help over a period to build the trust necessary to end past divisions, leading to an agreed and peaceful future.' This hinted at the possibility of unity through co-operation and European integration (Modernisation Theory: see Chapter 3). The British Government restated that it 'had no selfish strategic or economic interest in Northern Ireland'. The document was welcomed by the SDLP and widely among opinion in the Republic. Nationalists claimed that Hume–Adams was the basis for the Joint Declaration and illustrated the power of the pan-nationalist front. The Taoiseach, apparently in preparation for Irish unity, undertook to examine Southern political life for any elements which might be seen as a threat to unionism's way of life or ethos. The unionists received a reaffirmation of the principle of consent and the Irish Government promised to change its constitution to fully reflect the principle of consent in Northern Ireland. At the crux of the document was an attempt to reconcile self-determination with the consent of the people of Northern Ireland:

> The British Government agree that it is for the people of the island of Ireland alone, by agreement between the two parts respectively, to exercise their right of self-determination on the basis of consent, freely and concurrently given, North and South, to bring about a united Ireland, if that is their wish.

The UUP's reaction was muted; Molyneaux did not endorse the document but did not oppose it, and argued it was not a sell-out of the Union. The loyalist paramilitary groups, the UVF and UDA, paralleled the UUP's position by neither accepting nor rejecting the Joint Declaration. Ian Paisley's DUP rejected the Joint Declaration and criticised UUP acquiescence in it. An opinion poll suggested that the DUP might be more in tune with unionist opinion in Northern Ireland. This suggested that, overall, 56 per cent of the people of Northern Ireland supported the Joint Declaration, and 87 per cent of nationalists but just 43 per cent of unionists. Given the tendency of opinion polls to overestimate moderation, the UUP's position appeared to be out of step with its voters (*The Guardian*, 22 December 1993). Rising dissent and talk of mutiny led to a leadership initiative to explain the Declaration to the membership and a hardening of the UUP's stance on the resumption of the talks process (Cochrane 1997 pp. 320–3). The British Government attempted to soften the impact of the Downing Street Declaration on unionism by declaring its intention of setting up a Northern Ireland Select Committee and claiming that there would be no amnesty for republican prisoners. Of great significance for the subsequent history of the peace process, the government also insisted that the IRA would have to decommission its weapons before taking part in all-party talks (*The Guardian*, 17 December 1993). The Irish Deputy Prime Minister, Dick Spring, also announced that the IRA would have to hand over their guns (Duignan 1995 p. 136). The UUP's lack of opposition to the Joint Declaration was 'pivotal' in helping to limit adverse unionist reaction in Northern Ireland as well as right-wing, pro-unionist dissent within the Conservative party, which had been antagonised by the Declaration (*The Independent*, 18 December 1993, Seldon 1997 pp. 429, 539, Major 1999 p. 450).

Republicans were surprised that Major had signed up to the Joint Declaration in spite of his apparent dependence on Unionists for support at Westminster (Mallie and McKittrick 1997 pp. 271–2). Gerry Adams argued that in the Joint Declaration the British Government recognised, albeit in a heavily qualified manner, the right of the Irish people to self-determination and later claimed it marked 'a stage in the slow and painful process of England's disengagement from her first and last colony' (Patterson 1997 p. 253). The republican movement did not endorse the Declaration; indeed, it called for its 'clarification' by the British Government and set up a peace commission to consult the republican movement. Galvanising republican discontent with the declaration, Bernadette McAliskey argued, 'It cannot be sold, that's the difficulty Gerry Adams is in ... Gerry Adams cannot sell this thing, that's the beginning of the story and the end of the story in reality' (Sharrock and Devenport 1997 p. 316).

'Pan-Nationalism' and the 'Tactical Use of the Unarmed Struggle'

The British Government refused to 'clarify' but did 'explain' the Joint Declaration for Sinn Féin. The likely parameters of a settlement had already been indicated in the leaking of an Irish Government document in November 1993; Reynolds suggested that the consent principle might result in reform of the Government of Ireland Act, and changes to Articles 2 and 3 of the Irish Constitution would be conditional upon cross-border institutions with executive powers (Patterson 1997 p. 253). During the summer of 1994 the republican movement considered an IRA ceasefire and debated a document called TUAS which some argue stands for the 'Totally UnArmed Strategy', while others maintain it stands for 'Tactical Use of the Armed Struggle'. This dispute may be a symptom of the Sinn Féin leadership's need to appease contrasting audiences: TUAS could stand for 'Totally Unarmed Strategy' to convince the republican movement's new allies in London, Dublin and Washington, but 'Tactical Use of the Armed Struggle' to traditional republican areas in Northern Ireland (Moloney, *Sunday Tribune*, 30 January 2000).

The debate within the republican movement was not so much about the morality of the 'armed struggle' but its effectiveness in bringing about the goal of a 32-county democratic socialist Republic. For the republican leadership to win the widespread support of the republican movement for an IRA ceasefire they had to demonstrate that the 'pan-nationalist front' (SF, SDLP, Republic of Ireland, USA, EU?, British Labour Party?) could be a powerful and effective alternative to violence. The substantial contributing factors which pointed towards the launching of the unarmed struggle were:

(a)   Hume's leadership of the SDLP;
(b)   the strength of the coalition government in Dublin;
(c)   Reynolds' lack of historical baggage and his knowledge of how popular a nationalist consensus would be among the grassroots;
(d)   the power of the Irish-American lobby;
(e)   the Irish-American lobby's ability to influence Clinton;
(f)   Britain's lack of popularity within the EU.

The TUAS document stated: 'It is the first time in 25 years that all the major Irish nationalist parties are rowing in roughly the same direction. These combined circumstances are unlikely to gel again in the foreseeable future.' (The TUAS document is reproduced in Mallie and McKittrick 1997 pp. 421–4.) The (contested) expectation that Catholics would be a majority in Northern Ireland within a generation and vote themselves into a united Ireland may also have played an influential role in persuading republicans to end the 'armed struggle'.

An 'intensive' consultation exercise culminated in a special Sinn Féin conference in Letterkenny in July 1994. There were reports of 'strong support' amongst nationalist opinion for a strategy which would combine mass struggle from below – through the mobilisation of a mass campaigning organisation – with 'politics from above', the diplomacy and negotiation being pursued by the leadership (Bean 1995 p. 26). Security sources suggested the IRA ceasefire required 'massive planning, massive consultation – a massive show of democracy on their part to keep their people behind them'. The internal debate was divided: the leadership favoured peace; the middle and higher levels did not think a ceasefire would work but were prepared to give it a chance, whereas the grassroots favoured war (Dixon 1997d pp. 14–15).

Conclusion

With the benefit of hindsight it is tempting to reinterpret history to suggest that political developments within the republican movement during the 1980s led inexorably and inevitably towards the IRA's ceasefire of 1994. From this vantage point, the nationalist view castigates those who ever doubted the sincerity of the IRA's conversion to a 'Totally Unarmed Strategy' (Mallie and McKittrick 1997). There are two main problems with this perspective: first, the upsurge of appalling republican violence suggested that IRA actions were a stronger indicator of republican intentions than Sinn Féin rhetoric about peace. Even those who later traced the 'Irish peace process' back to the mid-1980s believed in 1990 that the IRA was entering 'a military period'. Patterson argues: 'while there were certainly some republicans who believed that the armed struggle had become an obstacle to further progress, and the peace process was not in that sense a sham, it was, however, a much more ambiguous and contradictory strategy than many of its uncritical supporters would allow' (Patterson 1997 pp. 231, 225). Second, those convinced of the sincerity of the republican movement's shift towards peace and the permanence of the subsequent IRA ceasefire announced on 31 August 1994 were under the impression that the TUAS document stood for 'Totally Unarmed Strategy'. Later the weight of evidence – not least the end of the IRA's ceasefire in February 1996 – shifted and it appeared more likely that the IRA's ceasefire was not permanent and that TUAS stood for the 'Tactical Use of the Armed Struggle'. There was a very real fear that the IRA, after exploiting the benefits of an unarmed strategy (in terms of legitimacy and electoral support), would then return to violence stronger than ever before and better placed to destabilise Northern Ireland.

10
Bridging the Gap? The Peace Process 1994–2000

Introduction

Prior to the IRA ceasefire of 31 August 1994 there appeared to have been little convergence in the public positions of any of the parties to the conflict, and no obvious convergence in public opinion. Both loyalists and republicans could believe they had won. In this climate it was difficult to see what kind of agreement might 'bridge the gap' and win the acquiescence, if not consent, of both republicans and loyalists. The Irish Government concentrated on soothing republican fears and demonstrating to the republican movement the effectiveness of the political path by championing the nationalist cause. The British Government had to perform a 'dual role': they had to deliver concessions to nationalists to underpin the IRA's ceasefire and reassure them they would be dealt with fairly in any negotiations. Simultaneously, they had to reassure unionists and bring them to the negotiating table with republicans. The British Government would push the Unionists 'to a line beyond which they will not go' while the Irish Government pulled 'the Republicans to a line beyond which they will not come'. The remaining gap would be negotiated by the political parties in Northern Ireland (*The Observer*, 5 February 1995).

Ceasefire Reactions

The roles assumed by the British and Irish Governments during the peace process are illustrated by the contrast in the reception the IRA's ceasefire received in Dublin and London. The Irish Government's task was to keep the republican movement on board and demonstrate to it the benefits of the non-violent, political path it was apparently taking. They therefore quickly accepted the IRA's ceasefire as permanent and within days Adams was received into the pan-nationalist family through a public three-way handshake in Dublin. Sinn Féin was also swiftly admitted to the Republic's all-Ireland 'Forum for Peace and Reconciliation'. In November the Republic released some republican prisoners.

Paralleling Irish support for the republicans, the British Government expressed unionist scepticism of the IRA's intentions. The UUP leader, James Molyneaux, assured unionists that no secret deals had been done and shared the British Government's concerns that the IRA's ceasefire declaration had not stated that it was 'permanent'. A significant body of unionist opinion felt that the British Government had done a secret deal with the IRA in return for the ceasefire. The loyalist *Newsletter* was wary about 'the real intent of the republican leadership' (*Newsletter*, 1 September 1994). For the DUP the ceasefire was a tactical ploy by the IRA to win concessions from the British Government, part of a British strategy to push Northern Ireland out of the Union. NIO officials met with loyalist paramilitaries to let them know that the Union was safe and no secret deals had been done with republicans to bring about the ceasefire (Rowan 1995 pp. 117–18). On 16 September the British government took steps to reassure unionists by declaring its commitment to a referendum on any package for the constitutional future of Northern Ireland. Six weeks after the IRA's cessation, on 13 October 1994, the Combined Loyalist Military Command (CLMC), comprising the UDA, UVF and Red Hand Commando, declared a ceasefire.

Permanence and Decommissioning

Following the signing of the DSD the British insisted that the IRA's handing over of explosives would figure high on the agenda of the 'exploratory talks' and would have to take place before all-party talks (*The Guardian*, 17 December 1993). There would be three principal, and highly symbolic, steps for Sinn Féin on the way to all-party talks:

(a) exploratory dialogue with civil servants;
(b) direct contact between representatives of the British Government and Sinn Féin;
(c) an invitation to all party-talks with unionists.

Public opinion polls confirmed the difficulties of bringing republican and unionist parties into all-party talks. Protestants were sceptical of the IRA's ceasefire, believing that the IRA had called a ceasefire because they had cut a deal or had an ulterior motive. They were keen to see tangible evidence of the IRA's intentions and over-whelmingly (92 per cent to 5 per cent) favoured decommissioning (of both loyalists and republicans) as a precondition to Sinn Féin's entry into all-party talks (*Irish Political Studies* 1995 p. 309). The loyalist paramilitaries refused to decommission unilaterally but would do so if the IRA also began decommissioning, and in the meantime the loyalists would not strike first. Catholics were more convinced of the sincerity and permanence of the IRA ceasefire than Protestants, although a plurality of Catholics (46 per cent to 37 per cent) also wanted to see decommissioning by the paramilitary organisations (*Irish Political Studies* 1995 p. 309). However, as decommissioning became a more hotly contested issue between nationalists and unionists in the peace process, Catholics began to fall into line with their political leaders who opposed decommis-sioning.

The importance of the permanence of the IRA ceasefire was that, if sincere, it prevented Sinn Féin from using the threat of a return to violence at the negotiating table with the constitutional parties. The implicit threat of a return to violence would bolster Sinn Féin's bargaining position in all-party talks (its political support was only 10 per cent to 12 per cent). The republican movement, given its scepticism of British Governments and their intentions (particularly in view of its perfidy during the 1975 ceasefire), was opposed to declaring a 'permanent' ceasefire which robbed the movement of its bargaining power and could be interpreted as a surrender. Towards the end of September Adams implied that the ceasefire was not necessarily permanent but contingent: 'None of us can say two or three years up the road that if the causes of conflict aren't resolved that another IRA leadership won't come along because this has always happened' (Bew and Gillespie 1996 p. 70). The Sinn Féin leadership may have been unable to deliver a 'permanent' cessation but the wording of the ceasefire was more than even the RUC Chief Constable had expected (*The Guardian*, 22 May 1996).

The British Army had long believed there was no purely military solution to the conflict in Northern Ireland (Chapter 5). There were reports that senior British Army officers 'have long believed that the IRA really does mean to abandon its military campaign' (*The*

Economist, 27 January 1996). This judgement of IRA intentions may have led to the pragmatic approach adopted by leading figures in the security forces – the RUC, the British Army and MI5 – towards decommissioning. The army and RUC placed no importance on the handover of weapons since the paramilitaries could rapidly re-arm; they were more concerned with the will and intention of those with weapons (*The Guardian*, 16 November 1995). Indeed senior soldiers and policemen suggested privately that pressing the IRA or the loyalists on the issue of disarmament could be counter-productive since it might lead to increased pressure on the republican leadership and the breakdown of discipline (*The Economist*, 11 March 1995; see also *The Observer*, 1 January 1995). The RUC Chief Constable argued – as did his top officials and the Irish police, the Gardai – that Adams could not persuade the IRA to decommission before negotiations: 'He doesn't have that much control over them' (Mitchell 1999 p. 30). Michael Oatley, a former MI6 officer who had been involved in secret talks with the IRA, also acknowledged the leadership's problem with its grassroots. Weapons were dispersed under the control of local cells: 'Volunteers are not sheep. All joined to pursue an armed campaign for agreed objectives which have now been modified. Discipline in the face of such changes has been remarkable. Leaders can but lead; confidence in new policies takes time to spread' (*The Sunday Times*, 31 October 1999).

The republican movement had been notorious for its splits. The chances of a permanent end to violence and a workable settlement would be reduced if significant numbers left the Provisional movement for more hardline paramilitary groups, such as the Irish National Liberation Army or the Continuity IRA, or established new breakaway groups, such as the Real IRA (established 1997). The British Government and the security forces therefore had a vested interest in seeing that the Sinn Féin leadership retained control of a united, disciplined movement and that splitters and dissenters were dissuaded. It was probably essential in the short term at any rate for the Provisionals to retain at least some of their weapons not only in order to maintain discipline within their own ranks, but also to 'police' the extremist factions who might try to usurp the IRA's position and exploit difficulties within its ranks (Rowan 1995 p. 101, Mallie and McKittrick 1997 pp. 400, 405). There were reports that in the run-up to the ceasefire, the Provisionals had established a team to deal with dissent and to ensure that the INLA and the Continuity IRA did nothing to endanger the peace process. If the Sinn Féin leadership was pushed 'too far' for concessions (e.g., on decommissioning) during the peace process then the danger was that the SF leadership would not be able to maintain unity.

There is evidence that the Conservative Government, to some extent, shared the RUC's analysis of the republican movement, the conditionality of the ceasefire and the problems facing the leadership. As Major recalled, 'Adams and many in the Provisional leadership seemed committed to a political process, but the IRA remained in full and active readiness' (Major 1999 pp. 461, 470, 477, 478). In January 1995 Patrick Mayhew told a group of sixth formers, in what he thought was a private meeting, that Gerry Adams' ability to control the 'hard men' in the republican movement was vital to maintaining the IRA ceasefire and that it 'would be a disadvantage to everybody' if he was replaced.

> To some extent we have got to help Mr Adams carry with him the people who are reluctant to see a ceasefire, who believe they might be betrayed by the British Government. If the hard men say, 'What did Gerry Adams do? We have called a ceasefire but got nothing sufficient in return', then Mr Adams will take a long walk on a short plank and be replaced by someone much harder. (*Irish Times*, 9 January 1995)

Also that month, Peter Brooke praised Adams as a 'brave' and 'courageous' man (Mallie and McKittrick 1997 pp. 408–9).

Decommissioning and Demilitarisation

The British Government probably did not expect the IRA to declare a *permanent* ceasefire and the security forces advised it that the IRA would not decommission. But there was also evidence that the IRA might well contemplate '*demilitarisation*'. This could be interpreted to mean all-round demilitarisation of paramilitaries and security forces or else the reduction of the British military presence. Prior to the ceasefire Martin McGuinness had spoken of a 'total demilitarisation' of Northern Ireland involving the IRA, loyalist paramilitaries and the British Army, which may have encouraged the British Government to believe there could be movement on this issue (*Sunday Tribune*, 31 July 1994). He reportedly told Reynolds and

Spring, 'We know the guns will have to be banjaxed' (Duignan 1995 p. 151).

The question of permanence and decommissioning was of symbolic importance to both republicans and unionists. Republicans saw a permanent ceasefire and decommissioning as tantamount to surrender, leaving the Catholic community defenceless and themselves vulnerable to British treachery. For unionists, decommissioning represented a tangible symbol of the republican movement's intention to end the violence. If the republicans did surrender weapons it would be an indication of the leadership's ability to deliver its movement. Decommissioning also represented a test of the resolve of the British Government to defend the Union. The unionists had little reason to trust the word of the Conservative Government: it had negotiated secretly with SF while publicly denying contacts, conceded to SF demands for the clarification of the DSD and then retreated from its insistence on the permanence of the IRA's ceasefire. The British Government had publicly insisted on decommissioning and the permanence of the IRA ceasefire; if it reneged on these pledges, what price its guarantees over consent and constitutional change?

Nationalists and republicans have claimed that the British Government introduced the decommissioning issue only after the IRA's ceasefire in order to deadlock the 'peace process' (for example, McGarry and O'Leary 1996 p. 358). However, there is considerable evidence that the decommissioning issue was raised by both British and Irish Governments *before* the IRA's ceasefire, and John Major claims that if anything the Irish Government made the running (Major 1999 pp. 470–2). In October and December 1993 Patrick Mayhew stated the British Government's demand for decommissioning. Again after the Downing Street Declaration the British argued that the handing over of guns and explosives would be dealt with in exploratory talks after the IRA had declared a permanent ceasefire and full negotiations would start once the IRA had handed over 'all its arms and proved that it had permanently renounced violence' (*The Guardian*, 17 December 1993; see also Bew and Gillespie 1996). In an interview on 8 January Adams criticised Mayhew, Hurd and Major for repeating their demand for an IRA weapons handover (*Irish News*, 8 January 1994; further recognition of the decommissioning demand by Adams came in the *Irish News*, 14 January 1994 and 26 February 1994; see also Bew and Gillespie 1996 p. 46). The Irish Government also demanded the decommissioning of IRA weapons well before the IRA ceasefire (Bew and Gillespie 1996 pp. 35, 54, *Irish Times*, 16 December 1993).

The Irish Government supported decommissioning prior to and immediately after the IRA ceasefire but then shifted its position. Contemporary newspaper reports suggest that Reynolds believed IRA decommissioning would not reach the agenda until sectarian murder had been brought to an end, and that paramilitaries would have to be disarmed soon: 'Both governments should be shortly in a position to organise and implement a full demilitarisation which will require the co-operation and participation of the paramilitary organisations' (*Irish Press*, 22 September 1994, *Irish Times*, 22 September 1994, *The Independent*, 1 September 1994 on sectarian murder and IRA decommissioning; see also Bew and Gillespie 1996 p. 74). By October 1994 both governments had plans for decommissioning, although the Irish were arguing that decommissioning could only be achieved when all-party talks were well under way (*Irish Times*, 22 and 25 October 1994). On 17 November 1994, Albert Reynolds resigned as Taoiseach in a storm of domestic controversy. He was replaced by a Fine Gael/Labour Coalition led by John Bruton, who had a reputation as being more sympathetic to unionism than his Fianna Fáil predecessor.

So why did the Irish Government shift its position on decommissioning after the IRA ceasefire? This is most convincingly explained as arising out of the dual role which the Irish Government was expected to play during the 'peace process'. Like the British Government, which had to champion unionist interests while pushing that community towards accommodation, the Irish Government had a responsibility to push republicans towards the 'centre ground' but also to champion their interests (Duignan 1995 pp. 125, 138). In the wake of the ceasefire, pan-nationalism moved to shore up the Sinn Féin leadership and demonstrate the benefits flowing from the 'unarmed struggle'. If the Irish Government had broken ranks with the 'pan-nationalist front' and lined up with the British Government against Sinn Féin over decommissioning, this would have represented a severe blow to the credibility of the republican leadership's unarmed strategy and undermined the IRA's ceasefire.

The British Government claimed that it had to deliver on decommissioning to have any prospect of bringing about all-party talks (*The Times*, 16 December 1994). But Major attempted to avoid turning the surrender of guns into a precondition for progress and in October 1994 a distinction was drawn between the decommissioning of explosives (Semtex), which were not used for defensive purposes, and guns. In January 1995 it was suggested that the IRA might decommission their offensive weaponry and that this might be linked to prisoner releases and withdrawal of troops to barracks during daylight hours. The gap between the British Government's public insistence on decommissioning and its private view of decommissioning's futility was 'every day wider'. What the government was seeking was a gesture from the Provisionals, the sudden 'discovery' of Armalites in the Republic, 'Something to calm the increasingly fragile nerves of its Ulster Unionist allies that this peace process isn't leading them inexorably down a path to somewhere they would rather not go' (*The Guardian*, 17 January 1995). The new Irish Taoiseach, John Bruton, said both governments were agreed that the decommissioning of weapons was 'not a pre-condition' to all-party talks and rejected suggestions that the British were deliberately stalling and attempting to keep SF out of talks.

The Framework Documents: Overbalancing?

The Framework Documents were published on 22 February 1995. They are composed of two sections: the first contains the British Government's understanding of where agreement might be found among the parties on new institutions for Northern Ireland, while in the second section the British and Irish Governments present their best assessment of where agreement could be found concerning new political arrangements between Northern Ireland and the Republic and between the two governments. The proposals were 'strongly commended' to the parties (p. vi). They suggested the establishment of a power-sharing Northern Ireland Assembly and executive, with a system of checks and balances to protect minorities alongside a North–South body with considerable 'executive, consultative and harmonising functions'. Separate referendums in Northern Ireland and the Republic would be called to endorse any settlement. There was also an implicit threat to unionists that if they attempted to collapse any settlement, North–South co-operation would continue.

The Framework Documents were laced with the rhetoric of 'harmonisation' and North–South co-operation which nationalists had long interpreted as paving the way to Irish unity (see Chapter 3).

The Irish Government and Opposition were 'well-satisfied' with their achievement. The republican leadership's response to the documents was 'enthusiastic' and Adams commended its 'all-Ireland character' (*Irish Times*, 23 February 1995).

The principal unionist parties were united in their condemnation of the Framework Documents which they felt were another step down the slippery slope to Irish unity (Cochrane 1997 p. 334). Unionists feared that 'harmonisation' and the all-Ireland focus of the documents would lead 'inexorably to joint authority between Belfast and Dublin', with the North–South body acquiring more and more powers, thus becoming an 'embryonic all-Ireland government' leading ultimately to Irish unity ('Response to Frameworks for the Future' UUP, 10 March 1995). The policy areas for harmonisation suggested to unionists an ideological project of constitutional engin-eering to produce Irish unity rather than pragmatic co-operation. Furthermore the Assembly was so hamstrung with checks and balances that it would be deadlocked, leaving the North–South institution and the Anglo–Irish process to dominate. Unionists were looking for a final settlement, not an interim step towards Irish unity. Protestants and Catholics, like their political representatives, reacted very differently to the publication of the Framework Documents. A narrow majority in one poll believed the Framework Documents 'form the basis for a lasting peace'. While 73 per cent of Catholics agreed with this statement only 36 per cent of Protestants did, and 58 per cent of Protestants and 49 per cent of Catholics thought the documents 'will eventually lead to a united Ireland' (*Irish Political Studies* 1996 pp. 257–8).

Why did the governments produce such an apparently one-sided document? It has been claimed that the British Government simply miscalculated, and using the papers from the Mayhew talks they attempted to construct a balanced document without taking into account the changing political context between 1992 and 1995 (NIO source). This account appears less than convincing. Major had consulted Molyneaux over the Joint Declaration but he did not do so over the Framework Documents, even though he was aware by October 1994 of the UUP leader's increasingly difficult position within his own party (Major 1999 p. 465). A more likely explana-tion of the 'one-sidedness' of the Framework Documents is the British and Irish Governments' need to deliver concessions to the nationalist community in order to underpin the Sinn Féin leader-ship's position and entrench the IRA ceasefire. All-party negotiations would then allow some dilution by unionists (Bew, Patterson and Teague 1997 p. 211). Although Major later argued that unionists misunderstood the Framework Documents, in his memoirs he appeared to accept that they were tilted towards nationalism. In negotiating peace in Northern Ireland balance was important: 'If one side was happy I knew I had probably got it wrong. If my proposals attracted no more than grumbling and grudging acquiescence from both sides, I was perhaps on the right track' (Major 1999 p. 469, 492).

The consequence of entrenching Adams' position was the discrediting of Molyneaux's 'inside track' strategy and the end of his leadership of the UUP. In March 1995 the UUP rejected the Framework Documents and Molyneaux was faced with a damaging 'stalking horse' challenger for the leadership. His challenger claimed the UUP leadership since 1984 had 'totally miscalculated the Government's intentions and misled the pro-Union majority as to the security of the Union'. In August 1995 Molyneaux resigned the leadership. 'With Molyneaux no longer leader, Unionist opinion, on which any future constitutional settlement hinged, would be less biddable. And without a willingness on the part of the Protestant community to yield, no lasting settlement would be found by Major's government' (Seldon 1997 p. 529).

The alienation of unionists after the publication of the Framework Documents and the plight of James Molyneaux suggested that the British Government would have to work harder to keep unionists on board the peace process. In May 1995 the North Down by-election was won by the UK Unionist Robert McCartney, whose campaign was based on opposition to the Framework Documents. In July there was a confrontation at Drumcree between Orange marchers and nationalist residents in Portadown which crystallised unionist alienation and resentment at the course of the peace process. David Trimble, the MP for Upper Bann, played an important role in the Drumcree dispute and was subsequently elected, to the dismay of the British and Irish Governments, to replace James Molyneaux as party leader. He was supported by the grassroots of his party, as the most 'hardline' of the candidates, but not by the party hierarchy or fellow MPs.

The British Government's pursuit of the peace process, in spite of its 'understanding' with the Ulster Unionists in July 1993, suggested that the Unionist MPs at Westminster did not have a veto on British policy. Since July 1993 the British Government had continued its secret contacts with Sinn Féin; concealed these contacts; negotiated the nationalist-sounding Downing Street Declaration; 'clarified' the DSD for Sinn Féin after refusing to do so; accepted the 'permanence' of the IRA's ceasefire; watered down its commitments on decommissioning; and finally signed up to the nationalist-oriented Framework Documents. These were published after Major's support had fallen so low that he needed UUP support to command an overall Commons majority. In March 1995 the Sinn Féin chairperson told a conference that 'John Major, by the very act of publishing the Framework Documents in the teeth of opposition from right-wing Conservatives and the Unionist leaderships, has demonstrated that his government is not totally hostage to the mathematics of Westminster' (Bew and Gillespie 1996 pp. 89–90).

The US Charade: Adams' Visa and 'Washington 3'

The US Government played its part in the pan-nationalist front. US influence was believed to have won Adams his first visa to the USA in 1994 and forced the British to drop their exclusion of SF from an investment conference in Belfast. In 1995 Adams wanted to visit the USA again and to raise funds for Sinn Féin. The British again publicly opposed such a move and wanted the US Government to use its leverage with Sinn Féin to make progress on the decommissioning of IRA weapons before all-party talks could take place. In private, however, Mayhew told US officials that he wanted SF to 'seriously discuss decommissioning' rather than the handover of weapons before entering talks. Nancy Soderberg, Deputy National Security Adviser, described 'a complete disconnect' between what Mayhew asked of the US Government in private and his stronger public statements for decommissioning later the same day when he announced 'Washington 3' (O'Clery 1996 p. 191; and see below).

Patrick Mayhew's behaviour in not emphasising to the USA the importance of an arms handover could be interpreted as a complete blunder; or else the British Government, perhaps convinced of the moderation of the unionist electorate, may have believed that in spite of the publication of the Framework Documents it had room to push unionists further by taking steps to water down the conditions necessary to bring Sinn Féin into talks. Again, privately, the British Government may not have been too distressed at the decision by the US president to lift the ban on Adams and allow him to raise funds in the USA. This decision would also bolster the credibility of the SF leadership's unarmed strategy by demonstrating its influence in the USA. The British Government's publication of the Framework Documents and its weakening of the decommissioning conditions in Washington 3 resulted in rising unionist and Conservative back-bench dissent. The British Prime Minister made a public show of his fury at Clinton's decision over the Adams visa and refused to take the US President's telephone calls for five days (*Irish Times*, 15 March 1995, O'Clery 1996 p. 195). Later, Clinton praised Major for taking 'brave risks' in making peace 'within the context in which he must operate' (*The Daily Telegraph*, 18 April 1995). According to a source close to Clinton, by April 'the President had developed a genuine respect for Major and figured he was trying to do the right thing and understood why Major might need to make a gesture by not taking a phone call' (O'Clery 1996 p. 219).

Mayhew's announcement of the 'Washington 3' conditions for SF inclusion in all-party talks represented a further softening of the British Government's position on decommissioning. For Sinn Féin *to join all-party talks*:

(a) republicans must demonstrate a willingness in principle to disarm progressively;

(b) there should be agreement on the practical modalities of decommissioning;

(c) there should be actual decommissioning of *some* arms as a tangible confidence-building measure and to signal the start of a process. (my emphasis)

The British Government's line on decommissioning had been cloaked in ambiguity. Initially the British Government had demanded 'substantive progress' on IRA decommissioning before they could enter into talks *with ministers*, let alone all-party talks. In Washington Mayhew was arguing that British ministers would meet SF if there was a 'willingness in principle' to disarm progressively (*Irish Times*, 8 March 1995). In May 1995 Michael Ancram met a SF delegation which prompted the UUP to refuse to meet the minister while he was engaged in such talks (*The Independent*, 11 May 1995).

Explaining the Decommissioning Deadlock

John Major's principal interest was to see a successful peace process resulting in a stable accommodation between unionism and nationalism, which could only improve his re-election chances. The security forces had long held the view that there could be no purely military victory over the IRA. In spite of his dwindling support at Westminster and problems with his backbenchers Major had advanced the peace process, suggesting he was not the prisoner either of his own backbenchers or the Ulster Unionists. The UUP's influence at Westminster was limited; they could bring the Conservatives down but opinion polls suggested the result would be a Labour government with a large majority and without the need for UUP support. A former adviser to Patrick Mayhew argued that Major's ability to help unionists was 'severely limited': 'Mr Trimble ... cannot compel the Government to adopt a Unionist agenda and Mr Major is unable to find the means of delivering it without risking the central achievement of his period in office – peace in Northern Ireland.' The most that Trimble 'could expect to achieve is to exert a negative influence on events' (*The Guardian*, 18 January 1996).

The demand for decommissioning had been jointly made by the British and Irish Governments prior to the ceasefire and was not a post-cessation invention. The British Government was under pressure from unionists to maintain their position on decommissioning. The difficulties of unionists in negotiating directly with republicans had been signalled prior to the ceasefire. At the UUP's party conference in October 1993 the party reacted angrily to suggestions that it would engage in talks with Sinn Féin even after decommissioning (*Sunday Tribune*, 17 October 1993, Bew and Gillespie 1996 p. 21). Ulster Unionist MPs insisted that decommissioning take place while Major 'has had little or nothing to say on this subject, and it does not appear to be of over-riding concern in the Republic' (*Irish Times*, 1 September 1994, *The Guardian*, 1 September 1994). Pro-unionist Conservative cabinet members and backbenchers appeared more motivated by security issues (for example, decommissioning) than the Framework Documents, and tended to take their cue from the UUP (Mallie and McKittrick 1997 pp. 351, 352). This suggests that the primary influence on decommissioning was coming from the Ulster Unionists rather than from Conservative unionists (Seldon 1997 p. 484), although it is difficult to disentangle the two factors. Newspaper reports suggest that there were 'significant ministerial and inter-departmental differences of opinion' on the handling of the peace process. While Major was determined to push the process forward he was constrained by Michael Howard, the Home Secretary, and other right-wingers on the Conservative backbenches (*The Independent*, 3 August 1995). Gerry Adams acknowledged the constraints on Major but the peace process was 'the only positive thing he has going for him' and could put him in the history books (*New York Times*, 25 April 1995).

The British were 'demilitarising' and had retreated from their demand for IRA decommissioning before Sinn Féin representatives met ministers. The Irish and US Governments were both urging a gesture by the IRA on decommissioning in order to secure entry into all-party talks with unionists (*Irish Times*, 24 June 1995). In May Bruton and Major had described such a gesture as 'not so much a requirement from both governments, but a necessary step for Sinn Féin in talks with other political parties in Northern Ireland' (*Irish Times*, 24 June 1995). In June 1995 the British and Irish Governments agreed on a joint effort to break the deadlock over decommissioning. Dick Spring wrote to John Bruton, setting out the essential reasons for the deadlock over decommissioning:

> The essential difficulty as I see it is that the British Government, already in a vulnerable position, is afraid of movement away from its Washington tests, because there is nothing to protect its flank. On the other hand, those who believe that the British Government has the power to persuade the Unionists to engage in dialogue in the absence of progress on decommissioning are suffering from a delusion. And our own best assessment suggests that the Sinn Féin leadership is powerless to force the issue with their hardliners, even assuming they want to. (Quoted in Mallie and McKittrick 1997 p. 356)

There was some recognition even within Sinn Féin that it was the pressure from unionists and their reluctance to sit down to negotiate with Sinn Féin without any gesture on decommissioning which underpinned the decommissioning demand from Britain. In January 1995 Sinn Féin's newspaper argued: 'Today the Dublin government, the RUC and Garda chiefs, and many political parties agree that the issue of arms should not be pushed forward as an obstacle to the peace process. One suspects that even John Major does not believe that this should happen' (Patterson 1997 p. 275). In February 1995

Martin McGuinness 'revealed that Northern Ireland Minister Michael Ancram informally admitted that the British Government was relatively unconcerned but could not persuade unionists to negotiate with Sinn Féin without a guarantee on removal of arms' (*An Phoblacht*, 12 February 1995, quoted in Davis 1997 pp. 40–1).

While the Irish understood the British Government's problems with Unionists, Spring's best assessment was that the Sinn Féin leadership also had little room for manoeuvre and that the republican grassroots were getting restless (Mallie and McKittrick 1997 p. 356). The difficulties encountered by the Sinn Féin leadership with its dissidents may explain why by September the Irish Government had moved more into line with the republican position on decommissioning. According to Major, 'In private Adams and McGuinness were reasonable. They had boxed themselves in, and seemed to want help in getting out' (Major 1999 p. 477).

On 5 September the Irish Government pulled out of an Anglo–Irish summit scheduled for the following day. The Irish Prime Minister, John Bruton, had been coming under pressure from Sinn Féin, John Hume, Dick Spring and the Fianna Fáil opposition 'not to be seen to be embracing London's insistence on some form of IRA disarmament as a pre-condition to all-party constitutional talks' (*The Guardian*, 6 September 1995). The summit also looked set to embrace the option of an international disarmament commission to which SF also objected (*The Economist*, 2 December 1995). 'Senior republicans' later warned that Britain was close to its goal of splitting the nationalist consensus by winning Bruton's support for decommissioning: 'It's going to be very difficult for Mr Bruton as Taoiseach. By seeming to echo Major the whole image going out is that the nationalist consensus is gone. It was on that basis that the IRA gave their ceasefire' (*The Guardian*, 25 September 1995). One report suggested SF warned Bruton there would be 'blood on the streets' if he met John Major at their scheduled summit and agreed a 'twin-track' process: decommissioning and talks (*The Guardian*, 21 February 1996).

In order to preserve the IRA ceasefire the US Government and Irish Government had to make sure 'the whole image going out' was of a pan-nationalist consensus driving back the British. According to Major, 'The Irish were clearing every step they took with the Provisionals; and the Provisionals kept upping the ante' (Major 1999 p. 478). Days after the cancellation of the Anglo–Irish summit Dick Spring moved to restore this image when he argued against any decommissioning before all-party talks (Bew and Gillespie 1996

p. 118, 8 September 1995). In October Spring was claiming that 'The crucial point is that the guns are silent.' Both the British and Irish Governments believed that their respective 'clients', the unionists and the republicans, could be pushed no further (*The Independent*, 7 September 1995). British ministers reportedly believed the IRA should decommission out of conviction, but also because the government believed it should reflect unionist concerns, in parallel to the way the Irish Government reflected nationalist interests (*The Independent*, 6 September 1995).

The Mitchell Report and the End of the IRA Ceasefire

On 28 November the British and Irish Governments announced a 'twin-track process to make progress in parallel on the decommissioning issue and on all-party negotiations'. The two governments had 'the firm aim' of achieving all-party negotiations by the end of February. The governments would 'invite the parties to intensive preparatory talks to reach widespread agreement on the basis, participation, structure, format and agenda to bring all parties together for substantive negotiations'. These matters for discussion would include 'whether and how an elected body could play a part'. An international body, chaired by US Senator George Mitchell, was to be established to 'provide an independent assessment of the decommissioning issue'. The governments would not be bound to accept its recommendations, which were advisory, but 'will consider carefully any recommendations it makes and give them due weight on their merits'.

George Mitchell's report on decommissioning was published on 24 January 1996. It concluded that 'the paramilitary organisations will not decommission any arms prior to all-party negotiations'. However, there 'is a clear commitment on the part of those in possession of such arms to work constructively to achieve full and verifiable decommissioning as part of the process of all-party negotiations'. Major claims that Mitchell privately admitted that 'he was stretching a point for tactical reasons': that is, there was little evidence that the IRA would decommission, but this optimistic interpretation helped to push the peace process forward (Major 1999 p. 486). The Commission recommended that 'some decommissioning take place during the process of all-party negotiations rather than before or after'. Those involved in negotiations should affirm their total and absolute commitment to what became know as the 'Mitchell Principles' of democracy and non-violence.

The British Government struck a compromise between unionist and republican positions: the unionists would get an 'elected body' (rather than an assembly) while the republicans would be allowed into all-party talks without *prior* decommissioning. Decommissioning would take place during all-party talks as envisaged by Mitchell. John Major told the Commons, 'The government believe that such an elective process offers a viable alternative direct route to the confidence necessary to bring about all-party negotiations. In that context, it is possible to imagine decommissioning and such negotiations being taken forward in parallel' (House of Commons, vol. 270, col. 354, 24 January 1996). Patrick Mayhew, according to *The Guardian*, 'publicly insists the IRA and loyalists must hand in some weapons before talks, but in private is prepared to accept whatever proposals will ensure that Unionists will talk to Sinn Féin. Interested in an assembly if it will bring David Trimble along' (*The Guardian*, 20 Janauary 1996).

Unionists, although critical of Mitchell's failure to insist on decommissioning, were relatively contented. They endorsed the elected body but their position was ambiguous. This was sufficient to indicate that they might well take part in all-party talks without prior decommissioning. But it also allowed them to defend their flank from Paisley by insisting that the need for decommissioning had not been removed. The DUP was also prepared to join an elected body that contained Sinn Féin members.

Nationalists reacted with outrage over the British Government's stance, although this compromise had long been trailed and was winning support with the US Government, the British Labour opposition and even the Irish Government (Mitchell 1999 pp. 33–8, 40). Publicly nationalism had to remain united against the British to persuade republican hardliners that the pan-nationalist front was still united, powerful and could deliver through the unarmed struggle. Privately, however, the Irish Government had reacted positively to Trimble's suggestion of an elected assembly and probably realised this was the most likely grounds for a compromise which would bring both unionists and republicans to all-party talks (*The Guardian*, 16 November 1995, Major 1999 p. 480).

On 9 February 1996 the IRA ended its 18-month ceasefire by detonating a bomb in the Canary Wharf area of London's docklands killing two, and injuring over 100 others. The IRA's operation had been planned from the previous October or November, even before the Mitchell Commission was established (Patterson 1997 p. 285). Unionists argued that the IRA bomb demonstrated that the ceasefire had not been permanent and vindicated its view of the ceasefire as a tactic. Nationalists and republicans, on the other hand, tended to blame the British Government's intransigence and its interpretation of the Mitchell Report for bringing about the end of the ceasefire.

During the first IRA ceasefire the balance of power had shifted radically against the republicans. In 1994 the 'pan-nationalist front', which was to be the driving force behind the republican movement's unarmed strategy, consisted of Reynolds, Clinton, Hume and, arguably, also Kevin McNamara, keeper of the British Labour Party's pro-nationalist Irish policy. By February 1996 John Bruton had replaced Reynolds and Mo Mowlam had shifted Labour's policy towards the centre. Clinton was supportive of Major's compromise on elections to get round the deadlock on decommissioning and may have drawn closer to the British Government as the two deployed troops in Bosnia (O'Clery 1996 p. 227, p. 232, Seldon 1997 pp. 621–2). According to John Major:

> Throughout the seventeen month ceasefire, intelligence from all sources, overt and covert, had shown that much of the Provisional movement dissented from Adams's 'unarmed' strategy, and saw the ceasefire as no more than a tactic. Factions within the IRA did not want to be locked into the peaceful negotiations for which we were striving, and had been gearing up for a renewed campaign. (Major 1999 p. 488)

Reviving the Peace Process

The British and Irish Governments accelerated the pace of the peace process through a joint communiqué released on 28 February. This prompted accusations that the governments had moved in response to renewed IRA violence. The two governments demanded a restoration of the ceasefire and agreed 'that an elective process would have to be broadly acceptable and lead immediately and without further preconditions to the convening of all-party negotiations with a comprehensive agenda'. At the beginning of negotiations all parties with an electoral mandate would have to make clear their total and absolute commitment to the Mitchell principles of democracy and non-violence. The participants 'would also need to *address* ... its proposals on decommissioning' but this implied that actual decommissioning would not have to take place before the talks, including SF, started (my emphasis). Sinn Féin could take part in negotiations if the IRA reinstated its ceasefire and signed up to the Mitchell principles of democracy and non-violence.

The Forum elections on 30 May 1996 were the first elections to be held since the 1994 IRA ceasefire and were an important indicator of how the peace process had affected public opinion in Northern Ireland. The assumption of those in the British Government and others that there existed a 'moderate silent majority' in Northern Ireland to sweep away the region's 'intransigent politicians' is comparable to the hopes of 1972–74 (see Chapter 6 above and Dixon 1997b) and was severely shaken by the Forum elections, and also by the second confrontation at Drumcree in July 1996.

Although one in four people in Northern Ireland had voted for a party with a paramilitary wing, some of these votes could be interpreted as votes for the 'peace strategy' being pursued by those parties and, in SF's case as a vote for the reinstatement of the ceasefire. Sinn Féin, in spite of the end of the IRA's ceasefire and criticism from nationalist politicians, did better than expected, achieving its best ever result in a Northern Ireland election. The disastrous performance of the UUP against the DUP was of considerable importance for the fate of the peace process. The UUP, which had taken a more conciliatory approach to the peace process, crashed to its worst ever electoral performance (apart from European elections), while the DUP's hardline stance appeared to be reaping dividends and put pressure on David Trimble not to be seen to be 'too compromising' by softening his stance on SF entry into talks. The IRA failed to restore its ceasefire and its bombing of Manchester's city centre (injuring 200 people) and its murder of Garda Jerry McCabe hardened opinion in Britain and Ireland. When all-party talks started on 10 June Sinn Féin were prevented from taking their seats.

Drumcree and the Security Dilemma

The confrontation between Orange marchers returning along their 'traditional' route from a service at Drumcree Church through the nationalist Garvaghy Road area of Portadown raised tension in Northern Ireland and led to an annual confrontation during the peace process. The Orange marchers saw themselves exerting their democratic and cultural right to march on the 'Queen's highway' along traditional routes which they had walked for over 100 years. At the time of the Anglo–Irish Agreement, unionists marched through the nationalist 'Tunnel' area of Portadown in spite of government bans. This led to violent clashes with the RUC and the march was subsequently re-routed along the mixed Garvaghy Road area. In recent years the Garvaghy area had become overwhelmingly Catholic and the residents more resistant to the parade. Marchers argued that nationalist protest was IRA-inspired since the newly-formed Garvaghy Road residents' association was led by Brendan Mac Cionnaith, a former republican prisoner, whom they refused to meet.

The nationalist residents of the Garvaghy Road objected to what they saw as a 'triumphalist', intimidating, sectarian parade passing through an overwhelmingly nationalist area. The nationalists demanded 'parity of esteem' and called for the marchers to return by the same route they had come. Dick Walsh argued: 'The right to march, now loudly proclaimed by the unionists and resisted by their opponents, was once among the demands of the civil rights movement. A right often officially denied by ministers of home affairs and unofficially by Mr Paisley's friends' (*Irish Times*, 20 July 1996).

The Drumcree march, like the decommissioning issue, was seen by nationalists and unionists as an indicator of the power of nationalism and unionism to influence developments in the peace process. After reaching an agreement in July 1995, Paisley and Trimble headed the march and danced a jig when they entered the town centre. This was seen by nationalists as triumphalist and breaking the spirit of the agreement; consequently relations were soured between nationalists and unionists. David Trimble's 'hardline' credentials were boosted at Drumcree and this probably contributed to his election to the leadership of the UUP the following September. The confrontations at Drumcree, which became annual events, took many observers by surprise, particularly those, such as the British Government, who had detected a gap between the moderation of the masses compared with the intransigence of the political elites (Dixon 1997d).

The conflict over Drumcree probably reflected polarisation within Northern Ireland, but also added to it. It represented an alternative indicator of public opinion to elections and opinion polls. The confrontation at Drumcree in July 1996 resulted in appalling violence and shocked observers and public opinion. Unionists tended, with some reason, to see the conflict as being engineered by republicans (*Irish Times*, 5 March 1997, O'Doherty 1998). Nationalists were more likely to portray the confrontation as an upsurge of community feeling aggravated by Paisley and Trimble's 'triumphant dance' the previous year. This time the RUC re-routed the Orange Order's traditional march away from the Garvaghy Road and there were fears that up to 100 000 Orangemen would converge on Drumcree to push the march through. This stand-off resulted in three days of rioting and sympathy protests across Northern Ireland which brought the region to a standstill. On 8 July Michael McGoldrick, a Catholic taxi driver, was murdered in neighbouring Lurgan. The reaction to Drumcree was symptomatic of unionist alienation from a peace process in which the British Government appeared to be weakening the Union by making concession after concession to republican and nationalist demands. The decision to re-route the Orange march was seen by unionists as a threat to their identity and an attempt to appease republicans who had engineered the confrontation.

The mobilisation of unionists exposed the vulnerability of the security forces in ways similar to that in 1972, 1974 and 1986. The RUC were stretched by widespread rioting and the Army had to be deployed. *The Independent* reported:

> substantial parts of the country seem to be largely in the grip of men in balaclavas who, through a mixture of menace and force of numbers, are posing a serious challenge to lawful authority. The security forces have made it clear that, with thousands of loyalist protesters active at spots all over Northern Ireland, they cannot guarantee free passage – even on major roads. The RUC is plainly almost at full stretch and more British troops are being sent in... almost elemental forces which periodically spring to the surface of Northern Ireland, are being unleashed. The current crisis... could let loose elements that no one will be able to control. (*The Independent*, 11 July 1996)

Trimble met the leader of the hardline paramilitary organisation, the Loyalist Volunteer Force, highlighting the 'grey area' between constitutional and unconstitutional politics. On 11 July, after a five-day stand-off between RUC and unionists at Drumcree, as well as trouble across Northern Ireland, the RUC Chief Constable allowed the march to go ahead. He feared that the confrontation planned for the following day would have brought thousands of Orangemen on to the streets and led to a widespread breakdown of law and order. He indicated that 3000 soldiers and police could not have contained 60–70 000 loyalist demonstrators and the security forces might have had to use live ammunition to stop the crowd (*The Sunday Times*, 14 July 1996, *The Times*, 15 July 1996). Following the RUC's decision to allow the Orange march to go ahead, there was serious rioting in republican areas which SF struggled to restrain.

During and after Drumcree 1996 there was low-level conflict across Northern Ireland. The RUC estimated over 600 Protestant and Catholic families moved during the week of the 'Siege of Drumcree' due to 'ethnic cleansing', resulting in 'probably the biggest single episode of demographic realignment in 25 years'. Up to £50 million of damage was done to property (*Irish Times*, 28 December 1996). In the aftermath of Drumcree nationalists boycotted Protestant shops, putting some out of business. Sinn Féin supported the boycott but denied they were orchestrating it. There were also incidents of attacks on churches, Orange Halls and civilian homes. Loyalists picketed a Catholic church at Harryville for 20 months in protest against a ban on an Orange march at nearby Dunloy (*Irish Times*, 4 December 1996, *Irish News*, 1 June 1998). *The Economist* commented: 'Intimidation and boycott are the stuff of Irish history. They are hard to prove and harder still to quantify, but their effects are poisonous and lingering' (*The Economist*, 3 August 1996).

The confrontation at Drumcree in 1996 highlighted, once again, the 'security dilemma': the limited ability of the security forces to cope with a mass uprising among unionists. There were fears that Northern Ireland could descend into all-out civil war. The new RUC Chief Constable, Ronnie Flanagan, later said: 'Northern Ireland cannot withstand another summer like this one. The intensity of the violence which our officers withstood was of a scale that I hadn't seen over 25 years. The country stared into the face of great difficulty and crept right to the edge of the abyss' (*The Independent*, 31 August 1996). Patrick Mayhew issued a statement after the Anglo–Irish Conference meeting on 18 July 1996 which claimed 'that he could not guarantee the RUC would be able to stand up to another Drumcree-type show of force'. Mark Durkan, SDLP chairman, said Mayhew was sending out a dangerous signal: 'People are getting a cue now from the Secretary of State that the way in which you impose or secure the outcome you want on a contentious march is to use local geography and mobilise numbers' (*Irish Times*, 20 July 1996).

The peace process had again reached deadlock. The polarisation of society in Northern Ireland indicated at the Forum elections and as a result of Drumcree constrained the possibility of movement towards the centre ground among nationalist and unionist political elites. British hopes in the 'moderate silent majority' – as with the first peace process 1972–74 – were again dashed. For Major the centre ground 'barely existed' (Seldon 1997 p. 662). In the wake of Drumcree Major appealed to the people of Northern Ireland to reject the extremes in Northern Ireland and look to the centre (even though these 'extremists' had just been 'rewarded' at Drumcree: see *The Independent*, 17 July 1996). Mayhew accepted the faults in his own 'civil society' analysis: 'For my own part, and I think for a great many people, the wish had been father to the thought that on each side ancient fires of hostility and fear had greatly diminished. They had not' (Mayhew speech to the British–Irish Association, 7 September 1996).

New Labour, New Peace Process?

On 1 May 1997 a 'new' Labour Government was elected with a 177-seat majority. Those who accepted the nationalist view of the peace process believed that a Labour Government, with its large majority and traditional sympathies for Irish unity, would easily succeed where the Conservatives had failed. Sceptics tended to interpret the breakdown of the first IRA ceasefire as arising out of the problems of bringing republicans and unionists simultaneously to the negotiating table and were therefore less optimistic about the prospects of swift progress.

The Labour Government's success in steering the peace process to the Good Friday Agreement in April 1998 could be taken as evidence that the Conservatives were foot-dragging. Yet in many respects the Labour Government's policy towards Northern Ireland followed that of the previous Conservative Government. In Opposition Labour had given bipartisan support to Conservative policy and in government it attempted to deliver the Conservatives' 'Mitchell Report compromise'. The unionists already had their Forum and the Labour Government offered Sinn Féin certain procedural guarantees, including an end date to all-party talks. Labour's fudge on decommissioning was not far from the Conservatives' aspiration that it should be dealt with in parallel, but not at the start of talks. Labour's task was made easier by the political credit that comes to a newly-elected government with such a large mandate. The relatively good showing for the UUP against the DUP in the General Election eased the electoral pressure on Trimble and facilitated his decision to enter all-party talks which included Sinn Féin.

The Labour Government attempted to balance reassurance to unionism with concessions to republicans to restore the IRA's cease-fire. Prime Minister Tony Blair delivered a speech which reaffirmed his belief in the UK. Northern Ireland would remain in the Union so long as that was the wish of the majority expressed formally through a referendum and endorsed by the British Parliament: 'This principle of consent is and will be at the heart of my Government's policies on Northern Ireland. It is the key principle.' Given Labour's adherence to this principle Blair argued, 'none of us in this hall today, even the youngest, is likely to see Northern Ireland as anything but a part of the United Kingdom. That is the reality, because the consent principle is now almost universally accepted.' Having sought to reassure unionism, Blair turned to Sinn Féin: 'The settlement train is leaving. I want you on that train. But it is leaving anyway, and I will not allow it to wait for you. You cannot hold the process to ransom any longer. So end the violence. Now.'

The Labour Government gambled that in their 'honeymoon period' after the election they could concede to Sinn Féin's demands, win an IRA ceasefire and also bring the unionists into all-party talks. If the IRA refused to declare a ceasefire then the peace process was effectively dead and the two governments could fall back on the all-party talks process, knowing they had made all reasonable attempts to restore the ceasefire. The IRA restored its 'complete cessation' on 20 July but its second ceasefire was met with more caution and scepticism than the scenes of celebration which accompanied the first one. The DUP's deputy leader, Peter Robinson, complained:

> They [the IRA/SF] can enter the talks. They don't have to indicate that they are permanently going to give up their violence, so they can take the gun out when they wish to again. They don't have to hand over any weapons in order to come in and they have got the framework document as the basis for negotiations. Why on earth would the IRA not call a ceasefire in all of those circumstances?

Following the IRA ceasefire, attention now focused on the Union-ist Party leader, David Trimble. If the UUP walked away from talks there would be no prospect of an agreed settlement. The fear of unionists was that a settlement might then be imposed by the British and Irish Governments and submitted to a referendum. Although the British Government had denied this in the past it had been sufficiently ambiguous to leave room for doubt. Trimble carried out a wide-ranging consultation exercise within his party. Ian Paisley warned Trimble that if he entered all-party negotiations he 'could find himself... a chief without Indians'. Although the UUP did not attend the start of talks on 9 September 1997, the UUP (along with the UDP and PUP) took their seats on 17 September in what many commentators agreed was a brave gamble. On 23 September the Ulster Unionists sat down at the negotiating table with Sinn Féin for the first time in 75 years. A leaked document later revealed Blair's appreciation of the risks which Trimble had taken for peace. He told the US 'Congressional Irish Lobby' that Trimble 'had come a good deal further than many Unionists wanted him to... It was important to remember that Trimble was under constant attack from Paisley and McCartney, so that giving comfort to the Ulster Unionists was vital' (*Irish Times*, 17 February 1998).

The talks process lasted from September 1997 until April 1998. The British Government attempted to balance concessions towards republicans with concessions towards unionists. Violence spilled over and both the UDP, the political wing of the UDA, and Sinn Féin were temporarily kicked out of the talks after violence by their military wings. The Heads of Agreement document in January 1998, as well as visits to loyalist prisoners by Mowlam and Trimble, helped to steady loyalist nerves about the direction of the peace process, and clarification a few weeks later of this document reassured republicans. The republican leadership had, to some extent, prepared its followers and voters for a settlement that fell well short of republican objectives. Gerry Adams had lowered republican expectations by talking in the summer of 1997 of a process producing a renegotiation of the Union. In the autumn of 1997 a splinter group of republicans balked at signing up to the 'Mitchell principles' and broke away to form the 'Real IRA'. Trimble was criticised for failing to prepare his party and supporters for the compromises necessary in any settlement.

Sunningdale cast a long shadow over the negotiations. A 'senior SDLP representative' said that his party was conscious of Trimble's difficulties and of the danger of a 'dramatic scenario with echoes of 1974' if unionists were pushed too far (*Sunday Business Post*, 5 April

1998). If the British and unionists had pushed the nationalists and republicans 'too far' then the Provisionals would probably have ended their ceasefire, while the alienation of the SDLP would have made any accommodation a distant prospect. The two governments once again appeared to be playing their role as champions for their clients in Northern Ireland. UUP sources claimed 'The Irish Government are fully batting for Sinn Féin and giving Sinn Féin a veto', and unionists expected Blair to 'do for us what the Irish Government appears to be doing for the nationalists' (*Irish Times*, 8 April 1998).

The Good Friday Agreement

The outline of the Good Friday Agreement (or Belfast Agreement) which was signed on 10 April 1998 was widely anticipated, and to a considerable extent dictated by what was deemed to be 'politically possible'. The Agreement, which resulted in two periods of devolution (December 1999–February 2000 and May 2000–) comprised the following.

A Northern Ireland Assembly

This is a 108-member assembly, elected by proportional representation (single transferable vote), to have legislative and executive power over those matters formerly the responsibility of the Northern Ireland departments. The Assembly is constrained by checks and balances to prevent majority domination. Members of the Legislative Assembly (MLAs) have to indicate whether they are unionists or nationalists (or 'other') for the purpose of cross-community voting. There are two alternative special voting procedures which can be triggered for key decisions. Firstly, *parallel consent*, in which a majority of both unionists and nationalists present and voting must support a proposal. Secondly, *weighted majority* where 60 per cent of MLAs, including 40 per cent of both nationalists and unionists, must be in support. This element of the GFA has been criticised for entrenching and legitimising communal division rather than attempting to transcend it. A consultative 'Civic Forum' has been formed which comprises representatives of business, trade unions, the voluntary sector and others with expertise.

An Executive

The First Minister (Trimble, UUP) and Deputy First Minister (Mallon, SDLP) were elected by a procedure which required cross-community support. The rest of the 10-member executive (3 UUP, 3 SDLP, 2 SF, 2 DUP) was appointed by the d'Hondt formula and reflects party strengths in the Assembly, guaranteeing executive positions for all parties with sufficient popular support.

The North–South Ministerial Council

This brings together those with executive responsibilities in Northern Ireland and the Republic and covers 12 subject areas. There are six areas of co-operation (Transport, Agriculture, Education, Health, Environment and Tourism) and six implementation bodies (Inland Waterways, Food Safety, Trade and Business Development, Special EU Programmes, Language, Aquacultural and Marine Matters). Decisions on the Council are taken by agreement on both sides, with each side being accountable to their respective parliaments.

The 'British–Irish Council and Intergovernmental Conference'

The aim of this is to bring together representatives of the assemblies in Britain and Ireland to promote 'the totality of relationships among the peoples of these islands'.

Equality, Human Rights, Victims

The European Convention on Human Rights has been incorporated into UK law. In addition there will be a Bill of Rights for Northern Ireland. A Human Rights Commission and an Equality Commission have been established. The Northern Ireland Victims Commission is part of a programme of reconciliation work.

RUC Reform

An independent commission, under the Catholic former Conservative Northern Ireland Minister, Chris Patten, reported in September 1999, proposing radical reform of the RUC.

Decommissioning and Prisoners

The GFA said little about decommissioning, committing the participants to use 'any influence they may have, to achieve the decommissioning of all paramilitary arms within two years'. Those paramilitary groups who had not established or maintained a 'complete and unequivocal cease-fire' would not qualify for early release of their prisoners, who would all be released within two years.

A Balanced Settlement?

Inevitably, pro-GFA unionists and nationalists presented the Agreement to their supporters in very different terms. For unionists it entrenched the Union and was a disaster for republicans, while for republicans it was a further step towards Irish unity. The North–South bodies were a key concession for pro-GFA nationalists and republicans. It could be argued that they formed the embryo for a government of a united Ireland which would gradually develop through a process of Modernisation and harmonisation (see Chapter 3). Nationalists and republicans also gained from a strong commitment to the equality agenda, security, justice and language reform. Republicans could also take comfort from proposals for the swift release of paramilitary prisoners. A Sinn Féin Ard Fheis endorsed the Agreement and the leadership called for a 'Yes' vote, North and South, in the referendum. A poll at a Sinn Féin special conference of 138 delegates found 44 per cent who said they could accept the agreement, 28 per cent who said they could not and 28 per cent 'don't know's (*Sunday Tribune*, April 1998).

Republicans opposing the GFA – the Real IRA, the Continuity IRA and the 32 County Sovereignty Committee – argued that it represented the defeat of the republican movement. The 'armed struggle' had not been fought to see the legitimation of British rule in Ireland, the restoration of 'Stormont', the end of Sinn Féin abstentionism, acceptance of the principle of consent and the repeal of Articles 2 and 3. The all-Ireland referendum endorsing the GFA overturned the result of the all-Ireland 1918 General Election from which republicans claimed a democratic mandate for armed struggle. The Commissions on equality, human rights and policing were all British-appointed.

The pro-GFA unionists argued that they had stood and fought for the Union while the rejectionist unionists had run away. The GFA had preserved the Union, removed the Anglo–Irish Agreement and restored power and democracy to Northern Ireland. The East–West 'British–Irish Council and Intergovernmental Conference' was also an important recognition of the British dimension of the settlement and a counter-weight to the North–South body. The repeal by the Irish Government of Articles 2 and 3, and their replacement endorsing unity by consent, strengthened and entrenched the Union. Prisoner releases would happen regardless of the GFA and it was expected that decommissioning would take place before Sinn Féin sat in an executive. It was argued that the anti-GFA unionists had no alternative to the Agreement and unionist intransigence would result in an acceleration of the Anglo–Irish process under direct rule.

Unionist misgivings about the GFA were reinforced by the strong republican embrace of the Agreement. Anti-GFA unionists attacked the GFA on several key issues:

(a)   'terrorists' in government without any IRA decommissioning;
(b)   the early release of IRA prisoners without any decommissioning;
(c)   parades and the expected decision to ban the Drumcree parade;
(d)   provisions in the agreement for North–South bodies;
(e)   later the issue of RUC reform became an important bone of contention.

Six out of ten UUP MPs at Westminster, the Loyalist Volunteer Force and the Orange Order opposed the GFA. The mainstream loyalist paramilitaries and their political wings (UVF, UDA and UFF) supported the GFA. David Trimble managed to win over the UUP executive (53 votes to 23), and the Ulster Unionist Council, which consists of grassroots activists, voted by 72 per cent to 28 per cent (540 votes to 210) in favour of the Agreement.

The Referendum

The Good Friday Agreement attempted – like previous British–Irish agreements – to be all things to all people. During the negotiations, Trimble told his executive that his bottom line was that before

Sinn Féin had got into the executive it would have to drop its abstentionist line and begin decommissioning. The UUP leader believed he
had reassurances from Blair that the process of decommissioning
would begin immediately after the assembly came into being in June
1998 (*Sunday Tribune*, 12 April 1998). In the run-up to the referendum
on the GFA the Labour Government encouraged the belief among
unionists that Sinn Féin would not get into any executive without
decommissioning, but did not state this unequivocally. The *letter* of
the Agreement did not insist on IRA decommissioning before Sinn
Féin participated in the executive, but the British Prime Minister
cultivated the *impression* among unionists that this was the *spirit* of
the Agreement. These assurances had been phrased in a way to give
him 'wriggle room' at a later date. During the referendum campaign
he reassured unionists over prisoner releases, decommissioning and
participation in the executive. In a speech during the referendum
campaign to the Royal Ulster Agricultural Society, Blair set four
tests to clarify 'whether the terms and the spirit of the agreement are
being met and whether violence has genuinely been given up for
good' which would become 'more rigorous over time':

(a) a clear commitment that there was 'an end to violence for good'
     and that the 'so-called war is finished, done with, gone';
(b) the ceasefires had to be complete and unequivocal and this
     included 'punishment beatings' and the need for the dismant-
     ling of paramilitary organisations;
(c) 'full co-operation with the Independent Commission on
     Decommissioning';
(d) no other groups to be used as 'proxies for violence'.

These reassurances, like those given to Trimble during the negotiations of the GFA, were carefully worded to give the public impression of support for the unionist position, but were sufficiently
ambiguous to avoid a cast-iron commitment.

The referendum was passed by 71.1 per cent to 28.8 per cent on a
high 81 per cent turnout in Northern Ireland. It was calculated that
the referendum passed with the support of a bare majority of Protestants and an overwhelming majority of Catholics. An exit poll for
RTE, the Irish television company, suggested that 51 per cent of
Protestants and 99 per cent of Catholics supported the Agreement
(*The Independent on Sunday*, 24 May 1998, while a *Sunday Times* poll
found 96 per cent of Catholics and 55 per cent of Protestants in

favour). The 'Yes' campaign had the support of the media, the British and Irish Governments, most of Northern Ireland's politicians and several influential figures, including the former RUC Chief Constable and 'policeman's policeman', Sir John Hermon. Analysis of the referendum result suggested that the 'Yes' vote in the Unionist camp was bolstered by 140–160 000 new voters, most of them Protestants, who came out to support the Good Friday Agreement (*Sunday Tribune*, 25 May 1998). There was a real danger that if these voters did not turn out for the Assembly elections that the anti-GFA unionists could win sufficient seats to deadlock the Assembly. In the Republic the referendum was passed by 94 per cent to 6 per cent on a low 56 per cent turnout.

In the wake of the referendum result Blair backed down on the spirit of the commitments made during the campaign. The British Government refused to enact legislation which linked the release of paramilitary prisoners to decommissioning. Neither did it insist that the IRA decommission before Sinn Féin entered the executive. At the Assembly elections in June 1998 the UUP suffered their worst ever result (apart from European elections). The DUP came within 3 per cent of the UUP vote and the anti-GFA unionists won a total of 27 seats, just three short of the 30 seats needed to deadlock the Assembly. The high turnout for the referendum campaign, which was thought to have brought out 'Yes' voting unionists, was not repeated for the Assembly elections.

Stretching and Bridging?

Although the Good Friday Agreement had been endorsed in the referendum by a majority of both Catholics and Protestants, they were each probably endorsing contrasting interpretations of the Agreement. The impasse over decommissioning, which dated back to before the IRA's first 1994 ceasefire, continued to dog the progress of the peace process. As the Agreement was implemented expectations were once again deflated on both sides, but particularly among unionists. According to opinion polls, unionists believed that nationalists had gained more from the GFA and increasingly opposed it. Reflecting this the British and Irish Governments first put pressure on the Sinn Féin leadership to stretch its constituency by moving on decommissioning and thereby taking pressure off the hard-pressed UUP leadership.

The UUP leadership attempted on several occasions to circumvent the decommissioning impasse. But by February 1999 it was clear to the *Irish Times* that Trimble was in no position to move on decommissioning and survive as leader of the party (*Irish Times*, editorial 3 February 1999). The Irish Prime Minister put pressure on the IRA by insisting that failure to decommission was incompatible with participation in an executive (*The Sunday Times*, 24 February 1999). An opinion poll published on 4 March 1999 suggested the depth of public division over the decommissioning issue. A clear majority of unionists now opposed the GFA (59 per cent to 41 per cent); 68 per cent of unionists opposed allowing SF into the executive without decommissioning; 20 per cent would allow SF in with some IRA decommissioning, but 34 per cent insisted all arms be surrendered. Nationalists overwhelmingly supported the GFA. The two governments published the Hillsborough Declaration on 1 April 1999 which stated that decommissioning was 'not a precondition but an obligation' under the GFA. It proposed that nominations be made to the executive before IRA weapons are decommissioned but that power not be transferred to the executive until around the same time as the IRA decommission. The SDLP and the US Government supported the Declaration, isolating Sinn Féin.

The Hillsborough Declaration did not produce the hoped-for shift in the republicans' position on decommissioning. The Sinn Féin leadership had also been experiencing continuing problems in trying to preserve the unity of the republican movement. The RUC continued to be sceptical about the usefulness of decommissioning since this might remove discipline and lead to splits (*The Economist*, 9 May 1998). The Real IRA had carried out the Omagh bombing in July 1998, the worst single outrage of the troubles, killing 29 and injuring 310. Remarkably, Adams condemned the bombing and there were subsequent reports of the IRA 'policing' the RIRA. In March 1999 a leaked republican briefing complained that the movement had 'been pushed too far' (Bew and Gillespie 1999 p. 390).

Having failed to move Sinn Féin, pressure was now applied to the UUP leadership. Within weeks of the Hillsborough Declaration Trimble was being urged to accept a deal which promised no decommissioning, but the UUP leader was constrained by internal party resistance. In the European elections which followed, the UUP slumped to their lowest ever share of the popular vote. The two anti-Agreement candidates won 31.4 per cent of the vote, while the two pro-Agreement candidates secured just 20.4 per cent. The UUP were almost pushed into fourth place by Sinn Féin, who doubled their share of the vote. In July 1999 Tony Blair intensified pressure on the UUP and attempted to spin the parties into Agreement. In *The Way Forward* document, the two governments wanted the UUP to support the transfer of power and the establishment of the executive in return for assurances that IRA decommissioning would follow shortly after. Blair claimed that there had been shifts within the republican movement which represented a 'historic and seismic change in the political landscape'. There would be decommissioning within days of the devolution of power, and the handover of weapons within weeks. Unionists felt that Blair had offered no guarantees about decommissioning or evidence of this 'seismic shift' in republican thinking; later, Adams criticised Blair's 'seismic shift' comment for the problems it created with his own grassroots. The SDLP refused to guarantee that they would stay and work with the executive if Sinn Féin was expelled for failing to decommission. David Trimble offered to 'jump together' with Gerry Adams, but the UUP would sit in the executive with SF if the IRA simultaneously decommissioned. Power was devolved to the Assembly and executive, but there was insufficient cross-community support for the institutions to work. As *The Times* commented, 'Having felt duped by the referendum promises Unionists were not going to allow themselves to swallow soundbites again' (*The Times* editorial, 16 July 1999).

Both the Sinn Féin and Ulster Unionist Party leaderships continued to face considerable difficulties in managing their parties, and increasingly each recognised the other's problems. Nevertheless in November 1999 David Trimble declared his willingness to sit in an executive with Sinn Féin without decommissioning, but he promised to withdraw from the executive in February if there had been no IRA decommissioning. On 2 December 1999 power was devolved to the executive and Assembly. After just 10 weeks of devolution the 'seismic shift' in the republican movement that Blair perceived in the summer of 1999 had not resulted in the surrender of any weapons and the British Government – fearing the demise of Trimble's leadership – suspended the executive and the devolution of power. According to *The Economist*:

> Senior British politicians say they have no doubt that Messrs Adams and McGuinness are sincere in wanting peace. And they are prepared to accept that Sinn Féin's leaders are struggling, so far in vain, to get hardliners in the IRA to hand over even the very

few weapons that would be needed to get the process started again. Whatever the rights and wrongs of decommissioning, the British seem to have judged that Mr Trimble was under more immediate internal threat than Messrs Adams and McGuinness.' (*The Economist*, 19 February 2000; see also *The Observer*, 30 January 2000)

Unionists were unhappy not only with the failure of the IRA to decommission, but also the implementation of the Patten Report and the key ministerial posts taken by Sinn Féin in the executive. Martin McGuinness became Minister for Education while Bairbre de Brun became Minister for Health, Social Services and Public Safety. The majority of unionist opinion appeared to be opposed to Trimble's leap of faith (i.e., getting on for half the UUP plus the anti-GFA unionist parties). Following an IRA statement in May 2000 which promised to 'put weapons beyond use' David Trimble, having survived a serious leadership challenge and narrowly won the support of the governing council of his party, once again took the plunge and devolution was restored to Northern Ireland on 29 May 2000. The attempt of the peace process to 'bridge the gap' between nationalists and unionists, after 30 years of 'real' and 'propaganda' war, continues uncertainly. The leaderships of both the UUP and SF are under considerable pressure as they continue to try to sustain the Good Friday Agreement.

Conclusion: A Critique of a Nationalist and a Unionist View of the Peace Process

The problem for the British Government in defending its position in a high-profile way against both nationalist and unionist critiques is that these defences can be used in the propaganda war against it. For example, emphasising the positive and long-term role the British have played in the peace process is likely to antagonise some sections of unionist opinion. On the other hand, emphasising the continuity of British policy and impracticality of Irish unity is unlikely to convince republicans to enter a peace process which they believe will result in Irish unity.

The account of the peace process presented here casts serious doubt on the influential nationalist and unionist views of the peace process described at the beginning of Chapter 9 (an analysis of the peace process is presented in the Conclusion).

The nationalist view can be critiqued on several grounds.

1. *There was no radical shift in British policy under Brooke which opened the way for the IRA ceasefire.* Since the early 1970s the British had wanted to bring the IRA into the political process but the republican movement, believing it was winning, rejected these overtures. If Sinn Féin had been admitted to all-party talks without a ceasefire the unionists would probably have walked out. The British position on its strategic or economic interests and Irish unity had changed little since the early 1970s, and successive British governments had kept the lines of communication open to the republican movement.

2. *The British government played a pivotal role in driving the peace process and it was not principally an Irish affair.* British politicians since at least 1989 (with 'contacts' dating from 1990) had been investigating the possibility of bringing the republican movement into the political process. The 'back-channel' contacts and public speeches by Brooke and Mayhew indicated a British commitment to bringing Sinn Féin into the political process even while IRA bombings continued.

3. *All-party talks without Sinn Féin were 'worth a penny candle'* since they represented an important incentive for Sinn Féin to end IRA violence.

4. *The British did not deliberately obstruct the peace process or artificially establish decommissioning as a barrier for Sinn Féin.* The British government's interests in Northern Ireland were for stability and an agreed settlement (see Conclusion). John Major was more likely to benefit electorally and secure his place in history if he could pursue the peace process to a successful conclusion. There is evidence of British determination to push the 'peace process' in the British Government's contacts with SF dating back to 1990, its efforts at confidence-building; negotiation of the 'nationalist-oriented' Downing Street Declaration and Framework Documents; and its watering down of commitments on decommissioning. John Major advanced the peace process even though he was operating under significant constraints from domestic public opinion; a precarious parliamentary majority and then minority; Conservative backbenchers; and the need to keep unionists 'on board'. The impasse over decommissioning flowed more from the need to reassure unionists and bring them into the peace process than to secure his parliamentary majority, as the Irish Government acknowledges in its private correspondence with the British. This problem was exacerbated by the apparent polarisation of opinion within Northern Ireland. The Labour

Government, even with a large parliamentary majority, has struggled to overcome unionist insistence on decommissioning.

There are several key problems with the unionist view of the peace process:

1. *The peace process is not a 'surrender process'.* Britain's primary interest in Northern Ireland lies in stability and this is most likely to be achieved by reaching a historic accommodation between nationalism and unionism (see Conclusion). If the British have been trying to disengage from Northern Ireland since 1921 why has it – having succeeded in withdrawing from the biggest Empire the world has ever known – failed to pull out? If Britain has been trying to disengage since 1921 then this would suggest that Britain has had no selfish strategic interest in Northern Ireland not only since the end of the Cold War in 1989, but even before the Cold War started in the 1940s. Presumably, the end of Britain's economic interest in Northern Ireland also dates from the 1920s. If this is the case then surely the British have had better opportunities to quietly slip Northern Ireland out of the Union during the past 75 years rather than going through the current, high-profile, peace process? Britain had considerable incentive to coerce Irish unity during the Second World War but this was impracticable. During the recent conflict the most likely occasion for British withdrawal was the mid-1970s following the collapse of power-sharing, but this course of action was seen to be disastrous by both the British *and Irish* Governments. Britain's primary interest in Northern Ireland is stability and this is unlikely to be achieved through withdrawal (see Chapter 7).

2. *The peace process is not motivated by the economic effect of the bombing of the City of London in 1992.* The government's public overtures to Sinn Féin date back to the Brooke Speech in 1989 and secret 'contacts' were initiated in 1990 well *before* the City of London bombings. For a long time Britain has not had any economic benefit from remaining in Northern Ireland. The Baltic Exchange bombing may have increased the economic incentive for Britain to reach a settlement, but this was more likely to be achieved by reaching a stable accommodation than through a withdrawal resulting in destabilisation.

3. *British public opinion would probably support the expulsion of Northern Ireland from the Union.* The vulnerability of unionism is that it tends not to be seen in Britain as part of the nation. Opinion polls have consistently shown support for withdrawal from Northern Ireland and any solution which would rid Britain of this issue.

However, withdrawal would probably not result in a stable resolution to the conflict due to the strength of unionist resistance to a united Ireland as illustrated throughout the conflict.

4.   *Harmonisation and North–South structures are unlikely to erode unionist opposition to Irish unity.* The problem with this is that all the evidence (see Chapter 3) suggests that economic integration does not necessarily lead to political integration or the erosion of national identities. In spite of the harmonising institution of the EU and the alleged onset of globalisation unionists have, if anything, become more opposed to Irish unity and an Irish identity than they were 30 years ago.

11

Conclusion: The Politics of War and Peace

Introduction

This conclusion reviews and draws together the themes and arguments of the book to show how the concepts of power, ideology and 'reality' can provide a convincing explanation of the recent conflict, and in particular of the peace process. An attempt is then made to assess the interests of the key parties and governments to the conflict and their power – through both the 'real' and propaganda war – to realise these interests. Why has the British Government been unable to impose a settlement on the conflict? What are the limits to its powers and that of other parties? How might a more democratic peace be constructed in Northern Ireland?

Explaining Northern Ireland: Power, Ideology and 'Reality'

As previously noted, there was a widespread expectation in Britain and Ireland at the time of partition that it would only be a temporary measure and that inevitably, Ireland would be reunited either in the British Empire/Commonwealth or in an independent united Ireland (Chapter 3) by, among other things, the forces of Modernisation. While Modernisation Theory has become discredited, the widespread acceptance of its assumptions produced and continue to produce real effects in the attitudes of politicians and public. The British and Irish could justify their non-interventionist approach towards Northern Ireland by trusting in the inevitability of a united Ireland. Unionists increasingly interpreted Modernisation Theory as a threat to their position in the UK, particularly perhaps when this theory had such currency among the British.

281

O'Neill's attempts to weld Modernisation Theory to a more 'moderate', accommodating attitude towards Catholics was backed by the British Government, the BBC and the *Belfast Telegraph*, but met fierce resistance from unionists inside and outside his party. This limited the ability of O'Neill to back up his rhetorical gestures towards Catholics with concrete, material concessions, which alienated unionists without satisfying Catholic demands. It was into this volatile environment that the civil rights campaign marched, sparking off an unanticipated explosion from below of Catholic resentment and frustration at discrimination in the expanding public sector. This agitation for civil rights was mixed in with more traditional anti-partitionist sentiment, and republicans played a leading role in the movement's establishment (Chapter 4). Just as O'Neill experienced considerable difficulties leading unionism, the leadership of the civil rights movement was pushed more from below than led from the top.

During the period 1968–71 the British Government attempted to bring Northern Ireland up to 'British standards' of democracy in the hope that this would result in the resolution of the conflict. The British were ideologically ill-equipped to deal with communal conflict and quickly became disillusioned and frustrated when it appeared resistant to their reformist efforts to resolve it. The desire of the British to limit their involvement resulted in dependence on the Unionist Government to balance the reconciliation of nationalists without undermining its political position among unionist 'hardliners'. There had been considerable sympathy in Britain for the demands of the civil rights movement, but when the British Army was deployed on the streets of Northern Ireland and came into conflict with both nationalists and unionists, a process of British alienation from the region began.

The limits on Britain's power to police Northern Ireland 'impartially' soon became apparent. Leading soldiers dismissed the illusion of a purely military solution; the army could only 'hold the ring' while the politicians reached agreement and feared a 'nightmare scenario' where it found itself fighting a war on two fronts against both unionists and nationalists. The RUC were too weak to police Northern Ireland and until the local security forces could be built up – ideally on a cross-community basis – the British Army would have to remain in its 'policing' role. Certainly it was in the interests of republicans to draw the British Army into conflict, but the army's repressive approach to policing also contributed to its deteriorating relationship with nationalists. The British attempted to extricate themselves from Northern Ireland by involving Catholics in the government of the region and recruiting them in to the security forces, thereby legitimising the state. Alienation from the security policy of the Northern Ireland Government resulted in a withdrawal of Catholics from the locally recruited security forces.

Dependent overwhelmingly on Protestants to man the RUC and UDR, the danger was that policing the unionist community 'too stringently' could result in a lack of Protestants willing to join the security forces. It could also provoke the army's 'nightmare scenario' of a war on two fronts. It was this kind of calculation – the 'security dilemma' – which has constrained British security policy in Northern Ireland throughout the recent conflict, resulting in a structural bias against the nationalist community. This helps to explain the British state's reluctance and caution in taking on unionists in 1972–73, 1974, 1986 and 1996. The difficulties of managing British security policy were compounded by the strains 'counter-insurgency strategy' placed on civil–military relations and the problem of exerting close political control over the army. The repressive nature of security policy, and its anti-nationalist bias, conflicted with the attempts of British politicians to bring nationalists into a power-sharing settlement with unionists.

A bipartisan approach was quickly established by the two major parties to fight the propaganda war and maximise the chances of resolving the conflict (Chapter 5). British counter-insurgency strategy set great store on the importance of 'political determination' in order to defeat the IRA in the propaganda war. However, by 1971 there were signs that this determination was wavering and that the politicians' definition of the conflict was shifting away from an internal, domestic British conflict towards an 'international' or even 'colonial' conflict. There was considerable sympathy among British politicians, particularly but not exclusively in the Labour Party, for Irish unity. The introduction of direct rule, the growing involvement of the Irish Government and the opening-up of talks between the British Government and Opposition and the IRA raised further questions about the determination of British politicians to defeat the 'insurgency'. From the point of view of counter-insurgency strategy, increasing British ambiguity over the future of Northern Ireland encouraged IRA violence by raising its hopes of victory. This ambiguity also exacerbated loyalist fears of forcible incorporation into a united Ireland. In 1971–74 a 'Protestant backlash' developed, culminating in the UWC strike, partly in response to what loyalists saw as the successful deployment of violence by republicans which had produced major concessions from the British. Loyalist violence and unionist mobilisation against both nationalism and the British state was 'successful' in checking the tendency among the British political elite (to some extent still wedded to Modernising assumptions) to see Irish unity as an option which could extricate Britain and leave behind a stable Ireland.

There have been important continuities in British policy throughout the recent conflict and these arise from the British Government's attempts to build accommodation in the centre ground of Northern Irish politics. There is a certain consistency to the British Government's 'inconsistencies and contradictions' which can be explained by its need to achieve 'balance' between unionists and nationalists while pragmatically keeping the lines of communication open to paramilitaries in the hope of drawing them into the democratic process. In order to achieve some kind of 'balance' between nationalist and unionist interests and claims, British Governments reassure nationalists (and even republicans) that they are 'neutral', Irish unity can be achieved by consent and they will be treated fairly in any peace process. At the same time the British Government must also reassure unionists of their place within the Union by championing their cause and opposing Irish unity without the consent of a majority in Northern Ireland. The 'contradiction' in the British position in declaring its opposition to talking with terrorists and then engaging in talks (1972, 1975, 1981, 1990–) can be explained most convincingly by reference to the propaganda war between the British Government and the IRA for the support of British, Irish and international opinion. The IRA and the British Army were not likely to defeat each other solely through military means but through a combination of the 'real war' and the propaganda war.

Initially, the IRA's emphasis was on the military struggle. Following the example of 'anti-colonial' liberation movements, the IRA hoped to demoralise British politicians and public opinion by killing sufficient soldiers to precipitate a withdrawal. Public opinion polls and the willingness of the British Government to talk gave republicans some reason to believe they were winning. Talking to 'terrorists' allowed the British to investigate the possibility of a negotiated settlement but ran the risk of lending the IRA legitimacy, a valuable resource in the propaganda war. It also raised fears among unionists that 'perfidious Albion' was about to sell them down the river.

There are considerable parallels between the first and second peace processes. The first peace process was unbalanced in favour of the nationalists, and so the chances of a successful settlement were therefore not maximised. Whether even a 'balanced' settlement would have led to a stable settlement in the polarised political climate of 1973–74 is questionable, particularly with both republican and loyalist paramilitaries attempting to bring down power-sharing. Nevertheless, in spite of considerable support for power-sharing from inside and outside Northern Ireland, from governments and the media, the 'moderate silent majority' failed to materialise and the failure of Brian Faulkner again illustrated the problems faced by unionist leaders in bringing their supporters to accommodation. During the second peace process (1994–) the power-sharing experiment of 1972–74 was a reference point for the parties. Seamus Mallon called the second peace process 'Sunningdale for slow learners', and there were considerable similarities in the two processes:

(a) faith in the 'moderate silent majority';
(b) negotiations with paramilitaries to bring them into the democratic process;
(c) a British declaration that it would accept the will of the majority in Northern Ireland if it favoured Irish unity and effectively that Britain had 'no selfish strategic or economic interest' (these declarations, it was hoped, would undermine the republican rationale for violence);
(d) British declarations of neutrality accompanied by statements of support for the Union;
(e) close co-operation between the British and Irish Governments;
(f) an attempt to 'balance' unionist and nationalist claims;
(g) a settlement at Sunningdale 1973 and the Good Friday Agreement 1998 on broadly the same ground: power-sharing and an Irish dimension.

Following the collapse of power-sharing in 1974 the stalemate between the parties and governments over Northern Ireland was more apparent. Various parties and governments had the power to combine and veto the preferred settlement of others, but none could impose its own agenda. The defeat of British policy 1972–74 by unionists was hardly compatible with the tenet of republican ideology which suggested that unionists were merely the puppets of British imperialism. Learning from this new awareness of unionist power, the Labour Government again considered independence for Northern Ireland as a more effective way of extricating itself from the conflict (this had been debated in 1969). This option, like withdrawal, was likely to result in civil war in Northern Ireland, resulting in the destabilisation of the island of Ireland with serious overspill effects for the UK.

The diffusion of power among the different parties to the conflict led to stalemate. The unionists had stood up to the British Government and its army and there was no reason to think that the IRA or the Irish Government would be much more successful in imposing its will on unionism in the event of a British withdrawal. There was no guarantee that the IRA would cease its 'armed struggle' in the event of a British withdrawal and be content only with a united Ireland run by the 'Free State' parties. The Irish Government took repressive security measures to deal with the IRA's military threat and also attacked republicans in the propaganda war. The IRA was able to sustain violence over a considerable period of time but not force the British to withdraw from Northern Ireland. Even if it could, the unionists represented probably an insuperable obstacle to Irish unity.

The British Government and the security forces could contain the IRA but might only militarily defeat it by using extremely repressive techniques which would probably have been counter-productive in the long-run. These would have alienated international opinion, destroyed the credibility of moderate nationalists (and with them any hope of an accommodation with unionism) and questioned the legitimacy of the British State. The continuing violence of the paramilitaries made attempts to construct an accommodation between unionists and nationalists more difficult. The unionists could prevent a British withdrawal through the threat and use of violence but could not gain integration or majority rule. All sides could exert their power to try to shift the political agenda in their direction but this was, to some extent, constrained by the power of other actors and the threat of destabilisation and all-out civil war.

Under the Labour Government 1974–79 there was an apparent drift towards integrationism, as both Labour and Conservatives courted the Ulster Unionists; however, it is doubtful whether this policy was seriously pursued. The pursuit of integration would antagonise international (particularly US) opinion, lose the British the co-operation of the Republic and alienate 'moderate nationalism', perhaps resulting in a drift of nationalists towards republicanism and a consequent increase in violence. The importance of underpinning moderate nationalism and winning security gains contributed to the signing of the AIA. There were also important intra-party and bipartisan pressures constraining either Labour or Conservatives from pursuing an all-out integrationist policy. British public opinion tended to favour extrication from the conflict altogether, but seems to have been appeased by continuing bipartisanship and the strategy of normalisation which decreased army casualties and attempted to contain the conflict. These constraints resulted in a considerable degree of continuity in British policy between Conservative and Labour governments. The extent of the constraints operating on British Government policy towards Northern Ireland are apparent in the shift of Conservative Government policy under Mrs Thatcher. In 1979–80 the Conservatives rejected their party's formal commitment to integration and Thatcher picked up where her Conservative predecessor, Edward Heath, had left off in 1974 by pursuing both power-sharing and, in 1980, an Anglo–Irish process.

By the mid- to late 1970s the British Government and the IRA were settling down for the 'Long War'. In order to win the propaganda war the British Government shifted its presentational approach of the conflict. The IRA were no longer to be treated as a political organisation, but were labelled 'criminals' in an attempt to 'normalise' the conflict and also undermine support for the IRA in the propaganda war. The IRA was also altering its propaganda strategy and attempting to mobilise a political as well as military movement. This 'mass propaganda' strategy resisted British 'normalisation' and resulted in the 1981 Hunger Strike and a propaganda victory for the IRA. Behind the scenes the British Government maintained contacts with the republican movement, undermining its own claim that the IRA were a criminal organisation. The successful entry of Sinn Féin into the electoral process during the Hunger Strikes damaged the British claim that the IRA was a criminal organisation which succeeded only through intimidation. The threat that Sinn Féin might replace the SDLP as the principal party of nationalists was a powerful force behind the Anglo–Irish Agreement in 1985.

The Anglo–Irish Agreement was not the rational, Machiavellian master-plan of Margaret Thatcher but the product of competing agendas in the civil service and the cabinet. They were responding to pressure from the Irish and US Governments but also to the turn of events in Northern Ireland, particularly the rise of Sinn Féin. The British Government in order to retain the hope of an accommodation, had to maintain some conception of 'balance' between unionist and nationalist interests. Push unionism 'too hard', as during the first peace process, and unionist public and party opinion would become too alienated to construct an accommodation. Push nationalism 'too hard' and this was likely to manifest itself in the more nationalist drift of SDLP policy in the late 1970s and the political rise of Sinn Féin.

The distinction between 'constitutional' and 'unconstitutional' politicians becomes blurred, particularly when a particular community feels itself under threat and constitutional means appear an ineffective way of defending political interests. The impact of the AIA was largely unanticipated: it provoked unionist rebellion, which the British Government struggled to contain, and the security situation deteriorated. Rather than coercing power-sharing, the AIA appeared to polarise politics as the SDLP engaged with republicans instead of conciliating unionism and unionism drifted away from devolution and towards integration. Yet one of the consequences of the AIA may have been to pave the way for the peace process and the GFA.

Analysing the Peace Process

The key to understanding the peace process is an appreciation of the difficulties that faced political elites in Britain and Ireland in bringing their parties and public opinion towards an accommodation. There is little evidence that public and party opinion, fed by the propaganda war and the experience of 25 years of violence and repression, was converging prior to the 1994 ceasefire. The political elites, assuming they were so inclined, would have to work hard to shift opinion to the point where a deal (such as the Good Friday Agreement) might bridge the gap between the parties. It was difficult to see where an agreement might be reached which was capable of being sold to both unionists and republicans. The Sinn Féin leadership had problems bringing their movement, if perhaps not so much public opinion, with them towards a settlement and these problems were recognised both by the RUC and the British Government. The leadership of the UUP also had considerable difficulties containing and leading unionist opinion. Prior to the IRA ceasefire in 1993 Northern Ireland faced high levels of violence, and communal tensions remained high during the peace process. These manifested themselves in opinion polls, elections and clashes during the marching season, most notoriously at Drumcree. In this environment how could the political elites lead their voters and supporters to a compromise settlement?

The polarisation of politics in Northern Ireland during the late 1970s and early 1980s was not conducive to the construction of an accommodation between unionism and nationalism. The confrontation and clashes between unionism and the British Government over the Anglo–Irish Agreement accelerated the ideological development of republicans by demonstrating, once again, the relative autonomy of unionism from the British State and the willingness of the British to 'face down' unionism. Brooke's public claim that Britain had 'no selfish strategic or economic interest' in Northern Ireland echoed similar British statements from the early 1970s. It reinforced the view that the conflict was essentially an internal one requiring accommodation between unionists and nationalists rather than one driven by British imperialism. The military struggle with the British was stalemated and continuing IRA violence inhibited any further electoral progress. In the Republic there was a movement away from traditional republicanism and towards unilateral moves to amend Articles 2 and 3 of the Irish Constitution. This, along with progress in the Brooke/Mayhew talks, threatened to further marginalise the republican movement. The end of the Cold War and other 'anti-imperialist' struggles, in South Africa and Israel/Palestine, also appeared to be moving towards resolution and were used by the Sinn Féin leadership to justify the unarmed strategy.

The view of leading members of the British Government was that a faction of the republican movement probably wanted to bring the conflict to an end and enter the democratic process. However, the problem remained as to how to bring the conflict to an end in a way that would maximise the credibility of the SF leadership, and therefore minimise the prospects of a major split in the IRA. The British and Irish Governments, Sinn Féin and the SDLP attempted to wind down the propaganda war by choreographing the peace process. The British had to play a 'dual role' and strike a balance between republicans and unionists. The British Government needed to draw republicans into a peace process and reassure them that their interests would be protected. Simultaneously, it had to publicly reassure unionists by championing their concerns and interests while attempting to push them towards accommodation. The Irish Government played a comparable role among nationalists and republicans. But the British Government had the added difficulty of taking responsibility for most of the decisions that moved the peace process forward, which tended to be seen by unionists as 'concessions to nationalism and republicanism'.

This made the British task of retaining the confidence of unionism all the more difficult. There is strong evidence of choreography in the back-channel contacts, the negotiations of the Downing Street Declaration and on decommissioning. Privately the British Government encouraged Sinn Féin and facilitated its path towards a peace process, acknowledging the constraints on the Sinn Féin leadership, while publicly it would reassure unionism by attacking and condemning the republican movement and displaying determined support for the Union. The Sinn Féin leadership needed to show republican activists and supporters that they could exert more power and influence through the unarmed struggle than they could through the armed struggle. The choreography of high profile 'defeats' for the British Government (for example, over Adams' visa for the US in 1995) would reinforce the Sinn Féin leadership's argument for the 'unarmed struggle'.

The failure of the IRA to declare its ceasefire permanent emphasised the importance of the decommissioning issue. This issue had been raised before the ceasefire and the British Government may have believed it was relatively unproblematic for the republican movement, which had declared its desire to demilitarise and remove the gun from politics. The Framework Documents seemed yet another concession to nationalism and while they may have helped, in the short term, to entrench the IRA's ceasefire, they did so at the cost of alienating unionism so that Molyneaux's position was fatally undermined. The 'balance' between unionism and nationalism had been upset. The British Government conceded further ground to nationalism on the decommissioning issue with 'Washington 3'. Unionists and their allies in the Conservative Party were digging in and insisted on movement on decommissioning before all-party talks. This reflected the alienation of the wider unionist community from the process.

The impasse over decommissioning was not an artificial barrier erected by the British. For unionists the British Government appeared to be in retreat before 'the pan-nationalist front', precisely the appearance that Adams needed to convince republican hardliners that the peace process was preferable to the armed struggle. Unionism was alarmed and destabilised by the British Government's apparent failure to defend the Union and its assertions of neutrality. Unionism's worst suspicions were aroused by the revelations of secret contacts between Sinn Féin and the British Government after these had been denied outright by the British Government. The Downing Street Declaration, the Framework Documents and British retreats on decommissioning were further evidence of the ability of the pan-nationalist front to set the agenda. The UUP leader, James Molyneaux, managed to reassure unionism of his influence with the government and mute its reaction to the DSD, although opinion was already shifting against his stance. The British Government attempted to get round the decommissioning issue but was constrained ultimately by the unionists who could not enter all-party negotiations without decommissioning. Quietly, Sinn Féin leaders acknowledged that the British Government was constrained over the decommissioning issue by the need to keep unionists 'on board' in the peace process. The ability of unionist leaders to bring their supporters and voters with them towards the 'centre ground' was severely limited as most indicators of unionist opinion suggested a hardening in that community's position.

The Irish Government privately, and to some extent publicly, appreciated the British Government's dilemma over decommissioning. However, the Irish Government, like the US Government, had to publicly fulfil its role in the 'pan-nationalist front' and take the nationalist part in disputes with the British, thereby demonstrating to republicans the effectiveness of the unarmed struggle. An impasse was reached by the end of 1995 with neither unionist or republican leaders having room for manoeuvre. The subsequent compromise announced by Major following the publication of the Mitchell Report seemed to be able to deliver all-party talks without decommissioning. The end of the IRA's ceasefire dashed these hopes.

The Good Friday Agreement of 1998, with its support for power-sharing with an Irish dimension, echoed the Sunningdale Agreement of 1973. As with the first peace process, the problems for the second peace process arose out of the ability of the political elites to sustain the GFA and deliver their respective constituencies to support the deal. The decommissioning issue had been (perhaps necessarily) fudged by the GFA: unionists felt the spirit of the Agreement involved decommissioning while republicans claimed the letter of the GFA involved no decommissioning before entering the executive. The pro-GFA parties and governments have attempted to choreograph movement on all sides to create an environment of trust and push the process forward. However, again and again the process has foundered on the rock of decommissioning and the limits of choreography and 'spin' to get round the 'reality' of no decommissioning. Both Sinn Féin and the UUP leadership appeared stretched to the limit by the concessions which brought about the two periods of devolution.

During the recent conflict violence and democratic politics have co-existed uneasily. Both nationalists and unionists have, through politics, mobilisation and the use and threat of violence, attempted to shift the political agenda in their direction. Loyalist and republican paramilitaries have used violence but nationalist and unionist politicians have also used the threat of violence to influence the political process. The relationship between some unionist parties, in particular Vanguard and the DUP, and the loyalist paramilitaries has often been close. When constitutional politics have failed, some unionist politicians have resorted to the threat of violence to prevent the erosion of the Union. Others have acted in ways which could reasonably interpreted as encouraging violence. The British and Irish Governments have attempted to reach accommodation with the paramilitaries but, in the process, have also risked the delegitimisation of democratic politics through this process. The attempt to bring paramilitaries into politics has recognised, and to some extent accommodated, the power of street politics and violence, although it should be remembered that liberal democracies often bow to those with extra-parliamentary (for example, economic) power.

Power and Interests

From the evidence presented in this book, we can attempt to define the (perceived) interests of various key actors and their power to realise those interests. Interests and power can vary over time, perhaps as particular politicians or governments learn the 'realities' and parameters of practical politics. The British Government is the most powerful actor, but it has been unable to impose its will on republicans or loyalists in Northern Ireland after 30 years of violence.

British Interests and Power

There have been widely contrasting interpretations of the British Government's interests and goals in Northern Ireland. On the one hand, republicans have emphasised the determination of British imperialism to retain the Union with Northern Ireland while some loyalists have claimed that Britain is in the process of withdrawing. Both tend to conceive of the British state as a very powerful, single, rational actor pursuing clearly determined goals. This conception was not borne out by our analysis of the AIA or the autonomy of the security establishment. The British state has sovereignty over Northern Ireland, an enormous capacity for violence and great resources which can be deployed in both the 'real war' and the propaganda war. However, it has been argued here that the *overriding* interest of British Governments is for a stable settlement, and its failure to deliver this indicates the limits of its power.

For a considerable period of time Britain has had 'no selfish strategic or economic interest' in Northern Ireland,

Economics   The region had long been an economic drain on the British exchequer.

Strategic   There is little evidence either that it was of overriding strategic importance to British policy-makers. The willingness of British politicians, particularly since the 1960s, to contemplate Irish unity or an independent Northern Ireland suggests that there was no overriding strategic interest.

Politics   Northern Ireland – with its violence and sectarian conflict – was often excluded from Britain's 'imagined community', something painfully apparent during the Falklands/Malvinas conflict and in opinion polls consistently showing British majority support for withdrawal. Even such keen supporters of the Union as Margaret Thatcher, signatory of the Anglo–Irish Agreement, are English Unionists whose interests and priorities do not necessarily coincide with those of Ulster Unionists.

Stability   The British Government's need for stability best explains its search for a settlement in Northern Ireland and its appeasement of whatever forces it felt were likely to deliver a stable settlement. First it pursued an internal 'British settlement' during 1969–71. Then, under the impact of increasing violence, it shifted towards an 'international' or, for some, a 'colonial' settlement in 1971–74, bringing the Irish Government on board and holding out the prospect of eventual Irish unity. The British-driven power-sharing experiment of 1974 illustrated the limits of British power to impose a settlement.

With the strength of loyalist resistance to power-sharing and Irish unity apparent, as well as the constraint of the 'security dilemma', there was consideration of withdrawal and independence in 1974–75. These options were unlikely to result in a stable Ireland, so the British reverted to direct rule and pursuit of accommodation between nationalists and unionists as events and the political environment permitted.

On the one hand, the limits of Britain's ability to coerce unionists into a settlement were seen by the failure of power-sharing and the AIA, which underlined unionists' ability to make Northern Ireland ungovernable. On the other hand, the British political and military elites largely accepted that the IRA could not in the long run be defeated by solely military methods (Major 1999 p. 492). The IRA's significant electoral support was apparent during the 1981 Hunger Strikes and this allowed it to sustain its campaign and undermine attempts to establish a power-sharing settlement among the other constitutional parties. Such experiences affected British calculations and set limits to what it perceived were credible policy options. The limited power of British Governments to achieve their interests in Northern Ireland is indicated by their consistent inability to achieve a stable settlement. The constraints operating on British policy shape its parameters which, while permitting short-term movement, have led to relative consistency in policy.

Unionist Interests and Power

Unionist interests lie in the preservation of the Union, but they are divided on the means to achieve this. The lack of *overriding* British strategic, economic or political interests in Northern Ireland and Britain's attempts to create a 'balanced accommodation' has further fed unionist insecurity about its commitment to the Union. The British Government has not been the sponsor of Ulster unionism in the way the Irish Government has supported Irish nationalism (Dixon 1995b). According to opinion polls, the citizens of the Republic tend to regard Northern Ireland as part of their nation, while the British on the whole do not. During the history of the recent 'troubles' it has been only in exceptional periods (when Unionist MPs have occupied a strategically important position in a finely balanced House of Commons) that British Governments have paid close attention to unionist interests. Significantly, there has been no campaign to sell the Union with Northern Ireland to the

'British electorate', which consistently favours withdrawal in opinion polls. The British Labour Party's record of support for Irish unity, and sympathy for this option among some Conservatives, underlines the asymmetrical relationship and isolation of unionism. In addition to this, northern nationalists have worked effectively to cultivate support and influence in the USA and Europe which unionists have not been able to match. It is this array of national and international forces that are ranged behind the nationalists (the so-called 'pan-nationalist front') which goes some way to explaining the oft-cited siege mentality of unionists. Given the 'unreliable' record of success-ive British Governments on Northern Ireland, it is hardly surprising that unionists are insecure about their constitutional position in the UK and have regarded both the first and second peace processes with such suspicion.

Since British Governments have not been a great source of support or comfort for unionists, they have fallen back on their own resources, including the threat and use of violence. It is during periods when unionists, with some reason, have seen their constitutional position under threat (1966, 1969, 1971–75/6, 1986, 1991–93, 1996) that they have mobilised and violence has increased. Constitutional unionist politicians (like many other 'constitutional' politicians) have oper-ated in the grey area between democratic politics and the threat and use of violence. Fearing British manipulation of Northern Ireland out of the Union, unionist politicians have taken to the streets, threatened the use of force and advocated independence as the only way of resisting British power and coercion. Some nationalists hold these threats responsible for inciting loyalist violence against them. Vanguard in the early 1970s emerged from the UUP but had close relations with loyalist paramilitaries and threatened physical resist-ance. Ian Paisley worked alongside loyalist paramilitaries in the UWC strike, the abortive 1977 loyalist strike and in the campaign against the AIA.

At the same time, there has been considerable antagonism between the loyalist paramilitaries and the leaders of the principal uni-onist parties (including Paisley), who have condemned loyalist viol-ence. There is a difficulty in assessing whether unionist politicians (as with other politicians), in reflecting the outrage of some of their supporters, are attempting to incite further violence or, by venting frustration and letting off steam, limiting the prospect of that anger turning into violence. Without the physical resistance of unionists and the threat of violence it seems reasonable to suggest that the

British may well have eased Northern Ireland out of the Union. When the power of unionism has been demonstrated, as during the UWC strike in May 1974 and after the AIA, British (and Irish) political calculations have been reassessed. The unionists have had little success in the propaganda war and their power is limited by the lack of sympathy for them in Britain and internationally. However, unionism's capacity to mobilise its supporters, the violence of its paramilitaries and unionist domination of the local security forces give unionists the capacity to set limits on British–Irish initiatives.

Nationalist Interests and Power

Nationalists are united in their aspiration to a united Ireland but are divided over the means to achieve it. The nationalist SDLP has played a pivotal role throughout 'the Troubles'. As the political representatives of the majority of nationalists, the British Government requires SDLP co-operation in any power-sharing settlement and needs the party to be strong enough to fend off its Sinn Féin rival, unless SF replaces the SDLP and the IRA guns are silent. This majority status within the nationalist community gives the SDLP prestige and influence in the Republic, Europe and USA which it has exploited to significant advantage. The SDLP is able to draw on the sympathy of public opinion in the Republic of Ireland, and this is something that the Republic's political parties and government can ill afford to ignore. The SDLP has been scrupulous in its condemnation of violence from whichever source it has originated. Nevertheless, many of the founder-members of the SDLP were involved in the civil rights marches which could be interpreted as being designed to provoke confrontation. The violence and success of the republican movement has often rebounded to the SDLP's advantage. Anxious to stem the rise of republicanism, the British and Irish Governments have attempted to shore up the SDLP and undermine republicanism by making concessions (see the AIA). Since 1985 the SDLP has found itself in a pivotal position where it can either advance the peace process or the 'all-party talks' process.

The Irish Government has been in a position to exacerbate or ameliorate the conflict in the North. Articles 2 and 3 of the Irish Constitution lay claim to Northern Ireland and have been seen by unionists as legitimising the IRA's violent campaign. In 1969 republicans were encouraged to fight by their perception that the Irish Government would come to their rescue. There have also been allegations of the Republic's lack of resolve to deal effectively with the IRA. The 'Arms Crisis' of 1970 involved allegations of Southern ministers funding and arming the IRA. On the other hand, the IRA was, perhaps increasingly, seen by the Irish political elite as a direct threat to the stability of the Republic, particularly once the extent of unionist resistance to Irish unity became apparent. Containing the IRA and preventing civil war in the North spreading into the Republic have created a strong incentive in the South for a stable settlement to 'the Troubles', and some have detected the emergence of a partitionist, 26-county nationalism. Since 1972, if not before, the British have seen an important role for the Irish Government in promoting peace in the North, first at Sunningdale and later through the British–Irish process initiated in 1980, producing first the AIA and subsequently the GFA. British–Irish co-operation has deflected international criticism from Britain and has been effective in the 'propaganda war' against the IRA, particularly in the USA.

The continuing violence of the IRA's campaign during 'the Troubles' has contributed significantly to the polarisation of public opinion and enormous suffering. But it has also proved a powerful tool for drawing the attention of the British Government to republican grievances. The mobilisation of republicans during the Hunger Strike and Sinn Féin's successful entry into electoral politics were catalysts to the signing of the Anglo–Irish Agreement. While the IRA has been unable to beat the British militarily, its violence has helped to heighten tension and undermine British constitutional initiatives. Sinn Féin has been able to exert electoral pressure on the SDLP to prevent it entering an accommodation with unionists. The history of the republican movement has been a history of splits, and the leadership is constrained in its ability to move towards accommodation by hardline activists within the IRA and the wider republican movement.

The US Government has an interest in actions which gain it Irish-American support and bolster its international and national reputation (through apparent political progress), but which do not alienate their loyal British ally. The impact of US pressure is difficult to assess but has generally been overestimated. During the recent peace process its influence has been deliberately overplayed to demonstrate to republicans the influence of 'pan-nationalism' and the advantages of the unarmed struggle. But the President also has an interest in taking his share of the credit for any settlement.

Power and the Propaganda War

The Power and Limits of British Propaganda

The British state has considerable resources to make a powerful impact on the propaganda war over Northern Ireland (Miller 1994 p. 274). But again, it is important to draw attention to the limits of this power. Although British press and broadcasting media are not subject to direct government control, the state has used its control of information, censorship and intimidation to influence the presentation of 'the Troubles' by the media (Schlesinger 1978, Schlesinger *et al*. 1983). The sensitivity of the British state to media portrayals of Northern Ireland suggests a sense of vulnerability to its impact on public opinion and its implications for the 'real' and propaganda war against the IRA. The British Government, with some reason, seems to have been more concerned with the impact of the portrayal of republicans on British rather than Northern Irish opinion (Dixon 2000a).

The British media has been largely sympathetic to the government's policy in Northern Ireland and has shared the government's attempts to rally and promote moderate opinion. The BBC–Northern Ireland (BBC–NI) during the 1960s supported O'Neill and attempted to emphasise the positive in community relations, stress the experiences which united the people, ignore sectarian divisions, marginalise 'extremists' such as Ian Paisley and manufacture consensus (Butler 1991, Butler 1995 p. 47). The *Belfast Telegraph*, the paper with the largest circulation in Northern Ireland and with a cross-community readership, strongly supported O'Neill's efforts at reform and subsequent unionist 'moderates'. The *Belfast Telegraph* attempted not only to describe the 'moderates' in Northern Ireland but to rally support for them and create a bandwagon effect. Like much of the British press, the *Belfast Telegraph* underestimated loyalist discontent. Before October 1968, the local broadcast media 'persisted with a bizarrely optimistic account of O'Neillism's command of a fictive centre ground' (Butler 1995 p. 47). The civil rights movement won the media battle, winning sympathy in the British press and in the BBC-NI (Butler 1991 pp. 109–12, Kirkaldy 1984 pp. 175–6, Parkinson 1998 p. 103).

Violence 'is thought to be an un-British way of solving political problems'. After 1969 the conflict was increasingly presented by broadcasters as one 'between equivalent warring tribes' (Schlesinger 1978 p. 236, Butler 1991 p. 110). The introduction of British troops in 1969 and the death of the first soldier in February 1971 further shifted the broadcasters' portrayal of the conflict. The British media supported the army as 'peacekeepers' between two warring factions, responding to events rather than impacting on them (Elliott 1976). Terrorism became the cause of the conflict and the IRA, killers of British soldiers and later bombers of Britain, emerged as the principal enemy (Schlesinger 1978 p. 205, Butler 1991 p. 110). Until the introduction of direct rule in 1972 'there was a structured institutional bias in broadcast journalism in favour of the "reformed" unionist position' (Butler 1991 p. 111).

As the violence further escalated following internment in August 1971, the broadcast media came under further political pressure which established the parameters of future reporting. Although the conflict with the IRA was not officially recognised as a 'war', for fear of giving legitimacy to the IRA in the propaganda war, the conflict was seen by the British Government and military as a war. Therefore the reporting of the conflict was 'war reporting' and the media were expected to offer support to the state in the propaganda war against the enemy. A myth had arisen in British military circles that it was the media which had undermined the USA's will to defeat the North Vietnamese (Dixon 2000a). Willie Whitelaw, the Secretary of State for Northern Ireland, warned the media of the dangers of lowering the morale of the security forces and argued that it was not possible to be neutral in the 'fight for freedom': 'Surely one is either for it or against it.' These sentiments were echoed in the right-wing press (Chibnall 1977 pp. 40–1). The broadcasters dropped their commitment to impartiality and came out in clear opposition to the methods of the 'extremists' (Schlesinger 1978 pp. 211–12, Curtis 1984 p. 10).

The British media's reliance on official sources further reduced its capacity for criticism of the conduct of the government or security forces. An indirect form of censorship was imposed which, while allowing reporting, inhibited any analysis of the underlying causes of the conflict. The source of violence was terrorism, 'the result of inexplicable, asocial forces' (Elliott 1976 pp. 5–3). Such covert censorship was arguably a more effective way of influencing public opinion than overt censorship, which would have discredited the media and thereby limited the effectiveness of the information they carried. Interviews with republican and loyalist paramilitaries were virtually banned. The broadcasters shared with the press a tendency to produce 'a series of decontextualized reports of violence and fails to analyse and re-analyse the historical roots of the Irish conflict' which left the British audience with a view of the troubles as 'largely incomprehensible and irrational' (Schlesinger 1978 p. 243; see also Elliott 1976, Butler 1995 p. 86). There was also overt censorship in the Republic. This may have contributed to Britain's problems in building domestic public support for sustaining its presence in Northern Ireland.

The effect of censorship was to overestimate the strength of 'moderates'. Butler argues:

> Without a wider frame of reference, the view was compounded that a 'few extremists on either side' were the cause rather than a symptom of deeper division. This encouraged the misapprehension that if the British could negotiate a 'reasonable' settlement between the parties, the good sense of the vast majority would prevail, isolating the tiny minority of malcontents. (Butler 1991 p. 111)

The power-sharing experiment attempted to unite moderates and isolate the extremists. The British Government was supported by the broadcast media and the *Belfast Telegraph* in its claim to have found a 'moderate silent majority' in favour of power-sharing. The British security services supported attempts to build moderation in Northern Ireland by undertaking a 'psychological warfare' or 'black propaganda' campaign against both republican *and loyalist* 'extremists', including William Craig and Ian Paisley (Curtis 1984 pp. 236–41, Foot 1989). In addition, the *Irish News* favoured Sunningdale, while the unionist *Newsletter* endorsed power-sharing and focused its criticisms on the Irish dimension of the Sunningdale package. The over optimistic hopes vested in a 'moderate silent majority' were dealt a knockout blow by the 'realities' of unionist politics and the subsequent defeat of 'moderate unionism' at the ballot box. This may have deepened the disillusion of the British public with any kind of settlement of the conflict and boosted support for the withdrawal option.

By 1975 coverage of Northern Ireland was falling away. The British Army's 'black propaganda' campaign was being exposed and losing it credibility as a reliable source of information. The British Government moved to wind up its operation, with responsibility for information being passed over to the RUC as the conflict was Ulsterised and the army took a lower profile (Miller 1994 pp. 78–9, 81). Learning from the failure of the broadcast media to create consent in the 1960s, the BBC proposed a state of 'balanced sectarianism' where the broadcast media would 'function as an honest broker, guaranteeing impartial representation between the various sectarian forces in the local polity' (Butler 1995 p. 73). The electoral success of Sinn Féin in 1981–82 represented a powerful blow to British portrayals of the IRA as criminals who sustained themselves through manipulation and intimidation and without popular support. 'Repeatedly obliged to give way to executive pressure, in 1969, 1971, 1974, 1977–78, 1979 and 1985, broadcast journalism had been reduced by degrees to a state of "culpable silence"'. For Butler, the limits of 'permissible reporting' are related to the shifting priorities of the state during the conflict (Butler 1995 pp. 79, 89).

While the British Government has considerable power to set and influence the political and media agenda over Northern Ireland, significant constraints operate on this. First, the support from the media for British policy was insufficient to sustain O'Neill or deliver a 'moderate' settlement in the first peace process. Indeed, public opinion appears to have polarised during 'the Troubles'.

Second, the British Government has also failed to persuade the British public against support for the withdrawal of troops. Although British policy emphasises consent and despite little public political support for the withdrawal option, opinion polls have consistently indicated that since the mid-1970s a majority of the British public supports withdrawal. Interestingly, there is evidence that, in the short term at any rate, IRA bombings and interviews with republicans have hardened British attitudes and reduced support for withdrawal (Dixon 2000a).

Third, the republican movement has scored 'propaganda' victories against the British Government, most notably during the Hunger Strikes and through its ability to reinforce the perception of the conflict as 'colonial'.

Fourth, David Miller has drawn attention to the role of British television in bringing about the release of the Birmingham Six and the Guildford Four in the face of obstruction by the state. Nevertheless, he argues that 'The media operate within a set of constraints in which power is clearly skewed towards the state' (Miller 1994 p. 277).

The IRA and the republican movement have been the particular targets of the British (and the Republic's) propaganda war. This is probably because republicans target British soldiers, bomb Britain and are seen as the primary threat to the stability of Northern Ireland. The loyalists are perceived to be reacting to republican violence. From the British State's point of view, since the IRA were the principal enemy it made sense to blame them for some loyalist killings in order to win the propaganda war. It may also have been felt that to draw attention to loyalist violence could lead to demands to take on the loyalists more forcefully and draw the army into its 'nightmare scenario' of a 'war on two fronts' (Elliott 1976 p. 5–3). This might also add to the disillusion of the British public with the whole conflict and accelerate demands for withdrawal.

There has been a tendency to assume that because the British media have focused most of their hostility on the republican movement that unionism has received favourable treatment. Some have argued that the media's obsession with IRA terrorism as the cause of the conflict has led to unionism being 'marginalised, absented and ignored'. It is argued that the underestimation of loyalist violence does not represent a pro-loyalist bias but a tendency to ignore unionism and its grievances (Butler 1995 p. 114, Parkinson 1998 p. 164). When unionism is considered it 'tends to be (mis)represented as a monolith' personified by Ian Paisley who has been subject to media hostility since the 1960s (Butler 1995 p. 114, Parkinson 1998). The 'reasonable' British are contrasted with the 'extremists' from both sides in Northern Ireland: 'The insistence on an extremist symmetry makes the Protestants almost as bad as the republicans. Indeed, from the standard British point of view, it makes sense that Protestants and Catholics are morally equivalent, for a binary system of identification legitimates long-suffering British neutrality' (Butler 1995 p. 115; see also Parkinson 1998 pp. 68–70, 166). Unionism has a poor media image and has largely failed to engage effectively in the propaganda war (Miller 1994 pp. 157–9, Parkinson 1998). The 'moderate' centre is occupied by the nationalist SDLP which has considerable media sympathy and is contrasted with republican and unionist extremists (Miller 1994 pp. 156–7, Butler 1995 pp. 115–16, Parkinson 1998 pp. 68, 108).

In those sections of the British press which support unionism this tends to be from a English/British rather than Ulster unionist perspective, sharing Ulster unionist concerns about security and IRA violence, but tending towards support for British Government initiatives (Parkinson 1998 pp. 89, 108, 121, 165). While the British are more concerned with the deaths of 'their soldiers' than the locally recruited RUC/RIR, unionists may correspondingly exhibit greater concern for the locally-recruited forces (Parkinson 1998 pp. 90, 96). *The Daily Mirror* (and the *New Statesman*) has broken ranks in the past to support British withdrawal but for English/British nationalist reasons – 'bring our boys home' and let the Irish get on with it – rather than out of any sympathy for republicans. In 1981

The Sunday Times came out in favour of withdrawal as a prelude to independence (its Insight Team had been sympathetic to Irish unity). In recent years the liberal *Guardian* newspaper has taken a position which has been sympathetic towards nationalists. Even right-wing magazines, such as *The Spectator* and *The Economist*, have expressed sympathy for Irish unity, and the right-wing press periodically despairs of Ulster (Parkinson 1998 pp. 49, 101–2, 103). But for the most part the UK press has taken a political stance broadly supportive of the Union but usually from a distinctively English/British unionist perspective.

How do we explain the failure of the British Government to win the propaganda war and dominate the audience's understanding of the conflict in Northern Ireland? Important sections of the people of Northern Ireland, both unionists and nationalists, have resisted British propaganda on the conflict. Even British domestic opinion has not proved as malleable as the political and military elites may have hoped (indicated by the extent of support for withdrawal). There has been an overemphasis on the power of the media to shape perceptions and less attention paid to the context in which the audience receives media messages (Miller 1994 p. 260). Philip Schlesinger has drawn attention to the excessive way research on the media has concentrated on the media itself and the privileged role of the state. He argues that we should not ignore 'the activities of other sources as this unnecessarily deprives us of empirical knowledge of how the battle for access is conducted' (Schlesinger 1990 p. 82). Media research suggests that perceptions are not shaped solely from the 'top down', by the state and the national or local media, but perceptions are also shaped by the audience itself. The public 'are active participants in the construction of meaning . . . both media and audiences are part of wider cultural political contexts that may either facilitate or obstruct the acceptance of certain kinds of representations' (Eldridge 1993 p. 31). It is possible to acknowledge the power of the media while at the same time accepting the importance of the cultural and ideological context for the shaping of perceptions. A media message may only be accepted when it reinforces the prevailing ideology and 'dominant values' of the communal group (Elliott 1976 pp. 1–13). The British Government's impact through the media may therefore be related to the socialisation and ideological disposition of the audience. It has more success at talking to its 'own people' than members of other communities, but even here, as British withdrawal support indicates, its impact is still constrained.

Just as the British State experiences difficulties manipulating British and Irish public opinion, so the nationalist and unionist political elites, as we have seen, encounter difficulties manipulating opinion within their own communities. While local elites may have the power of the party machine, activists and other sympathisers to promote their interests and account of 'reality' in the propaganda war, there are alternative sources of information available to activists and voters. Local cultures sustain ideological perspectives which compete with those of the British Government and also those of local elites. Local newspapers tend to reinforce communal ideologies and perspectives but also from time to time appear to have attempted to lead their readers towards the 'centre ground' (notably the *Newsletter* and *Irish News* during the second peace process).

There are important alternative sources of information apart from these local newspapers which compete for the attention of the people. There are the more obviously communal or party political media, the 'alternative press', the campaigning of pressure groups, but also folk memory, oral history, word of mouth accounts of events, rumour, marching organisations which can sustain an alternative culture and different perspectives and interpretations of the conflict. Jarman's work on parading draws attention to the way such practices 'have been shaped by the broader political world, and have been an important element in creating that world' (Jarman 1997 p. 253). People's direct experience of the 'reality' of the conflict is also likely to be a powerful influence on perception. If an individual has been beaten up, or witnessed violence or intimidation, then this could well have an impact on that individual's perception of the conflict(!). It could be argued that because the population of Northern Ireland are, relatively, so politicised they are likely to be particularly resistant to media or state manipulation. Loyalist and republican paramilitary organisations have a two-way relationship with the communities from which they spring and there are limits to the toleration of these communities for paramilitary violence and what are deemed to be 'legitimate targets'.

A Democratic Path to Peace in Northern Ireland?

By considering the inter-related role of structure and agency we have attempted to understand the extent and limits of the power of the various parties to the conflict over Northern Ireland. A popular explanation of the failure to resolve the conflict is to 'blame the intransigent politicians' who lack the skills, wisdom or integrity to reach agreement. While there may be some substance to this view, the account presented here has paid close attention to the limits of agency in order to tease out the structural constraints which operate on those politicians and the problems they have encountered in bringing their parties and public opinion to accommodation. The people have, from time to time, brought considerable influence to bear on the conflict in Northern Ireland, but this has not necessarily been in support of accommodation. The expectations of a 'moderate silent majority' were repeatedly dashed in both the first and second peace processes. If we try to compare the public stance of politicians with their political parties and voters there is evidence to suggest that from time to time the political elites have been a force for relative 'moderation' but have failed to bring their parties and/or voters with them.

A key question about the peace process is whether the 'structural' gap between unionists and republicans is too wide to be bridged by the political skills and power of the 'agents' involved in the process, or whether the ideological and material/class structures constraining the power of these agents is simply too strong for them to reach an agreement to which they can deliver supporters and voters. This leads on to the question of how, in the short or long term, can agents change these structures to facilitate accommodation? How can the 'centre ground' in Northern Ireland be strengthened? Is it possible to move from a negative peace, (the relative absence of violence) to a positive peace, where the underlying antagonisms are resolved?

A comprehensive and inter-related programme of reform aimed at undermining communalism and improved 'management' of the conflict could play a role in promoting an environment in which a settlement, such as the GFA, could be sustained:

1. There is, for example, a strong *class dimension* to the conflict in Northern Ireland which is often underestimated. Greater economic equality and improved life chances (including action against discrimination) for both working-class Protestants and Catholics seem likely to play a role, along with other measures, in bringing about an amelioration of the conflict.

2. Attention has been drawn to the difficult role played by the *security forces* in Northern Ireland and the 'security dilemma' which confronts policy-makers. But this should not be used as an excuse to prevent reform to make the RUC or army more

impartial and accountable for their actions. The deployment of excessive state violence, whether against nationalists or unionists, can be directly related to a deterioration of the conflict in Northern Ireland.

3. Integrated education and a host of *reconciliation initiatives* also have a role to play in undermining the communalism and material and ideological structures which perpetuate the conflict.

4. There are considerable difficulties in bringing about *ideological change*. Politicians and the media have overestimated their impact, and the benevolence of their impact, on public opinion. There are strong cultural influences which constrain their ability to shift opinion and these are related to other material reforms mentioned above.

5. The intensity of the Northern Ireland conflict has varied over time and has responded partly to British and Irish *conflict management*. As British and Irish politicians have explored the parameters of the conflict and what is perceived to be politically possible, they *generally* appear to have learnt to manage it better (although they too have been constrained by their own communal, ideological assumptions). The environment of constitutional insecurity, largely created by the British (and, to a lesser extent, the Irish) Government, has exacerbated the violence and the prospects, particularly for unionists, of moving towards accommodation.

6. There has been a general *failure to understand Ulster Unionism*, and its sense of vulnerability and isolation which have 'real' substance behind them. Lacking empathy with unionism, there is a tendency among British politicians to push unionists 'too far' towards a settlement and thereby undermining moderate unionism.

There has been a considerable degree of secrecy, manipulation and choreography by the political elites in Britain and Ireland of party and public opinion during the recent conflict and particularly during the second peace process. This may reflect a trend among politicians to emphasise the importance of 'appearance' over 'reality': 'as political actors and media have grown dependent on each other, politics has become not only a persuasive but a performance art, in which considerations of style, presentation and marketing are equal to, if not greater in importance than, content and substance' (McNair 1995 p. 189). An attempt has been made to stage-manage politics and 'spin' the people of Northern Ireland into an accommodation, rather than persuade supporters and public opinion to support the peace process based on a 'realistic' understanding of the balance of political forces and a sense of the politically possible. For some, the goal of a settlement justifies the means to achieve it. However, it is precisely this lack of democracy, accountability and openness which has contributed to the kind of political environment that these measures are now argued to necessitate. There are limits to how far unionists or nationalists can be manipulated without addressing the 'real' grievances of the various constituencies. Northern Ireland has a highly politicised public which generally has a close relationship with its political leaders, and so its susceptibility to 'spin' and 'stage management' is correspondingly reduced. Manipulation and deceit eats into the culture of democracy, producing cynicism and resentment. The result of this is that the GFA is balanced precariously on still seething reservoirs of hatred between unionists and nationalists. The possibility of a more democratic, open and informed debate about the future of Northern Ireland does exist, which could challenge communal ideologies (both within Northern Ireland and outside it, in Britain, the Republic and the US), unmask the 'realities' behind the propaganda war and bring public and party opinion towards an accommodation which would be more stable for being popularly reinforced.

Further analysis on the politics of Northern Ireland can be found on the author's web site:

   www.nipolitics.com

Bibliography

Adams, G. (1987) *The Politics of Irish Freedom* (Dingle: Brandon).

Anderson, D. (1994) *14 Days in May* (Dublin: Gill & Macmillan).

Armstrong, Lord R. (1993) 'Ethnicity, the English and Northern Ireland: Comments and Reflections', in D. Keogh and M. Haltzel, *Northern Ireland and the Politics of Reconciliation* (Cambridge: Cambridge University Press).

Arthur, P. (1984) *Government and Politics of Northern Ireland*, 2nd edn (London: Longman).

Ashe, F. *et al.* (1999) *Contemporary Social and Political Theory* (London: Open University Press).

Aughey, A. (1989) *Under Siege: Ulster Unionism and the Anglo-Irish Agreement* (Belfast: Blackstaff).

Barritt, D. P. and Carter, C. (1962) *The Northern Ireland Problem* (London: Oxford University Press).

Bean, K. (1995) 'The New Departure?', *Irish Studies Review*, no. 10 (Spring).

Benn, T. (1988) *Office Without Power – Diaries 1968–72* (London: Hutchinson).

Benn, T. (1989) *Against the Tide – Diaries 1973–76* (London: Hutchinson).

Bew, P. and Dixon, P. (1995) 'Labour Party Policy and Northern Ireland', in B. Barton and P. Roche (eds), *Northern Ireland: Policies and Perspectives* (Aldershot: Avebury).

Bew, P., Gibbon, P. and Patterson, H. (1979) *The State in Northern Ireland 1921–72* (Manchester: Manchester University Press).

Bew, P., Gibbon, P. and Patterson, H. (1995) *Northern Ireland 1921–94: Political Forces and Social Classes* (London: Serif).

Bew, P. and Gillespie, G. (1993) *Northern Ireland: A Chronology of the Troubles 1968–1993* (London: Gill & Macmillan).

Bew, P. and Gillespie, G. (1996) *The Northern Ireland Peace Process 1993–96: A Chronology* (London: Serif).

Bew, P. and Gillespie, G. (1999) *Northern Ireland: A Chronology of the Troubles 1968–99* (Dublin: Gill and Macmillan).

Bew, P. and Patterson, H. (1985) *The British State and the Ulster Crisis: From Wilson to Thatcher* (London: Verso).

Bew, P. and Patterson, H. (1990) 'Scenarios for Progress in Northern Ireland', in J. McGarry and B. O'Leary (eds), *The Future of Northern Ireland* (Oxford: Clarendon).

Bew, P., Patterson, H. and Teague, P. (1997) *Between Peace and War: The Political Future of Northern Ireland* (London: Lawrence & Wishart).

Birrell, D. (1972) 'Relative Deprivation as a Factor in Conflict in Northern Ireland', *Sociological Review* 20, no. 3.

Birrell, D. and Murie, A. (1980) *Policy and Government in Northern Ireland* (Dublin: Gill & Macmillan).

Bishop, P. and Mallie, E. (1987) *The Provisional IRA* (London: Corgi).
Bleakley, D. (1972) *Peace in Ulster* (Oxford: Mowbrays).
Bloomfield, K. (1994) *Stormont in Crisis* (Belfast: Blackstaff).
Blumer, J. G. and Gurevitch, M. (1995) *The Crisis of Political Communication* (London: Routledge).
Bowman, J. (1982) *De Valera and the Ulster Question 1917–73* (Oxford: Clarendon).
Boyce, D. G. (1995) *Nationalism in Ireland* (London: Routledge).
Boyle, K. and Hadden, T. (1994) *Northern Ireland: The Choice* (Harmondsworth: Penguin).
Brett, C. E. B. (1970) 'The Lessons of Devolution in Northern Ireland', *Political Quarterly*, 41.
Brett, C. E. B. (1978) *Long Shadows Cast Before* (Edinburgh: John Bartholomew).
Brivati, B. *et al.* (1996) *The Contemporary History Handbook* (Manchester: Manchester University Press).
Bromley, M. (1989) 'War of Words: The *Belfast Telegraph* and Loyalist Populism', in Y. Alexander and A. O'Day (eds), *Ireland's Terrorist Trauma* (London: Wheatsheaf).
Bruce, S. (1989) *God Save Ulster: The Religion and Politics of Paisleyism* (Oxford: Oxford University Press).
Bruce, S. (1992) *The Red Hand: Protestant Paramilitaries in Northern Ireland* (Oxford: Oxford University Press).
Bruce, S. (1994) *The Edge of the Union: The Ulster Loyalist Political Vision* (Oxford: Oxford University Press).
Bruce, S. (1999) 'The state and pro-state terrorism in Ireland', in R. English and C. Townshend (eds), *The State* (London: Routledge).
Bulpitt, J. (1983) *Territory and Power in the UK* (Manchester: Manchester University Press).
Burton, F. (1978) *The Politics of Legitimacy: Struggles in a Belfast Community* (London: Routledge & Kegan Paul).
Butler, D. E. (1991) 'Ulster Unionism and British Broadcasting Journalism, 1924–89' in B. Rolston (ed.) *The Media and Northern Ireland* (London: Macmillan).
Butler, D. E. (1995) *Trouble with Reporting Northern Ireland* (Aldershot: Avebury).
Byrne, S. (1995) 'Conflict Regulation or Conflict Resolution: Third-Party Intervention in the Northern Ireland Conflict; Prospects for Peace', *Terrorism and Political Violence*, vol. 7, no. 2 (Summer).
Callaghan, J. (1973) *A House Divided* (London: Collins).
Cameron Report, (1969) *Disturbances in Northern Ireland*, Cmd 532 (Belfast: HMSO).
Campbell, J. (1983) *F. E. Smith* (London: Jonathan Cape).
Canning, P. (1985) *British Policy towards Ireland 1921–41* (Oxford: Oxford University Press).
Carruthers, S. L. (1995) *Winning Hearts and Minds: British Government, the Media and Colonial Counter-Insurgency 1944–60* (London: Leicester University Press).
Carver, M. (1989) *Out of Step* (London: Hutchinson).

Cash, J. D. (1996) *Identity, Ideology and Conflict: The Structuration of Politics in Northern Ireland* (Cambridge: Cambridge University Press).

Castle, B. (1980) *The Castle Diaries 1974–76* (London: Weidenfeld & Nicolson).

Castle, B. (1984) *The Castle Diaries 1964–70* (London: Weidenfeld & Nicolson).

Chibnall, S. (1977) *Law and Order News* (London: Tavistock).

Clarke, L. (1987) *Broadening the Battlefield* (Dublin: Gill & Macmillan).

Cochrane, F. (1997) *Unionist Politics and the Politics of Unionism since the Anglo–Irish Agreement* (Cork: Cork University Press).

Connor, W. (1972) 'Nation-building or Nation-destroying', *World Politics*, 24, no. 3 (April).

Conservative Party (1969) *Conservative Party Conference Report* (London: Conservative Central Office).

Coughlan, A. (1986) *Fooled Again? The Anglo-Irish Agreement and After* (Cork: Mercier Press).

Coughlan, A. (1990) *C. Desmond Greaves, 1913–1988: An Obituary Essay* (Dublin: Irish Labour History Society).

Coulter, C. (1999) *Contemporary Northern Irish Society* (London: Pluto).

Cox, M. (1997) 'Bringing in the "international": the IRA ceasefire and the end of the Cold War', *International Affairs*, vol. 73, no. 4.

Crossman, R. (1977) *The Diaries of a Cabinet Minister 1968–70* (London: Hamish Hamilton and Jonathan Cape).

Cunningham, M. (1991) *British Government Policy in Northern Ireland 1969–89, Its nature and Execution* (Manchester: Manchester University Press).

Curtis, L. (1984) *Ireland: The Propaganda War* (London: Pluto).

Darby, J. (1976) *Conflict in Northern Ireland* (Dublin: Gill and Macmillan).

Darby, J. (1994) 'Legitimate targets: A control on violence?' in A. Guelke (ed.) *New Perspectives on the Northern Ireland Conflict* (Aldershot: Avebury).

Darwin, J. (1988) *Britain and Decolonisation – The Retreat from Empire in the post-war World* (London: Macmillan).

Davis, R. (1997) 'Have the Northern Ireland Ceasefires of 1994 Ended "Zero Sum Game and Mirrored Thinking"?' in A. O'Day (ed.), *Political Violence in Northern Ireland* (London: Praeger).

Devlin, B. (1969) *The Price of My Soul* (London: Collins).

Devlin, P. (1975) *The Fall of the N.I. Executive* (Belfast: published by P. Devlin).

Dillon, M. and Lehane, D. (1973) *Political Murder in Northern Ireland* (Harmondsworth: Penguin).

Dixon, P. (1993) 'The British Labour Party and Northern Ireland 1959–74', unpublished PhD thesis, University of Bradford.

Dixon, P. (1994a) 'European Integration, Modernisation and Northern Ireland 1961–75', *Etudes Irlandaises*, no. XIX–1.

Dixon, P. (1994b) '"The Usual English Doubletalk": The British Political Parties and the Ulster Unionists 1974–94', *Irish Political Studies*, 9.

Dixon, P. (1995a) '"A House Divided Cannot Stand": Britain, Bipartisanship and Northern Ireland', *Contemporary Record*.

Dixon, P. (1995b) 'Internationalization and Unionist Isolation: A Response to Feargal Cochrane', *Political Studies*, vol. 43, no. 3.

Dixon, P. (1996a) '"A real stirring in the nation": the Crisis of the British Army over Northern Ireland', in G. Stanyer (ed.), *Contemporary Political Studies* (the collected papers of the PSA) (London: Longman).

Dixon, P. (1996b) 'Explaining Antagonism: The Politics of McGarry and O'Leary', *Irish Political Studies*, vol. 11.

Dixon, P. (1996c) 'The Politics of Antagonism: Explaining McGarry and O'Leary', *Irish Political Studies*, vol. 11.

Dixon, P. (1997a) 'Consociationalism and the Northern Ireland Peace Process: the Glass Half Full or Half Empty?', *Nationalism and Ethnic Politics*, vol. 3, no. 3.

Dixon, P. (1997b) 'Counter-insurgency strategy and the crisis of the British state?', in P. Rich and R. Stubbs (eds), *Counter Insurgent States* (London: Macmillan).

Dixon, P. (1997c) 'Paths to Peace in Northern Ireland (I): Civil Society and Consociational Approaches', *Democratization*, vol. 4, no. 2.

Dixon, P. (1997d) 'Paths to Peace in Northern Ireland (II): Peace Process 1973–74, 1994–96', *Democratization*, vol. 4, no. 3.

Dixon, P. (1998) 'Comment on *The Conservative Stewardship of Northern Ireland 1979–97*', *Political Studies*, vol. 46, no. 3.

Dixon, P. (2000a) 'Britain's "Vietnam Syndrome"? Public Opinion and Military Intervention from Palestine to Yugoslavia', *Review of International Studies*, vol. 26, no. 1.

Dixon, P. (2000b) 'British Policy Towards Northern Ireland 1968–2000: Balance, Continuity and Consistent "Inconsistencies"', Paper delivered to the Political Studies Association, LSE, London.

Dixon, P. (2000c) 'The Northern Ireland Peace Process: From Conflict to Choreography', Paper delivered to the International Political Science Association, Quebec.

Donoughue, B. (1987) *Prime Minister – The Conduct of Policy under Harold Wilson and James Callaghan* (London: Jonathan Cape).

Downey, J. (1983) *Britain, Ireland and the Northern Question* (Dublin: Ward River Press).

Duignan, S. (1995) *One Spin on the Merry-Go-Round* (Dublin: Blackwater Press).

Eldridge, J. (1993) 'News, Truth and Power', in Glasgow University Media Group, *Getting the Message: News, Truth and Power* (London: Routledge).

Elliott, P. (1976) *Reporting Northern Ireland: A Study of News in Britain, Ulster and the Irish Republic* (Leicester: Centre for Mass Communication Research).

Evelegh, R. (1978) *Peace Keeping in a Democratic Society: The Lessons of Northern Ireland* (London: Hurst).

Farrell, M. (1976) *The Orange State* (London: Pluto Press).

Faulkner, B. (1978) *Brian Faulkner, Memoirs of a Statesman* (London: Weidenfeld & Nicolson).

Fay, M. *et al* (1999) *Northern Ireland's Troubles: The Human Costs* (London: Pluto).

Feeney, V. E. (1974) 'The Civil Rights Movement in Northern Ireland', *Eire-Ireland*, vol. 9, no. 2.

Feeney, V. E. (1976) 'Westminster and the Early Civil Rights Struggle in Northern Ireland', *Eire-Ireland*, vol. 11, no. 4.

Fisk, R. (1975) *The Point of No Return, The Strike which Broke the British in Ulster* (London: André Deutsch).

Fisk, R. (1983) *In Time of War* (London: Paladin).

Fitzgerald, G. (1991) *All in a Life* (Dublin: Gill & Macmillan).

Flackes, W. D. and Elliott, S. (1999) *Northern Ireland: A Political Directory* (Belfast: Blackstaff).

Foot, P. (1989) *Who Framed Colin Wallace?* (London: Pan).

Furedi, F. (1994) *Colonial Wars and the Politics of Third World Nationalism* (London: I. B. Taurus).

Gailey, A. (1995) *Crying in the Wilderness: Jack Sayers: A Liberal Editor in Ulster 1939–69* (Belfast: Institute of Irish Studies).

Gillespie, G. (1998) 'The Sunningdale Agreement: Lost Opportunity or an Agreement too far?', *Irish Political Studies*, vol. 13.

Goldsworthy, D. (1971) *Colonial Issues in British Politics 1945–61* (Oxford: Oxford University Press).

Goodall, D. (1993) 'The Irish Question', *Ampleforth Journal*, vol. XCVIII, Part 1 (Spring).

Gordon, D. (1989) *The O'Neill Years, Unionist Politics 1963–69* (Belfast: Athol Books).

Graham, J. A. V. (1982) 'The Consensus-forming Strategy of the NILP', MSc thesis, Queens University Belfast.

Gudgin, G. (1999) 'Discrimination in Housing and Employment under the Stormont Administration in P. J. Roche and B. Barton (eds.) *The Northern Ireland Question: Nationalism, Unionism and Partition* (Aldershot: Ashgate).

Guelke, A. (1988) *Northern Ireland: The International Perspective* (Dublin: Gill & Macmillan).

Hadden, T. and Boyle, K. (1989) *The Anglo-Irish Agreement, Commentary, Text and Official Review* (London: Sweet & Maxwell).

Haines, J. (1977) *The Politics of Power* (London: Jonathan Cape).

Hamill, D. (1985) *Pig in the Middle, The Army in Northern Ireland 1969–85* (London: Methuen).

Harkness, D. (1977) 'The Differences of Devolution: The Post-War Debate at Stormont', *The Irish Jurist*, vol. xii.

Harkness, D. (1993) 'Never the Twain: Belfast–Dublin Relations Since 1920', *L'Irlande Politique et Sociale*, vol. 1 no. 3.

Harkness, D. (1996) *Ireland in the Twentieth Century: Divided Island* (London: Macmillan).

Hay, C. (1995) 'Structure and Agency', in D. Marsh and G. Stoker (eds), *Theory and Methods in Political Science* (London: Macmillan).

Hazelkorn, E. and Patterson, H. (1994) 'The New Politics of the Irish Republic', *New Left Review*, vol. 207.

Heath, E. (1998) *The Course of My Life: My Autobiography* (London: Hodder & Stoughton).

Hewitt, J. (1991) 'The roots of violence: Catholic grievances and Irish nationalism during the civil rights period' in P. J. Roche and B. Barton (eds.), *The Northern Ireland Question: Myth and Reality* (Aldershot: Avebury).

Hillyard, P. (1988) 'Political and Social Dimensions of Emergency Law in Northern Ireland', in A. Jennings (ed.), *Justice under Fire* (London: Pluto).

Hogg, Q. (1975) *The Door Wherein I went* (London: Collins).

Holland, J. and Phoenix, S. (1997) *Policing the Shadows* (London: Coronet Books).

Howe, G. (1994) *Conflict of Loyalty* (London: Pan) .

Hunt Report (1969) Report of the Advisory Committee on Police in Northern Ireland and Belfast.

Hurd, D. (1979) *An End to Promises* (London: Collins).

ICBH (Institute for Contemporary British History) (1997) Anglo-Irish Agreement Witness Seminar, 11 June.

Ignatieff, M. (1996) 'Articles of Faith', *Index on Censorship*, no. 5.

Irish Political Studies (1986–2000) Yearbook of the Political Studies Association of Ireland (Limerick: PSA Press).

Jarman, N. (1997) *Material Conflicts: Parades and Visual displays in Northern Ireland* (Oxford: Berg).

Jenkins, R. (1991) *Life at the Centre* (London: Macmillan).

Kelley, K. J. (1988) *The Longest War: Northern Ireland and the IRA* (London: Zed).

Kelly, H. (1972) *How Stormont Fell* (Dublin: Gill & Macmillan).

Kennedy, D. (1988) *The Widening Gulf* (Belfast: Blackstaff).

Kenny, A. (1986) *The Road to Hillsborough* (Oxford: Pergamon).

King, C. (1975) *The Cecil King Diary 1970–74* (London: Jonathan Cape).

Kirkaldy, J. (1984) 'Northern Ireland and Fleet Street: Misreporting a Continuing Tragedy', in Y. Alexander and A. O'Day (eds), *Terrorism in Ireland* (London: Croom Helm).

Kirkaldy, J. (1986) 'English Cartoonists: Ulster Realities', in A. O'Day (ed.), *Ireland's Terrorist Dilemma* (Lancaster: Martinus Nijhoff).

Kyle, K. (1975) 'Sunningdale and After: Britain, Ireland and Ulster', *The World Today*, November.

Lawrence, R., Elliott, S. and Laver, M. (1975) *The Northern Ireland General Elections of 1973* (London: HMSO).

Lawson, N. (1992) *The View from Number Eleven* (London: Bantam).

Lichbach, M. and Zuckerman, A. (1997) *Comparative Politics* (Cambridge: Cambridge University Press).

Loughlin, J. (1995) *Ulster Unionism and British National Identity since 1885* (London: Pinter).

Lynn, B. (1997) *Holding the Ground: The Nationalist Party in Northern Ireland, 1945–72* (Aldershot: Avebury).

Mair, P. (1987a) 'Breaking the Nationalist Mould: The Irish Republic and the Anglo-Irish Agreement', in P. Teague (ed.), *Beyond the Rhetoric: Politics, the Economy and Social Policy in Northern Ireland* (London: Lawrence & Wishart).

Mair, P. (1987b) *The Changing Irish Party System* (London: Pinter).

Major, J. (1999) *John Major: the Autobiography* (London: Harper Collins).

Mallie, E. and McKittrick, D. (1997) *The Fight for Peace: The Secret Story of the Irish Peace Process*, rev. edn. (London: Mandarin).

Marsh, D. *et al.* (1999) *Postwar British Politics in Perspective* (Oxford: Polity).

Mason, R. (1999) *Paying the Price* (London: Robert Hale).

McAllister, I. (1977a) 'The Legitimacy of Opposition: The Collapse of the Northern Ireland Executive', in *Eire-Ireland*, vol. 12, part 6.

McAllister, I. (1977b) *The Northern Ireland Social Democratic and Labour Party: Political Opposition in a Divided Society* (London: Macmillan).

McCann, E. (1969) 'Interview with Peoples' Democracy', *New Left Review* no. 55, May–June.

McCann, E. (1974) *War and an Irish Town* (Harmondsworth: Penguin).

McCullagh, M. (1983) 'The Political and Sectarian Significance of Changes in the Occupational Structure in Northern Ireland', *Social Science Teacher*, vol. 12, no. 2.

McGarry, J. and O'Leary, B. (1995) *Explaining Northern Ireland* (Oxford: Basil Blackwell).

McKeown, M. (1997) 'The Impact of the 1947 Education Act upon Roman Catholic access to academic secondary education in Northern Ireland', *Irish Education Studies*, vol. 16, (Spring).

McKittrick, D. *et al.* (1999) *Lost Lives: The Stories of the Men, Women and Children who Died on a Result of the Northern Ireland Troubles* (London: Mainstream).

McNair, B. (1995) *An Introduction to Political Communication* (London: Routledge).

Miller, D. (1993) 'Official Sources and "primary definition": the case of Northern Ireland', *Media, Culture and Society*, 15, 3.

Miller, D. (1994) *Don't Mention the War: Northern Ireland, Propaganda and the Media* (London: Pluto).

Miller, D. and McLaughlin, M. (1996) 'The Media Politics of the Peace in Ireland' *Harvard International Journal of Press/Politics* 1(4) Fall.

Mitchell, G. (1999) *Making Peace* (Heinemann: London).

Moloney, E. (1980) *The IRA* (Dublin: Magill).

Moloney, E. and Pollak, A. (1986) *Paisley* (Swords: Poolbeg).

Morgan, M. (1987) 'The Catholic Middle Class in Northern Ireland: Myth or Reality?', *Ireland: Politics and Society*, vol. 1, no. 3.

Morgan, M. and Taylor, R. (1988) 'Forget the myths: here's the real story', *Fortnight*, October.

Murray, G. (1998) *John Hume and the SDLP* (Dublin: Irish Academic Press).

Nagel, J. and Olzak, S. (1982) 'Ethnic Mobilisation in New and Old States: An extension of the competition model', *Social Problems*, vol. 30, no. 2.

Needham, R. (1998) *Battling for Peace* (Belfast: Blackstaff).

Nelson, S. (1984) *Ulster's Uncertain Defenders: Protestant Political, Paramilitary and Community Groups and the Northern Ireland Conflict* (Belfast: Appletree).

Northern Ireland Office (1972) *The Future of Northern Ireland: A Paper for Discussion* (Belfast: HMSO).

O'Brien, B. (1993) *The Long War: The IRA and Sinn Féin 1985 to Today* (Dublin: The O'Brien Press).

O'Brien, C. C. (1972) *States of Ireland* (London: Hutchinson).

O'Clery, C. (1986) *Phrases Make History Here* (Dublin: The O'Brien Press).

O'Connor, F. (1993) *In Search of a State: Catholics in Northern Ireland* (Belfast: Blackstaff).

O'Clery, C. (1996) *The Greening of the White House* (Dublin: Gill & Macmillan).
Ó Dochartaigh, N. (1997) *From Civil Rights to Armalites: Derry and the Birth of the Irish Troubles* (Cork: Cork University Press).
O'Doherty, M. (1998) *The Trouble With Guns: Republican Strategy and the Provisional IRA* (Belfast: Blackstaff).
O'Farrell, J. (1998) 'Divided People, Divided Press – Interpreting the poisonous silences in a fractured society', *Media Studies Journal*, vol. 12, no. 2.
O'Halloran, C. (1987) *Partition and the Limits of Irish Nationalism* (Dublin: Gill & Macmillan).
O'Leary, B. (1997) 'The Conservative Stewardship of Northern Ireland, 1979–97: Sound-bottomed Contradictions or Slow Learning', *Political Studies*, XLV.
O'Leary, B. and McGarry, J. (1996) *The Politics of Antagonism*, 2nd edn (London: Athlone).
O'Malley, P. (1983) *The Uncivil Wars: Ireland Today* (Belfast: Blackstaff).
O'Malley, P. (1990) *Biting at the Grave: The Irish Hunger Strikes and the Politics of Despair* (Belfast: Blackstaff).
O'Malley, P. (1994) 'Northern Ireland – A Manageable Conflict?', *The Irish Review*, no. 15 (Spring).
O'Neill, T. (1969) *Ulster at the Crossroads* (London: Faber & Faber).
O'Neill, T. (1972) *The Autobiography of Terence O'Neill, Prime Minister of Northern Ireland 1963–69* (London: Rupert Hart-Davis).
Owen, E. A. (1994) *The Anglo-Irish Agreement: The First Three Years* (Cardiff: University of Wales Press).
Parkinson, A. (1998) *Ulster Loyalism and the British Media* (Dublin: Four Courts Press).
Patterson, H. (1986) 'British Governments and the Protestant Backlash 1969–74', in A. O'Day (ed.) *Ireland's Terrorist Dilemma* (Lancaster: Martinns Nijhoff).
Patterson, H. (1997) *The Politics of Illusion: A Political History of the IRA* (London: Serif).
Patterson, H. (1999) 'Sean Lemass and the Ulster Question 1959–65', *Journal of Contemporary History*, vol. 34, no. 1.
Porter, N. (1996) *Rethinking Unionism* (Belfast: Blackstaff).
Power, P. F. (1977) 'The Sunningdale Strategy and the Northern Majority Consent Doctrine in Anglo–Irish Relations', *Eire-Ireland*, vol. 12, no. 1.
Prior, J. (1986) *A Balance of Power* (London: Hamish Hamilton).
Purdie, B. (1983) 'The Friends of Ireland: British Labour and Irish Nationalism 1945–49', in T. Gallagher and J. O'Connell (eds), *Contemporary Irish Studies* (Manchester: Manchester University Press).
Purdie, B. (1986) 'The Irish Anti-Partition League, South Armagh and the Abstentionist Tactic 1945–48', *Irish Political Studies*, vol. 1.
Purdie, B. (1988) 'Was the Civil Rights Movement a Republican/Communist Conspiracy?', *Irish Political Studies*, vol. 3.
Purdie, B. (1990) *Politics in the Streets* (Belfast: Blackstaff).
Rees, M. (1973) 'The Future of Northern Ireland', *Contemporary Review*, vol. 223, part 1290.
Rees, M. (1974) 'Northern Ireland', *Contemporary Review*, vol. 224, no. 1297.

Rees, M. (1985) *Northern Ireland: A Personal Perspective* (London: Methuen).

Rose, Paul (1981) *Backbencher's Dilemma* (London: Muller).

Rose, Peter (1999) *How the Troubles Came to Northern Ireland* (London: Macmillan).

Rose, R. (1971) *Governing Without Consensus: An Irish Perspective* (London: Faber & Faber).

Rose, R. (1976) *Northern Ireland: A Time of Choice* (London: Macmillan).

Rose, R. *et al.* (1978) *Is There a Concurring Majority about Northern Ireland?*, Studies in Public Policy no. 22 (Glasgow: University of Strathclyde, Centre for the Study of Public Policy).

Rowan, B. (1995) *Behind the Lines: The Story of the IRA and Loyalist Cease-fires* (Belfast: Blackstaff).

Ruane, J. and Todd, J. (1996) *The Dynamics of Conflict in Northern Ireland* (Cambridge: Cambridge University Press).

Ruane, J. and Todd, J. (1999) 'The Belfast Agreement: Conflict, Context, Consequences', in J. Ruane and J. Todd (eds), *After the Good Friday Agreement* (Dublin: University College Dublin Press).

Ryder, C. (1992) *The Ulster Defence Regiment: An Instrument of Peace?* (London: Mandarin).

Ryder, C. (1997) *The RUC: A Force Under Fire* (London: Mandarin).

Scarman Report (1972) *Violence and Disturbances in Northern Ireland in 1969*, Cmd 566 (Belfast: HMSO).

Schlesinger, P. (1978) *Putting 'Reality' Together* (London: Methuen).

Schlesinger, P. *et al.* (1983) *Televising Terrorism: Political Violence in Popular Culture* (London: Comedia).

Schlesinger, P. (1990) 'Rethinking the Sociology of Journalism: Source strategies and the limits of media centrism', in M. Ferguson, *Public Communication: The New Imperatives* (London: Sage).

Seldon, A. (1997) *John Major* (London: Weidenfeld and Nicolson).

Sharrock, D. and Devenport, M. (1997) *Man of War Man of Peace? The Unauthorised Biography of Gerry Adams* (London: Macmillan).

Sinn Féin (1993) *Setting the Record Straight* (Sinn Fein: Belfast).

Sluka, J. A. (1989) *Hearts and Minds, Water and Fish: Support for the IRA and INLA in a Northern Ireland Ghetto* (London: JAI Press).

Smith, D. and Chambers, G. (1991) *Inequality in Northern Ireland* (Oxford: Oxford Univerity Press).

Smith, M. L. R. (1995) *Fighting for Ireland? The Military Strategy of the Irish Republican Movement* (London: Routledge).

Smyth, C. (1987) *Ian Paisley: Voice of Protestant Ulster* (Edinburgh: Scottish Academic Press).

Stuart, M. (1998) *Douglas Hurd: The Public Servant, An Authorised Biography* (London: Mainstream Publishing).

Sunday Times Insight Team (1972) *Ulster* (Hamondsworth: Penguin).

Sutton, M. (1994) *An Index of Deaths from the Conflict in Ireland 1969–93* (Belfast: Beyond the Pale).

Sutton, M. (1999) *An Index of Deaths from the Conflict in Ireland*, www.cain.ulst.ac.uk/sutton/index.html

Taylor, P. (1997) *The Provos: The IRA and Sinn Féin* (London: Bloomsbury).

Taylor, R. (1988) 'Social Scientific Research on the "Troubles" in Northern Ireland: The Problem of Objectivity', *The Economic and Social Review*, vol. 19, no. 2 (January).

Teague, P. (1993) 'Discrimination and Fair Employment in Northern Ireland', in P. Teague (ed.), *The Economy of Northern Ireland* (London: Lawrence & Wishart).

Thatcher, M. (1993) *Downing Street Years* (London: Harper Collins).

Urban, M. (1992) *Big Boys' Rules* (London: Faber & Faber).

Utley, T. E. (1975) *Lessons of Ulster* (London: Dent).

Wallace, M. (1982) *British Government in Northern Ireland* (Newton Abbot: David & Charles).

Walsh, P. (1989) *From Civil Rights to National War, Catholic Politics 1964–74* (Belfast: Athol Books).

Welch, D. (1999) 'Powers of Persuasion', *History Today*, August.

White, B. (1984) *John Hume: Statesman of the Troubles* (Belfast: Blackstaff).

Whitelaw, W. (1989) *The Whitelaw Memoirs* (London: Aurum Press).

Whyte, J. (1983) 'How much discrimination was there under the unionist regime, 1921–68?', in T. Gallagher and J. O'Connell (eds), *Contemporary Irish Studies* (Manchester: Manchester University Press).

Whyte, J. (1990) *Interpreting Northern Ireland* (Oxford: Clarendon Press).

Wilson, A. J. (1995) *Irish America and the Ulster Conflict 1968–1995* (Belfast: Blackstaff).

Wilson, H. (1966) *Purpose in Power* (London: Weidenfeld & Nicolson).

Wilson, H. (1974) *The Labour Government 1964–70: A Personal Record* (London: Weidenfeld & Nicolson).

Wilson, H. (1977) *The Governance of Britain* (London: Sphere).

Wilson, H. (1979) *The Final Term: The Labour Government 1974–76* (London: Weidenfeld & Nicolson).

Winchester, S. (1974) *In Holy Terror: Reporting the Ulster Troubles* (London: Faber & Faber).

Windlesham, D. (1975) *Politics in Practice* (London: Jonathan Cape).

Wright, F. (1973) 'Protestant Ideology and Politics in Ulster', *European Journal of Sociology*, vol. 14.

Wright, J. Wright (1991) *Terrorist Propaganda: The Red Arm, Faction and the Provision IRA 1968–86* (London: Macmillian).

Young, H. (1989) *One of Us?* (London: Macmillan).

A guide to further reading, articles and sources on Northern Ireland are available at

www.nipolitics.com

Index

Act of Union (1801)   3
Adams, Gerry   12, 35, 39, 121, 169,
    186, 230
  on Omagh bombing   275
  peace process (1988–2000)
      and   30–1, 220, 223, 224,
      241, 268, 276; ceasefire
      (1994) 246, 247, 248;
      decommissioning issue and
      249, 257; Hume–Adams talks
      216, 222, 232–5, 240
  rethinking of armed
      struggle   222–3
  visit to USA   254, 255
Aden   132
agency   27–9
Alderdice, John   17, 232
Alliance Party (APNI)   10, 16–17,
    138–9, 148, 185
  Anglo–Irish Agreement (1985)
      and   205, 206
  power-sharing experiment
      (1972–74) and   16, 133,
      141, 146
Amnesty International   170
Ancient Order of Hibernians   22,
    70
Ancram, Michael   255, 258
Anderson, D.   150, 151
Andrew, Robert   200, 202
Anglo–Irish Agreement (1985)   5–6,
    187, 190–214, 287–8
  explanations of   196–201;
      bureaucratic conflict
      199–200, 203; coercive
      power-sharing   200–1;
      external pressure   199; fear
      of Sinn Féin   197–8, 202–3;
      security policy   198–9;
      withdrawal option and   200
  nationalists and   9, 187, 194,
      197–8, 202–3, 204, 213
  negotiations   190–5

reaction to   204
reasons for signature   202–4
security issues and   191–2, 198–9,
    210–13
Thatcher and   5, 158, 189–92,
    197–9, 201–4, 206, 208,
    212–14, 287
Unionists and   14, 16, 154,
    155–6, 193, 195–6, 200–1,
    204–13, 214
Anglo–Irish Free Trade Agreement
    (1965)   63–4
Anglo–Irish Intergovernmental
    Council   180
Annesley, Hugh   223
Anti-Partition League (APL)   71–2
Apprentice Boys of Derry   13
Arbuckle, Victor   111
Arlow, William   167
Armstrong, Robert   199, 200, 203
Army   see British Army
Arthur, P.   55
Ashe, F.   27, 31
Atkins, Humphrey   178, 190
Atkins Initiative   177, 178,
    179, 180
atrocity myths   18
Attlee, Clement   53
Aughey, A.   195, 207, 208, 209

B Specials   86, 106, 107, 110–12
Ballymurphy riots   113, 114
Baltic Exchange bomb (1992)   230,
    279
Barritt, D. P.   69
Bean, K.   222, 223, 242
Begley, Thomas   234
Belfast   22
  residential segregation in   20
  Sinn Féin boycott (1920–22)   50
  violence in   25
Benn, Tony   108, 149
Bennett Report   170

318